The Lady and THE TYCOON

Rose Wilder Lane
(in 1962)

Rampart College

Jasper Crane
(in 1958)

Willard Stewart

The Lady and THE TYCOON

Letters of Rose Wilder Lane and Jasper Crane

Edited by
Roger Lea MacBride

The CAXTON PRINTERS, Ltd.
Caldwell, Idaho
1973

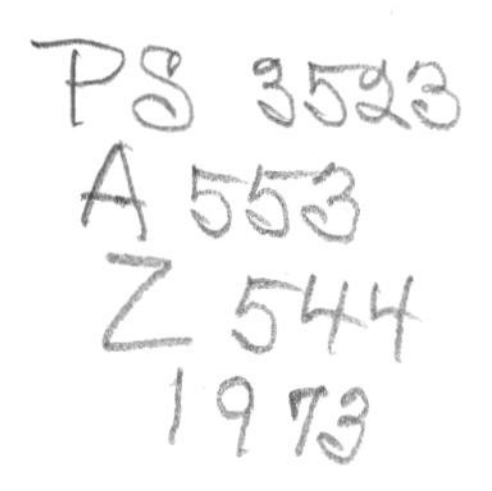

International Standard Book Number 0-87004-234-3
Library of Congress Catalog Card Number 72-78366

Printed and bound in the United States of America

90473

Contents

Dedication

For Abby

The Great Granddaughter Rose Would Have Loved

Foreword

I take pride in this exchange between The Lady and The Tycoon, because I was the friend who introduced them.

I first met Rose Wilder Lane through her *Give Me Liberty* in the *Saturday Evening Post.* Was I impressed!

In 1939 I had been made General Manager of the Los Angeles Chamber of Commerce, but there was no way to express my aspirations for freedom adequately through such an organization. So, with five of my friends and associates, I formed an ad hoc business which we named Pamphleteers, Inc. *Give Me Liberty* was our first pamphlet, and it yielded at least a nodding acquaintance with the celebrated Mrs. Lane. The Lady's remarkable letters to me began in 1943. Her first letter was a commentary on a speech I had delivered, "Our Battles on the Home Front."

As Roger MacBride has noted, Rose Wilder Lane gave up writing as a profitable profession about this time. However, the ideas that flowed in her mind were undiminished; writing was her compulsive trait. She had to have an outlet —someone who was receptive and responsive. For some years, I was one such person. Her frequent letters were always brilliant and lengthy—I recall one of seventeen pages.

I met Jasper Crane in 1946, during the formative days of The Foundation for Economic Education, Inc. He was one of the early Trustees of the Foundation and served prominently and with distinction until his passing in 1969.

Jasper Crane well qualifies as a tycoon in the sense of being "a wealthy and powerful industrialist." He was born in 1881 and graduated from Princeton University in 1901. He also received a M.S. degree at Princeton following a year of senior graduate work in chemistry and engineering at the Massachusetts Institute of Technology. His meteoric rise in the business world found him head of European opertions for E. I. Du Pont de Nemours and Company in 1920. He was made a member of Du Pont's Board of Directors in 1927; two years later, he was elected Vice President and a member of the Executive Committee. But it was not the tycoon in Jasper Crane that endeared him to me or really distinguished him; there is nothing unusual about being a tycoon in the U.S.A.

The gentleman, one of America's leading Presbyterian laymen, was also a scholar. His enviable library (including an extensive James Madison collection, which was bequeathed to Princeton University) was for his own study and enjoyment, not display. The study and practice of individual liberty was a passion with him.

Above all, however, was Jasper Crane's moral stature, featured by an absolute integrity. Never once, in our twenty-five years of intimate acquaintance, did he resort to expediency. He always reflected in word and deed what his conscience dictated as right. He was tolerant of disagreement but never of dissimulation. He was both righteous and tough-minded.

Jasper Crane was not celebrated but he was great—one of those rare oversouls who now and then grace humanity!

LEONARD E. READ

Irvington-on-Hudson
New York

Introduction

"Rose Lane is the greatest," said Bob LeFevre two years after her death. How right he was!

I knew her well.[1] She knew more about almost everything than anyone I have ever met. What a life she led!

Born in 1886 on a homestead claim on the prairie near De Smet, Dakota Territory (now South Dakota), she was the daughter of Laura Elizabeth Ingalls and Almanzo James Wilder. Her mother later became the author of the still widely popular children's books about pioneering days—the "Little House" series. Rose attended schools in Mansfield, Missouri (where her parents permanently settled) and in Crowley, Louisiana. Her first job after graduation was that of telegrapher for Western Union. As such, she worked in various parts of the country, the last being San Francisco. She then had a brief and highly successful career as one of the first female real estate agents in California, specializing in farm land in the San Fernando Valley. In 1909 she married Gillette Lane; the marriage was terminated by divorce in 1918.

Rose began a career as a free lance writer in the early teens, and later joined the reportorial staff of the *San Francisco Bulletin,* then under the editorship of Fremont Older. A fictional serial for *Sunset Magazine* was published as her first novel in 1919: *Diverging Roads.* During this period she also wrote *Henry Ford's Own Story* (1917), *White Shadows in the South Seas* (with Frederick O'Brien, 1919), and *The Making of Herbert Hoover* (1920).

Towards the end of World War I, the American Red Cross and Near East Relief sent her to the Balkans, to Russia and to the Near East to investigate conditions and to write articles about what she saw for the American public. During this era she was initially attracted, and then repelled by communist ideology and practice. She personally knew many of the Red leaders, such as Jack Reed

---

[1]I met her in 1945, as a schoolboy, became her attorney a decade later, and remained her close friend until her death.

(who now rests in the Kremlin Wall), and narrowly avoided jail in Russian Georgia.

After these travels Mrs. Lane settled for a time in Albania; she refused King Zog's offer of marriage. *Peaks of Shala* (1923) was about her experiences in the primitive areas of that country. She also translated from the French *The Dancers of Shamahka* (1923).

She permanently returned to the United States later in the 1920s, to live and write in Mansfield. During that decade and thereafter her short stories and articles appeared frequently in such magazines as the *Saturday Evening Post, Harper's, Country Gentleman, Good Housekeeping, Asia, The Independent, The American Mercury, Ladies Home Journal, McCalls, Sunset, World's Traveler* and *Woman's Day.* Many were later anthologized. In 1922 she won the second O'Henry Prize for the best short story of the year. Her Ozark novels *Hill Billy* (1925) and *Cindy* (1928) and her fictionalized biography of Jack London, *He Was A Man* (1925) added to her renown; at that time she was said to be the second highest paid author (after Somerset Maugham) in the United States. Her best selling novel of pioneer life, *Let the Hurricane Roar* (1933), was dramatized by Helen Hayes on radio and is still in print and selling briskly. In that decade she added to her works a book of short stories, *Old Home Town* (1935); an exposition of her own experience with totalitarianism and freedom, *Give Me Liberty* (1936); and another pioneer novel, *Free Land* (1938).

She bought a farm in Danbury, Connecticut, in 1938 and lived there for more than a quarter century. She discontinued writing fiction to emphasize her opposition to paying income and social security taxes used to support New Deal programs. She published *Discovery of Freedom* in 1943 as the exposition of her economic and political philosophy. At her death she was at work on a revision of this book, which I am now editing for publication. For several years during and after World War II she edited the National Economic Council's *Review of Books.* And she engaged in extensive correspondence with innumerable individuals in furtherance of her philosophic ideas. This book is a portion of her correspondence with only one such individual, but it is (I think) a sampler of her most illuminating observations.

A series of Rose's articles on needlework for *Woman's Day* magazine was published with numerous illustrations as the *Woman's Day Book of American Needlework* in 1963, which at this writing is still an offering of the Book of the Month Club.

In 1965 *Woman's Day* sent Rose to Vietnam to write about the war from a woman's point of view. Undoubtedly she was, at seventy-nine, America's oldest war correspondent. Upon her return she bought a winter home in Harlingen, Texas, where she enjoyed her life-long hobbies of remodeling her homes and creating gardens.

She enjoyed travel, adventure and homemaking. She read extensively; the fields of her interests were as broad as human experience. She was kind hearted, generous and resourceful. She knew virtually all of the prominent personalities of her active years, from Jack London and Sinclair Lewis to Bill Hart and Herbert Hoover. She was described, by virtually all who knew her well, as the most fascinating human being they had ever met.

Some of that fascination shines forth in this correspondence. The exchange of letters began in 1946 at the suggestion of a mutual friend, Leonard Read. Mrs. Lane, who hadn't met Jasper Crane, and who never suffered fools gladly, was initially a touch abrupt, as her first two letters in this collection reveal. But she got to know the Cranes on a visit to Wilmington, and formed a lifelong admiration for Jasper Crane's abilities. In editing the thousands of original pages I have of necessity omitted much engrossing material (such as, for example, how they saved the life of an anti-Communist Rumanian refugee who was on the verge of forcible repatriation) as well as the ephemeral. May those sins of omission not distort the authors' meanings!

Jasper Crane sent me the four thousand pages of this correspondence shortly after Mrs. Lane's death in 1968. I did not know him well, but I knew him well enough to say that he was indeed one of the remarkable men of this century. He was responsible for more specific actions of benefit to his fellowmen than any other person I have known or have heard about. No one will ever know how much he did or in how many areas he acted, because he was firmly opposed to any personal publicity. Since he was a man of action much more than a man of letters, the enormous scope of his greatness and goodness does not appear in this volume of correspondence. Take it from me: he was one of the giants.

Mrs. Lane and Mr. Crane—they both meant their correspondence to be fun, as well as to inquire, probe or edify. My deepest wish is that you enjoy it as thoroughly as they did, and as much as I did in the editing.

ROGER LEA MACBRIDE

Charlottesville, Va.
September, 1972

I

January 22, 1946

Dear Mrs. Lane:

I note with interest the reviews of books for the National Economic Council which you are making. I should think this would be an opportunity for fine service. No better start could be made than with Bastiat.

January 26, 1946

My dear Mr. Crane:

You misunderstand me if you think I regard anything I do as using "an opportunity for fine service." I am not trying to serve anyone but myself. I am really somewhat interested in keeping my small farmhouse and my own life. And have been for nearly twenty years now. If I seem ferocious, maybe that's the reason. But really, nearly everyone whom I've asked to my house has survived unharmed. The whole secret is in the fearless approach and steady nerve and eye.

Seriously, two groups of Americans are responsible for the present dangerous situation: the Big Business Men who are your associates and the "intellectuals" who may be said to be mine. I won't object if you say that business men left the job of thinking to the professional thinkers, who haven't done it. You'll find that I don't "pitch into" anyone; I am much more appalling than that; I actually say what I honestly think. It seems to me that the time is a little to late for anything else.

March 20, 1946

Dear Mrs. Lane:

When I talk about government regulations I mean that the police power of the State must be used to stop infringements of human liberty. For instance restraint of trade by business, domination of workers by racketeers and other practices that prevent the functioning of a free economy should be prevented.

March 22, 1946

Dear Mr. Crane:

As to the restraint of trade by business, that is impossible; the notion that money is power is another lie. There is no possible means by which the Du Pont Company can stop me (if I have the brains, and not a penny) from starting an enterprise that will eventually totally destroy the Du Pont Company. I can be stopped only by violence, by physical force. The Du Pont Company, desiring to stop me, has two possible methods: you can hire and pay a gunman to kill me or kidnap me, and gangsters to destroy my property; you cannot do this successfully if the State performs its proper function of protecting human rights (my right to life, liberty and ownership of property). Or, you can bribe enough Congressmen to pass an Act of Congress setting up a commission and requiring that anyone engaging in any enterprise in the field of Du Pont Company's activities must first obtain a permit from the commission and thereafter be "regulated" by the members of the commission. This act will be enforced by police force, which will as effectually prevent my competing with Du Pont as criminal force would do. You cannot use this second method, either, if the State is restricted to its proper function of protecting human rights, (my right to life, liberty and ownership). For "government regulation" is an infringement of my liberty and ownership.

If both lawless and legal violence are prevented, the Du Pont Company cannot restrain trade; it cannot prevent my competing with it and destroying it. You can then try to stop me by (1) offering me money for my idea and services, which I am free to accept or not, and, (2) by—to put this crudely—buying all the materials I need, and all the banks, and refusing to sell me materials or to give me credit. (The argument against this second procedure is on the socialist basis: that it is injurious to "the common good," in this country usually called "the public interest"). But either of these methods is simply an exercise of human rights, in the economic field of the free market. In the historic experience, neither of these methods actually operate to restrain trade. The Standard Oil Company is said to have used the second method; if it did, the method neither restricted trade in petroleum products, nor stopped competition with Standard Oil, as everybody knows. The actual restraint was exercised by the Federal power in dissolving Standard Oil under the Sherman Act; substituting forty-eight companies for one, with obviously an increase in overhead costs of producing and distributing petroleum products.

The so-called anti-trust acts actually are not Law; they are a substitution of personal State control ("government by men, not by law," tyranny) for Law. Law must *define* the *crime,* and Law must be applicable to all persons alike in all circumstances. The crime must be definable, defined, and provable by evidence.

Now it is impossible to define "restraint of trade." Every transaction in a free market is a restraint of trade, in that it IS trade. If I put a price on an article, I am restraining all buyers from obtaining that given article at a lower price. If I sell you a dozen eggs for fifty cents, I am restraining all other buyers from obtaining those twelve eggs from me. There is no transaction whatever in the free market, which a judge cannot decide is a restraint of trade. Enforcement of the anti-Trust Acts is, therefore, merely an exercise of police power in accordance with *personal* decision. And the basis of all these Acts is the socialist basis; they are presumed to protect "the common good." Certainly, their enforcement cannot protect human rights, which are the rights of the individual person: life, liberty, ownership.

The whole basis of the anti-Trust Acts is a delusion, the socialist delusion. No possible combination of business interests can possibly operate to restrain trade in a free market. Every such actual restraint is a use of force, lawless or legal.

Domination of workers by racketeers is carried out at present by legal police force. Earlier in the American labor movement, it was done (to a much less extent, of course, but it was done) by lawless force—by assault and murder of workers who resisted it. The prevention of racketeer domination of working men is police enforcement of Law protecting every individual person's human rights; life especially, in this instance. It is an arrant absurdity to demand that the State's police power stop the exercise of the State's police power; yet this is precisely what you (or at least, your words) advocate when you say "of course, government regulation is necessary." It is "government regulation" that gives racketeers domination of workers, and the way to stop it is not the use of more "government regulation," but the *abolition* of all government regulation, and the police enforcement of Law.

The State's police power at present enforces upon workers the hours they work, the wages they receive for their work, and memberships in labor unions and payment of labor-union dues; it is as nearly a return to serfdom as has yet been reached in modern industry and Paul McNutt's order of July 1, 1944 literally established actual serfdom for a time; if "government regulation" is not stopped, it will establish industrial serfdom permanently. (And American industrialists who welcome and help to enforce serfdom of their employees are idiotically in error in imagining that they can continue to do this and retain ownership of American industrial enterprises.) This use of police power to enforce encroachments upon the wage-earner's human rights, establishes the labor racketeer's power over the conscripted labor-union members. (And of course enables him to attack employers much more efficiently.) Instead of resisting and attacking this misuse of police power, which the racketeer is using against wage-earners and wage-payers, the wage-payers clamor for a further extension of this misuse, naively believing that *they* can turn it against the racketeer. Just as stupidly as the misled ignorant labor-union member who imagined that he could turn it against the employer, the Eric Johnstons and NAM leaders imagine that they can increase a force always greater than their own, and still control it for their purposes.

The blatantly obvious plain-common-sense course for American employers to follow, is to make common cause with their rank and file employees, against *this misuse of State power.* If the NAM had the sense that God gives little green apples, it would raise a battle cry of free labor and demand abolition of wage-envelope tax-deductions, with some such slogan as, All wages to the worker. They would stand up and refuse to act as tax collectors for the State without recompense; they would deny and refuse responsibility for taking their employee's money away from him without his consent. And the response they would get from rank-and-file wage-earners would astound them.

But no; instead of doing this, they not only support this plain robbery but they act as stooges for the robber-State, they do the actual job of taking the money, and then they cannot understand why "the masses" do not love them, nor why their employees will vote overwhelmingly to strike for "take-home pay." I swear, it is the spectacle of the Gadarene swine.

June 9, 1946

Dear Mr. Crane:

My visit to Wilmington was a wholly happy time in every sense, even the smallest details were all pleasant. I am truly glad to know you and Mrs. Crane, and I shall long remember your roses, the roast beef, and the Du Pont Hotel, which, these days, is an almost miraculous survivor of the Golden Age of American Hotels that we used to take for granted as normal. I do sincerely thank you and Mrs. Crane for your hospitality.

While I can't honestly think that I'd be as useful as one of a group engaged in doing the book that you and Mr. Pew have in mind, possibly I might be useful to them. "We are all socialist now" was true when it was said. I began to resist socialist thinking and to try to dig the tacit socialist assumptions out of my mind in 1920, perhaps earlier than most of the collaborators in such a book. If you would like me to act as a gadfly to their preliminary thinking, I'd be glad to meet them in that capacity, especially while they are doing the preliminary work on basic definitions. I am useful to honest thinkers, if only as an objector who attacks the taken-for-granted assumptions and forces them to examine and defend the bases of their thinking.

July 15, 1946

Dear Mrs. Lane:

I spoke to you about the project of a preparation of a "Treatise on Liberty" of sound character and comprehensive scope. The program is for a group of people who are experts in different fields to meet together once or twice a month for orderly and continued discussions of the various aspects of Freedom, the basic principles involved, with problems arising and the solutions to the problems, with a small staff of two or three competent persons to be continually engaged in the inquiry, assembling material for the meetings of the group and collating the conclusions arrived at. Finally, the leader of the group would put it together in his own words but with suitable acknowledgement to his collaborators.

The group so far constituted includes Dr. Donald J. Cowling—recently retired President of Carleton College, Minnesota, Ralph Robey—Economist, Dr. Norman Vincent Peale—of the Marble Collegiate Church of New York, Harold W. Dodds—President of Princeton University, and Felix Morley—Editor of *Human Events.* All of these have signified their willingness to cooperate in this activity, except Mr. Morley who may not be able to be present at the first meeting. Dr. Dodds is away from Princeton and we are not sure whether he will be at the first meeting. The first meeting of the group will be at the Princeton Inn, Princeton, New Jersey, Monday evening, July 29, to meet at six o'clock, have dinner, spend the evening in discussion and then have a session on Tuesday morning.

Can you be there? I know you sympathize with the idea but doubt whether it will bear fruit. That depends, it is true, on the soundness of the idea but also on the ability of those present to cooperate together. . . .

July 31, 1946

Dear Mr. Crane:

I did not and probably cannot thank you and Mr. Pew at all adequately for the meeting in Princeton.

The more I think of it, the more I believe that you may have begun a resurrection of American thinking. Of course one book, important as it may be, is only a beginning; what is needed is a whole school of thought, developing American principles from the point where their development was abandoned when the few first American thinkers died. I believe it is quite possible that such a resurrection of realistic thinking may come from a succession of such meetings as this first one in Princeton. I am sure that everyone there found it a most valuable experience.

Dr. Conkling's statement, and a conversation I had with him at breakfast, were most illuminating and suggestive. I do not know what books he has written (my ignorance is still my most valuable asset, constantly requiring remedying as it does), but I urgently hope that he will write, either a book or more books as the case may be. There is a need for such thought as his in print, and a terrible thirst for it.

I am not in a position to make a suggestion to Dr. Morley as to whom he may choose to include in the permanent group of his assistants; and I agree wholly with Mr. Robey's opinion that it should be a permanent group, unchanged during Dr. Morley's writing of this book. If I may, however, I will say this to you:

From the point of view of my own hope that the Princeton meeting was the beginning of the development of a whole school of thinkers and writers reviving American thinking, it is essential to attract young Americans. Our group represents, as a whole, a considerable prestige. This is discounted, however, by the charge that we are old—old fogies, old fashioned, reactionary, behind the times. The topsy-turvy view that collectivism is revolutionary, new, "the wave of the future" bringing the better world of tomorrow, captures the always essentially rebellious young people, especially young Americans. I do not know anyone else as young as Mr. Robey apparently is, who would be of any value as an assistant to Dr. Morley. But if Dr. Morley knows any young person whose assistance he could use at all, I would think that youth alone should be regarded as an asset, probably not for the immediate purpose of producing Dr. Morley's book, but to the possible future development of a whole movement in American thought.

The "Algonquin Crowd" took over the entire American literary field during the 20s. Its influence is still nationwide and incalculable in effect. While that group lasted, it stamped its imprint on all young American writers. It lasted only a decade because its ideology was essentially European; it wasn't an outgrowth from American history and traditions. Our group is American; our roots are here; and if we can attract young Americans, we'll bridge the present gap between real America and literary-academic America.

I doubt that much can be done to educate the writers, teachers, ministers of my own age. It was my generation that betrayed the American revolution; only a few of us woke up, halted, and began to fight our way back to American principles; it is typical that I was a socialist (and Dr. Watts, and Hazlitt and Hayek, etc., etc.) and Leonard Read was a new-dealer. You notice that every person of my age who is now "one of us" has smashed an established position, a career, and made a fresh start at an age when most people can't or think they can't do that. This majority who are hostages to their past fortunes make the set-up that young Americans now encounter. I think that our effectiveness immediately, now, is in making such breaches as we can in that set. If Mr. Mark Jones, for example, creates a publication hospitable to young American-revolutionist writers, that will be a break through the wall that now prevents such young writers from getting into print.

September 22, 1946

Dear Mr. Crane:

Unquestionably there is a definite turn in the intangible trends, a new tide that, taken (not yet at the flood, but) at the turn of the ebb. . . .

I must have expressed my optimism too crudely. These are the most dangerous times in history and I am convinced they will get much worse before they are better in any obvious or concrete terms. Since 1933 I have not been able to see anything in the near future but a terrific political, economic, social crash and chaos, with violence. What I mean is what I said to Mr. Hoover [Herbert, a personal friend whose biography she wrote.] two or three years ago: The darkest hour is not the time to despair of dawn. And since then, though the hour grows darker, I see so many indications of dawn that my optimism—which has doggedly been an evidence of things unseen, since the early 1920s—becomes confident, sometimes exuberantly so.

One great fact is that the European influence is gone, completely. Americans no longer look to Germany for lessons in efficiency and to France for leadership in culture.

English influence is negligible now and will become more so as British economy fails under socialism. The only foreign influence now is Russia and that is a push in the right direction. The issue is clarified; everyone knows that Russia represents communism. The time is past when collectivism came to this country disguised as the old, rich, wonderful art, culture, education, science, learning, philosophy, social sciences, social legislation of Father Europe showing crude young America the way to civilization. And this fact means, definitely and certainly, that the reactionary trends here since the 1880s are ended. It has gone far enough to end in a terrific and terrible crash, but it is ended. What comes out of the crash will be American.

I wholly sympathize with your attitude toward the radio. It certainly is painful; indeed I remember my making a small scene in your living room because bearing it was beyond my power of endurance. I have forced myself to hear enough to know what was being done on the air, essential to my education. No more than half an hour a day, two or three times a week, tells more about the important current facts than all the newspapers, publications and books. About two-thirds of the news broadcasters and commentators whom Big Business keeps on the air are Communist Party members or intentional fellowtravelers; General Electric, for instance, put on Granville Hicks, who openly announced his membership in the Party. Until recently, I listened nearly every Sunday evening to Drew Pearson (Lee Hats, at present) in order to know the Party line. It is interesting that within the past few months he is taking a position antagonistic to Russia. I don't know yet whether he is breaking with the Party Line or whether this is policy preparatory to the Party's going underground here.

I have canned 109 quarts of tomatoes from my garden and have a bushel to can today; this is a triumph because blight has literally destroyed nearly all tomatoes in this region. I have canned ninety-nine and a half quarts of beautiful chicken, young fat hens; and ninety-six of Gravenstein apple sauce. My corn crop was perfect; hybrid seed, mostly variants of Golden Bantam, bore abundantly, three and four ears to the stalk, all uniform and not one single cornworm or cornborer in the whole yield. Beans were harassed by groundhogs and did not do so well, the poor Kentucky Wonders had to climb beyond ground-hog reach before they could keep a leaf or set a pod; still it was a fair yield, now all in cans, and cabbages, carrots, beets, cauliflower, flourished beautifully. Eggs are scarce on the market here, being substituted for non-existent meat (not a scrap of meat in all Danbury) but I have three five-gallon jarsful of eggs in water-glass. Also I have a baby beef and a hog now nearing 300-pound weight, both boarding out so that I do not know them personally and will meet them only as pork and beef this winter. The Thorovian life isn't as simple as it seems in Walden Pond but it does have its values.

December 5, 1946

Dear Mr. Crane:

The group publishing *The Interpreter* is evidently part of the single-tax Henry George movement. This is explicit in the copy you sent me; I know nothing else about the publication or the persons publishing it.

The question is therefore basically the constant one: Are not-quite allies our enemies? On this question I agree with Lenin, whom I consider one of the greatest tacticians who ever lived. I think the persons and groups who are almost but not absolutely right are far more dangerous than the open adversaries who are wholly wrong. It's simply the question: which is more dangerous, the straightforward attacker, or the one in our own camp who will betray us to the attacker?

I have never been able to understand Henry George's followers, nor to get from one of them a straight answer to a straight question. They see *Our Enemy, The State* (the title of Albert Jay Nock's almost excellent book; he was a single-taxer) perfectly clearly, much more accurately than most of "us" do; and from this evidence they conclude, I can't concede how, that "The State should be the universal landlord" (to quote Henry George). This conclusion is total socialism; it would be if it referred to the soil, to "land" as commonly used; but their definition of land is "all natural resources." Their view is that all natural resources "belong to all humanity," therefore should be "owned by the community" i.e., by the Commune, which the State either is or represents (George is not clear on this point). They reason that when the State owns all natural resources, private ownership of all "products of labor" can be maintained. (They are staunch defenders of "private ownership.")

You know much better than I how true this would be in detail, if applied to the Du Pont Company. The State would merely own all sources of raw material and the raw materials themselves; the Du Pont Company would own its buildings, equipment, etc., and pay "rent" assessed by the State, for *use* of *all materials,* to The State. At present, the single-taxers contend, private ownership of materials is robbery; Du Pont robs "the community" by its ownership of materials (since all earth belongs to all mankind) and the proceeds of this robbery accrue to Du Pont Company as "economic rent." This explains, to them, the horrible increase of poverty in capitalism, which they take for granted as a fact.

Thus actually they are Marxists in principle; they differ from communists only in method. For forty years I have tried to get such intelligent leaders of the Georgeists as Albert Jay Nock and Frank Chorodov to explain their theory to me; simply to explain it. I believed for years that something was wrong with my head because I could not understand what seemed to be a self-contradiction in their thinking; I could not believe that there actually was a self-contradiction in the thinking of such apparently intelligent and certainly well informed persons. I am now certain that there is a blind spot in their minds. . . . If you can't understand it, they can only tell you to read Henry George.

January 22, 1947

Dear Mr. Crane:

It seems to me that there hasn't been a time of such confusion since the second to fourth centuries. We're all floundering in quicksands, really—trying to get hold of something solid. Truly I am not individualist in the sense of un-cooperative. (I'm working now on the Eleven Commandments, the Eleventh being a statement of the principle of cooperation as an essential of individualism.) And I'm not uncompromising in the sense of pigheaded porcupine—only in the sense of insisting that there ARE principles which MUST be discovered and defined by *reason.* I'm learning more and modifying my previous views all the time.

It may be impertinent of me to say this, but I shall say

it. It seems to me that you and Mr. Pew do not realize that you know infinitely more of value to the libertarian movement—that you are much more valuable to it *as persons*—than all the rest of this [Princeton] group put together, including me of course.

Have you read Sir Ernest Benn's *Confessions of A Capitalist?* If you haven't, I wish you would. If even one American who knows American industry as Sir Ernest knows business would write such a book, the effect would be enormous.

Look at this whole situation, in general. Here is the greatest achievement of mankind to date, an achievement unique in all history, and the only persons who know anything about it won't tell a word of their knowledge. The only persons who speak about it are parasites on it, who know no more about it than a flea knows of a dog. I can't understand why the American industrialist and capitalist imagines that the parasites (who *live* by biting him) are going to prevent him from being bitten.

I ask you: Precisely HOW am I going to defend Du Pont and Sun Oil Company? I can try—and do—to defend personal freedom; that's possible because I am a person, I know what I am, I know what personal life is and how it works and what the results of personal acts are; I can fight for *myself*. I can see that my being able to buy Du Pont glue and Dina (Dinah?) fuel depends upon the existence of Du Pont and Sun Oil, and—because I know some history and some political philosophy—I know they can't exist in collectivism. But I don't know how they work, I don't know precisely how collectivism works destructively upon them, actually I know nothing about them and *there is no means of my knowing*.

If you doubt this, just consider me as an applicant for your Du Pont job, or Mr. Pew's. And suppose I know all the books that all the economists have written, all the Brookings Institute reports and U.S. Census figures; say I've spent thirty years on research in libraries, and earned all the degrees of all the universities. You or Mr. Pew still wouldn't hire me as secretary to a third Vice President in charge of production; you'd know I couldn't help to run Du Pont or Sun Oil, because I wouldn't know how they run.

The only persons who know anything at all about how this unprecedented modern world runs are the men who run parts of it. And they won't tell. What staggers me is, why do they try to get me, or anyone like me, to tell? It's as if Stefanson returned from his years beyond all previous limits of exploration and urged someone who'd never left Delaware to write about those unknown lands, saying that he will help in every way he is able to do—which is paying for the writer's research in libraries.

So far as I know, Sir Ernest Benn is the only capitalist who ever told anybody about capitalism. His American counterpart is Mr. Paul Hoffman. Have you any idea why? I can't figure it out.

Surely Mr. Hoffman knows, or could learn, something about how Studebaker cars are made and marketed? Surely Mr. Sloan could find out how raw materials are turned into a Buick and sold to me on the installment plan? Everybody in this country wants a motor car. Just as everybody last summer wanted meat. People had found out (from black marketeers and inept politicians; certainly not from Swift and Armour) how cattle in Texas get into Danbury butcher shops as steaks and soupbones; they dimly saw that OPA stopped the process and Democrats and Republicans combined couldn't keep OPA meat controls.

Everybody who wants a motor car wants Duco finish and gasoline, but all that anybody (but the silent capitalist) knows about the process is that it's selfish greed for profits plus "economic imperialism" causing world wars. The parasites on Du Pont and Sun Oil tell everyone so; and he can see the profits with his eyes when he looks at your house or Mr. Pew's and compares it with his own. He knows that your incomes are fabulous. (The current SEP has a piece on a cheap columnist, Hedda Hopper. "Hollywood provides a substantial slice of Miss Hopper's annual income of $200,000. Miss Hopper further buttresses herself against possible adversity by guest performances . . ." etc. "Although she suspects that it is considerable, Miss Hopper has no very definite idea just how much her income of $200,000 really is. Her business manager knows. . . ." This is his information. And the reactionary Republicans talk about reducing taxes for these economic royalists, while these same greedy capitalists swipe the "holding taxes" out of a worker's wages every pay day!)

So I can tell him that he is the richest wage earner on earth or in history; I can tell him how much more he gets for how much less work than his father and grandfather did; I can tell him abstract principles. Nobody can tell him that his wages aren't meager in contrast to $200,000 a year; or that the capitalist doesn't take his wages (he has the slip of paper; so much deducted); or that getting a raise isn't the way to get a new car on the installment plan, with Duco finish and a tankful of Dinafuel. He isn't stupid; he knows there's something wrong somewhere now, that the car and the gasoline must be produced before he can get them and that something's wrong with production. But he can't know what is wrong because he doesn't know how capitalism works, and nobody who does know will tell him.

September 8, 1947

Dear Mrs. Lane:

Much is happening of a distressing nature, and I frequently think of your fundamental teaching. In spite of all discouragements let us keep our courage and do what we can about it.

September 9, 1947

Dear Mr. Crane:

Yes, there is a sound point of view from which everything in sight is disheartening. I have said since 1934 (I think, wasn't it then that the New Dealers stole the gold and repudiated the "will pay in gold" contracts?) that the worst time in history is coming. But it's like dying; you know you will, but you don't believe it. In Baku, when Lenin was carrying out his policy of overturning the basis of society by debauching the currency, I had to hire a porter to carry money enough to buy a railway ticket, and I know that exactly the same thing is occurring here, but the price of eggs scares me just the same, eighty-nine cents a dozen for eggs in August.

Yet I think that historians may regard these times as a renaissance. Probably the Renaissance was a heck of a time to be living in, everything upset and going to pieces in confusion. There certainly hasn't been in my lifetime anything like the quantity of thinking that's being done now.

What were you thinking about yourself, say thirty years ago? Well, make it thirty-five and I was thinking about selling California farm land and learning French and buying new clothes. And you and I are multiplied by many millions everywhere on earth. I am as certain as anyone can be of anything in the future that the twentieth century will end as the eighteenth did, with a great revival and resurgence of individualism. If you want something soothing to read, try Sterling Edmund's *Struggle For Freedom* (Bruce Publishing Co., Milwaukee: $4.50). Gives a nice long perspective.

September 15, 1947

Dear Mrs. Lane:

Your letter is much appreciated. The theft of gold from American people occurred early in 1935 (after the government had issued in December 1934 bonds redeemable in gold!) and was sanctioned by Supreme Court decision in April, I think. That woke me up too.

September 12, 1947

Dear Mr. Crane:

May I please ask your advice?

You have seen the piece in the current (September) *Plain Talk,* "Red Star Over Independence Square, The Strange Case of Edgar Snow and the *Saturday Evening Post.*"

The situation is this: Every writer, journalist and communist in the world knows when and how the Comintern took the key position on *Saturday Evening Post.* It is a major triumph of the infiltrating campaign, not only because it feeds millions of American readers the Party propaganda line, but also because it pays cash, a considerable share of Edgar Snow's salary, payment for the pieces, and royalties going into the Party funds and to that extent relieving Moscow. To Europeans, this capture of *Saturday Evening Post* is equivalent to, for instance my capturing control of *Pravda,* because since there has never been a free press in Europe, Europeans naturally regard all American publications as mouthpieces of our government, and

Saturday Evening Post is the chief of all of them, known everywhere. (Incidentally, the Party uses the current copy, in all countries, for its code messages, because anyone anywhere can carry a copy of *Saturday Evening Post* without attracting any notice.)

Now if it were possible to get Edgar Snow off *Saturday Evening Post,* the world effect would be worth more than the Truman and Marshall Plans together, in affecting opinion. Because it would show that, contrary to all former evidence, there exists in this country an opposition to the Comintern, an opposition informed, intelligent and strong enough to retake a major position that the Party has captured and holds. It would be more effective even than defending it all the time would have been, if that could have been done.

The opposition to such an effort of course is Mr. Fuller, the owner, and the big national advertisers who put up the cash. If even a few of the 2,500 advertisers can be induced to go so far as even to mention the matter to Mr. Fuller, I believe it might be done. It was to keep the advertising, of course, that Mr. Fuller went "left" and forced Wesley Stout, Garet Garrett and Adelaide Neall to resign; or, more accurately, to choose between their jobs and their self-respect.

You know I am a simple-minded person. I am just baffled; I cannot understand at all *why* the Big Business Men act this way. My mind can't get any hold on it, and goes blank. The proof that I do not know what to say to these advertisers is that everything I have been able to think of saying produces no results, no effect whatever.

So far as I know, you are the only one of the Du Pont executives who objected to supplying the Soviet dictatorship directly with goods. You convinced the others then, and I was so eager to know how you did it, because of my own many failures. You told me you said, "We can't deal with crooks and murderers." I have thought about this, for hundreds of hours altogether since you told me. Of course its effect was almost wholly in *your* saying it. And there is another element, another obstacle, in the advertising situation, but I do not know what it is exactly. I think it is somehow connected with the attitude to money. Actually there is no difference between shipping steel or oil or explosives to Russia, and giving Edgar Snow the money to send to Russia to pay for steel or oil or explosives, but in the minds of these advertisers there is some psychological difference; what is it?

September 19, 1947

Dear Mrs. Lane:

Your letter of September 12 is received, but I do not think that we can use the bludgeon that you suggest. A tactful discussion of this situation with Mr. Fuller by a number of his friends may be much more effective. That I am trying to develop. Let us hope that we can accomplish the important result that you suggest.

September 24, 1947

Dear Mr. Crane:

As to the *Saturday Evening Post* situation, of course it will be marvelous if Mr. Fuller's friends will discuss it with him tactfully. I shall hope and pray until I hear further from you.

I am certain that there really is complete agreement between us about it. I have failed to put my view accurately. I don't at all think that advertisers should use a "bludgeon" on publishers; actually I despise the publishers' attitude, all of it.

There was a time—which ended within my memory and experience—when publishers COULD not be bludgeoned and when advertisers accepted their responsibility. Those were the days of a free press, which has existed only once in history, only in the USA and only during the ninteenth century—regarding that century as fading away during the 1910s. I remember when we on the old *San Francisco Bulletin* under Fremont Older decided to print the Oxman letters (which proved that the whole law-enforcement apparatus of San Francisco had concocted and paid for the perjury that served as a pretext for sentencing Tom Mooney [a labor union militant in the 'teens] to death). Nobody hated Mooney more violently and vigorously than Older, who was the best hater, when he hated, that I have ever known. All the advertisers hated Mooney; so did all the labor leaders—

for quite different reasons. I had always been certain that Mooney was innocent of the crime for which he was convicted; he was a labor-dynamiter, not a killer; also there was sound evidence of the impossibility of his being within miles of the place where the bomb exploded. But it had been impossible to talk to Older, who raged at the very name of Mooney. When the Oxman letters were laid before him and he read them, he said, "My God, the man *is* innocent. We've got to print this."

The letters filled nearly a whole issue of the paper; fourteen solid pages of them. As soon as the first tearsheets reached Mr. Crothers (owner of *The Bulletin*) he came up to the editorial floor, pale, wild-eyed, shaking, saying to Older, "You're ruining us. You're killing *The Bulletin.*" Older said, "It's the truth. We've got to print it." Ten minutes after the paper was on the streets, advertisers began cancelling. Every display advertiser the paper had cancelled his contract, as of then. The composing room kept stopping the presses while the ads were chiseled out (being already in the metal, on the presses, they had to be cut out with chisels), starting and stopping again. The third edition and all succeeding ones that day went out with blank space where the ads had been. Meanwhile every prominent labor leader in town came storming into Older's office, calling him every foul name that labor leaders used then, pounding his desk, calling him a traitor, a renegade, a double-crosser, asking why the (adjectives) hell he hadn't let the (deleted) *hang?* They said, Mooney might have been some use as a martyr but WHY was Older saving the blankety blank's life? What was the big idea? And one thing was settled: that two-faced hypocrite, Older, would never again get away with his posing as a friend of Labor. Who had bought him off? Who was paying him? Where did Mooney get the backing to buy him?

Next day every labor paper on the Coast repeated this, and *The Bulletin* was out with no display advertising. Circulation soared, adding to costs of course and naturally temporary because no paper can hold circulation without advertising; people buy papers largely for the display ads, especially in the home circulation field which is the solid one. Crothers—who usually didn't begin to blur till late afternoon—was sodden-drunk early every morning and sat all day in his office muttering, "Ruined. Ruined."

Older said, "Well, if we're licked, we fought clean." Also he cursed Mooney, up and down and across, most eloquently, for minutes on end, frequently. If he could lay hands on the (deleted), he said, he'd hang the (deleted) himself, blank, blank, blank. Some of the staff began to worry about getting other jobs. But the department stores began to feel the pinch and began coming back during the third week, just as our home circulation began to sag. *The Bulletin* pulled through and held the San Francisco and northern California evening field as long as Older edited it (he went to Hearst some years later, and the *Bulletin* slowly died; Hearst bought the remnant finally and consolidated it with his *Call,* that Older was then editing.) Mooney, as you know, was not hanged; Labor got its martyr after all, and used him to great advantage all over the world, until he was pardoned only a few years ago, when everyone promptly forgot him.

What I am saying is this: When an advertiser accepts responsibility as an advertiser, and an editor, owner, publisher, accepts his responsibility, there is no question nor possibility of either using a bludgeon on the other. The attitude of the men who controlled Pacific Gas & Electric (and of each of their group, the "capitalists" who were the advertisers) was simply that they would not pay for activities which they did not approve, which they regarded as inimical to them and their objectives and interests. Older's attitude was simply that a publication exists to print facts and truth as the responsible person sees it; and there was none of this modern fallacy of "freedom of the press" on the Old *Bulletin;* Older edited it and not a word was printed in that that he did not endorse; anyone of his staff who wanted to print something else was wholly at liberty to quit and look for a job on a paper whose editor shared his opinions.

This acceptance of responsibility was the basis and source of the Great American journalism. (And, I surmise, of the growth of American industry and business, though I don't know as much about them.) It was already deteriorating in 1914. The advertisers should have stuck to their position and never paid for another line of *Bulletin* advertising.

Crothers should either have fired Older or stood with him. From about 1800 to 1870, that's what they would have done. In 1914, advertisers backed down because they saw immediate cash as more important than the free enterprise that their fortunes really came from (the golden egg more important than the goose that laid one daily). Crothers wobbled after that; he was afraid to fire Older and afraid not to, he didn't trust him and didn't want to lose him, and pestered and interfered till Older had to quit to keep any self-respect.

Every successful publication in this country was created by an editor; and every one of those men was a man whom nobody and nothing *could* buldgeon. Older, and for instance, Pat Calhoun, understood each other perfectly; they were the same kind of men. Older cost Pat Calhoun five million dollars (spent to keep Calhoun out of the penitentiary) and not a penny of the five millions went to pay Older's salary through *Bulletin* advertising. Calhoun wouldn't have paid it; Older wouldn't had accepted it. Arthur Vance of *Pictorial Review,* George Horace Lorimer of *Saturday Evening Post,* were the last of such editors. I don't know the record on the business side.

Graeme Lorimer said to me not long after his father died that there were no principles, policies, ideas any more in Curtis publications, "all we want now is circulation and advertising." He wasn't happy about it but he was resigned; that's the way it is, what can anyone do about it?

Patrick Henry said, "I care not what others may do, as for *me*—" George Horace Lorimer would have said, "The hell with what 'they' want; I'm running this magazine." If one man's accepting his own responsibility for his own acts is regarded by others as bludgeoning *them,* that's their fault; not his. God knows they'd still be naked, lousy, starving savages if they'd all gone on being bludgeoned by the opinions and acts of other persons; if nobody ever had stood up and accepted responsibility. Let them stand up on their feet and accept responsibility for what they do—or not; that's up to them. Somebody had GOT to do it, or they'll all go on sliding back into naked starving savagery.

At least, that is the way it looks to me. And probably I am somewhat emotional about it, because I cared for American writing, American publishing, the vigor and honesty, and soundness of a free press; and I saw it, and nearly all my life I've seen it rotted away into the cheap, immoral, venal, irrational, disgusting and destructive mess that it is now. But I try to discount for my own personal sense of outrage and nausea and fear; I try to *think* about the situation and I believe my view of it is rational.

I don't want to be misunderstood as ever suggesting, or approving, anyone's saying to anyone else, "You do so and so, or I will do such-and-such to you." That is a threat, an attempt to invade another's area of responsibility, to infringe human rights, to dictate another's decisions and acts. Du Pont did nothing of that kind when you all decided not to deal with the Soviet Union. What the company did then was to say, "*I* do this." And if asked why, "Because, the Soviet Union being what it is, this company cannot deal with it." This is not trying to dictate to Stalin, nor to destroy his regime. It is simply acceptance of Du Pont's responsibility for Du Pont's decisions.

If every American corporation's directors did this, of course, the Soviet Union would collapse. But that would not be the responsibility of the directors; it would be the responsibility of the men who created the Soviet Union so that it cannot survive if American corporation-directors act morally. If Du Pont's action so alarmed everyone in the Kremlin that they changed the Soviet regime, the change would be their responsibility, not Du Pont's. I do not think that Du Pont should dictate or try to dictate to the Kremlin, or threaten it; and I do not think that Stalin, Molotov, or anyone else should permit any threat or dictation to make him act contrary to his convictions. Even if his honest convictions are wrong, they are all he has.

When I say what I regard as a moral action by any national advertiser would make all publishers chase communists off their staffs, I simply state what I believe to be a fact. I think the publishers would act that way. I think it would be a wholly indefensible, immoral action, originating in their having no moral standards now, no convictions, no policy but grabbing the immediate dollar. And I amend my statement, which isn't accurate; not ALL publishers would act that way, only the big, respectable ones. The *Daily Worker* would go on publishing without an advertiser, it would go on if its editors and writers were outlawed, hounded by the police, forced to steal paper and ink and print in cellars, because the Communists do have convictions; on their crazy immoral basis they act morally; on their fallacy of "the individual is nothing," they act as individualists, each one responsible for his own undeviating adherence to The Faith. The Communist Press doesn't "give the public what it wants." There isn't money or pressure or any consideration on earth that would induce a communist publisher or editor to hire me or to print one word I write. That immoral-morality is their whole strength. Or may be only half of it, the other half being "our" lack of that quality, in so far as it is lacking.

* * * * *

[In her capacity as editor of the *National Economic Council's Review* of books, Mrs. Lane had reviewed a recent economics text book by one Lorie Tarshis. The book's approach to economics was heavily dominated by Keynesian and Marxist analysis. It appeared that the textbook had been adopted in a number of colleges throughout the United States, and Mrs. Lane and many who felt as she did about the book mounted a strong campaign to persuade those institutions to drop the text. A good many who had been unaware of the content of the book did so—and the angry publisher began to react strongly.]

* * * * *

Houghton-Mifflin, publishers of the Tarshis economics textbook have issued to their entire sales and contact staff this instruction: "If anyone mentioned to you Rose Wilder Lane's review of *The Elements of Economics,* refer him to *The Plotters,* by John Roy Carlson. The New York *Times,* of September 1 reports the appointment of Dr. Carl Shoup to the committee of three advisory economists to the U.S. Treasury now formulating the Government's new tax policy. Dr. Shoup read, endorsed and recommended *The Elements of Economics* in manuscript before publication. There can be no higher endorsement."

A member of the staff pointed out that John Roy Carlson is thoroughly discredited. He was answered, "Anyway, it's effective. Professors don't want to be mixed up with people that Carlson writes about."

The NEC sent a copy of the review with a covering letter suggesting that the recipient read the book itself, to all Trustees and Presidents of universities that have adopted it. The president of Oregon State College replied to Mr. [Merwin] Hart, [President of the National Economic

Council], more abusively than I fully recall but I remember bits. "In reply to your letter of . . . No. I have not read *The Elements of Economics* and I do not intend to read it. I have read *The Plotters* by John Roy Carlson. . . . Sir, you stink from foul associations. *The Elements of Economics* by Professor Lorie Tarshis most certainly WILL be used in Oregon State College." Mr. Hart replied, a grand letter, ending by saying that he is taking the liberty of sending copies of this correspondence to all members of the Oregon State Board of Education. I have sent a copy with personal note to all managers of Chamber of Commerce in Oregon and am now covering the Oregon Press in the same way.

October 9, 1947

Dear Mr. Crane:

If there are any developments in re Edgar Snow, of course I am intensely interested. Have you seen his piece in current *Saturday Evening Post* about the Communist leadership in France? nice, homely work showing that Communists are good neighborly home folks, as Stalin is good old Uncle Joe.[1] In conjunction with the emergence of the Comintern into the open again, and the *Plain Talk* reprint, it's a good article for our purposes. Of course it was in print before the *Plain Talk* piece appeared, too late to stop it.

October 19, 1947

Dear Mr. Crane:

A college president, President Harmon, of Drake University is my authority for the statement, not yet otherwise verified, that *The Elements of Economics* by Professor Lorie Tarshis which I reviewed in the *National Eco-*

[1]In fact Snow continued to write for the *Post* indefinitely. After it folded he moved over to *Life*. He died in early 1972 (two doctors sent by Chou En-lai in attendance), just before President Nixon's trip to Peking. *Life's* managing editor Ralph Graves wrote on February 25, "It had been Edgar Snow's intention to cover the trip for *Life* from the Chinese side, reporting the reactions of Mao and Chou as only he would have been able to do. We will sorely miss [his] expert words and insights. . . ."

nomic Council Review for August, is in use in General Motors Institute.

President Harmon underlines *General Motors Institute* and *The United States Coast Guard Academy* in his list of colleges using this textbook. He offers the list as proof that the book is "neither radical, socialistic, communistic, un-American or subversive, no more than Drake is."

We seem to have stopped its use in the Coast Guard Academy; so many letters have been sent out from headquarters saying it has not been issued pending a decision to be made and that meantime the old textbook is being used.

So far as I can learn, there ARE no good economic textbooks in existence, with which to replace Tarshis if or when we get his book out. It is no use trying to get an honest one written, until there is a sound thinker in an important university post who can and will write one. Because the first essential to publication of a textbook is that the writer be an employed Professor of enough standing and influence to guarantee the book's adoption by the university in which he is (for high school textbooks, high school teacher ditto). It is better if the textbook is co-authored by two (or more) writers in as many different institutions. The whole educational system is a vast bureaucracy which, like all such, operates to perpetuate itself, not for the end for which it is presumed to exist.

November 11, 1947

Dear Mrs. Lane:

Referring further to your letters about the Tarshis book I am glad to tell you that I am advised as follows by the head of General Motors Institute:

"He states that they reviewed Professor Tarshis' book entitled *Elements of Economics* and came to the same conclusion that you stated in your letter as to its type.

"As a result the book is not in use as a textbook by the Institute and is, therefore, not endorsed by General Motors."

November 13, 1947

Dear Mr. Crane:

Apropos absurdities: Can you believe (but it's actually true) that Houghton-Mifflin has solemnly appealed to the Civil Liberties Union (Roger Baldwin's outfit) seeking action against NEC and me on the ground that my review of *The Elements of Economics* is an invasion of, or injury to, Professor Tarshis' civil liberties? and has received a solemn decision of the Civil Liberties Union that action could not be undertaken without infringing upon the civil liberties of Mr. Hart and me. This decision bewildered Houghton-Mifflin executives; and disheartens them, too. Presumably (I have no report on this, but I surmise) they are asking each other, Is there no protection of free speech and academic freedom in this great democracy? If even the Civil Liberties Union cannot protect them, what can? Seriously, this is a rather dreadful comment on education, isn't it? Of course all Houghton-Mifflin executives are products of universities.

I assume you have seen Henry Hazlitt's new book *Can Dollars Save the World?* We absolutely MUST make this a best seller. Item of good news: Dr. Joseph Schumpeter, of Harvard, the Mount Everest of economists in the academic world, is as crazy about this book as I am. He will became emeritus in 1948, and then will be a fighter on "our" side.

December 1, 1947

Dear Mrs. Lane:

I think the steps that you have taken have already been successful and are effectively killing this book and a few more nails in the coffin ought to make it stay dead.

A great deal of pressure has been brought on the *Saturday Evening Post* in the matter of Edgar Snow, and I have had a frank talk with Walter Fuller myself but I am afraid that nothing is going to be done about it, at least right now.

January 22, 1948

Dear Mr. Crane:

Thank you for your note of yesterday. I believe that Yale's dropping the book is the beginning of its end, and wins this little campaign. It seems to me, too, that this Tarshis fight helps to start a much wider and more useful one, a generally questioning and active attitude toward schooling in general. Directly, it has initiated the Texas legislative investigation of all textbooks used in Texas. Groups in Arkansas are aroused, and in Oregon. There is more activity in direct relation to this August *National Economic Council Review* now than there was last year; in every mail I receive new letters, I mean from new correspondents, about it, with requests to send copies to other new persons. NEC has just ordered another reprint of 2,000 copies, of which more than half had been ordered before the reprinting.

* * * * *

[Mr. Crane had said that the difficulty of removing the Tarshis book from the institutions in which it had become lodged made him question whether the American Republic could be saved. Mrs. Lane responded—]

* * * * *

The Republic can't be preserved; it's gone now. Politically, the asset is in what remains of federal *structure;* the existence of the State Governments. When the Federal center collapses, as it will, centers of political power remain in the State capitals, which possess military force in State police and National Guard units. (Communists have always understood this; read Weisbond's *The Conquest of Power*. The obstacle to seizure of power in this country is unique, it exists nowhere else, it is the *federal* political structure. That is the reason why the Second and Third Internationals have worked for democracy here, and amended the Federal Constitution to that end; direct election of senators, income-tax amendment. That is why the New Dealers worked to centralize power in Washington while increasing democracy, and trying to supercede the States with the Seven Authorities, TVA the first, MVA the second, etc.) If there were political intelligence on our side, we would be capturing the

State governments now. However, the crash will compel that action.

The economic power really comes from the small units, upon which the huge ones are dependent. Say that there is a total crash, precipitated by "runaway" inflation and accompanied by political collapse, generally gangsterism and mob-fighting. Politically, the States will act to preserve order, with State police and National Guard. Economically, the localities will act to keep the economy functioning, as they do in, for example, a hurricane. The lineman will not wait for orders from a national center—as they do in England or France; they will act on orders from their local center, as they are accustomed to doing.

I have never expected—not since 1934—to preserve the Republic. The job is to rebuild the Republic. And the sooner we stop looking at Washington, the better. The real power is not in Washington. No more than the bills in your pocket are real money, or than "our highest national income" is real income. My God, how long are we going to go on believing that illusions are facts and trying to act as if they were facts?

This country isn't finished; it is still here and it will survive. Americans will pull it through the crash. Our great asset is intangible, it is in the minds and reactions of millions of persons. I said this all through the 1930s, when there was no evidence of it at all; and now the evidence is all over the place. This is the one country on earth in which *persons act*, as persons. The Vigilance Committee, the armed posse, is indigenous here. Human rights are the *assumptions* on which Americans act. The spontaneous reactions in this country are unlike anything anywhere else. We can depend upon it that the spontaneous reactions will be right. Americans will act to defend lives, liberty and property, theirs and their neighbors; and they will act to keep the economy functioning; they will act without orders.

What is needed is sound political and economic thinking. The spontaneous reaction is not enough. It is absolutely essential and it can be depended upon to support rational political action, but the rational thought is absolutely essential. And during the past ten years the effort to *think* in this country has become enormous, incalculable. A whole body of sound political thought is emerging, beginning to take form. It has seemed to me, and still does, that at present the only possible useful action is thinking; the clarification of one's own principles, and the expression of them. As the basis for sound thinking, a knowledge of facts is necessary. The more that American thinking can be communicated, the greater will be the strength of this country when the crash comes.

I don't think that any *action* now has any value or effect at all as action. The whole value of the Tarshis fight, as an instance, is its educational value; its value in informing citizens of the situation in the schools; its value in exposing economic fallacies; its value in stimulating activity and revealing America's enemies; its value in the experience of the aroused citizens; its value in showing them who their allies are and in putting allies in touch with each other. I wouldn't snap my fingers to take the textbook itself out of the universities; hundreds of similar ones would flow into the tiny gap. Stopping the Marshall Plan, or the federalization of education, or cutting the Federal budget, or defeating any of the unconstitutional "common good" measures now in Congressional committees, will make no difference. The value of all such fights is educational; every one of them strengthens the intangible force that will act effectively when the time comes for action.

Meanwhile if you'll try to ignore Washington and look at the "little people," the "common man," maybe you'll see more support for faith and optimism. I hope so; I do. Though I must say that these are tough times; sometimes I think even harder to live through than the 1770s-80s, and I certainly sympathize with General Washington, and also with his deserting soldiers, as I never did before.

II

January 30, 1948

Dear Mrs. Lane:

Your wonderful letter of January 22 is received and is very much appreciated. Indeed I was so much worked up over it that I talked very bluntly and emphatically over the telephone to a leading Wilmington character until my wife called me off! The particular point of this discussion was how to get things done, and I was pointing out that there is only one way to get things done—to make men free. It is simply appalling that so many people of benevolent purpose, yearning to accomplish good works, cannot grasp this point but are willing in one way or another to restrict human liberty in order as they fondly hope to promote the accomplishments they seek.

* * * * *

[Mr. Crane raised the question of whether it would be a good idea to subsidize various people to produce works expounding the principles and ideas of human freedom.]

* * * * *

February 1, 1948

Dear Mr. Crane:

Have you ever thought what giving away money does to the persons who earn money? as an *illustration only*, what Cecil Rhodes's subsidizing Felix Morley's schooling does to *my* schooling and my education? What Straight's subsidizing writers does to *my* writing? What Guggenheim's subsidizing Louis Adamic does to *my* books? What Carnegie's subsidizing Professor Rugg does to all decent educators?

You and Mr. Pew have done a great deal of useful work. There was a time when you had done nothing yet, and I assume that you began earning very little money in comparison with the amounts you earned later. Now try to imagine that when you began, when you took your first job, you had been offered at the same time another opportunity; twice the money, not for any real labor, but merely for pleasing someone else—say, as a play-companion to an agreeable fellow who was going yachting around the world for twenty years or so. Would you have taken the easy money? If you had, what would have been the results to *you*?

This is what the Americans who *earned* a lot of money have been doing steadily and constantly to all young writers, teachers, ministers, artists, students, for a half century. All these young ones have a choice: earn their living, or get an easier living by favoritism. The easier way is represented as an honor; it isn't only the cash, it's a prestige-advantage. It's a prize, a scholarship, publicity, fame. Just think! Instead of taking a job and earning a salary Jasper Crane was *chosen,* selected, honored, he wears a badge, he will be known his life through as Play-Companion to Mr. Yachter. He has won a Guggenheim Fellowship. He has a grant from the Carnegie Foundation. He is a Pulitzer Prize Winner. He goes from honor to honor, from Yachter to Messrs. Yachters; he speaks at banquets, he is appointed to commissions, he is honored and honored and honored and becomes President of Columbia, Honorary Ph.D. of seventeen universities, advisor to the President, emissary to China. He never has to earn a penny.

And all his misguided classmates, who did take jobs and did earn money, have no chance in competition with him. That one initial step, his taking unearned money, gives him a prestige-advantage (not to mention the financial one) over them all. What it does to him personally is another matter; it destroys him as a moral being.

This is an outrageous thing to do to human beings. It is so damned merciless, too. Mr. Benefactor preys on the weakness of other persons at their most defenseless, most helpless moments. He plans it that way. He offers unearned money often explicitly, to the "needy." He does it to the "poor, the struggling, the young." Sinclair Lewis had the guts to refuse the Pulitzer Prize; he was solvent at the moment. The Nobel Prize got him at a time when he was broke, deep in debt, not working, desperately needing both cash and a prestige-boost; and he couldn't stand out against it, especially as he'd have had to overcome Dorothy, too. All the pressures were too much for him at the moment. Earlier, or later, he might have been all right.

If Senator Ball really wants the Treasury to stop supporting subversive, anti-American enterprises, he should repeal all tax-exemptions. And triple tax all "non-profit" organizations; tax them one hundred percent of all gift-receipts. Let the churches, universities, schools, "social services," earn their money. The Sun Oil Company or Du Pont de Nemours is a genuine social service; that's how it gets money, by giving a real social service which people want and therefore are willing to pay for—by giving this service in exchange for the money which its beneficiaries want to pay for that service.

* * * * *

There is a vast quantity of writing about liberty and freedom, but the words are not even defined. So far as I know, only two persons ever agreed on a definition of liberty: Leonard Read and I. Leonard—I'm told not by him—has devised a parlor game, in his effort to get the definition into another head; I don't know with what success. The game requires two persons, one fly-swatter and a fly. One person holds the swatter but can move only as the other person tells him to move; the object of both is to swat the fly. This cannot be done, of course.

The idea of liberty is so new, so undeveloped and so little known that no vocabulary exists. People create words to express ideas; you and I have seen a whole vocabulary produced for the automotive and radio and airplane industries. (Remember when a car had no name? and when we called it "the machine"?)

Two words are needed, each developed as noun and verb (verb of course including adverb and adjective); one to mean: the natural, inherent self-control, therefore responsibility, of the individual person. The other to mean: conditions of environment which do not prevent the individuals exercise of his inherent self-control and responsibility.

If we use "Liberty" to express the first meaning, as in "endowed by the Creator with inalienable . . . liberty" then we have no verb, no adverb and adjective, corresponding.

If we use "freedom" to express the second meaning, then we have verb, adjective and adverb, as in "I am free,"

"They acted freely," "The slaves were freed," "To free the prisoners."

The lack, as yet, of knowledge of liberty, confuses the two meanings, which in reality are quite different. For example, no means exists of saying easily, "I am endowed by the Creator with inalienable liberty." "I am free" doesn't do it, because it expresses the other meaning, of the *release from imprisonment* or slavery and slides too easily into Roosevelt's "Freedom from want." That is, into the basic fallacy that liberty is a *grant* from an authority: i.e., that liberty is "liberties."

The idea must be grasped first; then the words created and the idea, by means of thought in word-symbols, developed. Not until then can a book be written. It seems to me that you are trying to pile up bricks, not only where there are no bricks and no straw but when there have been no brick-makers.

July 5, 1948

Dear Mr. Crane:

[Mr. Crane had sent Mrs. Lane a copy of a confidential letter he had written to Felix Morley attempting to bring Mr. Morley to see Mr. Crane's concept of christianity and of free enterprise. Mrs. Lane said that she was in thorough-going agreement with Mr. Crane's approach and added that she was unable to comprehend what Mr. Morley meant by the words "christianity" and "liberalism." She went on—]

As I once said in Princeton, if I exist it follows that a Creator (of me and of all things) exists; if there is Time, there is Eternity. Other persons may have means of perception that I haven't; and, since they say they have, I'll take their word for it; but so far as I am concerned, I have no means of comprehending the nature or purpose of God. I stop where the Moslem does and where some Jews do, at GOD IS. "Allah il allah." "I am that I AM."

Therefore I consider liberty as a principle existing in the nature of man within space and time; a general truth created by The Creator; an immutable fact within space and time, the *source* of which is both within and beyond space and time, the *source* being God who comprises ALL DIMENSIONS, creates all, is dimensionless and timeless.

It seems to me that liberty exists exactly as gravitation exists, a general principle in the nature of ponderable things. Isn't gravitation holy? Isn't it the Will of God that the sparrow (or Newton's apple) falls to the earth?

It seems to me that the purpose of human life is knowing the Will of God. If you consider this infinite creature, man, endowed by the Creator with senses, reason and self-control, but created totally ignorant, what other purpose of his existence on this planet is conceivable? Any human life is a continuous process in Time of acquiring knowledge of things within the dimensions of space and time, and these are all manifestations of the Creator's Will.

It seems to me that, since senses and reason are the means with which the Creator endows man, the holy method of learning God's will is the method called "scientific." This method begins by recognizing human ignorance and human limitations. A scientist does not attempt to deal with matters beyond space and time, nor to use other means than his senses and reason (admittedly limited, fallible, finite, inadequate to dealing with eternity and infinity). The scientist is meek. What did Jesus mean when he said, "The meek shall inherit the *earth*"? He did not say, the meek shall see God.

It seems to me that the great tragedy of these times is the dualism taught by the churches; historically the idea that came into Catholicism from Manichaeism and that Protestants took from Catholicism. Its result is that scientists (and the scientific approach generally) deny or disregard the (to me) plain self-evident fact that they are engaged in learning God's will; they have too little, or no, perception that their work is a humble approach to God, a way of prayer, and in that sense holy, an act of faith in God. They are condemned by the churches as engaged in *earthly* affairs which are, by definition in the dualist's view, essentially ungodly and evil; and, since they themselves accept this dualist concept of reality, they have little or no sense of the sanctity of scientific research, of its real character.

On the other hand, the theologians and philosophers and even any priest or minister, who simply hold beliefs obtained from other men's beliefs or evolved from their own mental processes and never subjected to tests of their truth, regard themselves and are regarded as peculiarly sanctified and holy, because it is assumed that they deal with unearthly matters which, by dualist definition, are superior to and opposed to the evil earthly ones. To me, it is obviously ancient pagan fallacy to regard the earth as created and ruled by the Devil, and reality as being war between the Devil's kingdom and God's. Historically the idea comes from prehistoric times when men did not understand and feared darkness, and worshipped the Sun which brought back light, so that day and night seemed to them engaged in war against each other and every evening, for all they knew, might be the final victory of the Dark which this time perhaps had finally killed the Sun. The idea survives in pure form among savages and barbarians; I have seen them worshipping on their knees, with tears of relief and joy, the morning star, and desperately fighting with rifles the attack of the Devil on the moon in an eclipse. In Europe and here, the idea survives in "the war between science and religion," in the reverence for the clergy and the lack of reverence for a discoverer of an electron, a plastic, or nylon. And in the belief that a person's life is a struggle between good and evil, the evil being his "natural" self and its desires and satisfactions. And, incidentally, in Felix Morley's condemnation of capitalism as "materialistic."

If my view is correct, i.e., if The Creator is One God (as Abraham said and Moslems say), then all things existing are expressions of His Will, and there is no Devil, no Principle of Evil, contending against a Principle of Good, in the universe; nor in any person.

Then the human struggle is between human ignorance and human knowledge. The "evil" is the result of man's acting upon a false concept of reality. This is plain enough; and accepted by everybody, in simple matters.

For example: Everybody knows that the horrible suffering in hospitals before the 1880s came from ignorance of anesthetics; that epidemics such as the Black Death came from ignorance of germs; that traffic accidents on the highways come from drivers' false concepts of distance, speed and momentum. If a man kills himself by his action in driving a car on a highway, nobody will call him anything worse than a fool. If he wrecks his marriage and his career by committing adultery, almost everyone will at once transfer his act to a "moral" plane, that is, to the concept of dualism, and he will be regarded as having engaged in the struggle between Night and Day, Darkness and the Sun, his "natural" self and his Soul, and as having chosen or fallen prey to Evil instead of joining forces of Good and "conquering" *himself*, i.e., his "natural" or earthly self which (in dualist theory) is inherently evil, being the Devil's kingdom. It isn't assumed that everyone "naturally" wants to kill himself; but it is assumed that everyone "naturally" wants to ruin his life and the lives of all other persons. It isn't supposed that nothing but supernatural Grace enables a man to drive a car safely and for his own benefit; but it is everywhere preached and believed that nothing but a mystic supernatural experience can enable him to direct his life correctly. It is simply assumed that anyone naturally wants to drive a car for his own good and that if he doesn't, he didn't know how to; but it is assumed (because of dualism) that everyone naturally wants to live his life for evil, and if he doesn't conquer and suppress that natural desire and isn't rescued by super-natural intervention from natural "self," all his acts and his end will be evil.

It seems to me that Human definitions are limited by human powers to finite matters (space and time) and that "good" and "evil" are human concepts, definable in no more than human terms. Because I myself have no mystic power, I know nothing about the nature of God. To me, good and evil are good and evil *to human beings*. And it seems to me that persons act in ways causing evil results to themselves and to other persons, because they are ignorant and misled by false concepts of reality.

I think that persons live "good" lives, in proportion to their knowledge of principles which exist in the nature of man and in the nature of human relationships; I think these principles are as "real" and "natural" as the principles of physics or chemistry or electronics (all principles being generally Truth applying to all particulars in their field; all being the Will of God). And I think that the greatest obstacle to men's acquiring knowledge of "moral" principles (principles of human nature and human relationships) is the concept of dualism taught by the churchmen, which blocks a "scientific" approach to the "moral" field of knowledge.

I have no ground on which to deny that some persons have means of acquiring knowledge, other than the human senses and reason; they say they have un- or supernatural means of communications direct with God, and I can't say they haven't. I know I haven't, and I doubt that many persons have. Certainly it is evident that when a majority of persons in any given time and place, cease to believe that goodness is obedience to churchmen, (still believing the dualist concept, that morals are in the supernatural world, opposed to the natural world) they have no guide whatever to their actions in relation to each other; they become wholly "immoral" with frightful practical results. This indicates that direct communication with God is not a common human power.

It is a historical fact that moral *principles* are almost unknown as yet. The only one ever stated is the one in the American Declaration: All men are born equal and endowed by the Creator with . . . life, liberty, ownership. Compare this meager knowledge with, for instance, the known principles of chemistry, or even of aerodynamics or electronics. In the field of morality, there is as yet little more than the Ten Commandments; and these are *commandments,* orders, they are not statements of principles. They have the relation to knowledge of morality that the signs, NO SMOKING, in a factory making explosives, have to knowledge of the chemical nature of explosives. It is advisable to obey them because the existing principles in the chemical nature of explosives are sound reasons for the command; and experience proves that if the command is not obeyed, the result is disastrous. But the signs, and the Ten Commandments, in themselves are a simple exercise of authority over the human will; and if the Creator endows man with liberty, which is free will, then God does not exercise authority over men's minds or acts. The Creator establishes *the principles,* His Will, in morality as in chemistry, and creates man endowed with free choice, senses, reason, self-control and responsibility, "free to do good or evil" and inevitably reaping the consequences of his action, by the inevitable working principles, in morality as in chemistry.

Now, if men begin (as they have recently) to grasp the concept of liberty—to have a glimmer of knowledge of the *principle* that every person has natural God-given self-control—they must deny the *authority* of God and the churches; they must accept individual responsibility. (They can't blame God for sickness or war.) If, at the same time, they keep the old primitive-communist concept of Authority, and the old pagan concept of the dual universe, the inevitable result is the "godless communism" which denies the existence of God, or any moral principles, of any force but physical force in a mechanistic universe.

The American statement of a moral principle (a principle existing in the nature of man) is the beginning of a scientific approach to morality. Human knowledge of morality today is no more developed than human knowledge of physics was when Newton stated the first principle of gravitation, or knowledge of electronics was when Franklin got a shock from the string of a kite. Persons live "good" lives by a groping combination of what their parents told them not to do with their natural impulses or "instincts," just as they didn't fall off cliffs for untold milleniums before Newton's alleged apple fell. We live in a primitive-savage state of morality; the Age of Reason has hardly begun and all the old taboos and the vested interests built on them are opposed to its development.

Returning to your letter, I agree with you that the problems in the field of human relationships (morality: including economics and politics) should be approached "in a really philosophical way." But I don't think that you and Felix define "philosophy" in the same sense at all. I think you mean what Franklin meant by the word when he established the Philosophical Society: and that Felix means what the scholastic thinkers meant. Franklin was scientific; he meant a *rational* approach to problems, realism. The scholastic thinkers and Felix are dualists; by "philosophy" they mean mysticism, the "spiritual" or "other world," the opposite to "natural" or rational, the opponent of "materialism" in thought or action. This is the reason why Felix disregarded economic facts; he doesn't regard such facts as within the field or scope of philosophy. The number of acres in the average farm, the percentage of share croppers or mortgages, the rate of increase in industrial wages, are all "this world" matters; they are material things, physical; in themselves as material things they are inherently evil, "natural" things to a dualist. Philosophy, to Felix or any dualist, belongs in the other and opposing world, in another plane of perception, finer, more ethereal, "spiritual" as opposed to "natural."

If I held his basic philosophic concept of the universe, I would have replied (in his place) to you and Mr. Pew that the facts you adduced proved his indictment of capitalism as materialistic; I would have said, "All these figures are very well in their place, but what spiritual or philosophic idea have you expressed? As I have said in my manuscript you are capitalists and you are materialists, as you have just shown that you are." In your place, I would have then replied as you do in this letter: "Free enterprise is moral and spiritual per se; the root of a free economy is the free spirit of man created free in the image of God, and the material goodness of its fruits to mankind is the principles in the universe that He creates. These material goods are man's reward for man's obedience to these principles which are the Will of God." But to make that reply, you must deny the validity of the concept of dualism, which Felix holds. You must say that Natural and Spiritual, matter and spirit, soul and body, are one; that God is One God, that His Creation is One Creation; that there is no opposition, no division even, in the Universe. And, I think, the corollary of this concept is that good and evil are temporal things and exist only in human life within time and space; that evil is a result of human ignorance of God's Will; and to say "God is good" is attempting to apply a time-and-space measurement to the Eternal and Infinite, to which it does not apply. The more accurate view, I think, is that Good is the result of man's knowledge of, and therefore action according to principles which are the Will of God operating in the universe; and the figures which you and Mr. Pew brought to Princeton are items of evidence to prove that. Aren't they? I think so.

For it seems to me that if God endows individual persons with liberty (and I am certain He does, as He endows all particles of matter in the universe with mutual attraction to each other) then it follows that men who know this principle and act according to it are acting in accordance with God's Will, knowing it and *choosing* to act according to it—as they do when they build a skyscraper and when they don't try to walk off its roof onto air. In both cases, the result of their so acting is a good to them. When people believed that the *authority* of God ordered walls to stand or fall, instead of knowing the *principles* of physics, they tried every imaginable way to persuade God to order their buildings to stand, including walling living persons into the corners of the walls, but none of these methods worked. In architecture, at least, God never was persuaded to use authority over the acts of man. In morality He doesn't, if He endows man with liberty. Felix doesn't understand that morality consists in principles of human relationships, relationships between persons (as physics is principles of relationships between inanimate things) and that morality includes all human institutions, organizations, states, corporations, markets, ALL relationships of persons to other persons. Politics and Economics are merely subdivisions of morality, artificial subdivisions made for convenience in research and thinking; as chemistry and electronics are subdivisions of physics.

How do you feel about the election? I am having some work done on my house and have met an unusual number of workmen since the Republican convention; I am surprised that so far every one of them has expressed (without any clue to my attitude) the same disgust and baffled anger that I feel. None of them read books or pamphlets; they get information by word of mouth and direct experience. None of them wants to vote for any candidate in sight. I was bowled over when I asked a good steady, sober, thoroughly respectable and respected electrician who he's going to vote for and he said slowly, "I am coming to the conclusion that voting does no good; nothing will stop them but guns."

July 20, 1948

Dear Mrs. Lane:

I appreciated so much your letter of July 5 and have read it several times. It came very opportunely for I have used some of your thought in preaching liberty to a distinguished clergyman and to a still more distinguished layman who are going to the meeting of the World Council of Churches in Amsterdam in August. This meeting should be very constructive, helping understanding, friendliness, and cooperation, but there are those who will be in attendance who present statist measures in the name of religion.

I, too, am not happy about the election. It does not look as though the politicians are going to save us. At a meeting of the Foundation for Economic Education recently one speaker listed the following that must be eliminated in order to preserve the Republic—progressively graduated income taxes, labor monopoly, printing press money, government subsidies, compulsory social security. Almost all present agreed with him but he went on to say that such a political platform would gain very few votes!

July 21, 1948

Dear Mr. Crane:

I wish I had been at the Foundation for Economic Education meeting. You can readily surmise, however, the reason why nobody else would wish that. Nobody alive can get away with that blatant snobbery unchallenged, if I'm there. (This refers to your mentioning the speaker who listed essential abolitions and "went on to say that such a political platform would gain very few votes.") Someone should have asked that speaker three questions:

1. Would such a platform gain your vote?

2. What is your factual basis for the assumption that you are intellectually and morally so far the superior of all but a "very few" other Americans? The assumption implies, (1) that you have a highly exceptional record for intelligence; please state ten instances of notably intelligent action on your part; (2) that your moral standards are clear, and that you habitually act according to them; please state ten instances; (3) that a majority of persons act unintelligently, as compared with you, and immorally, as compared with you; is this the case in the twenty instances you have mentioned?

3. As the exceptionally intelligent and moral person that you are, you are openly and vigorously standing for the abolitions that you know are necessary to save the Republic, are you not? What popular reaction are you encountering? please give instances.

If the Birmingham ticket can get on the Connecticut ballot I shall vote for it. If not, I shall not vote. My observation is that my contempt for Dewey and Truman is general among the "little people" in this neighborhood.

August 27, 1948

Dear Mrs. Lane:

I don't believe that our friend at the meeting under discussion considered himself superior to other Americans. He simply thought things through and most of them have not. In other words in my opinion it will take a long period of education to win public opinion against progressively graduated income taxes, labor monopoly, printing press money, government subsidies, compulsory social security, and other evils that must be eliminated in order to restore the Republic. Some of these can be licked easier than others, but there is no use in minimizing the tremendous job we have in front of us in order to secure liberty and to expand it.

January 7, 1949

Dear Mrs. Lane:

I am sending you a copy of the Du Pont employee magazine, *Better Living,* and of the Arlington plant magazine, *Plastimes.* In the latter, I thought you would be particularly interested in the pictures and text of the average Du Ponter's economic situation as presented by the president of the company, Crawford Greenewalt. It seems to me that this helps to give an understanding of the work of our company.

You may find the issue of *Better Living* "corny," but I do not think it is insincere, but rather mirrors the spirit that prevails.

January 14, 1949

Dear Mr. Crane:

Thank you for the Du Pont magazines. HOW I wish that all Europeans could see them. And the Russians. I can't decide whether to send these copies to England or to Germany.

Of course I don't think that *Plastimes* is "corny." These lovely good people, with their five-inch chrysanthemums and their weddings and babies. It breaks my heart, that they are so sweet and innocent and being destroyed—this whole world of simple people, being destroyed, without their knowing it, without their understanding or being able to understand that such creatures as their destroyers can exist. So innocent and trusting. Projecting their own images of what they are and want more to be, on such men as FDR and Wallace, and believing and trusting so humbly, their imagined greater goodness and kindness and wisdom and power.

Isn't there ANY way, through such an organization as Du Pont, to reach them at all? If it were possible, and I *can't* see why it isn't, just to run in these Du Pont publications a little ad of, for one good example, The Foundation's *Bill of Rights* pamphlet. Send a postcard for one copy, no charge; I can't imagine why the heads of such organizations as Du Pont apparently feel no responsibility at all for anything but the material, physical, aspects of the organization. Such magazines should have moral policies. This back-page ad—"meet competition—do good work—cut cost—improve quality"—quality of neophrene. Not a suggestion in the whole magazine, "improve yourself, widen your own view, learn more about your country, your citizenship. No opportunity offered for anything like that. WHY not an ad for that pamphlet?

January 22, 1949

Dear Mrs. Lane,

I appreciate your letter of January 14 and I am glad to be able to assure you that just what you suggest is being done. Every issue of our principal paper has contained thoughtfully designed material to press home these ideas.

August 27, 1950

Dear Mr. Crane:

I have forwarded to Dr. [F.A.] Harper the divinity student's letter that you asked me to send to him.

I would like to say two things to the young man: (1) Obviously, money, or "economic power", does not control men's thoughts or actions, since, if it did, and if its owners wished to, they would not let young Americans think and say what he does think and say about them. (2) His objection is to the use of *Government's police power* to suppress the individual freedom and human rights which God gives every person, and which he enjoyed in writing his letter. If he were correct in believing that Du Pont, for example, "controls" persons, then Du Pont can do this only by using the Government's police power upon those persons. Since Du Pont is not the Government, Du Pont could use Government's police power only by buying the officials whom his fellow citizens elect. If those officials can be bought then he is mistaken in trusting them. If they cannot be bought, then Du Pont cannot use their police power to "control" anyone.

Saying this would do little if any good; the young man's mind, if he had one, evidently has been shattered by his schooling. It has successfully substituted prejudices and fallacies for reason.

May 4, 1951

Dear Mrs. Lane:

I am very interested to read your excellent review of *The Great Idea.* I enjoyed the book very much and think it should be influential. It seemed to me significant that Henry Hazlitt, who calls himself an agnostic, reached the conclusion that the improvement of society can only be accomplished by moral principles for individuals and that these require the motivation of religion. I emphatically agree with that and, as you know, think that the particular faith which can "preserve the American form of government" is Christianity. I don't want to split hairs about deists and Christians and other points on which I have so little information, but rather rest on the simple faith in human and divine personality. The Christian Gospel seems to me to be the only logical explanation of life and to provide modificaton of human beings . . . .

May 5, 1951

Dear Mr. Crane:

Mr. Hazlitt, like Professor Mises, seems to me a sound economist, but oddly irrational in any other field of thought. Politically, for example, they both seem to me simply crazy; Mises in his advocacy of democracy, and Hazlitt in his crusade for abolishing the American political structure and substituting British parliamentarianism. In these political stands, both flatly contradict their economic views.

Now it may be that moral principles "require the motivation of religion." I don't know why; I have heard the statement so often that I have tried, often and for a long time, to figure out why, by myself; and I have looked for, and asked persons who say this for some explanation of this statement, without any result. Can you tell me why? Why do moral principles require the motivation of religion?

My present view is that moral principles exist in the nature of things on this planet, in the dimensions of Time and Space, exactly as physical, chemical, electronic, aerodynamic principles do. Du Pont, my radio tells me, "makes better things for more people through chemistry," that is, by means of human action in accordance with human knowledge of principles existing and operating in the nature of things on this planet. Does this knowledge and action require the motivation of religion?

If not, why does a knowledge of moral principles and human action in accordance with such principles, require the motivation of religion? If chemists discover enough about the existence and operation of God's Will on this earth to be able to act according to it and make nylon, from motives of curiosity seeking knowledge of truth and motives of self-preservation and self-advancement seeking profit, why cannot men discover enough about the existence and operation of God's Will on this earth to be able to act according to it and make "good" lives and "moral" societies, from the same motives?

It seems to me that human experience in this American experiment during the past century and a half, somewhat supports a hypothesis that they can . . . .

Didn't a human effort to act in accordance with the American principle make a small advance toward a more "moral" world? It abolished slavery, it abolished torture, it inaugurated American "neighborliness" (which exists nowhere else, and never has), it increased charity, and honesty, and hope; didn't it?

Please don't think that I am attacking religion . . . I am only saying that the "motivation of religion" seems to me irrelevant to practical action by living human persons on this earth.

Just at this point, I stopped to punch down the bread

I was making. I wish to make bread; to do this, I must know something about the nature of yeast, flour, milk, eggs and heat. These are all as God made them; all of them act according to God's Will, according to the principles *established* in their natures by their Creator. Men do not make, or control the action of, any of them; God does that. But to make bread, I do not need to know the nature of God; I need only to know something about *how* God's Will operates in yeast, grain, milk, eggs and heat. My motivation is a simple direct desire to eat bread. If Hazlitt means that bread can be accomplished only by principles (he must mean, by a human knowledge of principles) of course I agree; but when he adds that these (i.e., this knowledge) requires "the motivation of religion," I am stymied. And nobody tells me what he means. What is the connection between correct human action in making bread, and a *religious* motive?

What is the connection between correct human action of any kind *on this earth*, and a religious motive?

What is the difference, for example, between making bread and making peace on earth? Every normal human being wants peace, because—being endowed by the Creator with life—he wants to live; i.e., to function as God created him to function, on this planet. The difference is, that to make bread men must know something of the nature of things; to make peace, he must know something of the nature of man and of human relationships *on this earth.* Given that knowledge, can't men make peace on earth by acting according to principles established by the Creator in living men and their relationships, just as men now make bread—or nylon or airplanes—by acting according to the principles established by the Creator in inanimate things? Can't they make peace on earth simply because they want peace on earth, as they make motor cars? Why does "the motivation of religion" enter into one activity, more than into the other? What is the *relevancy* of belief in the Christian Gospel to either action? Can you tell me? I am bewildered.

Have you recently reread Thomas Paine's *Age of Reason?* If it isn't fresh in your memory I am certain that it will interest you. He wrote it, while in prison in Paris, in the Terror. I think his speech in the Assembly opposing its sentencing the King to death one of the greatest speeches of history. And that incident of his own sentence—one of the most fantastic details. You remember, I mean his door being chalked at night, and his writing all night to finish *The Age of Reason* before being guillotined at dawn; and leaving the cell door open because the weather was hot, so the hurrying guard didn't see the chalk mark and, in the excitement of Robespierre's assassination that morning, didn't count the prisoners loaded into the tumbrils; and Paine, to his great surprise, went on living. After all that hurry to get the last words of *The Age of Reason* on paper.

Did you see the New York reviews of Hazlitt's book? If I were to write a libertarian novel, and IF I got it published, would you bet me that it would sell a thousand copies?—I am revising *Discovery of Freedom* for European translation. A young Luxembourg Professor some how got hold of a copy of it and is avidly putting it into French, German and Italian. He wrote me a Christmas note saying he thanks God who gave him to "see the hope of such a great Cause" as individualism (by means of this book). Nothing of the kind has been remotely suggested to him by all his education; it struck him all of a heap. He believes it will astound and excite other Europeans; as it has him. Time will tell. The New York reviews damned *Discovery of Freedom;* it sold a few more than 1,000 copies, less than the first printing. I returned the royalty advance to the publishers.

May 10, 1951

Dear Mrs. Lane,

I also have noticed Henry Hazlitt's advocacy of the British political system and wondered why such a fine and sound person should have this aberration. I was taught this in college by Woodrow Wilson, but when I grew up I got over believing in this method of parliamentary procedure. So did he, but in quite a different manner! For he couldn't brook opposition.

. . . While I do not agree with you, I must admit that you have done much more thinking on this problem than I have, or indeed than I am capable of. Nor can I attempt to refute your logic. Above all I get from you, and it has been an inspiring principle, an appreciation of the unity of life. Yet without knowing much psychology, I do differentiate between reason and emotion. It still seems to me that we are motivated by the "adoration and service of God" (the dictionary definition of religion) even though we cannot comprehend Him intellectually. The greatest values in life—love, courage, duty, humor, integrity—are not simply matters of intelligence and reason.

This is way over my head. I have no business setting down on paper these immature thoughts, for I have no time to work them out logically and to find the right words. I know you will overlook the weakness in my hurried expression and get what I am driving at. After all, I think that your own letter supports my own belief. Knowledge alone will not make "good" life and "moral" societies. Education alone does not even furnish wisdom.

On the intellectual basis, I have never been able to obtain any understanding of things except the theistic interpretation. Nor can I discover any explanation for the Gospel and the Acts except the Incarnation. I don't emphasize conventional Christianity in many of those manifestations, nor would I dare to expound theology, but there is a wealth of meaning in the simple words of James, particularly when one appreciates that he refers to his own brother as Lord throughout his epistle—"But who looketh into the perfect law of liberty, . . . this man shall be blessed in his deed. . . . Pure religion and undefiled before God and the Father is this, to visit the fatherless and widows in their affliction, and to keep himself unspotted from the world." It is high time that the world did try Christianity.

It is good to read of the appreciation from abroad of the *Discovery of Freedom,* and that discovery after thousands of years is another example of how slow the process is of comprehending truth and right and learning how to act thereon.

III

May 29, 1951

Dear Mr. Crane:

Please forgive my delay in answering your good letter of the tenth and acknowledging the box of books received; thank you. I have been engaged in another revolt in a teaspoon here. It seems to have implications that may interest you; I'll tell you about it, hoping that a long letter won't be boring.

First, some background. You know the local government here is the Town Meeting. The Town's population is about 37,000, of which about 25,000 live in the City of Danbury, being subject to the City government which is subsidiary to the Town. From top to bottom the levels of jurisdiction are: (1) Federal (deriving its powers from the Sovereign States); (2) State of Connecticut; (3) Town of Danbury; (4) City of Danbury (enclosed in the Town).

Like all industrial cities, Danbury City is run by political gangsters, the ward boss system; administration usually Democrat, but bosses of both parties in coalition against citizens on any real issue. These politicians (both parties) of course backed by the local Big Business men (particularly Lees, of Lee Hats) have several times tried to effect what's called "consolidation" of Town and City; i.e., to bring the whole town under the city jurisdiction, which they control. Actually, this is like putting the General government under a State jurisdiction. But of course, practically nobody knows anything about political *structure*. Politicians in Stamford and Norwalk have actually done this, with disastrous effects. But the argument appeals to the city residents (the overwhelming majority of the Town's population) who now pay both city and town taxes, because it (the argument) is that, with consolidation, they would pay only "one tax." It appears to them that one tax is smaller than two taxes; they don't think far enough to ask, what will be the *amount* of this proposed one tax? Actual taxes have doubled in Stamford and Norwalk since their "consolidation," because eliminating the Town Meeting deprives the citizens of any control over taxes.

Last March, by sheer accident, a fruit-farmer here heard of a bill to abolish Danbury Town Meeting, which was in the General Assembly in Hartford. This was House Bill 656, "to provide a representative town meeting for the Town of Danbury." It provided that, next August, Danbury Town voters elect one representative for each 500 population, these representatives thereafter to have all powers now vested in the Town Meeting. This is, *they* could "consolidate" city and town by simple majority vote: thirty-one of them could do it. This farmer, Allen Farwell, had got out of Stamford because of the "consolidation" there, and now saw it pursuing him here. He appealed for help to the Independent Citizens' Committee, which a few years ago uprose in wrath and abolished the Danbury Zoning Commission.

Now this Independent Citizens' Committee actually never existed. It was only six persons, two of whom got scared and backed out, two more who became prudent and neutral, leaving two; Madelaine LaCava and me. Unexpectedly, the silent unnoticed second-generation-immigrant industrial workers, 4000 of them, suddenly appeared in Town Meeting and abolished the Zoning Commission, against the solid opposition of *all* political, *all* Danbury VIPs and the local paper. This phenomenon staggered everybody, including Mrs. LaCava and me; and it scared all our opponents out of their wits. Especially as The Independent Citizens Committee (as we called ourselves) apparently did it, and nobody could find that Committee. It couldn't be found because it didn't exist, but this explanation didn't occur to anyone, and the nebulous, ungraspable nature of these Independent Citizens made them even more frightening. All that could be learned was that Mrs. LaCava controlled this imponderable but terrific force, The Independent Citizens Committee.

So Mr. Farwell telephoned Mrs. LaCava, and she telephoned six others and we are now The Citizens-Taxpayer's Association. She and I (the Independent Citizens Committee) changed the name because, (1) we couldn't produce the Committee, and (2) the word Independent seemed to exclude registered Democrats and Republicans.

We learned that this House Bill 656 had been handed,

in a sealed envelope, to Lucy Coniff, Democratic Representative, by a Danbury lawer, a Republican, at the last hour of the last day for introducing bills, and she had introduced it without reading it. We asked the lawyer why he introduced it, and he said *he* didn't; he was acting for a client. Professional ethics and honor prohibited his revealing the name of the client. The bill had been referred to the Joint (House and Senate) Committee on Cities and Boroughs, and was sliding through unnoticed. The Danbury paper (Lee controlled) printed nothing about it. And did not print our letters about it in its letters-from-readers department.

So, we just worked; it was all we could do. We worked day and night, till we were near delirium from exhaustion. We held meetings in firehouses and garages all over the town, outside the city; we circulated a petition; we mimeographed and mailed thousands of handbills to addresses taken from the telephone book; at the last we stood twelve hours a day at the telephone and telephoned. On the day of the Committee hearing on the bill, in a heavy pouring rain, we took a cavalcade of sixty cars and a bus, flying American flags and placarded, SAVE DANBURY TOWN MEETING, through Danbury's main streets and on to Hartford, under State Police escort all the way; we filled the House chamber at the Capitol (to which the hearing adjourned) with 450 Danbury voters, and presented a petition signed by 2,350 registered voters, and an organized opposition program of fourteen speakers representing every segment of Danbury population: farmers, merchants, ministers, housewives, factory workers—and RWL, the—damn it!—"intellectual." Connecticut has seen nothing like it for a hundred years. House Bill 656 was killed in its tracks. The seven of us survived, barely. But another looming intangible Terror hovered in Danbury's political stratosphere: The Citizens-Taxpayers's Association.

"How many members had the Association?" The Bridgeport Herald respectfully asked Mrs. LaCava.

"And may we inquire what are your future plans?"

"The Citizens-Taxpayer's Association is organized to deal with local issues *as they arise*," she informed the reporter—and Danbury's worried politicians. The Danbury circulation of the *Bridgeport Herald* trebled that day. I went to bed; Madelaine LaCava did too after moving her bed to the telephone; Allen Farwell worked in his orchards —under arc-lights at night; it is spraying season. All the rest of us, except Perry Katz, work in Danbury factories, had done their day's work in them all the time. Perry Katz is our one rich member, dealer in real estate. He and his brother-in-law, our (for free) attorney, were undercover members until they spoke for us at Hartford. So the Citizens-Taxpayer's Association is almost wholly mysterious. In sight are only Madelaine LaCava, Perry Katz, Allen Farwell and one modest member, me. Who and where are the other thousands? The Hundreds who went to Hartford are not members, and say so when asked; they only responded to the call of the Association.

Now, two weeks ago, Perry Katz telephoned me about the Town Budget. He is a member of the Town Board of Finance. This Board has six members, three Democrats, three Republicans, appointed by the Town Selectmen and serving without pay. They draw up the Town Budget and submit it to the Town Meeting for approval. Perry was worried about the Board of Education budget, of $998,948.-56. With payment and interest on school bonds (carried in the General Budget) the school costs were roughly $1,200,-000, well over twice the cost of all other Town expenses combined.

The seven of us met at my house to discuss this. It is of course *impossible* to combat the Board of Education. By Act of the Assembly, it has autonomous power. No one outside it has any authority over its decisions or expenditures. It is also a solidly organized political pressure-group, a bureaucracy which has never been successfully resisted. It always works like the Communist Party, absolutely disciplined, obedient, monolithic. Whatever the Chairman of the Board of Education wants, he orders taken, and it is.

For example: Two years ago, Danbury Teachers packed a Town Meeting and took a $200 raise in salaries, plus an automatic $150 a year raise of all salaries annually thereafter. Last January (before the apparition of the Citizens-Taxpayer's Association), Madelaine LaCava and I went to a Town Meeting called to act on a proposal for a new school building. We arrived an hour early and could hardly get into the Town Hall. Teachers and High School students had every seat and practically all standing space. We did manage to wedge in. The Town Clerk moved an appropriation of $700,000 to build a new school. Instantly someone said, "Second." The Moderator said, "It is moved and seconded . . . all in favor say—" Madelaine said, "Mr. Moderator!" and the whole place yelled, "Out of order! Out of order! Sit down! Shut up!" Madelaine used a fog-horn voice and insisted; a motion before the house is open to discussion. The Moderator finally had to recognize her, and she said mildly that she wanted to ask a few questions. How many rooms were planned in this new school? How many pupils to a room? What materials were to be used? How was the figure of $700,000 arrived at? The Superintendent of Schools answered all these questions in a sneering contemptuous tone, and always the same answer: The proper authorities will decide at the proper time. As to the $700,000, he said the Board had decided to appropriate that amount. I said, then, that it would seem to me more businesslike, and a more prudent use of public money to decide the size and estimate the cost of the building before asking the Town Meeting to appropriate money to meet the cost. And I protested against the load of debt that every child is already carrying, and spoke to solid, cold hate. The Moderator then resumed, "All those in favor say Aye. Motion carried. Adjourn!" It was illegal of course not to allow a Nay vote. But who can fight such a thing through the courts?

(I forgot to say one reason for the attempt to "consolidate" is that the city is already bonded to its legal limit. Until that Board of Education raid, the Town had a negligible debt of a few thousand; this $700,000 bond issue still leaves a margin of some $500,000 possible bonded indebtedness before reaching the legal limit. Limit is proportioned by population by State law. The politicians want to get their hands on this half-million dollars.)

At my house we discussed the situation and decided that we couldn't risk an open fight. Defeat would wipe out the Citizens-Taxpayer's Association. As it was, we have a weapon—in the prestige of our Hartford victory—that we'd better save to use when we had some chance of winning again. I was uneasy about this expediency-argument, but I fell for it. Perry thought he could reduce the Board of Education's budget in the Board of Finance.

We went over it, and it was really appalling. Of 120 teachers, eighty already get $4,000 to $5,000 a year for 180 school days. Only eight get less than $3,000. All automatically get $150 annual raise. Four stenographers in the Superintendent's office get $3800 each. AND the automatic raise. (The First Selectman's Secretary gets $2,800.) The High School got a $10,000 automatic oil-heating system last year, supposed to reduce janitor costs; but the EIGHT janitors are still there, each getting the automatic $150 raise, and the proposed across-the-board $400 raise this year for ALL employees in the school system. All teachers were to get this $400 raise; and so were the Superintendent and Chairman, who now get $8,000 and $10,000. These janitors really annoyed us; they get extra pay for any cleaning they do, and extra for watching the children cross the street, although the General Budget appropriates an extra sum to pay the city police for this. Perry said he asked the Chairman of the Board of Education, in Board of Finance hearing, whether this janitor force could not be reduced since the new heating system was installed; the Chairman said, "Not possibly, these janitors were political appointments." The $400 across-the-board raise demanded, raised Town taxes two mills. And there are very few taxpayers in the Town whose hard-earned income comes anywhere near the teachers' now. These farmers and factory workers work the year round, and the factory workers pay heavy "deduction" taxes (which teachers don't) and how many of them come home with $4,000 a year?

Well, what Perry wanted was some moral support. He was going to insist on trimming that School budget a little, and he'd be outcast by all the city's VIPs when he did. He didn't want the Citizens-Taxpayer's (mythical) Association to be wrecked by open action, as such; he just wanted us to talk individually, and start a sort of counter-current in public opinion to support him a little. Maybe write a few letters to the paper, as individuals. So it was left at that.

But last Monday midnight, here was Perry yelling to us on the telephone. He'd lost, completely. The Board of Finance approved the School budget as submitted. The three Democrats on the Board wanted taxes raised as high as possible, because the city this year elected a Republican mayor; if taxes immediately jumped six mills, they'd elect Democrats in 1952. The two Republicans were with Perry, for trimming that budget a little bit, until the last instant. Then they said, What's the use? they'd only take a shellacking in a teacher-packed Town Meeting; so they voted with the Democrats. They turned on Perry and said, This is what you get for going to Hartford to save the Town Meeting. If we had any authority, we'd stay with you; but we aren't going to be the butt of a packed Town Meeting. So here was Perry, persona non grata all around and with no victory, desperately saying on the midnight telephone: "Look, Rose, you've GOT to DO something!" And I howling in reply, "How? What? We haven't any TIME."

Nobody but the few insiders knew anything about the budget. It wouldn't be printed in the paper till next day, Tuesday, an evening paper; and the Town Meeting to pass on it was called for Friday. The Citizen's-Taxpayer's Association might maybe have tried to do something, if we had time—but with only three days? And no means of communication, the paper being against us. And the whole Education pressure-group always permanently organized and acting like an oiled machine, ready to move into that Town Meeting at an hour's notice.

I had no idea this report would run so long. I do hope I am not boring you.

We had no time to meet or plan. Allen Farwell was working day and night in his orchards, spraying; the others were in the factories eight hours a day. Tuesday we got 2,000 postcards printed and all that night and Wednesday we were addressing and mailing them. One marvelous thing; people swarmed on Madelaine's telephone asking what the Citizens-Taxpayer's Association was going to about this raise of six mills in taxes. We concentrated on only one appeal: Be at the Town Meeting *before seven o'clock.* The meeting was called at eight. Our only hope was to get non-teachers into the Town Hall, enough to keep the teachers from packing it again. In the three days we got about 400. The Town Hall holds, with standing room, 500. The Board of Education commands 200 employees, and, with their adherents and high school students, turns out about 800. When more than 500 come to a Town Meeting, the customary procedure is adjournment to the High School Auditorium. On Wednesday, the Chairman of the Board of Education heard rumors of Citizens-Taxpayer's Association action, saw some of our early postcards, and cleverly rented the high school auditorium to a teacher's meeting from another town for Friday evening, thus preventing the Town Meeting adjournment there. The selectmen heard the same rumors, however, and apprehensively (such is the vague fear of the vague Citizens-Taxpayers) and spent $60 (of Town money) to rent the Elks Auditorium, IF it should be needed.

When we got to Town Hall at 7:00 p.m. Friday, we saw we had succeeded in mixing the crowd. It was about half-and half teachers and others, and about half in and half trying to get in. We carried adjournment to the Elks Auditorium, and news of that brought in a larger crowd, about 1,500 in all. They adopted the General town budget without debate.

The clerk then moved adoption of the Board of Education budget, this was seconded, and Madelaine offered an amendment—a Citizens-Taxpayer's amendment—reducing that budget $80,000 and recommending that the Board of Education apply this reduction to the proposed $400 increase in salaries. She was booed and hissed and applauded. The VIPs then advanced; two or three prominent attorneys, the Superintendent of Schools (Nothing, *nothing* he said is more wonderful, more precious, than a *child*), the Chairman of the Board of Education (Danbury, he said is entering upon a new era; new people are coming in. We must have the best, the very best, and only the very best, to attract the best people to Danbury. We all love Danbury). Our G.I. veteran member, who works in a hat factory, got the floor and read the schedule of teachers' present salaries; he said that even a hatter does not earn half as much, and some hatter said clearly, "And we *work* for ours." The minister of the First Congregational Church, leading representative of religion in Danbury, spoke eloquently of the great value of education for democracy in a democracy and appealed to the noble spirit of self-sacrifice for the good of all and the highest welfare of our beloved community; who, he asked, was not willing to sacrifice for the coming generation and the future of our country? and, he said a $5,000 salary is really very small when you consider—but that was a mistake; the factory workers booed him. Nothing so appalling had ever before happened in Danbury. We lost many voters right then; respectable people have nothing to do with scum that will boo the First Congregational Minister. So they voted for the teachers who booed Madelaine LaCava. (I wish I could stop trying to *explain* such things to myself.)

The appalled Moderator then lost his grip on the meeting. He tried to ask for a vote on the amendment to the motion, and several lawyers rose and wrangled about parliamentary procedure, getting him completely bewildered. It was a tactic; surely any attorney knows that a vote on an amendment to a motion comes before a vote on the motion, but they argued about it. Or maybe they don't know; the ignorance of Law School graduates is amazing. At the same time, we Citizens-Taxpayers (three of the seven of us) began to protest against a voice vote, on the ground that obviously many were present who were not Danbury voters. (Half of the teachers are not voters, and more than a hundred High School students were with them.)

We might have carried the amendment on a voice vote, but it would have been close. The attorney for the Board of Education moved (out of order, of course) that the vote be taken by the lists (of registered voters). But this would have taken all night, and every teacher would have stayed —or lost her job, while farmers and factory workers could not stay up all night and work the next day; some of them would have gone home. The meeting was in a turmoil, everybody shouting, the Moderator had completely lost control and the attorneys had hopelessly snarled up any parliamentary procedure, so I gambled on a long chance and moved adjournment to a ballot-referendum. Perry seconded this, the Moderator grabbed it as the only solid thing in reach, and we carried the motion. Adjournment to a ballot referendum the following Monday 3:00 to 9:00 p.m.

Our real difficulty was that we had no time to plan; we had to improvise. I gambled on the "masses" being right if they are informed, meaning that time was in our favor. But Republican members of the Board of Finance telephoned and bawled me out that night; they said we could have carried that meeting on a voice vote but that now, between Friday and Monday, the School Board and the Democrat organization would bring out the votes and lick us, sure; and if the Citizens-Taxpayers couldn't organize better than we had, we'd better stop this floundering around and plain quit. We'd thrown away a chance of winning and were licked now. What they didn't guess was that there isn't any Citizens-Taxpayer's Association; only Madelaine and Perry and me and four overworked others; Allen and the three hatters. Luckily, Danbury paper didn't know this, either; it reported the Elks auditorium meeting fully, with pictures; it interviewed Madelaine more respectfully, and it printed the schedule of teachers' salaries. Next day, it printed a half page ad of the Teachers' Association (which is a real Association) full of outright lies and tricky half-truths, showing that the poor Danbury teachers get less money than any teachers in Connecticut, which isn't true at all. Also, the teachers made the crazy mistake of threatening to strike if they didn't get their $400 raise.

So on Monday more than 4,000 voters came down to Town Hall and voted for our amendment, 3,300 to 700. And enough of them stayed, after the ballots were counted, to carry the amended motion by voice vote, *unanimously*. The teachers and their attorneys were there, but announcement of the result of the voting seemed to stun them; when the Moderator called for the Nay vote, there wasn't a sound. The attorney didn't even signal the High School students. He had about sixty there, boys. Before the voting, Madelaine asked them why they were there; they said, to study democracy in action. She told them that they had no right to vote in a Town Meeting, nor to crowd into it and keep voters out, but they answered—smart alecky, as boys of that age are if encouraged—that every child has a right to an education and they were entitled to be there because it was educational. The fact is that the teachers tell them to be there and mark down their grades if they aren't. Some of these boys apparently became a little uneasy about it, because they went to the School Board's attorney and asked him if they had a right to vote there.

He asked, How old are you? They said sixteen. He said, Sure you've got a right to vote here; yell your heads off when I give you the signal. Some of the teachers, after the vote, said loudly to each other that tomorrow they'd tell their pupils not to bother to learn anything, better grow up ignorant; an ignorant hatter made more money than educated teachers. This infuriated the hatters present. When the crowd was coming out of the Hall, groups of teachers stood on the sidewalks saying to others such things as, "I hope you're satisfied, you fools, you scum!" and "Just you wait, we'll show you!" "You think you're so smart, but wait! We'll get even!" The policeman from the Traffic intersection came up to join the one from the hall, and politely dispersed these teachers. The policemen were pleased and very grateful to the Citizens-Taxpayer's Association, because they are paid much less than even the beginning-teachers, even with the 10% raise that the Board of Finance gave them this year in the General Budget.

So this is the reason why I am so late in answering your May 10 letter. Hardly anyone has any idea at all of the conditions in the public schools. I think that something can be done in Danbury to clean them up a little. Though of course corruption, immorality, ignorance are inevitable in any system of compulsory State schooling. And it will take decades to get free schools in this country again. Maybe centuries.

I think the time has come for local *work,* local *action* of this kind. The mill-run of Americans is individualist, decent, moral, honest. And not as innocently trustful of Government, and therefore as inattentive to it, as Americans have been for two or three generations. A right action in opposition to the gangster-politicians gets active support now. And I think these amorphous local groups will be desperately needed, before this inflation is over. We are not going to make an organization here. The few of us, unorganized, can agree about what should be done—goodness knows, that's obvious enough— and we have proved three times, now, that there is plenty of support for a right action.

The difficulty is communication. That can't be overcome on a national, or even probably a State, scale without organization and money, but it can be overcome locally, without them. We have spent in all, in the three fights, less than $200, and that has been contributed to us voluntarily without our even asking for it. Several persons came up to me during the balloting last Monday, and asked who and where is our treasurer? As we haven't any, I said that really I didn't know. They gave me each of them, a dollar or two, to give to the treasurer. We have paid for the postcards, the bus to Hartford, the placards, and some two-line filler ads in the Danbury paper, and have about $10 left. The necessity is to reach "the masses," to break through the resistance of the VIPs. And State and National organization depends on the VIPs, has to be financed (and therefore is controlled) by them. There aren't enough non-socialist VIPs anywhere to support an organization.

* * * * *

Your letter refutes your statement that "such matters" are "way over my head." I agree with you that there is a distinction between reason and emotion, and that "the greatest values in life—love, courage, duty, humor, integrity—are not simply matters of intelligence and reason."

The difference between us is that I accept these values as existing in human nature, as an integral part of human nature, without trying to explain their origin. I do not attempt to understand mysteries which I, myself, am not equipped to explain; I simply accept them as existing realities. I don't try to answer the ultimate question—the question that all other questions lead to—"Why?" I take Creation as is, so far as I can perceive it, and proceed from that point.

It seems to me that I live in the space-time dimensions that I can perceive by means of physical senses and the human rational faculty, and that all my time and all my energy hardly suffice to deal with them. I have nothing to spare, to apply to efforts to answer such questions as: Why am I here? Why did a Creator create the universe and me? What is the Creator's nature and purpose? Why IS life? WHAT is life? Why and what are Infinity and Eternity? or *are* they? It seems to me—if I may say this without seeming flippant—that all such questions are up to the Power that is responsible for all Creation; I'm not, I didn't do it, I don't know what it's all for, I like it as it is, so far as I can know anything about it, and I have plenty to do without medding with God's affairs; let Him run them. I don't do so well at my own tiny job that I feel competent to cope with the Universe.

And I haven't any more confidence in theologians than in myself; actually, probably, less. I just don't believe all their explanations because, how do *they* know? They're human, too. It seems to me that human means of knowing are extremely limited, and enormously unused within their limitations; I accept the limitations and try to increase my knowledge within them. I am somewhat impatient with persons who don't know how to build a house or cook an egg or shine their own shoes and who tell me all about the Nature of God and the architecture of Heaven, as reported by profound thinkers who believed that the earth was flat. They seem to me to be misplacing their attention. Why don't they leave God's affairs to God, and attend to their own.

* * * * *

I have all the books on the list you sent me, except Brant's biography of Madison and Sherman's *How To Win An Argument with A Communist.* I am quite sure that this can't be done. It is easy enough to turn any non-Communist audience against a Communist, I've often done that. But it is not possible to win an argument even with a Henry George socialist. Collectivists are not of this world; they are not scientific-minded, not this-world realists at all; their minds work on a metaphysical logic-tight-complex basis, as the minds of insane persons do. You cannot win an argument with an inmate of an asylum who is convinced that he is Napoleon. He will win it. He will say, Who was Napoleon? He was a man who knew he was Napoleon, and everyone else knew it. I know that I am Napoleon; you do not know it, but if you and everyone else did know it, could you still deny that I am Napoleon? No, you could not. Therefore you must admit that it is you are ignorant of the fact, not I. A Communist reasons in the same way; his basis cannot be reached by argument.

Anderson's book, unhappily, disappointed me. I awaited it with the greatest anticipation, but probably I am too exigent; he compromises too much, for me. As Joseph Shumpeter did. It is good to compromise with *persons;* "there is so much good in the worst of us and so much bad in the best of us . . ." etc. But I think it is wholly wrong to compromise with ideas. Granted, that the most nearly accurate statement is not the whole truth, that the search for truth always brings men a little nearer (in the Time-dimension) to the whole truth, granted even that human beings may never, in Time, grasp a *whole* truth, still it does not follow that a false statement has *some* truth in it. Newton's First Principle of physics was very much less than is known about the nature of "matter" now; but a statement that "particles do not attract each other" would have been wholly false. There IS no compromise between Yes and No. . . .

* * * * *

Thank you, I would not want a set of McGuffey's Readers to stand idle on my shelves. They are great missionary works; I have equipped every receptive child whom I know with them. I could not get them into the school libraries here; could you, in Wilmington? In time, the Citizens-Taxpayer's Association may so disrupt the local school system that McGuffey's can be got into it. But that will take a long time.

Bethel (a neighboring village) Town Meeting cut the teachers' $400 demand to $300 in desperate battle, during the course of which a man rose and said that recently he passed the Bethel High School and (in school hours) had seen fifty or sixty children pulling the leaves off dandelions growing in the lawn; five teachers wandering among them, he said, and the Superintendent was superintending the activity; if children should be taught to pull leaves off dandelions, he said could not parents teach them to do this after school hours, rather than have it done at public expense? The Superintendent replied that he was happy to answer that question.

Modern education (he explained, kindly) does not impart information to our children, nor induce them to learn any skills; its object is wholly to develop intelligence, leadership, and attitudes—above all, ATTITUDES. Now—and he was confident that all present agreed with him in this—no attitude is more desirable, more fruitful in child or adult, than love of home. Long and earnestly the members of the Bethel Board of Education had conferred, and they had sought the helpful advice and instruction of the foremost experts in education (he gave names, degrees, dates of many conferences, in detail) all to the end of determining the best method of inculcating in the children of Bethel the attitude of loving attachment to the home. They had finally chosen the method used in the Danbury Teachers' College, and known as Do Day—a day wholly devoted to the students' *doing* something for their College, such as cutting the lawn, sweeping the floor, even on occasion he understood, going so far as to wash some windows, because loving is expressed in doing, and in doing on Do Day, students emphasized and deepened their love for the college-home. Inspired by this example, the Bethel School Board had decided that every child in their care should be required to DO for their school, which is their home for hours each day, in order that *doing* inculcate in them the home-loving *attitude.* He must stress again that *modern* educators value *attitude* far above anything else, indeed far above *all* else, that the school implants in the child. He would not contend (he said, with a little roguishness, a twinkle) that pulling leaves off dandelions had any usefulness that might be called practical, but (serious, now) we must never forget that attitude is, above all, the important thing. The Board had not found it best to engage all the children in this most valuable activity at the same time; they were divided into groups, so that at any time passersby would probably see some children so engaged. He himself would wish that adults in the community would share the *attitude* of affectionate responsibility for our children's school home which this activity is designed to inculcate in the children engaged in it, and refrain from taking shortcuts across the corners of the school lawn. He was prepared to agree amiably with anyone who thought that the children's activity had no permanent affect upon the dandelions in the lawn, indeed no practical usefulness of any kind, but he was confident that all present agreed that nothing can be more important than the *attitude* of love of home.

I can't think why I deliver this speech to you, except that I sat spellbound in the spellbound Bethel Town Meeting that heard it. (I was there as onlooking guest.) And maybe it spellbinds you. Nothing like McGuffey's Readers could be tolerated in a system so modern. But every literate teen-age child I know is fascinated by them; I know two children who have even learned to read from them.

If I dare ask you again, please do forgive the length of this letter? If you survive it as far as this, you find enclosed every good wish and my regards to your garden.

IV

July 18, 1951

Dear Mr. Crane:

Thank you for Brant's biography of Madison. It came early last week and I should have, and meant to have expressed my thanks then; nowadays I do nothing when I should. My gratitude increases with time, however, for I have been reading the book and enjoy it enormously. I have now nearly finished the first volume. It is certainly an exhaustive work and unusually interesting. Many of the details of Madison's early life I didn't know at all; and Brant's New Deal "slant" is so forthright and blatant that it is only amusing, not irritating even to me, who am so easily exasperated by such things. I am most eagerly anticipating the pleasures of reading the next two volumes.

October 27, 1951

Dear Mr. Crane:

Have you read Buckley's *God And Man At Yale?* It is having a real effect. I learned last night that it has frightened Yale into postponing its drive for funds, scheduled to begin now. The usual tactic of suppression by reviewers isn't working so smoothly; Sokolsky gave the book one of his syndicated columns; the *Daily News* reviewed it favorably; *Life Magazine* gave it an editorial; the National Economic Council has already sold 100 copies and ordered 150 more. I'm told that the coming issue of *The Freeman* has an article on the upheaval in Yale.

November 2, 1951

Dear Mrs. Lane,

I have Buckley's book but have only dipped into it so far. I persist in buying books and propose to keep on doing so, but it is impossible to find time to read all that are worthwhile, and I hate to skim some of the good ones too superficially.

I want to write Mr. [Winston] Churchill, although I know him very slightly, congratulating him on this new opportunity for service in the cause of freedom. [The Conservative Party had recently won election in England.] Not that I think he understands the philosophy of liberty, but he is opposed to socialism. What specific message should I give him?

Why I feel emboldened to write to him is this: Six years ago I sent a message to him that England would starve under socialism, and within a month he quoted what I had to say by improved wording. So now I want to write him promptly again.

February 22, 1952

Dear Mr. Crane:

My reply to your recent note has been delayed because I have been contending with that mystery lately named Virus X, though in my lifetime it has had other aliases. Remember influenza, la grippe, lung fever?

In November last you sent me two notes which I have not answered. The first about Churchill. It seemed to me typical that he quoted your words as his own. And I think that is indication enough that whatever he says means nothing at all—I'd better hastily explain, my goodness. I mean this: A person acts from his view of reality. What *you* say has meaning, because you believe what you say and you will act as you speak. But a man who picks ideas out of the air, as broadcloth collects lint, HAS no firm view of his own; he speaks to make an impression on others;

* * * * *

what he says has no connection with what he will do, because he will do whatever seems to him likely to impress others at the moment. I wouldn't bother to put words in his mouth; it would be more amusing to teach a parrot. Also, I do not believe that Winston Churchill is opposed to socialism. He likes to be Prime Minister of Great Britain; especially after his murderous fiasco at Gallipoli which was supposed to wreck his career permanently. But on his record, he is no more opposed to socialism than Lloyd George was. His opposition to socialism duplicates his opposition to the USA; in the early 1920s he *said*—AND how! that the USA was an uninvited, unwelcomed, unwanted and impudent intruder in Europe, that American attempts to interfere in European affairs were intolerable impertinence, that the USA should get out of Europe and stay out. Someone probably told him that, because it was truly intelligent and wise. It is fact that this country is inherently destructive of the Old World. But what he said had nothing to do with what he did; nobody more diligently dragged this country into England's idiotic next war than Winston Churchill. And I really think his demagogic eloquence is disgusting; it is so derived, so trashy and cheap.

His using your thought reminds me of my brief encounter with Mr. E. F. Hutton. This is a little incident that will entertain you. By some clerical error, Mr. Hutton's mailing department came to regard me as Chairman of the Board, and for months I received his imitation personal letters fervently impressing upon me the urgent necessity of educating the masses and urging me to improve the understanding of my employees without delay. At last, one of these exasperated me beyond bearing, and I wrote him briefly. To my astonishment, I received a handwritten reply, on the Long Island home stationery, engraved, of Mr. Hutton. I forget the contents; I forget my very brief reply except for its conclusion, and in a minute you'll see why I remember that. It was, If you Big Business men had the sense that God gave little green apples, you would act to save your property, your liberty, your lives; and that act would save the Republic. It is not "the masses" that need educating; it is the Mr. Huttons, and in my opinion you are not educable. Yours sincerely. . . .

I expected no reply and received none. But within the next two weeks I received inquiries from three unconnected correspondents, in three separate states. They inquired, Who is E. F. Hutton? Surely not *the* E. F. Hutton and Co.? Each one had received a letter from him which impressed them tremendously, and each quoted the same sentence that aroused their enthusiastic interest in Mr. Hutton. It was: If American Big Business men had the sense that God gave little green apples, they would act to save their property, their liberty, their lives, and that act would save the

Republic. If (Mr. Hutton continued) they would educate the masses. . . .

Snow has fallen here during all this week. If winter comes, it does seem that spring can't be farther away than if it were spring coming. The summer sun is much nearer Delaware than Connecticut. Do please give it my regards when you see it, and give them also to your garden. Meanwhile I send you all good wishes as always, and again my apologies.

February 28, 1952

Dear Mrs. Lane,

I'll have to let Churchill go on his own way! Yet I don't believe I condemn him too much for quoting others. We all do that. I don't know that I ever had an original thought in my life. You are most remarkable in that respect, that you think things out for yourself, and so few of us do. I have known for over twenty-five years that Mr. Churchill's thinking had its limitations; yet, he is a wonderful writer and an impressive talker, and he was a gallant figure in rallying the British for their independence. He doesn't understand this country—probably no Briton does. And the predominating philosophy ever there has been more increasingly socialist for over forty years or more.

March 6, 1952

Dear Mr. Crane:

Your letter of February 28 came this morning, and I can indulge myself in the luxury of an immediate reply because I am the victim of surely one of the funniest of self-inflicted calamities: I sprained both my thumbs in enthusiastically upholstering my furniture. The situation is all the funnier because I completed only two chairs; all the others are standing woebegone, nakedly stripped to their skeletons. And how peculiar the innards of the most dignified armchair look, you've no inkling at all, unless you've taken one apart. And do you appreciate your thumbs at all correctly? Are you kind and grateful to them? You'd be surprised to discover all the things you can't POSSIBLY do without their unflagging, faithful and too rarely rewarded assistance. Almost no activity is left to me but typing which fingers do.

A sentence or two in your May 10 letter keeps recurring to me, and I think I failed to make my own thought clear. You say that you "differentiate between reason and emotion," that "we are motivated by the adoration and service of God," that the greatest values in life are "not simply matters of intelligence and reason," and "knowledge alone will not make good life and moral societies."

It seems to me that we (human beings) haven't the means of apprehending any reality *whole*; we have to get at it piecemeal; we take hold of it by bits and pieces and—so to speak, reassemble them, by putting them in categories and arranging the categories. But we make the categories; actually they are artificial forms existing only in our minds. So it is useful, to our mental processes, to separate (for example) reason from emotion. We can see one category of human action—Newton's or Einstein's—as rational; and another—such as mob violence—as emotional.

But are reason and emotion actually separable? in human life or human action. Is any living person at any moment totally rational or totally emotional; i.e. wholly without any activity of the rational function? It doesn't seem to me so.

I think that a person is truly a unity; one indivisible. I think that reason is emotional and emotion is rational; and that the *whole* person acts. You observe for instance, that the kind, gentle, harmless person who is suddenly so emotional that in "temporary insanity," he kills someone, is not so irrational that he does it with a toy gun or by gripping his victim's arm instead of his throat. The Wright Brothers' discoveries in aerodynamics were highly intelligent and rational, yet Wilbur Wright writes that they were not thinking about making airplanes, really; they were just wanting to find out why some things happened. That is, they felt a strong emotion of curiosity.

Knowledge alone (I agree) will not make (leaving out the adjectives) life or society, because persons make their lives and their societies what they are, and no person *is* "knowledge alone."

But let me, in the hope of making my thought clear, transpose this subject from the making of life and society to the making of nylon. I trust that you know a lot more about the making of nylon than I do. *How* did men make nylon?

Human action—*acting* individual persons—made it.

Now the source of any human action, any action by any person is the profit-motive. That is, the person sees the possibility of obtaining a satisfaction of greater value (to him) than the value (to him) of the time-energy he must expend to get it. His *purpose* in acting is to obtain the satisfaction of a need or desire, but the *source* of his action is a profit-motive. You want a book. You walk to a bookshop to get it. You would not walk to San Francisco to get it, nor to New York nor to Baltimore; perhaps not even to the bookshop, maybe you telephoned for it. Unless the value to you, of having the book is greater than the value to you, of the energy and time required to get it, you do not act. If you do act, and don't get the book, you have operated at a loss, but nobody does this willingly. The *motive* of human action is profit.

I suspect that whoever began the action that eventually made nylon was trying to satisfy the same emotion that the Wright brothers wanted to satisfy: curiosity. He wanted an answer to a Why? and the value of that answer, was, to him, greater than the value, to him, of the time and energy that he used in hunting for it.

The answer, when he (or they) found it, was knowledge of principles existing in the *nature* of things. As Paine said, Men do not make principles, they discover them.

Persons always act according to their view of reality, whether their view is true—i.e. more or less coinciding with the reality–or false. What the reality IS, produces the result of the action. When you go to the bookshop for that book, your view is: that you can walk, that the street is safe for you, that the shop is open, that the book is there, that a clerk will sell it to you, etc. etc. If your view is approximately correct, your action achieves its purpose. If your view is false, your action is futile or disastrous to you. You determine your action; reality determines the result of your action. (What is called your "moral" purpose has nothing to do with the result of your action. I mean, you may have in mind to use the book kindly, maliciously, vindictively, to benefit or to harm yourself or others; your "goodness" or "badness" has nothing to do with the matter. You act according to your view of reality; reality produces the result of your action.)

So, men discovered certain principles existing in the nature of—whatever nylon is made from.—The process of discovery is, roughly, this:

1. By means of physical senses, I perceive an object.
2. By means of reason, I form a theory of what the object is.
3. I act as if my theory were true.
4. What the object is, produces the result of my action.

1-a. I perceive the result of my action.
2-a. I modify, or discard and replace, my first theory.
3-a. I act as if my modified or new theory were true.
4-a. What the object is produces the result of my action.—and so on.

When the theory (view of reality) coincides so nearly with the reality that a certain human action produces invariably (or nearly invariably) the same result, a principle is discovered, and stated. A principle is a *general* truth, always in all circumstances, applying to all particulars in its field. A principle is a Natural Law. Or call it the Will of God. It is a law established by the Creator in the nature of his Creation.

Men make nylon by taking I don't know what material thing or things, by acting in relation to that material according to the Law of that material's nature (which they have *discovered*, not made) and the reality of that material —what it IS, by its nature—produces nylon.

I do not know whether the men who do this (chemists, technicians, machine operators) are Catholic or Protestant Christians, Jews, Moslems, agnostics, atheists, theists, deists. Do you? Does it matter? Does it, I mean, make any difference in their ability to make nylon?

It seems to me that to make nylon the essentials are, a knowledge of the principles, or Natural Laws, inherent in the nature of certain materials, and a knowledge of how to act upon those materials in such a way that those Natural Laws will produce nylon.

Here I would like to add another observation: It is not necessary that everyone engaged in the actual production of nylon, or even more than a few persons, have this knowledge. Many of the producers may be incapable of understanding it, no matter how often or simply it were explained to them. It is enough that most of them want (for whatever reason, from whatever search for whatever satisfaction) to make nylon, and that they know that their *acting* in that certain way will make nylon. They will act in that way, to obtain—profitably—whatever satisfaction they want.

Do you think that this statement is correct, so far?

Now if we transpose this subject back to the making of life and society, perhaps I can express what I mean.

It seems to me that all persons, whatever their views (faith, knowledge, belief) of God, Heaven, immorality, in the sum: theology, must agree that living persons live on this earth and that society is relationships between persons living on this earth—at least, that earthly society is. The Catholic's Church Militant, Church Suffering, Church Triumphant, view does not deny that Church Militant is right here, on this planet. Living persons are here; any society of living persons is here. Christians may know that Heaven exists and atheists may contend that it doesn't, but surely both agree that it isn't here and now, and that human society is here and now (wherever elsewhere it may also be).

I think there is a common denominator of human needs and desires *on this earth.* I think that every living person wants the material "necessities of life"—food, shelter, comfort, health and pleasure; pleasure including all the satisfactions called emotional, cultural, educational, etc. etc. (actually I don't think they are separable.) I think that nobody within the very wide range of "normal," wants to be hungry, cold, sick, frightened, hurt or killed. In brief, living persons want prosperity, peace and happiness. The difficulty is that nobody knows HOW to get them.

I think that the method of making a humanly-satisfying complex of human relationships (society) by human action on this earthy is precisely the same as the method of making nylon by human action on this earth. This is to say:

It is essential that men discover the *principles* existing in the nature of living man on this earth. And this discovery is partially made and stated: All men are created equal and endowed by their Creator with certain inalienable rights (natural functions); *among* these are life, liberty, ownership of property. The United States of America are an experimental action. The result of this action demonstrates that the theory, so far, is approximately true.

Further, it is essential that men discover the principles

existing in the nature of human relationships on this earth. Relationships between persons are human action, reaction, interaction. The only one of these principles, these Natural Laws, so far discovered, is the Law of Supply and Demand, existing and producing the result of human *economic* action only. This discovery is enough to demonstrate the *existence* of principles in human relationships, and the possibility of a real "social *science*" but it is less of a beginning of such a science than Newton's First Principle was, of the present science of physics—which now includes chemistry, aerodynamics, electronics, goodness knows what, I don't. Because economic action is an infinitesimal part of human action, an essential part but always a small one and today the very smallest, at least in this country. All the aspects and elements of the whole person are expressed in his constantly profit-seeking action, and all his actions are acting relationships with other persons. The field of a real social science is enormous. The discovered Law of Supply and Demand hardly more than indicates that the field exists and can be explored.

I think that the making of human society on this earth satisfying to human needs and desires *on this earth* is as "practical" as the making of nylon.

I do not think that such a society can be made by human obedience to Commandments which (whether or not Divine Revelation originally) persons receive on, or from, the authority of other persons. It seems to me evident that the Ten or Eleven Commandments rest on actually existing principles, but nobody knows the principles or tries to learn them, discover them, scientifically.

(Let me use another metaphor to explain my meaning. If, with the "Thou shalt not steal, lie, covet" of the Mosaic Law there had been another prohibition, "Thou shalt not walk on the rim of a cliff," would there have been no use in Newton's discovering and stating his First Principle? from which men have since developed all the branches of physics. The attraction of particles to each other, gravitation, certainly is a Natural Law, a principle existing and operating in the nature of things in "this world": it is certainly the Will of the Creator; and it is the reason why a person [for his own welfare on this earth] should not walk on the rim of a cliff. Everyone "instinctively" fears the unwiseness of lying, stealing, and murdering—as the recurrent and always anonymous and spontaneous creation of the "common law" shows. The *ultimate* answer to, "Why shouldn't I walk over the edge of a cliff?" is, "God forbids, God will punish you if you do." Because there is no ultimate explanation of gravitation other than it is God's Will. But the whole science of physics which is the area of human knowledge between that question and its ultimate answer, is not only enormously useful to living persons, but it serves to keep them from falling out of all the windows of all the skyscrapers all the time; because when they were young and asked Mama "Why can't I?" she replied not theologically, but "practically," "You'll fall if you do, you'll be hurt." Mama may never have heard of Newton, but her *certainty* came from the existence of a science of physics in a few men's minds; because in the fourteenth century she believed that angels and demons might support the child in the air.)

I do not think that a "good" society can be made by human obedience to the Judeo-Christian Commandments because I don't think—or observe—that persons are naturally obedient. If the obedience were there, the "good" society would be; witness the ants and bees and bison. A person is unique; many persons are enormously diverse. Persons are inquisitive, adventurous, inventive, experimental, not obedient. They do not adjust to environment; they create their environment; and they do it by perceiving, thinking, acting experimentally, daringly. Whatever is, is a challenge to them; they attack it. Give them a commandment, and they say, "Why?" Answer that, "Because I say so!" and they respond, "You and who else?"

To make a good society, with nothing but human beings and the Commandments, it really is necessary to *enforce* the "social order." . . . And, since it is not possible to make any "good" by physical force, in fact the enforced social order, or good society, is not social nor order nor good. If it is as religious as is possible, it is feudalism. If it is as anti-religious as possible, it is what's called totalitarianism.

So it is my view that persons will make a prosperous, peaceful, humanly good complex of human relationships on this earth when there is a science of praxeology, of human action in space-time; a moral-social-political-economi-cultural science.

Scientific knowledge is narrowly limited. Scientists don't answer philosophical, theological, metaphysical questions; they don't answer, What? Why? they only answer How. Nobody knows what an electron IS; or why it is; or what is its purpose in being or in acting as it acts. A scientist doesn't deny the validity of those questions nor the existence of answers to them but they are outside his field of work; as a scientist, he is seeking only an answer to How? he wants to know *how* the electron *acts,* and *how* (for instance) a hydrogen molecule reacts to the electron's action. Science is knowledge of nothing but space-time relationships.

But human society on this earth is space-time relationships between *acting* persons.

It is human *action* that creates these relationships; that makes "society" what it is. What a person IS, and WHY he is, are questions outside the social field. For example: You do not steal. The reason may be morality, religion, a Freudian complex, fear of being caught, indifference to material things, or possession of too many of them—the reason is important only to you; and WHY you ARE—whether you are an accidental result of meaningless forces as a materialist believes, or a child of God, created in His image whose beginning being, and end are in God—doesn't affect the social complex, either. Given the fact that in *action* you do not take property from anyone else without his consent, the property of everyone else is safe with you, no matter what or why you are.

I hope I need not emphasize that I don't mean the answers to What and Why have no importance. I mean only that men make nylon without answering those questions in making nylon; and that men can make humanly satisfying human relationships—a "good society"—when they have the same small, limited knowledge of the principles of interhuman action that they now have of the principles operating in—and producing the result of—interaction between persons and the chemical elements of whatever they make nylon from.

If I steal, what happens in the field of space-time relationships between me and other living persons? Nobody knows; there is no answer to that. The only answer is the *ultimate* one: God says, Don't steal; he will punish you if you do. That answer is thousands of years old, and obviously it has not stopped stealing or even noticeably diminished it. There's an "instinctive" feeling that stealing is inadvisable; as there was an "instinctive" fear of falling long before the apple fell on Newton. But this vague awareness called conscience, plus the theological threat, aren't strong enough to overcome everyone's desire, also "instinctive," to take what he wants when he can.

I don't think, as that silly Rousseau did, that persons are naturally "good." We are naturally self-controlling, naturally responsible for our actions because we control the, naturally profit-seeking, naturally rational-emotional. A person will make himself prosperous, safe (peaceful) and happy. IF HE KNOWS *HOW*. When most persons know how to do that, the by-product of their success will be the good society. At present the whole area of possible knowledge of the principles producing the results of persons' *actions* in relation to each other is a vacuum; as the whole area of the science of physics was in the fifteenth century.

It seems to me certain that, if I steal, I injure myself. I mean an actual, practical, "this world" injury. I don't know *how*, I don't know the principle that will produce the result of my action; nobody knows. But in a vague general way the contrast between living conditions in this country and in countries such as Arabia where stealing is more prevalent seems to demonstrate Franklin's Honesty is the best policy. Persons will follow the best policy for themselves in their actions when the *principles* whose operation makes certain actions profitable (and others unprofitable) to them are *known*. It isn't necessary that everyone understand these principles, or even be capable of understanding them; but it is essential that some men know them, it is essential that there be a science of human action. A poetry, an emotion, a theology, aren't enough to determine the actions of enough persons to make a "practical," an actually existing human society on this earth in which human actions will satisfy human needs and desires.

I have now indulged myself beyond all bounds; and I send this intolerably long letter only because there is no compulsion upon you to read it all at once or to read it at all. If I begin a reply to your reference to the British, there'll be no stopping me. With every good wish,

March 25, 1952

Dear Mrs. Lane,

I appreciated your letter of March 6 greatly, but have the same comment as before that you should spend this energy in writing for a large public and give them your wonderful interpretation of fundamental ideas.

In your analogy about nylon, I think you will be interested to know that the first step in nylon was by a man who was trying to make a bigger molecule than anybody else had made; he had no thought whatever of making something that was useful. About one hundred and fifty men made technical contributions before nylon became a commercial article.

March 27, 1952

Dear Mr. Crane:

Thank you for your letter of the twenty-fifth. I am sure the whole story of the discovery of principles and the development of that discovery into the invention of nylon, and the technical problems solved in making its mass production possible, would be intensely dramatic and fascinating. Why the men who know such efforts and triumphs are so obstinately silent, I'll never understand.

April 18, 1952

Dear Mrs. Lane,

I have now received a copy of the *Princeton Seminary Bulletin* of last summer with the article by Ted F. Silvey, which I wrote was so false and yet appealing to some people.

What I would like is to be able to demolish the arguments tactfully but decisively.

April 27, 1952

Dear Mr. Crane:

The Silvey piece may be a deliberate act, intended to increase mental confusion and further imprint the collectivist assumptions by repetition. In that case, it is one more among thousands of skillful and successful writings according to Lenin's instructions. Or, it may be only one of tens of thousands of the effects of such writings. If this Silvey, whoever he is, believes that this article is his sincere and intelligent work, honest, then he is a hopeless fool who can understand nothing. If he knows what this article is and wrote it deliberately, then he is a fantastic destroyer, who will listen to no reason. The same description fits whoever approved this article's publication.

If you want to challenge this article—tactfully and decisively, as you wrote, I would suggest that you completely ignore it; write an original article of your own, with no reference at all to this one; and see if a rational liberal article can be printed in the *Princeton Seminary Bulletin.* For instance, a vigorous advocacy of an effort to establish (by peaceful means of education and eventual political measures) private ownership of the means of production; a theory based on the Mosaic Law and the Christian dogma of private ownership of property, and endorsed by economists from Adam Smith ("the invisible hand" of God) to the new Vienna school.

This is the point at which Science and Religion coalesce, are one: enjoining private ownership of property. Private ownership of property has never yet, in known history, actually been established; the doctrine of "eminent domain" and the State's authority to dictate a semi-owner's disposition of partially owned property (as in trade across frontiers, freight rates, etc.) have always remained even in these United States, where the Law of Moses and Christ has recently been most nearly obeyed in regard to ownership. I believe I am correct in saying that Christ did not describe the Kingdom of God on earth, in any detail; but He did definitely accept The (Mosaic) Law. It seems to follow that obedience to the Law, if universal among men, would establish the Kingdom. And in regard to property, the Law is clear; it commands private ownership of property. This is really a cause for Christian soldiers to rally to and march for. And I mean this seriously. If there is any spark of uncontaminated intelligence and energetic spirit in a seminary, such an article should at least stimulate some arguments.

I shall be glad to help so far as I can in anything you want to do about this Silvey piece, but as yet I can't see anything to be done with it but drop it in a wastebasket.

June 4, 1952

Dear Mrs. Lane:

It seems to me that what is urgently needed is a sound school of economics. The London School of Economics has been very influential—for the bad. A school of economics with a faculty faithful to freedom and righteousness and eminent in scholarship would have a great influence for good. Harding College in Searcy, Arkansas, is starting a school and can be depended on to be sound, but I doubt whether it will have sufficient prestige to be influential in university circles. College teachers are intellectually snobbish, and they will look up to a group that becomes outstanding in scholarship. Then the true fashion of thinking might begin to change and true ideas again begin to be respected.

June 5, 1952

Dear Mr. Crane:

The idea of a New School of Economics seems to be splendid. I am most enthusiastic about it. I think, too, that the time is auspicious for such a school. Because the destruction of Europe and the now well-known enmity of Russia to this country have ended, eliminated, the *impetus* of the reactionary movement; its effects remain and continue, but the reaction itself actually is ended—in the same sense in which winter ends in December. Tactically, too, there are now some means of publicity-support for such a school: *The Freeman, Human Events, Educational Reviewer,* several radio commentators.

My enthusiasm is for the *idea.* I am a bit skeptical about its being carried out practically, for several reasons.

First, financing. Such a school should be started with great enthusiasm and not much money. My vague memory (subject to correction) is that Beatrice Webb used all of a rather small legacy to found the London School of Economics; it was not at all prosperous financially when it did its effective work. Some money is needed, can it be got for an enterprise that is NOT non-profit?

It is an absolute essential that such a school be, itself, on a free enterprise basis. To champion, advocate, teach the economic necessity and value of profit-motive economic action from a non-profit basis is an impossibility. It is impossible in logic and it is legally impossible. Because it is logically impossible, the thinkers that such a school needs will not join it if it is a non-profit institution. And the insufficiently rational or honorable men who may try to do the impossible will be stymied by Federal restrictions and controls of non-profit institutions.

My observation is that men who can contribute money enough to start such a school insist that it be non-profit, I believe in order to avoid taxes somehow. I don't know why. Can't they lose the money in a free enterprise and somehow charge off the loss on income-tax returns? I am not—and hope I never shall be—in a "bracket" high enough to teach me the answers to such questions.

But there is the difficulty of financing, at all, any defense of a free economy on a free-economy basis.

Second, where is the faculty of such a school? Ludwig von Mises has prestige, and he is sound in economics, indeed a pioneer in that field; but in politics he is irrationally and obstinately a democrat; he ADVOCATES, passionately and fervently, "the rule of the majority," and every effort to discuss this with him, or to explain to him the American political principle of restriction of "rule" has come up against his obstinacy. Hayek, of course, both opposes and advocates Bismarck's Sozialpolitik. Orval Watts is a trained economist, sound and consistent; is there another one? There was, probably still is, a small group of economists (Anderson was one of them) who published some fine pamphlets; I can't quite recall the name of the others just now. But they would not price, or sell, the pamphlets because, as one wrote me, they would not "commercialize" them.

It will be extremely difficult to find as many as three or four economists theoretically sound. Sound theory is much more important than prestige, of course; but at least some prestige would be desirable. Though unless I am mistaken, the London School of Economics made the prestige of its group. Prestige was really all that Beatrice Webb wanted in life, and she founded the School to help her get it.

June 10, 1952

Dear Mrs. Lane:

I appreciate your letter of June 5 and agree with all you say. I, too, believe that Orval Watts is one of the best men in the country for such an activity. While the suggested school would not be a profit-making institution in the sense that a surplus of receipts over expenditures would surely be realized, it would be a private institution and, therefore, subject to the discipline of profit and loss.

That is immaterial, however, because gifts to such a school, as for other education purposes, would carry the statutory exemption from income taxation.

You wonder why some men who can contribute money to such things seek to have tax exemption. The reason is very simple: at the rates of present taxation, Federal and State income taxes combined, a man with a high income pays, in the top bracket, ninety-two to ninety-four percent in income tax. The six cents that he retains out of every dollar income does not permit him to give liberally except out of capital. That is what most generous people are doing today, but the process has its limitations.

I enclose a letter from Dr. Eugene C. Blake, who is the titular head of the Presbyterian Church and a very fine person indeed. Naturally, I want to help him see the critical importance of freedom, so I discussed with him last year a point or two that had been made and then passed along to him the "all-about-everything" memorandum. His reply six months later is very favorable indeed, as you will see, but he needs a thoughtful statement to answer the difficulty that so many of these high-minded people have. I have had the same reaction in a recent discussion with a most outstanding leader of Christian education. I want to be able to give these people an honest, thoughtful argument, which will help them over their difficulty.

I can tell them that free enterprise produces wealth rather than poverty, more goods and services for all the people. I can also say, as indeed Dr. Blake's letter admits, that equality of income is impossible. I could tell him further that a collectivist society is more apt to produce unearned rewards for the court favorite. I can give him the "shirt sleeves to shirt sleeves in three generations" argument. The point should be made that the right way to help the unsuccessful, shiftless, and unfortunate is on a local basis by the neighbors and not by some central bureau in a far-off capitol, but I would like to have put together an able and sympathetic answer to his problem.

June 11, 1952

Dear Mr. Crane:

Dr. Blake no doubt is a very fine, high-minded person and a blithering idiot.

The answer to his idiotic question is in the U.S. census, probably in any *World Almanac* on any news-stand, costing less than a dollar. *I* would like to ask: What is the duty of plain sensible people, when the fine, high-minded ones whom they clothe, feed, house, transport and shave and tend to take mental food (also offered them) until their brains rot away? Historically, what the plain sensible people always have done, eventually, is to slaughter these fine, high-minded ones.

Bastiat (who as a small businessman and then a small farmer, all-but peasant) used his mind and *thought* out what would be the economic effects of free enterprise, in the 1840s before anyone knew. He put these effects in the form of a formula, in a footnote in his *Sophismes economiques*:

"Suppose three periods during which capital increase, labor remaining the same. Let the total production of those periods be eighty—one hundred—one hundred twenty. It will be thus divided:

	Capitalists' shares	Laborers' shares	Total
1st period	45	35	80
2nd period	50	50	100
3rd period	55	65	120

Of course these proportions are given merely for the sake of illustration."

The theory they illustrate, of course, is this: In a free economy, current production of wealth increases in direct proportion to increase in capital wealth. Assuming human action in freedom, the operation of Natural Law (i.e., Adam Smith's "invisible hand," Ludwig von Mises's praxeological principles, or—I suppose—Dr. Blake's Will of God) will divide the wealth currently produced so that the *owners* of capital wealth will receive a portion increasing absolutely and decreasing relatively; the *users* of capital wealth in production will receive a portion increasing both absolutely and relatively.

(It is incredible to me that a man having Dr. Blake's presumable opportunities has not read Bastiat. And inexplicable that, after reading this theory and formula, he failed to refer to the U.S. Census to see what actually did occur—from simple curiosity, if without any other motive.)

. . . Figures in detail are too easily obtainable anywhere, I needn't bother to write them here. Bastiat's theoretical shift of income has occurred steadily, *at a constant rate,* from 1840 to 1930, in this country. (Nothing like this shift anywhere else, of course.) The over-all picture, roughly, is:

	Capitalists share	Entrepreneurs	Wage Earners	Total
1840	60%		40%	$ 2 millions
1930	16%	20%	64%	$75 millions

It is no more possible to answer Dr. Blake's question intelligently than to answer, "Why is a mouse when it spins?" Freedom of enterprise CANNOT "produce a society in which there is great wealth concentrated in the hands of a few and considerable poverty among the many." Dr. Blake might as well ask, "What is our political and Christian duty when water runs uphill, when the earth turns from east to west, when air is heavier than lead?" Doesn't Dr. Blake know any facts at all? Does he never LOOK at his country? How can he avoid seeing, if he ever glances at any city, town, highway or farm, that the salient characteristic of this country is *distribution,* not concentration, of wealth? Doesn't he know that even ownership of capital wealth is not concentrated?—that, for example, some 600,000 "among the many" own General Electric? What free enterprise produces most unexpectedly, is a society in which great economic *responsibility* is concentrated and great wealth is distributed among the many.

My indignation has just become amusement. It occurs to me that mentally Dr. Blake is the "unsuccessful, shiftless, and unfortunate" whom you are trying to help. Can such persons BE helped? I don't know. . . .

June 17, 1952

Dear Mr. Crane:

Thinking of the suggestion of a School of Economics, it occurs to me that it should develop itself from a spontaneous group—as in fact, the London School of Economics did. The Fabians were already a small group of mutually admiring forward-looking intellectuals meeting regularly though informally to exchange and polish each other's bright ideas, when Beatrice got that legacy and used it to found the School.

It was my happy, though brief, hope that in those Princeton talks we might find some tiny basis of mutual agreement, and enlarge it by discussions continuing in such a group.

If some sound economist would undertake, consciously, to make a *small* group of a few—even two or three—who basically agree, and who'd meet informally quite often to discuss their ideas and views, with no other motive than that—if that was truly their whole motive, they would become similar to the group called "the Vienna school." That isn't a school at all, of course; it was nothing but a few liberal economists in Vienna; but it became known, became called a "School" and stands for a definite economic creed recognized by all economists everywhere. The "Keynesian school" of economic thought is the same thing.

V

June 30, 1953

Dear Mr. Crane:

Roger MacBride, the Princeton undergraduate individualist of whom I think I spoke to you some years ago, told me an encouraging bit of news this week. He is now in Harvard Law School; a senior next year. He has published an interesting little book *The American Electoral College*; and Jim Gipson of Caxton Printers, the publishers, got him a job as a cub reporter on a Boise paper for this summer. He took me to dinner to celebrate these two occasions, and told me, among other news, that he was one of SIXTEEN young Princeton alumni who met recently to discuss ways of combating socialism in Princeton. The numbers surprised both of us, because during his four years in Princeton he had not been able to find one single non-socialist, among students or teachers. He found one, a student, in Harvard Law School, but almost immediately that one was drafted and sent to Korea. Roger has also had the satisfaction of explaining to Phillips Exeter Academy exactly the reasons why he contributes nothing to any alumni fund for that school; he will do so, he said, when it stops indoctrinating boys with socialism. The repercussions were quite pleasing to him.

August 16, 1953

Dear Mr. Crane:

Thank you for your note of the twelfth. I hope that you had a delightful summer in Canada. It's been almost twenty years since I was there; I was struck then by the amazing slowness of development, in contrast with the American. We crossed at the Soo (I forget the spelling) and drove from there to Montreal through pioneer country resembling Ohio a century earlier. Heavy forest, no towns, rarely a log hut surrounded by stumps with, often and strangely, a forlorn-looking man *sitting* in the doorway. In

Montreal I learned that the Government was vigorously encouraging western immigration and development, and that a gentleman was given free land, tools, a horse and a servant if he would pioneer out there. Evidently this was a correctly modified version of the American Homestead Act of 1862, which omitted to provide a servant for my father. But then, of course, my father wasn't gentry.

I didn't realize why not, until I mentioned somewhere in print that Wilders have been farmers since Magna Carta, and an indignant Wilder in Dartmouth wrote the editors demanding an apology and retraction, saying that Wilders are, and always have been, landed gentry. After thinking about this, I replied that I write in the American language; that in American, "farmer" is equivalent to "landed gentry" or "country family" in English, and "sharecropper" is equivalent to "farmer" in English—Dartmouth subsided, muttering feebly. Etymologically, he was helpless.

September 3, 1953

Dear Mrs. Lane,

As to the rest of your letter of August 16, we will have to go back to Chaucer (or was it somebody else?) "When Adam delved and Eve span, who was then the gentleman?" But seriously, you know, there is a vast difference between the thinking and practice in this country and in Britain. It isn't only the use of different words; we are freer, at least until the New Deal, from caste in this country than anywhere else in the world. I used to think we were improving in this respect, but now, alas, I am not so sure.

[Mrs. Lane, through correspondence with Jean Pierre Hamilius, the young Luxembourg professor, had come to regard him as a valuable representative of liberal, or libertarian ideas in Europe. She interested Mr. Crane in helping to supply his library, and otherwise to fund in a small way certain projects of his. Mr. Crane was happy to do so and Mrs. Lane commented—]

September 6, 1953

Dear Mr. Crane:

How truly Dr. Curtiss writes: "Mr. Crane is a good friend of Mrs. Lane." I am more grateful than I can say, and—if this will not seem gushing but as serious and simple as it is—thankful that there are a few persons like you. There is so much imitation friendliness, such gobs of it splashed all over the place by all the Eleanors, but the real thing is so very rare that most of the world's population never see it and cannot even believe that it exists. Why may I not say to you what I say to others? You are a rare person; there is nothing I value more than just knowing that there IS such a person. Who else would take such trouble to help an unknown young man in a distant place?

I've no idea who wrote, "When Adam delved and Eve span . . ." but it was somebody and it may well be Chaucer . . . though didn't he write a more antique English? Yes, that English feudalism! It has been Britain's Achilles' heel. If we had been wise enough, we would have known fifity years ago that its essential collectivism, combined with the British political structure, must *inevitably* wreck the Empire and ruin even Little England. And it's intrinsic, ingrained, invincible in Englishmen's minds. Colonel Stirling writes me from Tangier: "Egyptians are and historically always have been a slave race; they can only be ruled by a strong hand." Friends of mine here are an expert carpenter and his wife; one evening they took a young English guest of mine, and me, for a drive and a little supper. Some reference to his carpentry on a house we passed, by our host, startled the English girl, but she said nothing. At home, I said something like, "Aren't the Morgans nice?" and she said, doubtfully, "Yes, I can see that he is really quite superior to his class."

The incredible fact, constantly amazing me, is that people in this country actually *realized* the Marxians' announced objectives: the classless society, the "withered away" State, the economy of abundance, the steadily-diminishing-toward-abolition of poverty (in fact, the *abolition* of what is regarded as poverty elsewhere) by co-operation in producing and distributing goods, the distribution of property, *real* "public" *ownership* of production (Who owns General Electric, or General Motors?)—the incredible fact is that all this existed here, and NOBODY saw it. So far as I know, nobody ever has said it, publicly.

I remember, some thirty years ago, H. G. Wells' coming to this country: the Great Man, Fabian fore-seer of the coming socialist World Commonwealth. All we young forward-looking thinkers were in a fever of excitement, humbly aware of our American inferiority of course, few of us feeling worthy to approach him. Certainly I didn't. Three editors of *The Masses* (recognized by all as the best, brainiest, bravest that America could present) dared to greet him and welcome him. Max Eastman and Floyd Dell went to New York from Croton-on-the-Hudson to do this. Floyd's wife and I did not even think of sleeping that night; we waited palpitating, of course, to hear from Floyd every detail of the momentous occasion, every word spoken by the Apostle. Floyd returned about 3 A.M. His manner was subdued, not exuberantly glorified at all. He answered our eager questions briefly. It was evident that he had received an almost mortal blow. We soothed and encouraged and plied him with coffee. At last he blurted out the cause of his shock.

They had taken Mr. Wells to the Brevoort, given him a dinner regardless of cost, expressed their admiration, adoration, reverence, waited to hear his wisdom; he had said nothing but commonplace politenesses until they ventured humbly to tell him something of their own efforts in the class-struggle here. THEN he had spoken these terrible words: "There are no classes in these States," and had risen and said goodnight. None of them had been able to speak. —What did he mean? How could he have said *that?* H. G. Wells. I think nobody ever mentioned the incident again. I believe they all forgot it, quickly and completely. It's beyond human power to stare at your own idol's clay foot. I think they *could not* remember that H. G. Wells had denied the existence of Capitalist and Working Classes; they would have been compelled to believe that H. G. Wells was insane. I myself could not imagine what he could have meant, until I was in Europe and discovered what classes are. Americans who stay in this country don't know that.

It seems to me too soon to know how much damage the New Era, New Deal, Fair Deal period has done here. It may have done much more good. For the first time in my memory—since the 1890s—Americans are thinking politically; I mean, not in terms of party-politics but of political principles. If our perspective were long enough, perhaps we might see that the present confrontation of the USSR and the USA was made inevitable in 1776. Every action produces an equal and opposite reaction. The World Revolution was, is, intrinsically an attack on the whole Old World; on its basis, its philosophy, its concept of man and the universe. Of course there was a reaction, and—given communication between this country and Europe—this reaction produced effects here. Meanwhile, it also destroyed, successively, France, Germany, Britain. The process can be seen as a retreat of reactionary force, into barbarian Russia, where the reaction makes, so to speak, its last stand. . . .

The real conflict IS between Revolution and Reaction, centered now in this country and in Russia. And actually, the Nazis could not—did not—win, or hope to win, a war without Russian support. The latest fighting in Europe and in Asia was instigated in Russia. And it seems to me to be what the Communists say it is—essentially a *defensive* action. Not defensive in a military, but in a political sense. The men in the Kremlin do not *dare* let Americans come any nearer; they are afraid of Paines' "army of principles," they are terrified of the effects of Americans' success upon their subjects, if their subjects even suspect or guess what living in this country is like. They have made a trap and are caught in it. I do not believe that they dare to risk a military decision with these States, and I believe they do not dare risk anything like peace. The latest fighting showed them that in war their armies will desert; in peace, their subjects will starve, or (if the Iron Curtain is removed) be "Americanized." I see the Communist International as finally defeated now. Defeated, I mean, in the sense that France was ruined in the early 1800s; or that springtime begins in December. It is a curious fact in history that effects continue in Time after their cause no longer exists; I suppose because people's concepts of things are changed so slowly. Everyone goes on acting *as if* a Great Power that once existed, still exists, when it doesn't.

Surely it is a great gain, that Americans are aroused now, alert, aware of the whole world, and more and more thinking and talking realistically, as Americans did in the late eighteenth century. Twenty years ago, how rarely could we find anyone who had any political opinion. Or, really, any practical sense. Remember all the arguments about whether Roosevelt was, or was not, "sincere"? Is there any such controversy now about Eisenhower? I don't know; I don't get around much. But it seems to me that people now are asking, IS he going to reduce taxes? or, is He another New Dealer, or not? There is a lot of nonsense about Communists, but there is also—it seems to me—an increasing understanding of communism. I see words appearing with correct meanings: collectivists, individualists, even liberal. The "Conservative" (so-called) movement in the universities seems to me little more than a scramble; it is a back-to-medievalism movement, and I cannot see these millions of young veterans and their wives renouncing televisions, motor cars, radios, deep freezes, and airplanes for the placidity of, as Professor Kirk imagines and says, "a society of status." The universities seem to be in an intellectual chaos, which is a darn good thing; chaos is not influential. Deprived of faith in the Comintern, intellectuals really have nowhere to go but to individualism; and when that is fashionable among the Little Groups of Serious Thinkers, there'll be a great day coming. Even popular music has stopped whining and wailing; and families are large again. And Eisenhower is talking States rights and decentralized local government—only governors and mayors want Federal handouts raising any objections. This is no weather in which to be on the sunny side, but I can't help it.

October 3, 1953

Dear Mr. Crane:

Since writing you I have come upon an exact quotation and reference: Lincoln's on liberty. I believe I quoted to you, approximately, a remark credited to Lincoln in some report of his conversation but I can't give reference for it. I find in *The Ethics of Rhetoric* by Richard M. Weaver (Regnery) page 104:

"Lincoln's most explicit statement by far on the problem appears in a short talk at one of the "Sanitary Fairs" it was his practice to attend. Speaking this time at Baltimore in the spring of 1864, he gave one of these timeless little lessons which have made such an impression on men's minds.

> "The world has never had a good definition of the word liberty, and the American people just now, are much in want of one. We all declare for liberty; but in using the same word we do not all mean the same thing. With some the word liberty may mean for each man to do as he pleases, with himself, and with the product of his labor; while with others the same word may mean for some men to do as they please with other men, and the product of other men's labor. Here are two, not only different but incompatible things, called by the same name, liberty. And it follows that each of the things is, by the respective parties, called by two different and incompatible names—liberty and tyranny.
>
> "The shepherd drives the wolf from the lamb's throat, for which the sheep thanks the shepherd as his liberator, while the wolf denounces him for the same act, as the destroyer of liberty, especially as the sheep was a black one. Plainly, the sheep and the wolf are not agreed upon a definition of the word liberty, and precisely the same difference prevails today among us human creatures, even in the north and all professing to love liberty."

Of course my definition of liberty accurately applies to the action of each of the three (regarding wolf and sheep as metaphorically human). And if the shepherd be a figure representing the State (the policeman) then his action defends ("secures') the functional power, liberty, inherent in both sheep and wolf (regarded as figuratively human) because arresting, stopping, the wolf's action maintains an environment of freedom for the sheep and enforces, upon the wolf, the responsibility for his action which is inseparable from his control of it.

The error in Lincoln's metaphor is in his use of different species of creatures. A sheep is a wolf's natural prey and food, therefore wolves can eat sheep without injuring themselves. But persons are the same species; therefore one who injures another does injure himself. For instance, a person has a choice, whether to act productively or to rob a producer. If he seizes a part of the goods already produced, he reduces, today, the amount available to each of the other persons alive, and gets an unearned amount for himself. If he produces goods, he increased the amount available and since all goods produced MUST be distributed and (assuming a free market) he gets his equitable share.

It is obvious that by robbing others, he robs himself, because, obviously, if ALL human beings tried to live by not producing but stealing goods from others, none could survive beyond a limited time. So anyone's using his lifetime-energy in stealing, instead of in producing goods, reduces by so much the amount of wealth that potentially *could* be produced, and progressively diminishes in time the amount that he can get, even by stealing. If Lincoln's wolf were eating wolf-cubs instead of sheep, he would live well today with comparatively little effort, but in time he would be the only wolf alive, and starve to death. A shepherd who stopped his eating wolf-cubs would therefore be protecting his life (including his power to eat), for the cub-eating wolf really is in *process* of killing himself.

Chattel slavery really was an interesting illustration of this fact. The slave-owners were in process of destroying their own economy by maintaining slavery. That's why they could not win a military victory over the northerners. "Natural resources" were more abundant in the south than in the north, but wealth was progressively less in comparison because slavery inhibited the use of human energy in the south. So the southerner was hampering the use of his own liberty by suppressing the slave's use of his. The increasingly indebted slave-owner on his increasingly mortgaged property was unable to do much that he wanted to do, and the reason for his diminishing area of freedom was his denial of freedom to his slaves.

More and more southerners were seeing this fact and trying to get rid of their slaves; there were all kinds of plans for doing this. So many simply freed their slaves that most, if not all, southern legislatures passed Acts forbidding this—Acts intended to compel slave-owners to continue to bear their responsiblity for their slave-property, and to prevent an increase of the numbers of untrained, uncontrolled, unfed and unsheltered persons at large in those states. To evade these laws slave-owners moved temporarily into "free" territory, freed their slaves there, and returned. So laws were passed forbidding this. And laws forbidding such freed slaves to return to the slave State, on penalty of arrest, punishment and sale.

Meanwhile a custom of renting-out slaves was growing, and the rental charges decreasing; often it was possible to rent (instead of buying) slaves, for no more than the cost of supporting them—no payment to their owner. A large slave-owner in Louisiana chartered a ship, outfitted his slaves, some hundreds of them) gave each a sum of money, and shipped them all to Liberia. He had the very ingenious plan of getting rid of them by arrangement in advance; he agreed with them to pay each one a small wage weekly, he holding the money until it amounted to—if I remember correctly—$100 each, on condition that they all worked diligently and that no one of them could draw his wages unless all of them did; and that if or when the amount ($100? each) was accumulated he would, at his own expense, charter the ship, supply new clothes for all, pay them the money and land them in Liberia. This brilliant idea caught on, and several more slave-owners were using the plan when the war intervened. I hope you don't already know all this; not many do, but it would be just my luck to be boring you.

The whole situation hasn't even been studied, so far as I know; I have only scraps from source-records in historical libraries. It's a fascinating subject because it has all the elements—I guess I mean all the aspects—of the prevailing ignorance of political philosophy. The ancient, prehistoric, traditional custom, always *enforced,* therefore State-enforced in modern times; the opposition to it directed, not against its supposed beneficiaries; the indignant reaction of these supposed beneficiaries against the (actually unwarranted) attack upon them; the furious confusion of controversy on supposed moral and religious grounds; the mad impatience of the abolitionists, demanding that the State abolish an institution that the State was enforcing (so far as I know, not one voice asserted that the remedy was not State *action* but simple cessation of State action—parallel to the demand for and support of "anti-Trust" State action) and finally the useless and furiously brutal war. With the victims of the Slave-State fighting and dying to preserve it, and their kindly benevolent liberators doing them good in spite of them, so energetically that their descendants are still suffering from that kindness. And here again: Jim Crow, segregation, "white supremacy." A reaction, not against the Reconstruction period Federal tyranny in the south, but against its supposed beneficiaries, the negroes. Oh, well. Excuse it, please. I meant only to send you the Lincoln quote.

October 16, 1953

Dear Mrs. Lane,

Much beautiful thought is expressed in [the enclosed] statement, but isn't there a considerable element of collectivist philosophy in the discussion of "common life"? My own thinking is that a true community is developed by the voluntary association of individuals. A group formed or directed by compulsion or by the constraint of collectivist philosophy with its threat of compulsion may be a hive or a herd, but it is no real community in my understanding of that term. Am I impious in daring to be critical of such high-sounding phrases, or am I simply going batty from seeing and hearing and making contact with so much of what seems to me to be collectivism?

October 17, 1953

Dear Mr. Crane:

As to whether we are batty or not, please don't ask me. Perhaps our only reassurance is the (alleged, at least) fact that anyone who asks, Am I batty? isn't. Thus reassured, I often conclude, Then I am NOT batty—which eliminates the reassurance. The problem is logically insoluble; and empirically it's obvious that IF I am sane, very few other persons are.

Thank you for sending me the very interesting memorandum, returned herewith.

So far as the beauty of its thought is concerned, it seems to be beautiful as Ptolemaic astronomy was. Have you recently considered that lovely concept of the universe, and its antiquity? Imagine, more than three thousand years of Great Thinkers thinking and writing Great Books about those seven, or nine, translucent spheres enclosing this earth as the central jewel of Creation, the effable music of their revolving that only the angels hear, the diligent angels punctually propelling sun, moon and stars over their arcs, east to west above the earth and west to east beneath it, daily and nightly, and the 'waters above the earth' which the appointed angels let, or didn't let, fall as rain on the thirsty land. Thirty centuries, ninety generations gone in perfecting the beauty of that thinking—and it IS poetic, beautiful, its perfection hardly touched by the small clamor of the eccentric groups arguing about the exact location of the waters above the earth—were they above the outermost sphere?—or even by the minority group of fanatics insisting passionately that the spheres were not revolving spheres at all, but motionless oblongs. Imagine then, four centuries ago, that brash Galileo, impudently disregarding all that tradition and actually *looking* at the actual universe with a telescope!

The most delightful incident in all history, to me, is the student Galileo learning in the University of Pisa that heavier objects fall faster than lighter ones, and then—saying, Okay, let's see 'em do it—climbing the Tower and dropping two different weights which struck the earth simultaneously.

The memorandum is (to me) pure collectivism, nothing else but, and an admirable example. Really it is, both theoretically and historically, the pure essence of communism.

It *assumes* the existence, the truth, of the holistic concept of the nature of man. This is the vague, not *thought,* concept of primitive tribal savages whose language has no word for—no means of expressing the concept of—a person; no "I," "you," "he." It is highly intellectualized Greek—Platonic—view of man. . . .

The writers of this memorandum are, it seems to me, sincerely trying to *real*-ize their concept of the mystic *unity* of humanity; they are trying to create a *body* of men living super-naturally in this 'natural' world. The view is: In the mystic Being of Christ, all Christians ARE *one* being—a unity unified with HIM; therefore (and logically) *to the extent* that sinful men are cleaned of Original Sin, renounce and escape from the world, the flesh and the devil and live mystically, to that extent they live *as* one, in mystic communion, mystic community, in mystic "common." They deny and escape from self, from the ego, from "I," and become "we." Each is responsible "for the conduct and well-being of the group *as a whole,*" and the "whole" is responsible for the common conduct and well-being of itself, of all "as a whole." "Our . . . functions are the concrete expression of our common life." (Odd phrasing: it should be, "our function" if it expresses "our life." Still, one life may be regarded as having several functions: sight, hearing, liberty, ownership, speech, movement.)

Considered as organization, what these Seminarians are doing is based on Rousseau's theory of the *Contrat social.* The "group as a whole" is formed originally by a mystic General Will (I wonder how they define this Will theologically to which all individuals *voluntarily* surrender their own wills, their identities, their "I"; this surrender creates the Body of the General Will which thereafter is permanent; "the community must be a *reality,* not only as a confession of faith, but also . . . in *social life. . . . common life.*" The goal is a *living* commune; life itself shall exist in the Communal Being, rather than in persons.

Something of this antique concept of the nature of man remains in your own vocabularly—or mine, for that matter; I repeat, we have no vocabulary. You wrote: "My own thinking is that a true community is developed by the voluntary association of individuals." Rousseau *said* the same thing, and so does this memorandum, by implication.

Our difficulty is the absence of an accurate vocabulary. Our words do not serve as even approximately accurate symbols of the realities. The fact is that a "community" does not exist and and cannot exist. We have a noun; what we need is a verb. "Associations of individuals" are interactions of persons, each of whom has a desire similar to a desire felt by each of the others, (to go to a picnic, say) will act co-operatively to satisfy their desires. A number of persons whose similar desires cannot be satisfied in a short period of time (for many reasons, they all wish to build a house) will act co-operatively and, for economy of time, in groups determined by similar talents and abilities; i.e., in "specialization," "division of labor." A number of persons, having a great variety of desires and abilities, all of which can be variously satisfied by their acting cooperatively during a long or indefinitely long period of time (colonists want independence from Great Britain; increasing numbers want to make Ford cars) create an "organization (of any kind, for any purpose) is a *pattern* of human *action.*

All co-operation between persons follows a pattern of action in space-time. The husband goes to work in the morning, the wife stays at home and does the housework. Or, Sally makes the cake, Jane the sandwiches, Joe brings the ice cream and George drives them all to the picnic. Or, there is Du Pont—complex pattern of human actions which (how many) persons follow daily from 2 a.m. to 2 p.m. and from which numbers go out daily and numbers come in. Or there is a Government, an army, a labor union—organizations; all mental (or blueprinted; written) patterns that persons follow in their *acting.*

Now, what exists in all this is not a *thing,* an object, a reality that can be symbolized correctly by a noun, What exists is the *moving* of persons in space and time. Du Pont Corporation, for example, has no corporeal nor mystic *existence.* No substance. It exists as music does, or as dancing does. It is the moving of many persons in space and time, in complex patterns of action. They act in these patterns, as the Rockettes dance in other patterns. Some Rockettes, or some Du Pont employees, are constantly falling out and new persons are constantly coming into the pattern. But the pattern is a thought, an idea (which persons are constantly changing) and if living persons cease to act according to it, Du Pont will cease to exist. Just as the Floradora Sextette, or the clipper ships, have ceased to exist. The voluntary association of individuals does not form a community; it is nothing but individuals *acting* in association. the only reality is the person, each person.

Rationally, one would suppose that a theological seminary existed to satisfy the desires of persons to learn theology, to acquire knowledge of God. Like Du Pont, a seminary is an organization, a pattern of human action. Presumably, teachers who know God are there to teach, and students are there to learn. The basic assumption of this memorandum, therefore (if such suppositions are correct) is that the way to know God is to eliminate the self that seeks to know Him.

You say that "a group formed by compulsion or . . . threat of compulsion is no real community." I am fairly sure—though I haven't the data to offer—that compulsion is comparatively very rare in communism. Awareness of personal identity is recent in history and not widespread yet. The great majority of persons has always been communist, because the concept of the tribal unity is traditional. The Eskimo, for instance, and the American Indians a century ago, are (were) communists with no element of compulsion; unless the Eskimos abandoning their old 'members' to die as no longer useful to the commune, is compulsion.

Compulsion appears only after the discovery of personal identity. Before that, human lives are nasty, brutish, and *short;* people can't get from the earth enough food to keep them alive; but so far as I know, they don't use compulsion on each other within the tribe. The people in Russia were communists under the Czars; and those that I saw had had no contact at all with Government before the Bolshevik revolution. At intervals a tax-collector had appeared and taken some grain or stock; and now and then soldiers came and took the young men away—nobody knew where or why; but they were not 'governed' at all. They were communists as the Dukhabors are. And as students in Princeton seminary will be. The element of compulsion in this memorandum is simply the scapegoat idea; the "cleansing" practice of the Third International—the driving-out of those who are unworthy so that the commune remains pure and undefiled. In detail, it is evidently the modern Communist practice: first, an effort to drive out personal elements in the thought and action of the "deviating" person; then, if that fails, the expulsion of the "deviationists." This is the practice in monasteries and convents, too.

"The responsibility of each individual to the community" is another aspect of communism. The difficulty of being responsible *to* something that does not exist is obvious. The American idea was that a person is responsible *for* his actions, in Law. I have been wrestling with the meaning of "responsible," and haven't got it too clear yet. But, vaguely, I believe that the etymology of the word (respondere) is a clue to the fact. A person is responsible, i.e., his action causes a reaction *upon him.* A natural law, a Will of God operating in time-space (measurable in time-space dimensions) an as-yet undiscovered Principle of praxeology produces the reation, equal and opposite to this action (perhaps).

Anyway, a person is not responsible *to,* he is responsible *for.* The confusion arises from the person's acting in inter-personal relationships. For illustration, if I borrow money from you, I am responsible for its repayment to you; hence quite easily we slip into regarding me as responsible to you. In fact, I am responsible for my action in returning the borrowed money. And in practice, if I don't the reaction to my keeping the money is that my credit is no good.

Yes, of course communism is mystic. So are all religious creeds, aren't they? Theism per se seems to me within the category of rational knowledge, "science," but a dogma such as the doctrine of the Trinity, can it be anything but mystic? It is 'scientific' (hypothetically, at least) to say that all human beings are of one species; but to say that all persons in a group are One "in spirit" is mysticsm. True, perhaps; I don't know because I have no mystical perceptions whatever. Mystics say that they have mystical knowledge; and I do not see how anyone else can contradict them, nor how they can demonstrate their knowledge. Communists believe (and believe that they *know*) that human beings are members of a mystic super-individual Being; and they certainly have tried for thousands of years to demonstrate that theory. From the results of the attempted demonstrations, I myself judge that the belief is a fallacy. But to deny or doubt the existence of God seems to me to be irrationality carried to sheer insanity.

Or is it I who's batty?

All my best and anxious wishes to you, you Apostle of Discord! Would you sometime tell me what is the future of this memorandum?

November 5, 1953

Dear Mr. Crane:

I have just read a wonderful book, which I believe you would enjoy very much: *The Galilean Way*, by Jeremy Ingalls.

This book expresses so clearly and admirably a world-view of almost exactly mine that (of course) I am superlatively enthusiastic about it. I think it exactly expresses yours. . . .

You might, possibly, even find this book useful in discussions with some of your churchmen associates. Though I have begun to read *Protestant Thought in The Twentieth*

Century, a symposium edited by Arnold S. Nash (Macmillan), and I must say . . . Oh, no, I must not. Not in the presence of a gentleman.

December 14, 1953

Dear Mr. Crane:

I am indeed sorry that you have been having such a wretched time in the hospital, and Mrs. Crane has my sympathy even more, if possible. But there couldn't be better news than your recovery so rapidly.

Just the same, you really MUST be lazier than you want to be. I have not the slightest belief in any man's common sense about his health; not even in yours; and if I only could, I would be adding my insistence to all the feminine pressures upon you to keep you from brashly doing too much too soon. I hope you can be induced and persuaded and browbeaten into doing nothing but eating, sleeping, loafing and reading fiction at least until doctors URGE you to get back to work.

How long is it since you read Walter Scott? I have just recovered from a vicious assault of a most UNcommon cold, during which I re-read *Quentin Durward* and found it most amusing. It's odd, how these old novels have changed since we—I, at least—read them years ago. So far as I know, the only fiction written recently, and worth reading, is mystery novels and 'science fiction,'—Dorothy Sayers, Margery Allingham, Ray Bradbury, etc. Sinclair Lewis derailed American fiction; I sampled *Main Street* last week and date the wreckage from that. Hemingway then had written only *The Sun Also Rises* and *Farewell To Arms* which was a good job; and Hergesheimer, though self-consciously 'mannered' was still healthy; Ernest Poole (as I remember his work) was still American.

Lewis, I think, jumped the rails, and all the successful American writers since then have gone smash into the same ditch. If you haven't read Dorothy Sayer's mystery novels, do; they are literate and great fun. And there's a science fiction collection, *The Green Hills of Earth, in*—I think Penguin; anyway, paper covers—that's a good introduction to that field, if you don't know it. Marvelous story in it, about the famous six apes that, by the law of chance or is it probability, would in time produce all the world's literature just by banging away at typewriter keys. You will have a grand time with that story. A rich man, no scientist but humbly wishing to aid scientists in his small way, obtained the six apes, set them to work at six typewriters—and what do you suppose happened? according to the law of chance or probability.

February 1, 1954

Dear Mrs. Lane:

It is over two months since you sent me *The Galilean Way,* but my illness has delayed my reply. I read the book with great interest and almost complete approval. Two statements in it jarred me. One is the definition of Caesar with tyrannical government. My own interpretation of "Render unto Caesar" is simply government and, with this interpretation, we have Christ's teachings about the separation of Church and state and also the impropriety of calling on government to do things which we should do as individuals and in voluntary cooperation in the service of God. Her interpretation might lend support to government intervention in a way such that I do not believe the quotation should be used at all. (Page 154)

The other objectionable and still worse statement is (Page 151) "No one can become or remain materially 'rich' who has due regard for his neighbor, since tremendous wealth, as a private possession, is necessarily accumulated at the expense of one's neighbors." Does she believe in a predatory economy instead of a productive economy? Otherwise, I am in thorough accord with her book and gained a great deal from it. Its detailed teaching is most inspiring.

February 1, 1954

Dear Mr. Crane:

There's nothing to write you about, but I keep on thinking of you and hoping that you are having a pleasant and rapid convalesence—thinking and hoping so often and so much that I must do something about it. I have wild notions of sending you books (absurd, you HAVE books) and flowers (silly; you must have got far too many in the hospital), and even maybe one of these Get Well cards (all in such dreadful taste that, in a macabre way, they're funny; but would you be SURE that I mean you to laugh or would an awful doubt—Can she be serious?—annoy your mind?). You can rescue me from this predicament, as I know you want to and do rescue people from predicaments, only by getting quite well again quickly and soundly.

February 4, 1954

Dear Mr. Crane:

Yes, I saw those two errors in the book, too. And how idiotic can a sane person BE?—If ANY amount of wealth "is necessarily accumulated at the expense of one's neighbor's," then obviously *any* amount is. A billion dollars is only a billion times one dollar. If Jeremy Ingalls has a dollar "as a private possession," she necessarily accumulated it at the expense of her neighbor—or so she says.

But have you lately re-read that great work of the great originator of "free enterprise" economic thought: Adam Smith's *Wealth Of Nations?* Don't. Not until your health is bursting its seams. I first read it forty years ago, and no wonder I almost joined the Third International in 1919. When I reviewed Mr. George Montgomery's *Return To Adam Smith* (Caxton Printers Libertarian series) for NEC a few years ago, an illegibly dim memory made me vaguely uneasy, but uneasy enough to add to praise of Mr. Montgomery an implied reservation about Adam Smith. Since then I have been intending to re-read *The Wealth Of Nations* (even the title arouses suspicion) but got to it only last week. I am still quivering from shock. In one page, Chapter eight, "Wages of Labour," Adam Smith lays the firm foundation for all Marxists, from Karl to Henry George to Lenin. Marx must have read Smith; *Das Kapital* is nothing more than a fuzzy Germanic Hegelian-metaphysical elaboration of this page.—Jeremy Ingalls is one of 'us', a sound classical economist; her view of the "materially rich" is pure Adam Smith.

Have you seen Orval Watt's little book, just out: *Union Monopoly?* I think it is a grand job, so simple, and true—equal to or better than his memorable *So You Believe In*

Rent Control? I assume that he or Mr. Ingebretson has sent you a copy; the *Freedom Foundation* publishes it.

I am not happy at all about the Eisenhower Administration. But I never did like Ike; I began not liking him before anyone thought of using him to stop Taft.—Not that I liked Taft, either.—This country emphatically does NOT "need a leader", but I don't see how it can survive without a few men who cannot be "used".

February 8, 1954

Dear Mrs. Lane:

Thank you for your charming letter of February 1. I can't tell you how much I appreciate your kind friendliness in writing and the most interesting fashion in which you express yourself. I am glad to tell you that I am making an excellent recovery, suffering only a slight set-back when I tried to do too much, and believe that I am well on my way to better health than ever. Olive and I are shortly going to Florida for a three week vacation.

VI

September 29, 1954

Dear Mrs. Lane:

Mrs. Crane and I had a "once-in-a-lifetime" tour in Europe for over two months, getting a car and driving through the West and South of France and the North of Italy. It was very interesting and I learned a lot.

Our last stopping place was Venice, where I attended, for the first time, the annual meeting of the Mont Pelerin Society. I am glad to tell you that my reactions were very good indeed, and Leonard Read tells me that there has been a wonderful change and advance in the thinking of the members of this Society since it was organized seven years ago. All the members present, from England, France, Holland, Switzerland, Germany, etc., were believers in human freedom and the voluntary society. In fact, I feel that the time has now come when it would be desirable to hold a Mont Pelerin Society meeting in the United States, inviting a number of leading American intellectuals—mostly pinks—to be present as guests. They would be impressed, and I believe influenced by the expressed opinions of foreigners, many of them of much repute, where they wouldn't listen to American libertarians.

October 3, 1954

Dear Mr. Crane:

It is good news that you were at the Mont Pelerin Society meeting. Oddly enough, I, too, had thought of the Society's meeting in this country, and mentioned the thought to Jean Pierre, who is a member (I believe the youngest) of the group. Of course, the cost and the distance seemed to him prohibitive. Disregarding that, from his personal acquaintance with the European members and our common knowledge of their books, we both felt somewhat hesitant about the idea.

I have thought quite a bit about it since then. If you won't mind my saying this, I think it is tinkering with dynamite to promote such a project. It might possibly be all right, but if it wasn't it would be disaster. Will you please not think me too brash in giving you my view of it, unasked?

My view has one value: it is wholly disinterested. If there were money or prestige for me to be gained by a Mont Pelerin meeting here, it would be practically impossible for me to be wholly unbiased in its favor, wouldn't it?

All that interests you or me, and all that we could possibly gain, is satisfaction in the promotion of our ideas, the truth that we believe.

First. Excepting Jean Pierre Hamilius, not one European member of the Society is really reliable. I believe that, as Leonard says, they are slowly improving. But consider them one by one, and you find either, (a) that he has not grasped our basic individualist principle at all, that his basic *assumption* is communist, and that his words, liberty, freedom, democracy, rights, do not have to him at all the meaning that they have for us, or, (b) if he does dimly see what we mean, he thinks our view to be ideal, moral, spiritual, but not "practical", certainly not applicable in Europe, and he ends—like Hayek in *Road To Serfdom*—by recommending the course at which he points with horror.

Second. As a tactical matter, consider the European attitude to America?—hence, because of the collectivist basis of European thought, to any American. The European is as touchy and snappy as a pup with a sore ear; his European superiority is ingrained in him, taken for granted since he learned to talk; he *knows* that the USA and each of its parts—i.e., each American—is crude, uncultured, vulgar, materialistic and mercenary; yet here he is, a European whose Europe is wrecked, weak, sick, and dependent upon the bounty of this barbarous World Power. The normal reaction of the inferior to the superior is self-assertion; I'm as good as you are! The normal reaction of a dependent to the Lady Bountiful is hate. (He despises himself for being dependent; and because self-respect is essential to life itself, he diverts that contempt from himself, changes it to hate, and focuses it on the giver whose generosity actually is the cause of his being dependent.) So this is the *general* European attitude to the USA, more or less felt by very nearly every European because of their collectivist self-identification with their Nations, or with all Europe.

Now individually. Few, if any, European members of the Mont Pelerin Society *can* come to a meeting here, unless an American pays his expenses. It is one thing to be a guest when you can perfectly easily afford not to be. It is quite another thing to take food and shelter—even from a friend—if you are hungry, homeless and penniless.

This whole situation would be very much eased, if Americans still felt humble and inferior and eager to improve themselves by learning anything from any European, as we did a generation ago. But that is changed, too. As Felix Morley said, in the *Power In The People,* "it is impossible to be deferential to a dependent."

I think that European intellectuals—the Society's members—will come here more prepared to teach than to learn; and that Americans will expect them to learn rather than to teach. What was the Europeans' attitude toward the Americans in the previous meetings? Did Ropke, de Jouvenal, and the others, sit at Leonard's feet urging him to tell them the American political-economic principles, and show them the American way? Did they, in general, follow even Mises, as his "Vienna School" did? . . .

It seems to me not all impossible that they would go home to report more unfavorable impressions of this country. Partly because most persons nearly always see, not what they actually see, but what they expected to see; and partly because their own experiences at the meeting here won't please them.

Now, if it is undertaken—and if I may say so—I think that the worst possible tactic would be to invite (as you suggest) a "number of leading American intellectuals—mostly pinks—to be present as guests." If this is done, I will bet you—and I cannot stake more—my little Maltese dog, that the Europeans and these 'pinks' will instantly coalesce into a solid front and steam-roller right over any protesting American liberal there. Both groups will be reassured, more firmly convinced than ever that socialism is the irresistable wave of the future.

My view is that the effect of a meeting of the Society here, upon the American pink intellectuals, will be enormously greater if they are NOT invited, not permitted to be present. The pinks are European in theory and views; they remain deferential to Europe and Europeans. A meeting of European intellectuals with Americans, in America, to which THEY are not invited, will stun them, and, in their eyes, it will enormously increase the prestige of the Americans who are members of this new—and European—Society;

Americans whom, presumably, these European intellectuals prefer to meet and to work with, rather than with them, the pinks.

The Arthur M. Schlesingers take it for granted that they are the peers of the foremost European intellectuals; they simply assume that they will be invited, probably asked to address, any such meeting here. Such an invitation will be mere routine for them; if they come, they will greet their fellow socialists with pleasure and, with them, disregard the old-fashioned, reactionary non-socialist Americans. But NOT to be invited! They'll ask, What's going on here? Is this a bandwagon I haven't got onto? Can *I* be falling behind the avant-garde? Left behind?

The effect upon the Europeans will be somewhat similar. It should be taken for granted that they are liberals (or libertarians, if you prefer that word) and have no interest in meeting socialists here. As Jean Pierre said, Why waste time here on socialists? We have plenty of them at home. It should be assumed that they make the long journey to meet the *leading* American intellectuals, the leaders of the *new*, the American, thinking.

But, Mr. Crane, if this whole project isn't to blow up in your face, and all the costs in time and money be worse than wasted, it MUST be managed with a *firm* hand. It must not be muddled through all the muddle of petty personalities and whims and immediate personal interests and organizational rivalries. The Americans whom these Europeans meet and hear *must* each one, be picked for his convictions ONLY; and each must be an intelligent individualist . . . Orval Watts; Bradford Smith; Frank Hanighen; David Lawrence; Bill Johnson;—nowadays I forget *names*, names that I know perfectly well. Ingebretson; Rimanoczy; Harper.

I would urge that speakers—outside the Mont Pelerin Society membership—be invited to present as many facets as possible of the liberal movement here. Congressman Gwinn, and someone from the Los Angeles group, to talk on the Twenty-third Amendment that Gwinn has introduced in the House. Rimanoczy, to talk on methods of improving human relations in industry; perhaps showing one of his Foundation's moving pictures. Chodorov, to speak on taxation from the American-liberal point of view; with copies of his *Taxation Is Robbery* as gifts to the Europeans.

And so on. In sum, the meeting should be a shock and a revelation to the Europeans; they should listen to ideas and to facts that they have never heard of nor imagined. Let them have their Society meetings, and speak at them, mornings and/or afternoons; and every evening, or after-dinner give them an American speaker who will TELL them something startling, briefly; and be translated by a competent translator. Then they will go home with a wholly new view of this country and the American intellectuals.

October 18, 1954

Dear Mrs. Lanc,

I appreciate your letter of October 3 and will make no move toward having a Mont Pelerin Society meeting in this country. I defer to your judgment which is always wise in these matters, whereas I blunder along, I fear, and am not as effective as I wish I could be.

I do feel, however, that the members of the Mont Pelerin Society are a better lot than I expected that they would be. They have come a long ways in their thinking.

October 26, 1954

Dear Mrs. Lane:

Without any word from me on the matter, I have now received a letter from F. A. Hayek, President of the Mont Pelerin Society. When he returns from a trip abroad next June, "I shall have to begin organizing any Conference which we can hope to hold in this country about Easter 1956." He asks my help in financing this Conference which should be secured over the next couple of months so that he can go ahead next summer. I don't know just how to answer him. . . .

January 1, 1955

Dear Mr. Crane:

Happy New Year!

As to the "Mississippi Bubble" fraud called Social Security, what will happen is not only more inflation. Since the employed currently pay the "benefits," the time will come here, as it came in the Weimar Republic, when unemployment is so high that the employed CANNOT pay them; the infuriated defrauded people will then destroy the morally—as well as financially—bankrupt Federal Government.

I do not believe that public opinion polls correctly estimate general opinion in this matter. The inaccurate vocabulary "loads" the question. Nobody is opposed to social security. I am not. I am opposed to this fraud precisely because it destroys social security. Let the pollsters ask industrial workers, Are you in favor of withholding taxes? The amount of bootlegged labor everywhere, which anyone can see who looks for it, seems to me action louder than words, expressing a great deal of antagonism to "social security benefits." Why do so many persons risk jail rather than take them, if they want them?

I hope your new year will never fail to be amusing. If ever it threatens to, let me know and I'll tell you more bits of my autobiography—the snapshots I got in the Sanjak of Novi Bazaar, or how I met Buradin Pasha Vlora, or was arrested by the Cheka in Russia.

January 11, 1955

Dear Mrs. Lane:

When the *American Heritage* magazine changed its format, I promptly subscribed and received the first in December. Some if it is interesting and some of it is trashy. It is disappointing to me in that it does not seem to disclose any sense of inspirational values that Americans ought to have. I may be wrong about this. Anyhow, I am sending you this first issue, as you may be interested in seeing what this is going to be all about . . . .

January 22, 1955

Dear Mr. Crane:

As to *American Heritage,* I, too, subscribed immediately and am disappointed. There are no American historians—have been none since the mid-Nineteenth Century. About the 1880s, the universities here took *all* thinking back to Europe; it's a detail that American historians have seen this country from Europe ever since. So have everyone "educated" or, like me, unfortunately inclined to be "intellectual." Teachers, writers, editors, lawyers. The universities were European, anti-American, by the 1840s, with their enthusiasm for Fourier, St. Simon, Owen, all the leaders of the European reactionary movement . . . .

February 9, 1955

Dear Mr. Crane:

I am reading an interesting little book, *Laissez Travailler, Laissez Circuler*, by Dr. Andries de Graff, secretaire de l'Union Neederlandaise pour le Libre-Echange. I know nothing about this Union, but conjecture that it is a branch or affiliate of the British Free Trade Union. Booklet is published by Editions Sedif, Paris. I've not yet read more than a few pages, so don't know how sound it is, but the preface says that the title is a paraphrase of "laissez faire, laissez passer," and appendix discusses the origin of that phrase and says the origin is not established, but antedates the Physiocrats. Also it quotes a letter, que Du Pont de Nemours, a deputé a l'Assemblée Constituante . . . ecrit dans la preface d'un ouvrage de Turgot sur Quesnay:

"M. de Gournay, ayant été longtemps négociant, avait reconnu que les fabriques et le commerce ne peuvent fleurir que *Par La Liberte Et Par La Concurrence* qui dejouent des enterprises inconsiderées et menent restreignent a l'avantage due commerce les gains particuliers des auxspeculations raisonnables, qui previennent les monopoles, qui commercants, qui auguisent l'industrie . . . qui bassent le taux de l'interet, d'ou il arrive que les productions de la terre sont, a la premiere main achetées le plus cher qu'il soit possible au profit des cultivateurs, et revendues au detail le meilleur marche qu'il soit possible au profit des consommateurs pour leurs besoins et leurs jouissances. Il en conclut qu'il ne falliat jamais ranconner *ni reglementer* le commerce. Il en tira cet axiome: Laissez faire, lasser passer."

The book on Du Pont, which you kindly gave me some time ago, seemed to me disappointing because its writer failed entirely too much, even, the historically most interesting factor in the founding of the company here—the political philosophy of the deputy, Du Pont de Nemours, in France during the failure of the attempted French revolution. There must be a remarkable contrast between the development of Du Pont in this country and some parallel enterprise in the Europe that Du Pont de Nemours left when the revolution failed there. Some capable writer, like Orval Watts, really should do an adequate book on the Du Pont Company in the USA.

February 11, 1955

Dear Mrs. Lane:

I have not heard of the Free Exchange Union of the Netherlands but imagine that this society stands for the general idea of free enterprise instead of more narrowly for "free trade" only. The French society is doing a very useful work, which is called Association de la Libre Enterprise. Mr. G. Morisot is the executive of this and a man who is well acquainted with this country and thinks and works right along libertarian lines. The Editions Sedif, which publishes this circular, is a libertarian publisher. I don't know whether it is operated by a great worker for freedom named Lhoste-Lachaume in Paris, with whom I have frequent correspondence, but all of his writings are published by Editions Sedif. These people and many others work together with a group of Americans in the Mont Pelerin Society which, in my opinion, is gaining in strength. The big function here is to have the believers in liberty in the different countries correspond together and improve their mutual understandings.

It was not Pierre Samuel Du Pont who founded the Du Pont Company, but his son, Eleuthere Irenee Du Pont. So it would be lugging it in a little to talk too much about the elder man in writing the history of the Du Pont Company. Pierre S. Du Pont was quite a person—sound and able. His book on inflation, *The Dangers Of Inflation*, the American translation of which recently appeared, stood up very ably for the truth.

March 20, 1955

Dear Mr. Crane:

There was a snowstorm here Friday; deep snow on the ground yesterday morning, all melted by afternoon and the soil unfroze so that holes were dug for new trees ordered. I am planting this spring four dwarf apple trees, four dwarf pears and four *fuzzless* peaches and an apricot. My old peach and apricot trees bear wonderfully, most delicious fruit. I have never seen fuzzless peaches, but Stark nursery (Louisiana, Missouri) highly recommends them. My affectionate greetings to your own springtime gardens, and as always to you and Mrs. Crane.

March 24, 1955

Dear Mrs. Lane:

I don't know what fuzzless peaches are, unless they are nectarines, which are smooth-skinned peaches. I tried them and apricots but did not succeed with them. I got no fruit that was worthwhile from either on account of frost.

March 28, 1955

Dear Mr. Crane:

I am reading M. Lhoste-Lachaume's *Rehabilitation Du Liberalisme*, and I am most enthusiastic about it. It is the best thing I have seen, on either side of the Atlantic. You know how persnickety I am; maybe I shall find a flaw before I finish the book; but I'm nearing the end without finding one. The treatment of the direct causes of the 1929 crash is (I think) superb, and I don't see how the section on Social Catholics could be better. This means, of course, that he says—straight out and flatly, how wonderful!—exactly what I have thought of Rerum Novarum and Quadragesimo Anno. He is a Catholic? I infer that he is, when he coolly states that the Pope's socialism was simply a political tactic designed to entice the working classes.

Some of this book really should be translated for readers here. I'm afraid it is too European—too local—to attract a large American audience as a whole book. I would suggest to Frank Chodorov that Dean Russell translate the treatment of the 1929 crash, and the explanation of present conditions in France, to make two Freeman articles. This French view of the harm that the Marshall Plan did—what a pity that American readers miss *that.* Do you suppose that M. Lhoste-Lachaume would do those two articles—just lift them from the book—and submit them to *The Freeman?*

March 31, 1955

Dear Mrs. Lane:

I am ashamed to say that I have not read *Rehabilitation Du Liberalisme,* though I marked some passages in it and frequently quote them. There is so much that I ought to read, but don't seem to be able to get to it.

April 12, 1955

Dear Mr. Crane:

I have just read, four years late, *U.S.A. The Permanent Revolution* by the editors of *Fortune* and Russell Davenport. While I quarrel, of course, with some details and some assumptions—such as implied in the use of the words, liberal, progressive, etc.—in the main it is such factual truth and sound sense that I am enthusiastic about it. I am sending a copy to Jean Pierre. If you have not read it, I am sure you would share my view of it.

Yesterday was magical weather here; all that poets sing of Spring. And I set out fifteen fruit trees and one mock orange—*philadelphus viginalis,* should I say? I begin to suspect that your guess about "fuzzless peaches" is correct; although the Stark catalogue pictured them as large as the best of peaches and trumpeted them as the newest of discoveries, I find a printed label on one of them saying, bold as brass, *Flame Nectarine.*[3] Not that it matters greatly. I have one nectarine bearing so they should do well here, and I like nectarines. But—being a farmer's daughter—I bought this little place with a canny eye to its slope, which is south with protecting hill-shoulders east and west and my woodlots

[3]By 1971 the Stark Brothers catalogue had eliminated this gentle deception; the fruit was called "New Stark Nectarines, the delicious fuzzless peach."

higher in the north, so my scrap of land is ten degrees warmer in winter and cooler in summer than even my nearby neighbors' places. In summer the cool breezes flow downward across it. And hurricanes until now—my fingers are crossed—have leaped over it.

In justice to Stark's maybe they had to explain nectarines as "fuzzless peaches" to their largely midwestern market, in which "nectarines" may seem too exotic. I remember Luther Burbank showing me long ago in his Santa Rosa garden, the nectarine that he was making. It has a cousin, too, which I have not heard of since then; I forgot its name. One has a peach father and plum mother; the other, vice versa. Forty years ago, for goodness' sake.

Today is quite viciously cold, with prospect of snow before night. The whole world's weather went quite mad in 1914 and isn't sane yet—sane as it used to be. Meteorologists hoot at the fact, but it is one. Do you know that since the fifteenth century battle of Kossova the South Slavs in the Balkans had a hopeless folk-saying: The Serbs will be united again when spring flowers bloom in autumn;—roughly equivalent to, when hell freezes over? In 1914, during that frightful Serbian retreat, all the spring flowers bloomed in August, September and October, I was told; and certainly they did when I was there in the 1920s. All the best to you.

April 14, 1955

Dear Mrs. Lane:

Your letter of April 12 is received. I can't permit the record to stand that you being a farmer's daughter know all about horticulture with the inference that I am incompetent in that area! I will have you know that all of my generation of four sisters and one brother and myself, born in a solid city block, have green thumbs. In particular my peaches are famous. Only yesterday I was told that a neighbor said last summer that they were the most delicious he had ever eaten! And don't think that I haven't got the canny idea of slopes being protected by the rise of the land and planting trees to the North and to the West. My peach area basks in the sunshine of the slope to the East and South, though I must confess that the soil in that part of the garden is miserable sand and gravel, but the peaches thrive in it. The nectarines

—two varieties, Hunter and Sure Crop (evidently not too sure)—did badly so I finally took them out several years ago. Probably your variety has what it takes.

I, too, though so many years older, am still planting fruit trees. In fact, I have just planted one flowering tree that I am told will take ten years to bloom! That, I presume, is rather fatuous at any age of seventy-four years. But then, I knew a man who failed at business at ninety-one and refused to repine, saying that the only word to think of was "tomorrow." There is an old Arab story of a man who suggested to his son that he plant fruit trees, but the son replied that he was too old to expect to enjoy the fruit. Then he suggested it to the grandson, but the grandson felt it was too long to wait for the trees to develop and he might be dead in the meantime. So the old man planted the fruit trees and lived to enjoy the fruit for years.

I am almost ashamed to say that I never read *Let The Hurricane Roar* [Mrs. Lane's smash best selling novel—ed.] until last week and was thrilled by it, particularly the letter that was not sent listing the modern conveniences as compared to the old days. Then my wife read the book several days ago and said she couldn't put it down.

April 18, 1955

Dear Mr. Crane:

My goodness, I had no thought of casting aspersions on your green thumb! I have SEEN your gardens; remember? I was merely being snobbish about being a farmer's daughter; and say what you will, I shall maintain that you are not.

I wonder if you ever grew raspberries under peach trees? On my Ozark farm (southern Missouri, all-but Arkansas, altitude about 2,000 feet) that combination produced marvelous raspberries. I could never guess why. Perhaps the *light* shade?

Do you recall the story of the Professor that students became so exasperated by the quality of his mind that they penned him under a barrel and demanded a Yes or No answer to the question: Do you want to stay there? All night and next day he evaded and demurred, while relays of students held down the barrel and repeated the question, until finally he shouted "No" (and, as the students with a triumphant yell released him, leaped out and ran, concluding) "-body will ever know!" An old story dating before the days of Brain Trusts.

I am glad that you and Mrs. Crane like *Let the Hurricane Roar*. And it is nice of you to tell me so. Some of my short stories were as good, I think, but probably none of my other books. *Hurricane* was really about the 1929-30 depression—it was published during FDR's "Bank Holiday"—though few if any readers knew that it was. At least, they didn't consciously know, but that was the reason they loved it. It was a top best seller that year and into the next, and is still selling very well indeed.

May 22, 1955

Dear Mr. Crane:

I don't thank that propaganda has any appreciable effect in creating acceptance of the welfare state. Even compulsory State schooling would be ineffectual if conditions outside the schools remained American, or even if there were determined resistance to tyranny. The "little people" do not think in abstract terms; they think concretely, in terms of their own immediate responsibilities. They do their work and take care of their familes as best they can, in all circumstances. They accept the circumstances, however bad; partly because, in fact, they cannot change them. What can one factory worker DO, for example, about what he calls, "the damn 'holding' taxes"? He takes his pay envelope, minus wages that his employer takes from it; or he quits his job. If he quits, he'll never work again, because there is no employer who will not take his wages from his pay envelope. So he votes Republican and now he can't escape being robbed by ANY means at all; if he lives—gets any money to live on—he pays "self employment" tax. So he "accepts the welfare state." What else can he do? The man who COULD do something is an employer who would draw the line at robbing other men.

In one of those meetings at Princeton I tried to say this: the necessity for knowledge of principles increases in direct ratio to the extension of responsibility in space and time. If I slap your face, your reaction is immediate and *present*; I am instantly aware of it; you retaliate, here and now. I learn from direct, immediate experience what is the result, to *me*, of my acting incorrectly to you. I do not need to think, or to have any knowledge of an abstract principle existing in the field of human relationship.

I *feel*, I experience a result of my action which is such that hereafter I will not repeat that action. My next impulse to slap a face will be checked by memory or by subconscious "association of ideas."

But, I am Chairman of the Board of a world-wide organization, presiding at a meeting of Directors discussing policy in Timbuctoo. In view of the crisis in Vienna, the tension between London and Paris, the market situation in Liverpool and the inventory figures, the advisable policy seems to be to slap a face in Tokyo. It is so decided and we adjourn for lunch and afternoon of golf. The orders are transmitted correctly, and in Tokyo two men face each other. One says, I am very sorry, this is not my decision; in fact, I have fought against it with all my power; but this is ordered; I must slap your face. The other says, OK, it isn't your fault I know, I can't blame you; damn them!

I am contentedly playing golf, happily ignorant of any praxeological principle. But the principle exists, my action was contrary to it. I am responsible for that action, and the result of it will fall on me. Or perhaps, in time-measurement, on my children, my business, the hopes, interests, aims into which I have put my life. I may escape the direct result by dying soon, but my life-effort—whatever it was—will suffer it.

I doubt that any director of any Big Business enterprise in these States would pick a stranger's pocket on the street, even if he were penniless and hungry. FDR might have; you know the story of him asking the Attorney General whether he, the President, could do so and so; the Attorney General replying, Why, Mr. President, you *could* go out on Pennsylvania Avenue and knock down the blind beggar and take the pennies out of his cup; and FDR laughing heartily and exclaiming, Fine! so I'll go ahead! And doing it. But the basis of a free market is personal honesty, and therefore *American* business men are honest, with very few exceptions who don't become Big Business men. Yet here they are, all of them, picking their own employees' pockets, regularly every week, without a qualm, simply because FDR told them to. And they are not forgiven because they know not what they do—if they *don't* know, which seems incredible. Many of them do know but won't face the knowledge, they write me the most fantastic nonsense about their attorney's opinions and their public relations surveys and their ignorance of Constitutional law and, in short, their pitiable helplessness and irresponsibility for what they do. Edgar Monsanto Queeny even wrote me, laughing, that when I mention chemistry, "There I have you! Now you must stop saying that there are principles. As I wrote you before, there are no principles. There are no principles in chemistry. Chemists are making new discoveries all the time." Oh well. Let us raise a standard—the event is in the hands of God.

VII

May 24,1955

Dear Mrs. Lane:

Leonard Read made a visit here yesterday and said he had been grappling with the question of slavery and arrived at the following conclusions: Wild animals become tame in captivity. Slaves and serfs in time accept servitude. They have never been freed by their own uprising. So it seems to me not only have our intellectuals, whom I criticize so strongly, been conditioned to socialism by the jargon which they repeat parrot-like, but we businessmen—and I am as guilty as anybody else—have permitted the government to induce us to carry on practices that are not only opposed to the spirit if not the letter of the Constitution, but are in violation of the nature of man. If we, all or most of us, had refused at the start to do these things they couldn't have put all of us in jail; yet, almost no one made protest.

Do you know whether Vivian Kellems is still refusing to withhold taxes from her employees?

June 1, 1955

Dear Mr. Crane:

I don't know what Vivian Kellems is doing now. I met her only once, when I went with others to her factory to break the Connecticut wage-hour law for her; we were challenging the police to arrest us. (She got the law repealed.) She is not a thinker at all; she is executive *acting*, vigorous, fearless, honest, a fine person. When she was ordered to steal her employees' earnings, she simply reacted—as a "little man" does; she knew her eighty employees, they were persons to her, not ciphers on a balance sheet. Outraged, she was sure the order could not be real *American law.*

So she tried to get it into the courts, to have it declared —as she was sure it was—unconstitutional. The Federal Government, of course, has always prevented this. When I met her, she had been trying for, I think, a couple of years.

Treasury agents had walked into her bank and demanded some thousands of dollars from her account, which the bank gave them. There was no shred of legal basis for this act, because all her employees had, themselves, paid their taxes. So she was trying unsuccessfully, to get some backing from Big Business. If any big company—General Electric, say—would challenge the Act, something would happen. Vivian Kellems and those women in Marshall, Texas, are just ignored, browbeaten a little, and forgotten. For one thing, they haven't the money to fight to the Supreme Court, even if they could get a hearing in any court. The last I knew, Vivian Kellems had not got her case into court at all, but recently someone wrote me that he believed some minor judge had ruled in some case against her; whether her attempt to recover her money or not, I don't know. I have an impression that a minor court in Texas issued an attachment on all bank accounts of the women in Marshall. But "social security" for household servants is a dead letter, anyway; the servants won't stand for it and the Treasury can't enforce it, so it's just forgotten. The industrial workers are trapped, but household servants and women "by the day" escape. They really can't be cornered. As Truman said on the air, about the idea of seizing all the cattle "on the western range," to enforce OPA meat prices, "The distances are too great."

About Leonard's conclusions: wild animals have nothing to do with it. Because, (1) human beings are not animals; (2) an "individualist" wild animal, such as a lion (i.e. not a "herd" animal) normally copes with environment *as it is*—he isn't an environment-changing creature; and when he gets food without effort from persons, he takes it, just as he took it when he had to kill it. He no more attacks the feeder than he attacked the spring. He may become lazier, but his real nature is not changed.

Now, as to persons. They do not "in time, accept servitude." They *begin* in servitude. All infants are dependent, and naturally obedient. Children—with individual variations—remain so. Any lost child will obey any adult. Self-assertion, *self*-control, develop slowly. It is recognized in common law that children are not responsible for their acts. More than that, all known primitive tribes—savages and barbarians—are communist; their individual members regard themselves *as* members, not as whole persons; the

Tribe is, to them, the human Whole, the Power that controls and is responsible. They remain, like infants, dependent and obedient. This view of human nature prevails in all known ancient civilizations; it is THE historical Tradition, common to all persons alive. It is the basis of Greek thought, Roman thought, the Greco-Roman-Christian European civilization. The Egyptians who build the pyramids, The Assyrians, Chaldeans, Babylonians, Medes and Persians, were "slaves and serfs" of their Emperors, and never thought of not being. The Chinese have always been "members" of The Family, dependent and obedent. Chattel slavery—the ownership of one person by another—has always been universal, always regarded as natural, a normal situation and relationship. When the Prince of Hesse rounded up his peasants and rented them to George the Third to use in fighting the Americans, nobody saw anything unusual in that; and Frederick didn't like it—why?—because he thought the German Princes had better use their peasants in continental wars. It didn't enter anybody's head in Europe that a peasant doesn't belong to a Prince.

What Leonard sees as a relapse is actually a survival. The serfs and slaves are not deterioration from free men; they are simply not yet developed to free men. An American child now goes from obedient dependence on parents to obedient dependence in the compulsory state schooling system, then in the army, then in the compulsory-labor-union system in industry, under the compulsory withholding taxes and the company's pension system that prolong his dependence all his life. He does not "accept" servitude; he never knows anything else and his real attitude is the negative one of *not* rebelling against the customary. Who does? Do you "accept," say the wearing of shoes? Your feet are naturally bare. Have you ever given a single thought to going barefooted to your office? or even to the breakfast table? Have you reflected that shoes are an unnatural condition imposed upon your feet? Have you decided to accept shoes? Or had it simply never occurred to you to revolt against them?

June 1, 1955

Dear Mrs. Lane:

There is a group at Yale led by Gridley Wright that has established the Independent Library and, perhaps surprisingly, has not been interfered with by the University authorities. A year ago, I gave them a set of books on liberty and related subjects and have kept in touch with them.

July 7, 1955

Dear Mr. Crane:

THANK YOU for the copy of *The Independent.* This is wonderful. Oh, I shall yet be thumbing my nose at all the despairing prophets of doom! who have been pitying my optimism these thirty years. My wildest dreams didn't expect such a prodigy as this, so soon, from university students.

If I were picking flaws—and you know what a diligent, what an indefatigable, flaw-picker I am—I would object to *The Independent's* incautious use of the word, democracy, editorially; and, tactically, to its "free" distribution.

Free distribution is wrong, in principle; because "faith without works is dead (doesn't exist)" persons should practice what they preach, which in this instance means that a publication standing for economic freedom (the free market, the profit-and-loss economy) must, in acting according to its expressed conviction, operate *for* profit. Of course, it may not *make* profit, but economic printing (producing) and distributing a good IS an economic action.

Free distribution is a tactical error, because no one values what costs him nothing. As the editorial in this copy says, *The Independent* is "junk mail." If its producers do not regard it as valuable, why should anyone else?

In order to introduce this new thing to a market, an initial free distribution could be charged to advertising, but each copy should then be stamped SAMPLE COPY, and contain—or be accompanied by—an invitation to subscribe. And a *price* should be stated under the masthead.

I suppose that this false position is forced on *The Independent* by some Yale ruling? If so, I do hope that when its staff graduate they will take the library and the magazine off the campus and run it soundly as a free market enterprise in New Haven.

Meanwhile, it is certainly a most wonderful development. I am so GLAD. And I do thank you for giving me this delight.

July 20, 1955

Dear Mr. Crane:

Have you seen *The Attack on Big Business* by Professor John D. Glover? published by Harvard University Graduate School of Business Administration. If you have not read it I believe it would interest you. It is a splendid survey of the whole attack on Big Business, from Marx to popes Leo and Pius and the National Council of Churches, via the Carrs, Schlesingers, Lippmans, et al. A marvelous job. By a sound thinker. His mind seems to me congenial to yours.

Roger MacBride was here yesterday; he visited Jean Pierre Hamilius in Luxembourg while he was in Europe and attended one of Jean Pierre's classes. You will be glad to know that (he told me) he was amazed by the students. In compliment to him, the session was in English, and Roger said that Jean Pierre "actually has a whole group of young libertarians there!" He said their views were astounding; there is nothing like it in this country. And that class still has two years to go before they graduate, when they'll be "r'aring to go in Europe." Jean Pierre is really turning out a stream of young American revolutionists, Roger says. He is training them in pure Americanism, straight from Madison and John Adams, with flavors of Jefferson and Franklin and Paine. For this, you know, you are largely responsible because you gave Jean Pierre his summer in this country. . . .

August 22, 1955

Dear Mrs. Lane:

There is a noticeable turning to the right in Italy and France, too, where my wife and I visited three out of the last four summers. Of course, my observation would be superficial; but talking to simple people in those countries, I noticed a progression away from communism. Yet, I presume there is the barest beginning of a glimmer of understanding of freedom in the Latin countries. Here again, I am not going to criticize the other fellow, because in America we are going backwards in our thinking the past two years, and the idea of the welfare state is more firmly entrenched than ever. Have you read Garet Garrett's last book, *The American Story?* While the book is not as well balanced as it might be, he pours his thinking out in impressive fashion. The conclusion is sad—"What happened to you, thou American, in these fifty years?"

August 25, 1955

Dear Mr. Crane:

There seems to be something paralyzing in the possession of money and so-called "power." Groups of persons who have them seem to become impotent. Think of any major change in history—the Catholic conquest of pagan Europe, the Moslem conquest of the then-'civilized' world, the American revolution—they are always made by the poor, unknown, believed-to-be-helpless–"powerless"–people. Men who ACT. And act not for money, not for power, but *from* a conviction of truth, so strong it compels them to action, to action that seems hopeless against overwhelming odds. Christians who attacked Imperial Rome, only to be slaughtered and burned alive; desert Bedouin challenging the God and the power and the wealth of Mecca; frontiersmen and little farmers, in mobs, chasing the Royal Governors, and sailors on ships sunk by the Royal Navy, raising such hell here for almost a century that at long last even a few gentlemen "led" them.

Actually, it seems that power and money are always being *destroyed,* rather than "ruling," doesn't it? When you compare Marx with all the Royal Courts of Europe in 1848—or Lenin with the Five Powers and the USA, in 1914, when the Second International went to pieces as utterly as the First did in 1870. Even in my own little minor experience: Who could have believed in 1919, when the Palmer raiders were treating all "radicals" as lawlessly and even murderously as ever the Cavaliers treated the Scotch

Covenanters, when Floyd Dell and Max Eastman (sentenced to twenty years imprisonment, but out on bail pending appeal) were getting out *The Masses,* from penny to penny to unpaid printers' bills, and eating mostly on credit, and when men and women were out in the winter weather without winter coats or even enough food, hawking *The Masses* on street corners—who could have believed that in the 1940s *they* would be controlling the foreign and domestic policies of the United States? and world history.

I remember buying pancakes and coffee in Childs Fourteenth Street at the scrubwomen's hour one morning, for a man who was going to jail for twenty years, that day. He was a mild little man, nearly middle-aged, of no "importance," not a Tom Mooney or Jack Reed, for whom enough funds could have been gathered to pay for appeals, he was out on bail but had lost one lower court appeal. He sat there talking; he did not want to waste his last hours of freedom in sleep; and he said he didn't know why. Why he could never be like most people, and not care. He could do all right, he said, if only he didn't care. He had a newsstand once, a nice life, a room to himself in a boarding house, a fine landlady, friendly boarders, a good, clean place, he always paid the bill right on the dot, he had everything a man could want, and then he got caring about things till he couldn't stand it, so much suffering, so many people needed so much, seemed like he HAD to do something. Sure, he could do all right himself in the capitalist system, but the system was all wrong, it got so he couldn't stand it. The world hadn't ought to be like it is, and you just GOT to do something, don't you? Only most people don't. Well, that was all when he was younger. So he did his time for that, and when he come out he wasn't going to care no more, he was going to look out for himself from then on. And he did all right, too. He was doing fine; he had as good a wife as any man ever had, and two kids; she always took care of them. Kept them spruced up like that, and nice mannered, too, you can see from their pictures nobody'd want a nicer family, and they were saving up, going to buy a home; they had six hundred and forty dollars in the bank when he was arrested. The diner paid pretty well and she was careful and saving. And now that's all gone. Twenty years is tougher than life, they say; you got more chance of parole if it's life. Anyway, it's all gone now, even if there's an amnesty for political prisoners. His wife just couldn't understand. He couldn't understand it himself. He tried to be like other folks that didn't care, but when they really begun to make a decent world for everybody over there in Russia, he just couldn't stand it, to see it all ruined and not do anything. He just HAD to do what he could. WHY was he that way? It always looked to him like, if everybody did what they could do, there wouldn't be so much misery and poverty; everybody could have as much as he had, and more, and then he'd get to saying to himself, a man can't blame a system that he's in himself and don't try to change, and first thing he knew he'd be out on the streets selling leaflets or something; he just couldn't help it. And going to Party meetings. She said her and the kids ought to come first, and the truth was they did, only he HAD to do what he could, and she couldn't understand that, and you can't blame her. So now it's all over for him, but they'll keep on in Russia, won't they? They'd save the Revolution in Russia, didn't I think so?

He talked till dawn and then went to surrender himself and save the bail money for The Cause. A big man like Jack Reed jumped his bail (put up by a rich woman who agreed to his doing it) and went to Russia on the underground, but this was only a little man. I never saw or heard of him again. But those were the men who made Jack Reed famous and attached Eleanor and FDR to the social revolution, and put Alger Hiss and others in the State Department. Just as it was the forgotten Christian Jews and slaves who made pagan Europe ostensibly Christian in four centuries. And as it was the forgotten men who, from the 1660s to the 1760s, made the American Revolution. Such things are not done by writing checks; the work that is done for *money* is for *money*. It is action *for the change in human affairs,* that makes such changes.

A man who will pay his own expenses and go to a State capital to work for a bill, or against it, because he wants or does not want it, is worth more than sixteen hired lobbyists who work for their salaries.

Your news from Italy and France is cheering. Yes there seems to be a sort of leveling-out occuring over the world. In metaphor—which probably comes from my recent experience in the Connecticut flood—it is as if the frontiers had burst and the Revolution swirled out from here; all the currents are mixed, everywhere. From the 1770s to the mid-nineteenth century, the influence went out from here to Europe and Asia, overturning all the Old Regimes; then the counter-current, the socialist reaction, poured into these States, largely from Europe but from Asia, too (remember the vogue for Madame Blavatsky and theosophy for instance?). Now the whole world scene is a mixture, a confusion.

Well, the Founding Fathers began (as they knew) *world* revolution. I even wonder sometimes whether there wasn't a kind of inevitability in Wilson's abominable treachery to us all, that took this country into the British-German War and began World War. He was, of course, *personally* responsible for all the murder, destruction, horrible suffering of this continuing World War. But, given the factors—the Revolution plus the Reaction here—perhaps there was bound to be someone in the White House who would be stupid enough to start a World War with the idiotic notion that it was "war to make the world safe for democracy." The permanent factor in all human affairs being human stupidity, of course. Logically, the Revolution would conquer the world by the method that its founders intended, and Washington assumed in his Farewell Address. But the people in general, especially politicians, just ain't logical. (Sometimes I even suspect that I'm not, always.)

Yes, I read Garet's last book. I like him very much, and admired him; he wrote marvelously, even with flashes of genius. We never agreed in principle. He said that I am a mystic ruined by materialism, and that he was a materialist ruined by mysticism. (I don't agree with that, either.) He spoiled everything he wrote, for me, by always putting into it some contradictory flaw that threw away his basic position. I mean that he tried to fight for individualism on an always semi-collectivist basis. And above all, he was profoundly a pessimist. Hopelessness was his constant mood. Now of course pessimism is wholly irrational; it is a denial and rejection of the human rational function. Therefore it always involves a thinker in self-contradictions. Because he lives; he continues to live; and living without faith in life is an impossibility; and faith in life is optimism. So a living thinker who is emotionally attached to the image of himself as pessimist, and who therefore preaches pessimism (as Garet did) involves himself in manifest absurdities.

In my opinion, he also does incalculable harm to other persons. Living is a process of balancing between wanting to live and wanting to die—that is, between impulse to action and impulse to rest—and the pessimist's "vanity, vanity, all is vanity . . . What's the use? all is lost, lost, lost" had the effect of tipping that precarious balance toward inaction, toward death. Garet's *The Revolution Was,* for example, is a great bit of reporting, a piece of remarkable insight, and a great, most lamentable, detriment to the real, existing Revolution. Its effect is to discourage any impulse to act for the human rights that, Garet says, are already lost, hopelessly lost. Nothing remains but paying for the dead horse, or in other metaphor, why stupidly try to lock the stable door since the stalls are empty, the horse already stolen. There's nothing to do now, but sit and keen, wail with Garet for the happy past that is no more and can never be again. That attitude irritates me to near the point of frenzy. Not only that it's false but that it's so damned absurd. And Garet's presentation of it is so cleverly effective.

Here are you, for goodness sake, Mr. Crane! reading Garet and writing me, "The conclusion is sad—"What happened to you, thou American, in these fifty years!"

Okay, I'll bite: What DID happen to these Americans, in these fifty years? You and I—and Garet, if he would—remember 1905. How many Americans in 1905 ever gave a thought to any political principle? The current notion of socialism then was: Socialists are riff-raff, they are anarchists who use dynamite and shot McKinley; they advocate destroying the home; nice people are never socialists and socialists amount to nothing to worry about. But America and everything American are far inferior to Europe and anything whatever that is European; and in Europe, Germany is superior to all else. Germany is fifty years ahead of us in social legislation. Also in music and medicine and culture and happy life. As to politics, I'm Republican (or Democrat). Why? Because my family is; or because the silver-tongued boy orator from the Platte is for sixteen-to-one, which means: You shall not crucify mankind upon a cross of Gold; Bust the Trusts! In 1905, geography was in school books. Only a handful of Americans had a radius of knowledge, or even interest longer than fifty miles. In

San Francisco the "East" was Colorado; in New York, the "West" was Pittsburgh—and I speak now of the informed, the educated, the "upper-crust" persons. A very few of such Easterners traveled—humbly, for culture—in Europe. Most Americans had no concept whatever of the world beyond their home towns. Which means, no understanding whatever of their own country.

If "thou American" had no idea of the welfare state, he had no notion of objecting to it, either. He had never heard of Marx, or communism, or liberalism or individualism; if he had heard the words he would have had NO idea of what they meant—not even a silly one; and Russia was a place where the family fled in a sleigh over pathless snow and threw out the baby to halt the pursuing pack of wolves. If you really want to know what happened to thou American in these fifty years, just look at any newspaper or magazine dated 1905. I myself am all FOR what has happened to him since then. So are you; and so was Garet, actually; only Garet had a sickness in his mind, or temperament, or somewhere. He was desperately, passionately, hellishly, UNhappy—for no reason, so far as I could ever see, or guess—and he made his own picture of the world, of human life and history and the present situations, from that emotion. He was always looking for the Dark Forces that control Human Destiny and baffle all hopes and bring all efforts to nothing, nothing, nothing. He was always asking all the unanswerable Whys? Why am I born? Why is Life? Why is the Universe?—like a three-year-old child: Why? Why? Why? and, Why, Why? Why am I asking Why? Garet wanted to know. Because you do not use the sense God gave you, I replied. But his response, of course, was: Why? It's really too bad that he never saw how *funny* we all are.

October 3, 1955

Dear Mrs. Lane:

I agree with all that you say about the progress that has been achieved over the past fifty years. We have come a long way intellectually. Indeed, we were quite unsophisticated around the turn of the century as compared with our present knowledge and culture and also, I am afraid, our present self-esteem and self-righteousness. We have made marvelous scientific and technical advances and have multiplied the power of our hands so that we turn out almost unbelievable quantities of goods and services. Along with that we have less drudgery, more leisure and more appreciation of culture. We have music and art and literature far beyond the quantity and quality of the arts in America fifty years ago. We go to Church much more than we used to; membership and attendance have mounted steadily. Our education facilities have expanded tremendously. My Class of 1897 in Newark High School had only sixty members in a city of over two hundred thousand; now the city of Newark has twice the population and six high schools each graduating several hundred boys and girls. Our colleges are bursting at the seams; Princeton University, on which we conferred a favor (!) by attending, now can only accept one out of four or five boys who apply for admission. I know all of this, I have lived through it, with my eyes at least partly open. And I ascribe this progress, this marvelous expansion of release of human energy, to the freedom bequeathed to us by our forefathers, not all at once but in different steps over almost three hundred years. It is the result of devout people in a voluntary society, which is still functioning, though considerably impaired.

Yet, I can't be a Pollyanna. There is a limerick that has some truth in it:—

God's plan made a hopeful beginning
Then man burst his chances by sinning
We hope that the story will end in God's glory
But at present the other side's winning.

Your analysis of Garrett's state of mind is keen and interesting; yet, I have got a great deal out of reading his writings. I have always been happy. Still am. And optimistic. In the last analysis, my optimism is based on the thought that "America is the last resort of the human race" and that God will lead us to preserve and expand our freedom.

Gadgets aren't convincing to me. The late Lamont Du Pont, the finest man I ever knew, was not a churchman. But one day when I was burbling about all the advances of the present day and said "This is a new epoch in history," he replied, "Material things, technological developments, don't create a new epoch. That is caused by something that happened in Palestine nineteen hundred years ago."

A further look at life today and fifty years ago indicates to me that with all this progress in culture, as well as in technology, there has been a fearful regression. Perhaps we were simple minded at the turn of the century, but there were some virtues in us that we may have lost or may be losing. We did not analyze freedom then and prate about it; yet we instinctively believed in it and didn't barter it for security. The conversion of our Federal government into a welfare state, the socialization of twenty or twenty-five percent of our activities (which is still growing), the departure from the Constitution, the loss of the Republic constitute such a decline in our American life that, humanly speaking, our American civilization is doomed, though I stubbornly refuse to believe it. Right now the polls show that from 1953 to 1955 there have been large gains in the percentages of people who approve the Federal government aid to the public schools, Federal government housing, support of agriculture, expanded social security. Business men as well as the so-called intellectuals turn to the Great White Father.

I would sum up my feeling—and I presume it is a feeling rather than an intellectually-arrived-at conclusion—to say that we have slumped badly in many respects over the last fifty years, have lost many values, and are in grave danger, but that for the long pull I am optimistic. Rome had a fine civilization and was even becoming Christian, but it became a welfare state, declined and fell. Perhaps we will crash and another Dark Age will intervene. Even so, we will recover the light again one day. I simply do not believe in human perfectability and inevitable progress. This is nonsense. Only by God's guiding hand in history and the redemptive love of Christ can we realize what we ought to be, and there the possibilities are so unlimited that the prospect is heartening and enchanting. There may be many dips in the upward curve, but let's fight the present Reaction right now and try to prevent a collapse and eclipse with all the suffering and sorrow that there would be entailed.

And through it all we must, as indeed you do, preserve our humor. I thought as I read your letter, that it used to be said in New York that the West began in Rahway, New Jersey! You move it out to Pittsburgh. A very observing foreigner said of the American cities that Boston looked down on New York, Chicago resented New York, but Philadelphia didn't even know New York existed. As to Boston and its culture, you may recall the story of Miss Palfrey who at eighty-six years of age started to learn Hebrew; when asked why at her age, she replied that she soon expected to meet her creator and wanted to be able to talk to Him in His language.

Hurray for Wilmington. I often say, "Il faut cultiver notre jardin," for one mustn't say it despairingly.

October 5, 1955

Dear Mr. Crane:

Your interesting letter of October 3 came this morning and I infer that it is the one that didn't come yesterday—What a sentence! Idiotic as it is, I expect you'll know what it means.

I have just read a book that I believe will interest you: *"Work And History," an Essay on the Structure of Civilization*, by Paul Schrecker. Princeton University Press, 1948. It may be out of print; I got my copy from Schulte's Bookstore, 80 Fourth Avenue, New York City, where I buy all books that I do buy because they're second-hand, remainders or review copies and cheap. I think this is an important book. It is all that I know about its author, but he is a thinker in the Vienna School line. He takes the Human Action view of Mises into all aspects of human life—which, in sum, he calls "civilization" and in contra-distinction to non-human "nature," and he analyzes it—"civilization"—*structurally*. He is an original thinker, and an individualist though individualism is not explicit in this book.

For the reason that your view is transcendental and mine isn't I cannot agree with you about "materialism." I cannot see, actually, in fact, any such thing as materialism. Nobody ever wants any *material thing*. No human being ever, in any circumstances, even for an instant, is a "materialist." All human desires and all their satisfactions are intangibles. Nobody wants any "gadget." Do you want a car? Just *look* at the thing—metal, glass, cloth. Of course you don't want it; what you want is transportation, speed, quicker contacts with other persons, lifetime saving—i.e.

more value contents in *life enjoyment* of wider sense, sharing that enjoyment with family and friends, etc., etc. All intangibles. You don't want a *house*; you want shelter, comfort, cleanliness, beauty, perhaps evidence of abilities of mind and character, called "success." A starving person, even, does not want *bread*; he wants life itself. This scorn of "materialism" seems to me to be either a shallow and thoughtless cliché, or an expression of frustration, despair, envy, hate—as in the general European and Asiatic "contempt" for this country's "sordid materialism." Europeans flaunt their "culture," Nehru flaunts Indian "spirituality." America, they say, has nothing but plumbing; how low, how vulgar, how contemptible, a country that values bathrooms while Europe loves art and India has a soul.

Well, okay, I'll raise right now the flag of the bathroom. What IS a bathroom? It is cleanliness, health and all other values of human *life* on this earth: leisure, learning, art, culture, because it releases human beings from life-wasting drudgery. Paris can have its art—and its "working class quarters" where pale people live in airless, windowless rooms, wear dirty clothes on unwashed bodies and use the pavements and gutters as dogs do. Europe can have its rich old culture and England its imperial pride, and their bourgeois homes and hotels where the "slaveys" heat water on stoves in basements and lug jars of it up flights of stairs, fill tin tubs, and lug the dirty water down the stairs again, day after day and year after year till they die. Give me American bathrooms; give me the country where pumps and pipes are the working class, where "gadgets" *serve* the values of human life, and human beings have a life-time to *live*. India can have its "spirituality" and its over-populated land, and under-fed, hungry, overworked, dirty, sick people sitting in the dust half-naked, with flies swarming on their babies' eyes and holy cows eating the little food they have. India is "spiritual" because it hasn't enough to eat. Starvation fills anyone's head with—Well, you have never been hungry; you don't know. And who wouldn't dream of the bliss of not-being (Nirvana), whose experience of "being" was the Indian's? India has nothing to "teach the West," and Europe has nothing to teach the USA—except what NOT to do and to be.

And speaking for myself, I am all FOR "American materialism."

I cannot understand Mr. Lamont Du Pont's view. How can anyone say, for one tiny example, that synthetic fibers don't "create a new epoch?" For thousands of years, thousands of living persons spent their lives caring for worms, unwinding filaments from the cocoons, spinning, weaving, making a little cloth for a few 'way up there "high class" persons to wear. Meanwhile, the others, the low-class servants of the worms, humbly wear rags. It isn't a new epoch, when a few skillful, clean, well-fed, healthy persons tend machines pouring out beautiful cloth for everyone to wear? and all of them have an abundance of life-time to use "all the powers that God for use has given?"

Will you forgive me if I say that "something that happened in Palestine nineteen hundred years ago" seems to me to have created no new epoch during eighteen hundred of those years? The period began in hunger, disease, oppression, cruelty, massacres, wars, torture and ended in the same. It began with Romans killing Jews and ended with Christians killing Jews and killing each other and Moslems.

If there is value in human life—and can we say that there is no value in what God hath wrought?—it seems to me that a "new epoch," in terms of those values, is only now beginning. And it seems to me to begin with the beginning of man's approach to knowledge of God's "natural" laws through the use of those means—the "senses" and the rational faculty—with which God has endowed human beings; the approach called "scientific."

By the way, wasn't it Newman who said, "to live is to change, and to be perfect is to have changed often?" I must confess that I don't know what he meant; except vaguely that he seems to have attached some value to living. I don't believe in human perfectability, or in the inevitability of progress, either, of course; my goodness! I don't believe any such transcendentalist theories. And if I'm not mistaken, it wasn't the inevitability but the *possibility* of human progress—improvement—that was such a radical and horrifying theory in the seventeenth century. Benjamin Franklin, as a youngster, believed in that possibility, with a few other young radicals; that was one of the reasons why he was so shocking in Boston that when he grew wiser he found it prudent to begin his serious career in Philadelphia where his radical ideas were not so well known. I don't know where the inevitable progress theory came from; its kind of idiocy suggests that it came from the Physiocrats. It's inherent in the Marxian philosophy of course. And in the Hegelian thesis-anti-thesis-synthesis historical philosophy, which is a secularization of the Christian tenet of the superrational synthesis of collectivism and individualism, by Grace. What Chesterton called "the wild paradoxes" of his Catholic faith.

It seems to me that to regard any human action as inevitable is to deny the existence of liberty—the inalienable function of self-control intrinsic to a human being. It is not human choice, human action, that is inevitable; it is the *result* of the human action. A person controls his own action; Natural Law—the Will of God established and operating in Creation—produces the result of the action. That fact, really, is the basis of all "science," isn't it? It is by acting, observing the result of the action, thinking about it, and repeating this process, that persons learn something about the operation of Natural Law. If the *result* were not inevitable, science would be impossible. The kind of knowledge called scientific (always only approximate as it is) depends upon God's non-intervention with the Laws established in the nature of the universe.

November 1, 1955

Dear Mr. Crane:

If you have not read Joseph Wood Krutch's book, *The Measure Of Man*, I would urge you to do so. I have just read it and think it is *fine*. Also I think that it is very nearly perfect—as nearly as perfection is possible—for use upon the bemused "intellectuals." It is a marvelous, gentle and davastating attack upon the mechanistic *basis* of most contemporary thinking.

Danbury was much more damaged by the October flood than by the flood in August. The two have left the main street wrecked, and ruined many business and industrial firms. I myself survived with only minor losses of equipment; my house was not damaged. There was chaos for awhile, with martial law and without water or electric service, and neighbors taking refuge with me when unable to reach their own houses. Mr. Harding's famous "normalcy" has come back to my little household now, however.

November 7, 1955

Dear Mrs. Lane:

Your letter of October 5 was tremendous, and I only wish that I could discuss some of these points with you. They can't be dealt with by letter with any satisfaction at all.

I agree with almost all that you say in your letter, but with important reservations. Certainly in the light of history and what we know of the character of homo sapiens, one could not reasonably expect the new epoch to burst into full bloom nineteen hundred years ago. Rather, it is almost literally true that "Christianity has never yet been tried." After its first marvelous progress, it was perverted into a state, institutionalized religion. There was a collapse into the Dark Ages with spots of light from time to time through the centuries. After eighteen hundred years there was a dawning of understanding of some of the fundamental ideas of man's life and freedom, and this was manifested in different areas of life—religion, economic and political.

It may well be that we will have another Dark Ages. Certainly the behavior of man in the best of countries is shameful, and progress is only possible and redemption feasible through repentance and consequent understanding. I don't know much about "practical historical factors." All I know is that we human beings are not angelic and are not going to become so by some purely natural development.

The head of the Independent Library at Yale writes that they are having a discouraging time, banging away at the stone wall without chipping it. I have just replied to him that for twenty of them to meet several times a month will accomplish more than they realize.

Mansfield, Missouri
November 20, 1955

Dear Mr. Crane:

Probably, as you say, we think alike but can't perfectly express our meanings because we—human beings—cannot think or speak *meanings*, but only symbols of them.

Essentially what I try to do is to say that it is possible—and, I think, most desirable— to regard the nature of man as a scientist regards the nature of an atom; that is, as a thing *given,* prioristic, existing *as is,* acting according to Laws that human senses and human reason can discover, approximately. This is an arbitrarily restricted view, to be understood as arbitrary and restricted. It does not deny nor affirm, but merely excludes for purposes of (restricted) observation and thought, the whole field of religious truths.

When you say, Progress is only possible and redemption feasible through repentance and consequent understanding, I agree of course; but do I know your meaning of "repentance?" The word is used to symbolize a "conviction of sin" and a spiritual change caused by Divine Grace. There is another meaning which I'm sure everyone knows from ordinary experience; the repentance that follows and is a consequence of understanding. You drive your car without chains on an icy pavement, and skid; you say to yourself, I'll not do that again, I'm lucky I'm alive. And you don't do it again. Isn't that repentance and reform? And is it not a "purely natural development?"

I certainly agree, too, that "human beings are not angelic." But my arbitrarily restricted—and temporary—view does not include angels nor their qualities. It may be—and, for my present strictly limited purposes, it IS—that living persons on this earth are *human,* having wholly human nature, human functions, human qualities and powers, which (I think) have not yet been sufficiently observed and thought about. To observe this human creature and try to discover the Law of its nature, we must not be distracted by attention to angels, nor by the question of whether this human being should or will or can *become* an angel; the simple question before us is, What IS this human being? A living person on this earth is, obviously, an acting energy. To know ALL that a person *is* may be as impossible as to know all that any energy (electronic, for example) is—its source, its purpose, its essential being; after all, we living creatures are not the Maker of all things including us. But some approximate and tentative knowledge of the nature of man surely can be obtained by learning (as with the electron) HOW it *acts* and what results its action produces.

It may be that trying to be, or to induce others to try to be, angels—meaning super "natural" beings on a non-earthly plane of being—is not the method of improving human relations here on earth; as all the rites of all religions turned out to be not the method of eliminating pestilences and famines. Some simple "natural development" of that rare uncommon quality called common sense—such as the repentance of the skidding motorist—about war, for instance, or Government, really could prevent another Dark Ages, don't you think?

VIII

Mansfield, Missouri
November 25, 1955

Dear Mr. Crane:

It was such a pleasure to hear your voice, almost like seeing-and-talking with you again. I did enjoy it. Thank you.

When you spoke of a Foundation for the purpose of fostering liberalism, and I asked you, How? I understood you to indicate that you were not considering methods at the moment, but would like my view of a Foundation per se.

First, a Foundation is an "organization"; that is, it is an established pattern of human action, existing as a pattern-idea in human minds and as a repetition of human actions in space and time.

Now of course I know the profit-values of cooperation and that for many purposes an established pattern of such action is essential. Certainly it is enormously profitable to all enterprises in which achievement of their purposes is measurable. But I do not forget Mohammed's view of organization for intangible and immeasurable purposes. As you know, he emphatically prohibited ANY organization in the field of religion.

His reason for this prohibition was "practical" and, I think rational, intelligent. It was that persons in an organization tend to work for the existence and expansion of the organization, rather than for the organization's *purposes*. When the purpose is a measurable achievement, that fact concentrates attention and effort upon it; a traders'-organization of a caravan aiming to reach a certain market within a certain time and to trade the caravan loads profitably there, or General Motors having the purpose of making a certain number of cars and selling them within twelve months, has a *measure* of success or failure constantly before it (them). The organization, while essential, is a means to serve the end. But, in Mohammed's view (and at least tentatively in mine), when the purpose to be achieved is intangible and immeasurable, the means (the organization) becomes—to persons in it—itself the end to be served.

He drew this conclusion from observing the history of organized Judaism and organized Christianity. His was "the faith of Abraham and the Prophets"—individualism. He thought that organization had substituted means for end; that the greatest of the Prophets (Christ of course) had attacked the *organization* and revived the true faith; that its organization in the Church had again subordinated purpose to means. He reasoned that truth could be preserved and promulgated in human minds only in the absence of its establishment as purpose of an organization. The practical result of his theory was that the religious concept of the individualist nature of man dominated the civilized world for eight centuries and produced the richest culture in history and by far the most progressive age until the American. This result, I think, demonstrates some value in the theory. At least, it does not dismiss the theory from consideration, as does the result, in practice, of the collectivist theory.

Second, the purpose of a Foundation is to achieve some intangible, immeasurable end (such as social service or general welfare) by giving away money. This raises the question of what money IS, and what is its correction function in human relationships. I have wondered whether money CAN be used correctly in relationships other than those named "economic." Money itself is a commodity; and a commodity used as a means of exchanging other commodities.

Supposing the object of its use to be the general welfare of humanity, certainly a dollar invested in, say, Alexander Graham Bell's new invention, was enormously more productive of the desired result than a dollar given to the "poor." The Bell Company is daily preventing and diminishing more poverty than the Community Chests temporarily relieve in a year. (Not to mention the Bell Company's social and cultural effects.) May it be that money belongs wholly in the "economic" field of human action and should not be used—is ineffective or destructive—outside that field? (Excepting, of course, its uses in directly *personal* need of friendliness. If I may call upon Mohammed again, you remember that he said: It is a sin to give alms without also giving yourself.)

Third, a Foundation's purpose in giving away money to "educate" persons in general, has several aspects that seem questionable to me. It is a use of money to change unknown persons' beliefs and concepts. Isn't there a discrepancy between this means and the end desired? CAN money affect beliefs? It is an attempt to *teach,* in the sense of an active effort to affect passive minds. But nothing CAN be taught in that sense; everything must be *learned.* The activity must be the learner's, not the teacher's. You can lead a horse to water but you cannot make him drink. The thirsty horse *need* not be led; if free, he seeks and finds water, and drinks.

In sum, my thoughts about Foundations as such are these:

1. An organization for any intangible, immeasurable purpose tends to use—waste—human time-energy in perpetuating and expanding the organization, rather than in achieving its purpose.

2. A Foundation gives money on a non-"economic" basis, that is, not on the free-market profit-motive exchange-of-values basis. Is this not a misuse of money? CAN money actually have other than an "economic" function?

3. Since a Foundation's achievement of its purpose is immeasurable, there is no standard by which to determine the value received in exchange for money given. If the givers are conscientious, they do not simply give money to their personal favorites; they try to expend it for achievement of the organization's purpose "objectively," without regard to personalities. But they have no way—there is no way—of measuring an intangible value in relation to the concrete market-value of money, and, since persons cannot be eliminated, it seems to me that their effort tends to distort them, producing veniality, hypocrisy, parasitism, self-deception—Owen Latimores.

I think that the success of the many existing Foundations in promoting collectivist fallacies and resulting political action is no argument for the potential value of a Foundation in promoting liberalism. On the contrary, does it not suggest that a *method* which demonstrably produces reactionary results will not produce progressive ones?

A Foundation is non-profit. How, then, can it stand for the rightness of the profit-motive in human action? How can it assert the fact that profit-motive *exists,* as a natural, essential, inalienable element in ALL human action? How can it show, specifically, the proved great value of a "profit-motive economy" in increasing human welfare in all its aspects—material, social cultural? Being itself non-profit, how can it do otherwise than advocate a non-profit "system"? by example, if not openly by precept.

Being a non-profit organization, a Foundation submits to the State's supervision, acts only within limits which administrative agencies of the political power place upon it and upon the expression of convictions held by persons in it, representing it, or receiving its donations. Itself submissive and obedient, how can it represent or advocate correct American resistance to, and limitation of, the political power? (In practice, as you know, it cannot—and keep its non-profit political privilege.) Accepting imposed limits upon free speech and free press? Being itself not a free enterprise, how can it urge others to defend the freedom of enterprise?

The non-profit Foundation stands as a prominent example of submission to the existing political power and of unresisting, willing obedience to its arbitrary decrees. (It does this, of course, for what its organizers and directors believe to be its effect upon persons. Freedom is an environment in which NO use of physical force upon a person, or persons, prevents or impedes or stops the individual's use of his own God-given powers, under his own *self*government. Any person who uses these powers to injure others should be—and is, by a correctly functioning state—deprived of his freedom, removed from that environment. But a group of persons organized as a State (and therefore having the legal monopoly of the use of physical force upon other persons) who use force in an attempt to *govern* others are encroaching upon the others' inalienable power and function of *self*-government and freedom can be preserved only by resistance to that encroachment.

If those statements are true, HOW *can* a non-profit organization, enjoying a State-granted privilege of tax-exemption, permitting a State encroachment upon its members', employees' and beneficiaries' self-government, accepting and imposing State-decreed limitations upon expression of opinion and reports of fact, obeying the State's orders prohibiting any action whatever in the whole field of relations between man and State—How can such an organization stand, in anyone's eyes, as a defender of freedom? And, when it does not itself stand for freedom—even for its own—how can it effectively urge or induce others to do so? With money?

A free publisher can publish free and sound books. What can money do? It can support a writer; but any writer worth reading can support himself—and will, will insist upon it; and any writer eager and able to express convictions will express them. Money can subsidize a book's publication; thereby it removes the publisher's profit-incentive and makes his promotion and sale of the book feeble and futile. Money can buy and give away books; which therefore nobody will value and few will read, because a give-away seems worthless to everyone. Books given to libraries are seldom kept in them, because cataloguing a book costs more than the book, so a librarian willing to spend the cost of cataloguing a book, buys the book. I really do not know what money can do.

I do sympathize with you in your evident problem (while selfishly being glad that it isn't mine), and I am sorry that I cannot be helpful to you in solving it. My only suggestion would be *little* charities, small and personal, struggling little private schools like Bera and School of the Ozarks, the little group that's trying to supply slates and pencils to schools in Greece and Africa—places where a little money can be greatly helpful to human lives.

It is not money but *action*—personal, cooperative, FREE action that will save the Republic. It is those twenty students in Yale, and the three or four that you—actively!—may get together in Princeton, and other groups like them, hundreds of such active groups now, who will do that. Truly they will. The other side is not winning!

December 1, 1955

Dear Mrs. Lane:

Let me digest your letter a little further before attempting to reply to it. Meanwhile, the thought came to my mind that there are five duties or practices in Islam, and one of these five is the giving of alms to the poor. They surely should be on a wider basis than the bare necessities of life to those that are starving.

Mansfield, Mo.
December 5, 1955

Dear Mr. Crane:

The mail brings me this morning a comment: "Intellectuals are the champion confidence men" seems to me a gem of accurate observation.

This is not impugning the honesty of these eager-beaver grabbers of subsidies. They (in general) first deceive themselves; which is the first essential to salesmanship of any dubious product. (This is the reason that I, when a salesman, first most carefully, suspiciously, investigated what I was considering selling: in order NOT to deceive myself about it, but to have genuine confidence in it, based on fact and proof.)

Another instance, doubtless, of discrepancy in vocabularies: I don't quite know what you mean by alms "on a wider basis" than aid to the starving. An imperative in Islam is alms, as you say, and it is guarded by the prohibition of giving alms without giving one's self. That is, almsgiving is kept on the individualist basis. I'm sure you and I agree that there IS no "wider basis" in the human world than the individual person. An instance of Moslem alms was your aid to Jon Ovezea; you went to Ellis Island to see him, you gave not only assistance but yourself. So did Merwin Hart and Mr. Pew. Meanwhile, during the whole eighteen months that we spent in saving his life, the organized aids to immigrants were speeding hordes of communists through Ellis Island, many of whom in passing told Jon Ovezea what a fool he was; he had only to join the Party to get out. And others who didn't were shipped back to their countries in Red hands; so many succeeded in killing themselves enroute that they were being handcuffed and locked up on the ships at the time that we finally got Jon shipped to Honduras. That is an evil of *organization*. Most of the persons involved were more merciful, but in the organization they felt constrained to obey orders. That time that Jon was shipped back to Rumania (and three of the others shipped with him had killed themselves before we got him off the ship at sea) it was one of the guards who shipped him who saved him, by secretly telephoning me after he got off duty. He did not give his name, even then.

William Volker—a Lutheran!—also practiced Moslem alms for decades before he died. He lent money to literally thousands of individuals, personally; it was known widely throughout the Midwest that anyone in need could always see him, and he would give help, though nobody knew WHO he helped because his own requirement was that the persons helped would not tell. Since he died, several persons now successful and active individualist-liberals have confided to me that Mr. Volker helped them through times of desperation. He gave help that no organization could, because of its necessary rules and impersonality.

No one in Islam was hungry, because every household was a source of food and shelter and friendliness. And of thanks for the opportunity of practicing the faith. Of course there is a great deal of "westernization"—and socialism—in the Moslem countries now. But even as late as 1915, when the Armenians rose in arms behind the Turkish armies defending the Caucasian frontier against the Russians and military survival required the mass-movement of the Armenian population away from the rear of the Turkish troops at the front, all the Turks' houses along the route of march were opened to the (enemy and Christian) Armenian refugees. The convoys were absorbed and given hospitality in the Moslem households all the way from Van to Scutari and Damascus. No Red Cross ever did a finer job than the unorganized Moslem faith did then. It is not simply a question of giving "bare necessities of life to the starving:" any charitable organization does that, more or less. Never to give alms without giving one's self also is a wide basis, isn't it? Can there be a wider one? Isn't the difference between writing a check for the Community Chest and taking a friendless stranger into your home as a friend, precisely a difference in, so to speak, width? Of course we agree completely. I just don't know quite the meaning of your words.

December 16, 1955

Dear Mrs. Lane:

I think you perform a service in pointing out the dangers of organization. The members of such organizations too often become pre-occupied with the organization itself. I have seen that in many different kinds of organizations.

Yet, I believe in organization provided it is on a voluntary basis. I have long said that the outstanding feature of American life has been cooperation. The difference between America with our relatively high degree of freedom and proliferation of such numerous and so many different kinds of voluntary associations and foreign countries which have in varying degrees collectivist philosophy and government points this up very strongly. Though many have been unwisely conceived and badly run, America would be a very different and much poorer place without all these voluntary assciations.

So I believe that foundations are good provided they have high purposes and are properly managed. I am sure I get from you very wise and desirable warnings about the dangers, but I can't go all the way that a foundation must necessarily be an improper set up. There are many rocks in the waters, but I hope they can be avoided.

A private college does enjoy a tax-exempt status from the state, but its usefulness has not been destroyed by that. I am still going to believe in private education rather than to go over to the public school.

December 29, 1955

Dear Mr. Crane:

Thank you for your letter of the sixteenth, which reached me this morning. (What on earth is happening to postal service?—a purely rhetorical question.)

In the old days of the "dawn in Russia," enthusiastic writers whose "capitalistic market" price was tops—Jack Reed, Art Young, Bob Minor—wrote their brilliant best for *The Masses* and made it a brilliant, popular, influential magazine. *The Masses* paid them $10, or $5 or nothing if the printer wasn't paid. They wrote for *The Masses* because there they could say what they wanted to say. The editors, too, edited *The Masses* because they wanted to; Max Eastman, Floyd Dell, the editors, got $15 a week IF the printer was paid. *The Masses* was a free enterprise, started (like *Reader's Digest*) with barely capital enough to pay the printer's first bill. It seems to me that it was run on fairly sound business principles. The overhead was the least cost; the magazine sold at a very small profit; the revenue went for material and manufacturing costs, the aim was larger production and wider distribution; and the venture succeeded. Before it was suppressed during the war, it was paying writers and artists $25 to $50 and the editors were getting their $15 regularly every week and always paying the printer's bill promptly in full. As for popular support and subsidies, in this century's teens they were as rare for communism as they are for individualism now. In this respect the situation recently seems to me the exact reverse of the situation then; and it was enterprises like *The Masses* that reversed it.

Of course there is an element now that didn't exist then; the governmental pressure. The collectivists are using political power to suppress free enterprise, as the simple grafters of fifty years ago never dreamed of doing. In those days, the police merely wrecked the office and clubbed you over the head. Now the tax collector gets you.

How totally I agree with you about co-operation, "the outstanding feature of American life." I believe it demonstrates a praxeological axiom: Given an environment of freedom, human beings act in co-operation.

Rousseau messed up thinking by his theory that human beings are naturally "good." It isn't a question of "good" and/or "evil" at all. It is simply a question of what human beings ARE, per se. One thing we are is profit-seeking. Without a profit-motive, there is NO human action. This is a fact so obvious that hardly anyone sees it. . . . The profit motive is essential to ALL human action. Therefore, human beings co-operate; because the profit, to each, from co-operative action is greater than each can obtain, for the same expenditure, from isolated action. If there is no restraint put upon them—that is, in an environment of freedom—all persons act co-operatively, in every way that their imaginations can devise, from the farmers "trading work," and the log-rolling and husking bees and quilting parties to General Motors and Rotary and N.A.M.

Alas, I fear that we shall never agree about foundations. I may never lose my conviction that any "privilege" granted or obtained from the State is destructive to the "privileged." I think it is a fact, historically demonstrated, that State action intended to "benefit" a group causes an equal and opposite reaction, not against the State, but against the group "benefited." I think—as random examples

—that this reaction occurred against the French aristocrats during the French Revolution; against the negroes in the South after "Reconstruction"; against the subsidized railroads in the "Bust the Trusts!" movement that made the socialist Interstate Commerce Commission and the Antitrust Laws and gave great impetus to the whole reactionary movement here; I think it is occurring now against the labor unions. Especially I remain convinced that freedom from State control cannot be advocated, maintained, defended, by accepting State control in return for a status of "privilege." I think that the usefulness, to human rights and freedom, of tax-exempt private colleges and churches HAS been destroyed; which of them now is on the right side in the Man versus State struggle?

I may not always wholly agree with you but I do know that, whatever you do, you believe it is right; and that's the best that any of us can do. So you always have my sincere good wishes for your success in all your undertakings.

January 20, 1956

Dear Mrs. Lane:

I, too, believe in the influence and importance of work in a garret, and I am always suspicious of affluence. Yet, many developments which have been so strategic have been financed in one way or another. Coming right down to today, some of the activities of the big foundations seem to be quite reprehensible, but I have not gone over to the belief that all eleemosynary institutions should be deprived of tax exemption.

So, I am going ahead with my own little foundation and hope it may do some good; but it will, by the way, have no paid employees.

Mansfield, Mo.
January 27, 1956

Dear Mr. Crane:

Now, about tax exemption. It seems to me that there are two *ways* of looking at any situation actually existing; the strategic and the tactical. The basic *point of view,* of course, is fundamental principle. We look at the situation from the individualist liberal point of view; i.e., we know that ownership of property is an intrinsic, inalienable function of the individual person. Therefore, "thou shalt not steal" is axiomatic; anyone who takes property from anyone else by any other means than voluntary exchange is an aggressor invading a "natural" (God-given) human right, an intrinsic *function* of the living human being. Taxation, therefore is armed robbery.

From this point of view, the long-range strategy is abolition of all taxation. Such an achievement now, or in any near future, is as impossible as abolition of chattel slavery was in Greece or Rome. Taxation is a tradition as old as the State; or as slavery; it will require centuries if not milleniums to get it into people's heads that force is no more essential in getting them to pay for adequate police protection and its legal restriction TO protection, than force is essential in getting them to work productively. There are even amusing aspects of the really very exact parallel between taxation and slavery; speak of abolishing taxation now and you get a perfect echo of the reaction to abolition of slavery a few decades ago. But how could we maintain civilization, how could we even live, with nobody to do the hard work? But, you are MAD; how could we have law and order, civilization, safety, with nobody paying taxes to Government? It is the slave's DUTY to pay taxes and—as Mrs. Roosevelt says—cheerfully. Oh, well.

Tactically, it is at least possible to protest that the traditional robbery should be indiscriminating. If we are robbed, let us all be robbed equally. When the train is stopped and the armed bandits enter the passenger coach, they add outrage to injury if they leave one man his watch and another his wallet and pass the third one by with an indulgent smile, saying, "Keep your cash, old-timer, you raise cattle and we like beef." You see of course the assumption underlying such an attitude, the assumption that makes it outrageous and is the basic assumption of taxation; that our property is not OUR property which they are taking, but that it is their property which they are disposing of as they please.

Historically—as you know, I'm only asking you to remember it here—that is the origin of taxation; not, in the beginning, an assumption but an unquestioned assertion, that all property belongs to The Tribe and when a Strong Man (priest or chief or king) usurps power to rule the tribe, ownership of all property passes to him. As he owns and rules all persons comprising the Tribe, he owns of course all possessions too. He takes anything that he wants to use or to give anyone, and lets his subjects have the remainder. That was the situation here in Missouri until 1804, remember. In 1797 the King of Spain gave Moses Austin the lead mines here and forty square leagues of land.

That was not the revolutionary assumption underlying the tax clause in the Federal Constitution. The House of Representatives, before the adoption of the Sixteenth Amendment, had power only to tax the State *in proportion to their ascertained population.* That is, property belongs to individuals; it can be taken only by their consent given to their elected representatives. No taxation without representation.

This isn't a superficial question of whether or not persons who are tax-exempt do nothing "reprehensible." Or do everything admirable and desirable.

If you will examine the real basis, in your own mind, for believing that some eleemosynary institutions should be tax-exempt, you will discover that it is a collectivist assumption. You are thinking unconsciously in terms of Society as an Entity, as a collectivist mystic Being, entitled to provide for its own welfare as all real beings are. You are thinking in some such terms as, A Nation needs spiritual guidance, it needs charity and culture and education, these are all good things and should be encouraged and fostered, they are for the good of all, therefore all should (*be compelled to*) contribute to them. Persons who are organized into recognized groups and who are working only for these common goods should not be taxed. Q.E.D.

But the reality is that some persons—individual men—who by tradition are engaged in robbing everyone else, let some potential victims go free because—also by tradition—*they,* these armed robbers, regard them as engaged in labor for the Common Good.

And, not only by rational theory, but in demonstrable fact, the practical result is that these privileged workers for the Common Good are working for an increasingly collectivist—Common Welfare—State. They could not logically work for greater individual freedom, which can be achieved

ONLY by diminishing the power of the State which is their direct benefactor; nor logically advocate a change in general thinking which contradicts their own Common Good position; and in the actual situation they cannot legally do anything of the kind, because the string tied to their privileged status is a prohibition of any "political" propaganda or action. It is absurd to attack, for example, the Ford Foundation's Fund for the Republic, for doing what it does; it can't do anything else, either logically or legally.

None of what I have said applied to your Foundation; I mean, it isn't attacking it; I am not referring to it. In so far as it is an escape from taxation of course I am for it. Defending one's property from robbers is a basic human right, a natural human function. When an armed man walks into my house and demands my money or my life, he gets my money, with (in the circumstances) my consent; but if I can hide any of it from him by ANY means whatever, I shall do that, with an absolutely approving conscience. If you can save any of your money from the tax-racketeers and continue to exercise even a part of your own lawful control of its uses, by all means do so with my applause.

But I do think that you are undertaking a very delicately dangerous enterprise, because (I think) that what I have said does apply to all tax-exempt organizations, *in principle.* If your Foundation outlives you, what then? Into whose hands will it fall? What assurance is there that the logical and legal pressures on it will not result as they do result in all the big Foundations? The Carnegie, Guggenheim, Ford, etc., etc., etc. These are, of course, wholly rhetorical questions, expecting no answers from you.

IX

August 23, 1956

Dear Mrs. Lane:

I do feel there is some hope in the situation. We are hearing more voices for freedom. Even at the present Republican National Convention lip service at least is being paid to freedom and it is quite interesting to note that the speakers on the first two days have all been libertarians and the Socialists have been lying low. They will be heard from later on. At any rate, it isn't as blatant as it might be in proclaiming alien philosophy.

There is an increasing amount of freedom literature. The trend is still up. *Human Events* has now reached a circulation of over 28,000; *The Freeman* about 45,000, more I presume than any other magazine of opinion. You have always been optimistic for the future of liberty. It is a rough road, but some progress is discernible.

August 27, 1956

Dear Mr. Crane:

I, too, was struck by the change of tone in the Republican convention. In that respect, Knowland's and Nixon's speeches were quite good, I thought; and of course Mr. Hoover's was. If only they would suit the action to the word—But they will come off the platform to promote Marx-Bismarck's 1880s Sozial-politick—calling it "new"; are they ignoramuses (ignoramusi?) or just plain liars? And though I am personally fond of Mr. Hoover, who can forget his record in office? I love him but I would never vote for him again. As for Ike, I do NOT like him and never did. If I vote, I shall vote for the Independent ticket in Connecticut, throwing away my vote as the Socialists threw away their votes, from Debs to Thomas, until finally they could vote for FDR. I think the stay-at-home non-vote will be a bit larger this year than in 1952 or '48. The Republican voice was American but the hands are the hands of the Demopublican "Liberal."

Yes, I am optimistic—as I was in the 1930s and have been ever since. It amused me to hear Mr. Hoover's optimism, after all these years that he has sighed wistfully and shaken his head at mine. I hope he really feels it now. The difference between optimism and pessimism is simple eyesight; pessimists are shortsighted, and what they see is real and all they say is true, but—

I'm pleased to know the rising circulation of *Human Events* and *The Freeman*. Of course the trend is changing—when didn't trends change? As I used to say in the 1930s, the darkest hour is not the time to despair of dawn. I don't know whether the trend can change quickly enough to stop "Social Security" before it destroys the USA as it destroyed Germany, but whether it does or not, the Revolution can't be stopped now. It really has smashed the Old World—already, in not yet two centuries; what a stunning surprise 1956 would be to Adams, Madison, Jefferson! I was thinking this morning, perhaps the Administration in Washington are reactionary at this moment; it may be that their "middle of the road" policy is really maintaining a global equilibrium. Imagine what might happen if Eisenhower for instance, were throwing this country's weight into the World Revolution with all the enthusiasm and energy with which Lafayette and Jefferson carried it into Europe and wrecked France in the 1790s. Possibly the eggheads and Communist agents in Washington are in fact merely carrying out a holding operation, maintaining this shaky armstice while the Third International fails and fades away from—in Marxian words—"Its own internal contradictions." If that should prove to be true, maybe the ridiculous and contemptible actions of "our leaders," which now make Americans so miserable and ashamed, can someday be forgiven—*the actions,* not the "leaders." Because the responsible ones want to win elections, not to save the world or serve the Revolution, nor even to give Americans Peace and Prosperity and Progress.

August 31, 1956

Dear Mrs. Lane:

I agree with your political comments; yet, it seems to me almost amusing for these groups in Texas, Louisiana,

Virginia and New Jersey putting up Coleman Andrews for president this year, though I know and admire most of the men interested in this movement. Also, I thoroughly agree with Mr. Andrews about the iniquity of the income tax! Yet, I don't believe this particular movement will get very far from the home plate. Nor would I be willing to throw away my vote for it.

I shall vote the Republican ticket, believing that the candidates and platform are markedly superior to the Democrat. I like Eisenhower and believe he is sincere but very ignorant on some of the fundamentals. He is badly advised by the little group of people closest to him, particularly his brother Milton.

Congress, both parties, are to the right of the White House, and the important issue is to elect to the Senate and House as many men as possible who believe in America rather than the alien philosophy that has pervaded the New Deal, the Fair Deal and the Raw Deal. Yet, you are probably right, though it goes against my grain to say so, that the position of the present executive has been only what could be expected of public opinion. A really sound believer in freedom and the United States of America, like Bricker or Byrd, could not have been elected and if he were would have been so far to the right of Congress as to almost risk impeachment. What we must keep on working for is to get wider understanding of the fundamentals of individual liberty, personal responsibility, voluntary cooperation, the free market, and limited government. Then undoubtedly, pray God, we will have an American government once more, and I definitely feel that we must look to His leadership, and guiding hand in history, to rescue us from the morass into which we have marched.

September 4, 1956

Dear Mr. Crane

I believe Hans Sennholz has in mind a quarterly in the 'way high up stratum of technical economics, something like *Econometrica*. The kind of thing that I, for example, COULD not read. (I can only nibble around the edges of *Econometrica*.) Hans would have Mises taking up cudgels for Fisher against Bohm-Bawerk—that kind of thing—to the vast excitement of their peers in the top stories of ivory towers, where actually the ideas and "trends" of the next century are always being hatched. Far, far over *my* head.

Dear Mr. Crane, it's fantastic how well we agree in fundamentals and how frequently we diverge in surface matters. Now I am serious about the Coleman Andrews Party, and I shall change my plans in order to be here to vote for the splinter Republican candidate, Viviam Kellems, in Connecticut. I agree with you, of course, that these movements "won't get very far," (at least, not soon) and I also agree completely with the statement of the Andrews Party's Vice Presidential candidate on Fulton Lewis's broadcast last Friday: Americans have had no vote since 1932, the choice has been between Tweedledum and Tweedledee, "and I am against both of them," he said; and this new ticket on the ballot in twenty-eight states is, (1) an opportunity for Americans to register a choice, and (2) an experiment to find out what actual support there is in these States for American Constitutional Government as opposed to Federal usurpations of State powers and to surrender of American sovereignty to international groups, through the United States.

That is the opportunity that I have been longing for, all these years; and I welcome with the greatest joy this offer of a way to *register* my own political philosophy—to "stand up and be counted," as one who believes what I believe.

I am so tired of voting, "Yah," or "Da," like someone in Nazi Germany or Soviet Russia—what difference does it make that the one party has two heads?—that I did not intend to repeat the farce this year. Vivian Kellems is, and represents, nothing that I *stand* for; in my opinion she expresses only an emotion which I feel, not a principle nor a policy. But now that the Andrews group is in the political field, with principles and with a policy, a vote for Kellems will be regarded as part of the same movement. I hope that the Kellems group will join that movement, so that I can vote for Andrews, too. In any case, I shall stay here until after the election solely in order to *vote*. . . .

My vote will be only a NO—one little negative; and it will be in a minority, in a "majority rule" situation. Therefore it will not "get very far"; actually it will "get" nowhere. But the *only function of a vote is negative.* The franchise is NOT a "ruling" power, ever; it cannot be, in the nature of things. Because each person is endowed by his Creator with inalienable liberty. You can vote for Smith, but you cannot control Smith. When you vote for Eisenhower, you have no effect on Eisenhower; the effect is upon Stevenson against whom you say, NO—a negative effect. A vote has a negative, but never an affirmative, power. Only ask yourself, what is the effect of a Russian's vote? when all he can say is, Yes. Would the effect be any different if he said nothing?

Now the practical effect of a minority NO—an Andrews vote— in this country this year will be, of course, in ratio to its size; therefore I think it is my civic duty, as an American citizen in addition to my moral duty to myself—to add my one vote to it. But however small it may be, it will have some effect upon the politician's complacency. It will strengthen the hands of the so-called "right" elements in both parties. In Connecticut it may have the effect of defeating the Republican ticket. It may even be large enough to repeat the pattern of the Republican vote in 1856 —and, after four more years of socialism in Washington— the Republican vote of 1860.

The Andrews-Party candidate on Lewis's broadcast said what we all know: A political party comes up from the grass roots, it is not imposed from above. The Republican Party originated in 1856 because the opposition party then refused to state the issue that divided the American people at that time. The same situation exists now. The opposition party refuses to state the issue; the new party states it.

The issue is constitutional government; division of powers, between legislative, executive and judiciary and between Federal and State; restriction of governmental power; individual freedom; American sovereignty.

I also wonder, what is the use of all our working to get wider understanding of basic principles, if, when a party, platform, and candidates standing for our principles appear, we are not to vote for them? By what other means than voting CAN we "have an American government once more," —except violent revolution? If I believed that God intervenes in elections, instead of leaving such responsibilities to you and me, I would have been praying day and night during these twenty years that He would raise up such a new party as Coleman Andrews is heading this year. I cannot think of any other third alternative to the alternatives of Communism or violent revolution in this country. Because both major parties are thoroughly socialist in theory and practice now, and the inevitable end of their practices is totalitarian communism.

I am unable to believe that God will do anything at all to save us from the consequences of our own acts, because I do believe that He has given every person liberty—which is control of, and therefore responsibility for, his acts; and because, while I regard myself as wholly incompetent to comprehend the nature of God, I really cannot feel that the Creator of this marvelous universe is more viciously evil than I am. And certainly if I had a guiding hand in human history, I would not have tossed all the simple human beings of Russia, China and all eastern Europe into the hell that they are in now. I am part of this universe that God creates, and I take no pleasure in cruelty; why should I suppose that He does? I can believe that, having made man with liberty and reason, and having established a universe of Law, the Creator gives human beings the opportunity to learn, by trail and error—by acting and experiencing the consequences of acts—what the Law is, and how to live according to it. If God intervened to protect us from the consequences of unlawful actions how could we learn that? Such intervention, by human beings, in human affairs, is the way to make juvenile delinquents.

September 14, 1956

Dear Mr. Crane:

Speaking of amusing, have you ever happened to read *The Mad Forties?* If you haven't, and if you want a bit of useless but entertaining—and, in its way, enlightening—reading, I'll be delighted to lend you my copy. I say lend, because it is out of print, it is one of my darlings, and I would not part with it, permanently, for a pretty. (Is "for a pretty" only an Ozark expression, I wonder?) *The Forties* are the 1840s; the book is a dead-pan, historically accurate report of the activities and beliefs of our country's intellectual-cultural leaders of those days; the reader supplies the parallels with the 1940s. It is really a book about today's intellectuals—depending on the reader's collaboration; as my little novel, *Let the Hurricane Roar* was about the 1929-30 depression, though on the surface a simple "pioneer" story. A reader who doesn't collaborate can learn from *The Mad Forties* all about water cures, phrenology (the "new science" in Yale and Harvard), Emerson, the Alcotts, and other pioneer thinkers, abolitionists, free lovers, women's rights, and Modern Times. I take it all with hearty laughter, but Dick Cornuelle—to whom I lent the book—says it is, and also it isn't so funny; he hunted down a copy for himself but doesn't know where it belongs on his book shelves. Whatever else it is, it is authentic American history. Though not in any other book that I ever heard of; certainly in no textbook—Imagine *laughing* at Brook Farm!

October 2, 1956

Dear Mr. Crane:

I have read with interest the pamphlet you sent me, *Education For What?* Your question: Is it good, sound, important? puts me into a bit of a quandry.

Some details startle me, coming from Dick Rimonoczy. Dr. Coulter I don't know. Who and what is he? apparently a churchman. —How does this pamphlet come to bear the ISI imprint? —Who is the, here un-named, author of the *Layman's Guide,* from which this pamphlet is a partial reprint? —Who is financing the publication of either or both? —If I knew the answers to those questions I could have a sounder opinion of the booklet. Nothing exists in a vacuum. A book that I might regard as invaluable to you or me I might not recommend to a college freshman. Heroin is worth life itself to a mangled person allergic to morphia; heroin is worse than death to a drug addict. How can anyone answer a question: Is heroin good?

Page 4. —A so-called conservative maintains that a child should maintain the principles underlying the society into which he was born; a progressive regards society as changing and himself as modifying existing institutions.

First, logically this is not the contrast intended and implied. *Principles* can be, and are, maintained and institutions (which are human actions) changed. This passage gives a false impression of a contrast, but its real implication is that maintaining principles is maintaining a status quo (into which he was born") and resisting any change, any progress. The implication is false, and its effect upon ISI members is certainly not to be desired.

The real contrast is not between conservatives and progressives, of course. But if these authors adopt the lying labels, then the contrast is that the "conservative" knows that principles *exist*—natural laws not made nor changed by human beings; and the "progressive" declares that "There are no principles," and that man makes the world whatever he wants to make it.

Page 5. —"Under the theory that there is no God who created man, that man is simply a superior animal. . . ." ?????! God does not create the animals?

This sentence means that, if there is no God, man as well as all the rest of the universe including animals is self-created or accidental; whereas, if God created man, it is only all the rest of the universe, including animals, that is not created by God. The sentence *says* that if there is no God, man is an animal; i.e. the universe including man exists un-created. This is the pure mechanistic materialism of the Marxian theory, accepted as being true of everything existing, except man whom God created. —So far as I know, such a view as this has never been expressed elsewhere, by anyone. Even the concept of the "natural" world as being "the Mystic Body of Satan" (and the Church being the Mystic Body of Christ) isn't materialistic; it conceives animals [Nature] as being super-naturally created.

Page 8. —Egyptian totalitarian collectivism, "Although completely authoritarian, must have been a pretty good system" because it produced Moses! —This sounds like a pulpit pleasantry. Not from any Fundamentalist, either. According to the Bible it was years as a fugitive from Egyptian justice, plus direct orders from Jehovah, that produced Moses.

Pages 10-11. —Including the chart. I protest that here is injustice to the Sophists. They were embryo individualists. They emphasized self-development, the individual's existence per se, a person's being an integral unit in an environmental society; an idea in contrast to the collectivist concept of Society as the human Unit in which a person was merely a negligible particle. In a vacuum, this text will pass as accurate enough, but in freshman college year, the chart's conclusion, as the Sophists objective: "The Greek most likely to *get ahead*" amounts to slander.

There is a "slant" here. A contrast is strongly implied, between nationalism, patriotism, service to the state and to existing social institutions, on one hand, and ruthless "selfishness," dog-eat-dog, jungle morality, the getting-ahead, getting on top, fat Capitalist, on the other hand. I think of the effect on the college freshman coming from years of schooling in the viciousness of competition, the values of social adjustment and altruism and socialism and service to the nation and free books, free lunches, free schooling from the state-to-be-thanked-for-everything-good. Most young Americans automatically reject the "frankly self-centered," and the idea of "getting ahead," here combined with doubting, questioning, and lack of conscience. They need no *more* contempt for "getting ahead."

Page 16. —Here begins the advocacy of compulsory State schooling. The text is true in a narrow sense; no outright lie in it. But the impression given is false. It is as if a twentieth century Communist quoted eighteenth century opponents of "monopoly." The Humanists opposed the Church monopoly of education; they wanted secular schools, and being collectivists (as everyone still is, more or less) they did not think of free schools but of State schools. The quotation from Luther, page seventeen, shows the attitude: compulsory military service warrants compulsory schooling. But Americans once had free schools and a free militia. The opposition here, now, is not between Church and State, it is between freedom and compulsion. And this text is for compulsion.

Notice page seventeen, the slippery shift from compulsion in the Luther quotation to "state *support* in education" given as "the essence of the Reformation" three paragraphs later. It is true that the Reformation was largely reactionary; after a millenium of the Church's effort to synthesize the thesis (collectivism) and the antithesis (individualism), Luther and Calvin (stimulated by Aquinas's support of human reason) gave up the effort and stood for the thesis. Hence came nationalism and the Divine Right of Kings and modern totalitarianism. But all this is omitted; there is no space for it in this booklet—even if the authors wanted to include it. Catholic students may know it; but Protestants are a majority and to their ignorant young the

Reformation—if they have heard of it at all—means their churches, their religious faith. And it says here that "from the standpoint of education" compulsory State schooling is "the essence" of their religion.

Pages 17-18. —Notice the contrast, in text and in charts, between Luther & Bacon. Given the simplification, the charts are correct. If you look at them, you see that they balance each other. Luther omits science; Bacon omits religion. Luther's aim is "the informed Christian"; Bacon's is "Scientific man."

Now in the text, Luther's was the *first strong voice* to cry out for tax-*supported* education, a means to man's *salvation* and *freedom;* he wanted the *"common man"* taught to read, *equipped to be good;* his approach was *simple and direct;* he began the Reformation.

Bacon was a nobleman; his *pet scheme* was to find out how to make the forces of nature serve humanity; *historical circumstances* made his proposal *popular;* his position is *impaired* by his omission; he went to an *"unreasonable"* length; he made a substantial but *limited* contribution to *Humanism.*

Why this bias? Is there such antagonism between "the informed Christian" and "scientific man"? Isn't religious faith totally-destitute of-knowledge-of-"forces-of-nature" as "limited" as all scientific knowledge totally-destitute-of-religion? Neither, of course, can actually exist in any living person. But regarded as concepts, isn't one as "unreasonable" in its lengths as the other? Luther created the Lutheran Church; Bacon created the modern world which Du Pont Company may serve as a symbol. They can be taken as contrasts, for the limited and crude purpose of this pamphlet; they can be shown as two sides of historical development and education; either can be criticized as one-sided—as the charts show them. Is it truthful to "slant" the comments on them as this text does?

Page 31. —Under the head: *Fourth.*

Philanthropic money ready and eager to finance education *"was"* important "because the American policy of local control of education at that time meant that there could be no central government agency to approach for research funds."

How unfortunate.

Page 35. —Notice that "conservatism requires *indoctrination,"* recommends that students (ISI members, reading this) "shall be *trained* to *accept* facts and *conclusions* from *others,*" assumes that orderly change requires that the child be *"indoctrinated* in" (not simply told or taught) "the basic beliefs and *customs* on which the society is founded," recommends that students should be *made* to qualify "in certain basic *scholastic* subjects, *whether they want to or not,*" and *"Made* to compete with each other for high grades," while Deweyism assumes "That all learning is within the learner," that the student learn from experience, while applying his "common sense" and being "encouraged to re-examine and re-evaluate beliefs and customs and support such changes as seem desirable."

When you were eighteen, which of these attitudes would have appealed to you more? Or do you remember that the prevailing desire among students was to be indoctrinated, trained to accept conclusions from others, compelled to learn Greek and Latin, or chemistry and mathematics, whether they wanted to or not? Did they want to maintain the status quo, or did they feel like supporting such changes as seemed to them desirable.

So how am I to answer your question: Is this pamphlet good, sound, important?

As a primer of philosophy, suited in my schooldays to (McGuffey's) *Fifth Reader* Class, I think it good in its charts and passable in text. The charts give a graphic quickly grasped and easily remembered, crude concept of the basic views of most important philosophers. The only objection to them, on the ground of accuracy—soundness—is the depiction of Sophism. (I think.)

October 7, 1956

Dear Mr. Crane:

You get the NEC service, don't you? I'd guess that you agree with Merwin Hart more closely than I do—on immigration quotas, for instance. But some of the Council Letters make me suffer from my poverty. I wish, I wish, I am WISHING that I could send Council Letter No. 392, *Dependence And Servitude,* to every member of Intercollegiate Society of Individualists. That would cost $180 for postage alone, to 6,000. Never mind; anyway ISI will do, in reverse, what the intercollegiate Socialists began doing in 1904.

About the year 2,000 I'll meet you at the gold bar of Heaven and say, Didn't I tell you so? Didn't I say, down there sixty years ago, that the twentieth century would end as the eighteenth century did? in a great liberal movement, this time world-wide?

RWL

N.B. Of course I don't mean a nontemperance "bar." I mean the one from which the blessed damsel leaned down, and the stars in her hair were seven.

October 10, 1956

Dear Mrs. Lane:

I am not ready to make a definite appointment with you at the bar. Rather, considering the great disparity in our ages, I might make the retort that a canny old Scot made to a Salvation Army lassie who asked him to give a shilling to the Lord: "I'll be seein' him long before you do, and I will give it to him myself."

October 17, 1956

Dear Mr. Crane:

Everywhere I look nowadays, I see someone who believes that two and two are four, and someone who believes that two and two are six, and in the interests of harmony and the hope of ironing out difficulties, and always the basic assumption that all opinions are merely beliefs conditioned by social environment or economic determinism or historical necessity, I see them conferring and compromising and concluding (as correct compromising should conclude, of course) that two and two are five. This conclusion proving, in practice, to be unsatisfactory to both, there is nothing to do but call another conference, in the interests of harmony and the hope . . . etc., etc., etc.

I began in 1939 to argue that a third party is the only practicable political solution. And to be informed by more informed persons—George Horace Lorimer, for example—that it was absolutely impractical, because of the Solid South. Of course, I approach the question from the "theoretical" side. When an actual political issue exists, there are only two possible means of deciding it: a peaceable political action (which in USA twentieth century is voting) and a violent political action, either coup d'etat or civil war. The second is impossible here and now, because, (1) the federal organization, consisting of forty-nine separate political entities, organized and *armed* (State Police and State National Guards) prevents any successful coup d'etat, and (2) the present issue is not along geographical lines, which are essential to civil war. Therefore, the only possible decision (in this time and place) of the actually existing issue, between totalitarian communism and freedom, is the peaceful one. For this, the essential is two political parties, opposing each other and offering voters a choice between the two opposing political principles at issue. Therefore, either two such parties must appear, or violence must ensue—violence which can only be chaos, widespread and general chaos as in Germany in 1933, since the federal structure and the absence of geographical division make both civil war and a successful coup d'etat impossible. Hence a new political party is the only "practicable" method to use. Q.E.D.—Not that this reasoning was Q.E.D. to the political Big Boys to whom I have offered it occasionally.

X

Mansfield, Missouri
January 5, 1957

Dear Mr. Crane:

I assume that you are not too pleased by Eisenhower's happy reception of the mandate for "modern" Republicans. But I have no news here at all, except such bits as may come by post from loving friends.

January 17, 1957

Dear Mrs. Lane:

The world has gone mad in its worship of the golden calf of government. All over the place supposedly intelligent and certainly high-minded people are encountered who actually believe that the way to better housing, elimination of poverty, more abundant living, better education, and above all security, not to mention peace on earth, is by government action with increasing powers, larger resources, and less freedom of choice by people. Perhaps the most maddening manifestation of this reactionary philosophy is the "middle way" between totalitarianism and anarchy. (That is how some of us are stigmatized.) The militant "liberalism" and pro-communism of the '30s has markedly subsided or perhaps been converted into the torpor of "moderation," that partnership of government and people (and little John Q. Public gets it right in the neck!) guarantees perpetual prosperity and peace. I read in last Friday's newspaper that the President has launched a campaign against inflation. He is, of course, the chief instigater of inflation but there may be some comfort in government's disowning its own offspring.

Mansfield, Mo.
January 20, 1957

Dear Mr. Crane:

WHO said there is no Santa Claus? —Let him be reprimanded severely. Here I have, not only such a good letter from you, but—in its midst—surprise! your offer to buy books for the Freedom School's Library. I had no Christmas in '56 but here it is, on the nineteenth day of '57. I am really quite excited, and I do *thank* you.

This will take some little time for thinking. I have sent a note to Mr. LeFevre, asking him what books he has already, and what wishes he has in mind. I have written Ken Templeton for the Volker list, if there is one. I am making a list to send to Schulte's in New York with an inquiry, Can they supply them? Because Schulte's second-hand books have always been in excellent condition, and why should we waste money on new ones if discounted books can be had? A library book is almost immediately a "used" one, anyway. I am going to try to make that little library a really fine one in its field; and I believe at no great cost, for the field is not extensive, of course. If the titles of some desirable books occur to you, would you let me know? I have only my memory to rely upon here, since all my own books are in Danbury, and my memory lately has some startling holes in it.

I am indeed frantically busy. No help of any kind is available here, and I am houseworking, nursing, cooking, and figuring out diabetic diet at high speed all day long. The Springfield doctor is in charge by telephone. We hope to be able to take my mother[4] to Springfield on February 11, for blood-sugar test and further examination. She is holding her own and perhaps gaining a little strength. I wish she would stay with me in Danbury but of course I understand her attachment to her home. My own difficulty is that I have no opportunity to read or write except during the nights when she is sleeping.

As to the general situation, don't you think that it is improving? It seems to me that your "supposedly intelligent and certainly high-minded" collectivists are—shall I say?—an ebbing of the wave of the past. After all, the

[4]Laura Ingalls Wilder age ninety, author of nine immensely popular children's books about her pioneering childhood, published by Harper & Row.

whole world has been collectivist (in theory and therefore in attempted practice) for a known sixty centuries, and it seems to me that the change made in the past two centuries is almost incredible and certainly most encouraging.

Shorten the view to these two past centuries, and what do you see? The eighteenth century impact of the individualist revolution upon collectivist Europe, causing an immediate (1789 to 1793) and most powerful reaction; the anti-individualist reaction of very nearly all European thinkers (backed by the traditional collectivism of all the "little" Europeans) which was implemented in organizational terms by the First, Second, Third Communist Internationals; which successively wrecked France, Germany, Russia, England and increasingly through the nineteenth century influenced thought and action in the U.S.A.

You can see the impact-reaction pattern, in little, in every country on earth; from 1789 to 1917. It has wrecked the whole Old World—the pre-eighteenth century human world on this planet. Can anyone expect "order" to result between 1917 and 1957? It took forty years (1775-1815) even to establish the survival of the USA (some 5 million persons) on a basis of "order." Here are some two thousand millions of persons, violently shaken out of their "traditional" patterns of thought and action. What can we expect but confusion of mind and of irrational actions on this earth for a much, much longer time than forty years?

Naturally, the collectivist concepts remain in the minds of innumerable "supposedly intelligent" persons. But I think, not that "the whole world has gone mad" but that the whole world is showing symptoms of a beginning sanity —after sixty centuries of madness.

Regarded as an historical "movement," the *organized* reaction culminated in Spain, with Franco's defeat of the Third International there. The fragments of the Second International organization (Hitler; Mussolini) never had a chance, actually; they were doomed by *being merely* fragments, by being based on nationalism instead of on a concept of the nature of man. (It is always a *general* concept of reality that survives in history—whether true or false, it must be believed to be a universal principle. For example, Ptolemaic astronomy. A concept that lasted for four millenniums, and yielded only to an equally general concept, Copernican astronomy. None of the narrower attacks upon it had any force.) The Second International ended in 1914 when the German Social Democrats voted war credits to the Kaiser. Hitler and Mussolini and Norman Thomas—its fragments—were historically irrelevant, nothing but bits of flotsam, left floating. (I said this in the 1930s, and of course was hooted at. But where are they now?)

The Third International is now going to pieces. The dominant European intellectual influence is waning—or gone—all over the world. So much for the past two centuries.

I certainly agree with you that the "middle way" nonsense is maddening; frequently it maddens me. But I think that really it is only a symptom of the inevitable confusions, and what did confusion ever accomplish, practically? It also shows that the "middle wayers" are abandoning their former firm collectivism and just don't know where to go from there. They're floundering in self-contradictions. And they act as opportunists, just snatching at every passing straw that they hope will keep them afloat. They may do a lot of immediate harm, but nothing fundamentally important, nothing permanent, or, rather, "long run." (Nothing, of course, is permanent, in human history.) They'll evaporate as Hitler did.

January 30, 1957

Dear Mr. Crane:

The parcel from you arrived some days ago, and until today has been treasured like a Do Not Open Until Christmas present. Today, after perilously skidding to town in a blizzard and fetching the week's groceries, and after disposing of dinner and dishes and ashes and filling the stove with greenwood for the night, I rewarded me: I opened the parcel. Thank you.

I have read avidly, with applause, the copies of your letters to Hayek and Mr. Henderson's to the National Council of Churches; and I have gulped the entire Mises *Anticapitalist Mentality,* and read the first seventeen pages of *Foundation of American Freedom.* This, I see, is most intensely interesting, and not to be gulped. It promises a view of Calvinism new to me, and probably an added explanation of the American historical phenomenon, which I have never been content to ascribe to the Physiocrats and Locke. You may remember that I have suggested that actual human experience here, plus Bible reading, seem to me a more tenable hypothesis for the unprecedented American action. If the Physiocrats and Locke explained it, obviously the action would have occurred in Europe. Dr. Davies enlists me—in seventeen pages—by his intelligence and also by his reference to St. Thomas Aquinas. Who is, I know, a Catholic saint, but who also seems to me to be the origin of the Protestant Reformation and, indirectly of course, of the Communist Internationals. Surely it was perilous to introduce into scholastic thought the emphasis on natural law, and the endorsement of human reason? without discarding the collectivist concept of human nature. Prolong that line far enough, and wouldn't it arrive, via Hegel et al., at "scientific" materialism and secular—"godless"—communism? assuming of course that a German-metaphysical and "one-track" mind did the prolonging, as Marx did.

All the rest of your gifts remain to be enjoyed; I am expecting to revel in the Burpee's catalogue and in the December *Free Trader*. Deryk Abel sends it to to me, but my copies are stranded in Danbury. Also, I shall be interested in [Secretary of Agriculture Ezra Taft] Benson's booklet; I've seen nothing he has written, or said. Though I know he must be acrobatic to survive among the modern Republicans in Washington. I truly do thank you VERY much.

I am sending you a letter and list that came this morning from Bob LeFevre. If you have time to consider the list, would you please add your comments to mine, and return it?

Sending you this list is only a tentative preliminary. The Freedom School is a summer school: July, August. There is quite a bit of time. I am only making a definitive list now. Ordering nothing until you finally approve it. My own list isn't hatched yet. A few of my titles are on this one, but I would certainly add Huxley's *Brave New World* to the fiction, and N. J. Birrel's *Man's Emerging Mind* to—what category? science? And Haskell's *New Deal in Old Rome* to history (or politics) ? and *The Mad Forties*. . . . (I have pasted on the inside cover of my copy the portraits of John Dewey and seven of his confrères, the great figures of Progressive Education in the 1930-40s. The writers did a perfect dead-pan job, straight reporting, no comments, but debunking the pseudo-intellectuals could not possibly be more superbly done. It is hilarious farce and at the same time blood-chilling.) One has to take *Man's Emerging Mind* to restore one's equilibrium. I do seriously believe that most persons will—in a long, long time—become rational and that the human world will eventually cease to be barbarian and begin to be what we mean by the word civilized, once applied to such revolting bestiality as prevailed in ancient Rome? And now we use the word to mean something that doesn't even yet exist.

Incidentally—and NOT apropos—isn't Mises a bit mistaken about American society? IS there an American "Society"—*le monde*—of the rich, excluding the intellectuals and artists? I don't know; I've met only a few very rich Americans, most of them hospitable to me. I guessed that Professor Mises misses here, the class distinctions of Europe and because he doesn't find *le monde,* infers that it exists behind gold curtains. But perhaps it actually does. Does it? Please tell me.

He is certainly wrong about American farmers clamoring for "tariffs, subsidies, and 'parity prices.'" The European peasants want, and get, "protection"—tariffs—but American farmers fought the "protective tariff' from 1800 to 1896; while the "infant industries" became the "soulless corporations" and the Trusts. Even as late as 1933, when Garet Garrett and I drove all over the Midwest, the farmers in general were not wanting AAA or any other Federal interference. In Kansas I met a rabble-rousing New Dealer from Washington who took me to a farmers' meeting where he spoke with real conviction and eloquence. The audience listened absolutely noncomittal, until he worked up to an incandescent peroration: "We went down there to Washington and got you all a Ford. Now we're going to get you a Cadillac!" The temperature suddenly fell below freezing; the silent antagonism was colder than zero. That ended the speech; the whole audience rose and went out. The orator later said to me, "Those damned numbskulls! the only thing to use on them is a club."

Sometime later, in a hotel lobby in Branson, Missouri (summer resort on White River) I met a young man almost in tears, totally woebegone and despairing. He had spent seventy days in Stone County, working day and night, he said, house to house, up hill and down, over those horrible roads; he'd gone to every house, he'd used every persuasion he could think of, talked himself hoarse, and he had not got even ONE man to take a $2,500 loan from the government; and those wretched people needed everything; why, their children were barefoot, some of them lived in *log cabins*—could I believe it? They NEEDED to be rehabilitated, I had no idea what rural slums they lived in; and here he offered them a loan from the Government; amortized, twenty-five years to pay it, more time if they wanted it; he offered them horses, and tools, even a car, anything almost and they just wouldn't take it. They didn't talk or act like such fools either. He couldn't understand it. He HAD to get some of them to take Government help or he'd lose his job. What was wrong with them? could I tell him? could I help him?

In southern Illinois there was a Terror. The Government men went into that county and took no nonsense; they condemned the land—every farm; offered the owners $7 an acre, or nothing; this was a model project, tearing down houses, building new roads, surveying a Community Center all blueprinted. The people were frantic and furious; they hired lawyers, who told them they could do nothing; they tried to get the facts printed. No newspaper dared do it. The county was listed as rural slums, the land as eroded. When I asked to be shown erosion, the answer was, it is sheet erosion. That is, the constant effect of rainfall on all earth. There was not an eroded ditch in the County. Every farm was well cared for, every house in repair, painted, cared for—simple frame houses, a few without electricity or plumbing, but many with both. One family had lived there since an ancestor came with George Rogers Clark; another was a depression-refugee from St. Louis, all savings invested in the farm at $25 an acre. None of them wanted to be rehabilitated. None of them would speak to Garet or to me until we *proved* that we did not come from the Government. Garet was dumbfounded when men surrounded the car and demanded that proof; luckily he had it, by chance . —And these are the people said to be demanding subsidies! That was a story—Communist Terror in Illinois. (The manager of the project was a Party member.) Neither Lorimer nor any other editor would print it, of course. The truth about this country never does get into print.

February 1, 1957

Dear Mrs. Lane:

I am sending you the fourth and fifth volumes of Brant's Biography of James Madison. The fifth volume isn't as good as the preceding ones, but then Madison at this stage of his career wasn't as appealing as when he was developing and fathering our Constitution.

I hope the world-wide situation is improving, but it is difficult to find evidence to support that view. There is more discussion of freedom; there is more agitation for freedom. If this war that communist Russia is carrying on against the rest of the world breaks out into all-out violence, the casualties will be beyond all experience or comprehension, but the military power of Russia will be destroyed. Yet, that doesn't solve the problem. These international criminals always come back for a second licking. Hitler may have been but a bit of flotsam, but he certainly raised hell.

* * * * *

Mrs. Lane's mother, Laura Ingalls Wilder, died on February 10 in Mansfield, Missouri.

* * * * *

XI

March 21, 1957

Dear Mrs. Lane:

In response to the questions in a letter from you, I wrote several months ago that I would prepare a memorandum of the connection of freedom and Christianity. I have done this with fear and trembling, for I am not a theologian and it has taken me quite a while to put the pertinent thoughts together. I trust the enclosed memorandum may be of interest to you. If there are gaps in the train of reasoning or statements that appear to you to be erroneous, please let me know and we will see if we can get them straightened out. You have helped me so much in getting these matters straight in my own mind that I hope I may be of service to you in making a logical summary of these important ideas.

I was very sorry indeed to hear that you, quite naturally, were tired out, but trust that you are recovering your health and strength. I am waiting to get through you the final list of books that I am to present to the Freedom School Library.

HEADINGS OR SUMMARY OF CONNECTING FREEDOM WITH JUDEO-CHRISTIAN TEACHING

The idea that thinking beings can evolve by chance from primordial matter is untenable. We, therefore, postulate a Supreme Being who thinks. If we see a clock running, we must have the presumption that there is a clock maker and someone who winds up the clock.

We cannot solve the riddle of the universe by external observation. Scientific discovery and research do not reveal the nature of matter or energy. We finally arrive at Mathematical expressions. Within ourselves, however, we learn two things: a belief in right and wrong and that we do wrong and not right. Moral law in all ages and in all peoples varies but little; we believe, therefore, that moral law and all other laws are the design of God, the Supreme Being. Yet, we see within ourselves that we disobey His laws, and the problem of evil arises. The problem of evil is not solved by a philosophy of dualism, nor indeed can we expect a complete solution. It must remain, as all ultimate truth remains, a mystery. The most reasonable and satisfactory concept is the unity of life, the creation of all nature by one God. He created man in His own image, i.e. self-controllable persons; free, therefore, to disobey His will, to do wrong.

From the universal moral standard in human beings we believe that God is not only all powerful and all knowing, but righteous. The concept that He might be a merciless judge and not a loving God is overwhelmingly unacceptable except to queer or psychopathic people. The early Hebrews though of Yahweh as a tribal god; but as Judaism developed after the Captivity, the concept of God, loving mankind, arose.

Then what would a loving God do when He sees us believing in righteousness but doing wrong? He would surely reveal Himself to us, not only in nature and through inspired souls but by establishing contact with us in space and time. So Judaism foretold and Christianity proclaimed the coming of God to earth in human form. Almost all other religions in history and in the world, so largely true but lacking the true message of the Incarnation, include a story of this kind and thus support the belief of the coming of God to earth. Islam, with its sturdy monotheism, has the weakness of lacking this understanding of a loving God visiting His children.

Jesus stated categorically that He was God. He was either an impostor speaking and living a monstrous falsehood or it is true. The historicity of the Gospel message has been so well established, and by recent findings so fortified, that insofar as they were able to write accurate history the writers of the Bible attest to the deity of Christ. Moreover, His story—character, deeds, sayings—just cannot be imagined to be a fabrication. It just does not seem humanly possible for such a story to be made up.

And what did He teach? No collectivism with its philosophy of force, but together with the reaffirmation of the moral law His new Commandments of love of God and love of neighbor. He told of the lost sheep, the prodigal son, the humble publican, the repentant sinner, the good Samaritan, the talents. "Blessed are they that mourn; for they shall be comforted." The Gospel is sufficient for every human need. He spoke of truth, liberty, the responsibility of the individual, purity, sincerity, unselfishness, service. He revealed the true relationship of man to God the Father. He suffered the agony of physical death in atonement for our wrong doings.

The happenings promptly after Christ's death and Resurrection emphasize the truth and glory of the Gospel. The Book of Acts, written by a careful writer, is simply overwhelming. There just does not seem to be any other explanation of what was said and done, as recorded in that book, than the Christian message that God had visited the earth in physical form.

And in subsequent history the Church, consisting of His followers, is the body of Christ, the necessary physical organisms—brains to think, lips to speak, hands to do—for contact with mankind to carry on the work of reconciliation. We live in space and time, but they are mysteries. We talk of matter and energy, but don't know what they are. God must believe in matter, for He invented it; He approves of human bodies, for He designed them. As God was revealed to us by the Incarnation in physical form, so the risen Christ maintains our touch with infinity; and His followers are witnesses throughout the earth.

The Church, too, with its human make-up and in spite of its divine ordination went wrong. It got into many by-ways, sideshows, and improper thoughts and practices, but it is the only agency to carry on the sublime ministry. Over the past two thousand years there have been bursts of light, the torch has been raised, and again and again passed along to others by a long list of teachers, prophets, martyrs, scientists, artists, writers, leaders. There developed truer understanding of the nature of man as a person created in the image of God. Here it is important to note that as von Ranke, the historian, reported "Calvin was the virtual founder of America." At first that sounds preposterous, because he and his followers were, according to our ideas, intolerant in so many ways, but they were much more tolerant than the customs of their time. It is precisely in the countries where Calvinism prevailed—Switzerland, The Rhineland, Holland, France (until the religious reaction),

England (until the Restoration), Wales, Scotland, and America—that the ideas and practices of freedom developed. In America though only eight percent of the population were members of Christian churches, the book of the colonists was the Bible. Their philosophy was predominantly Calvinistic. They developed the concepts of freedom of worship, limited government and the free market. Towards the end of the eighteenth century came almost simultaneously the great accomplishments of the individual, free exercise of religion, separation of church and state, division of labor, freedom of markets, and strictly limited government, all stemming from moral philosophy and Christian tenets.

Thus, the connection between freedom and Christianity is both theoretical and actual. God created self-controllable persons, visited us to reveal Himself, and continues with us working through human agencies to reconcile us to Himself by free processes of persuasion, sacrifice and love. In actual history this fundamental truth is demonstrated. In spite of all back slidings and short comings, there has been upward and forward movement, not by any perfectability of human nature but by the workings of revealed religion. Without that, slavery persists. Insofar as Christianity is practiced, higher ideals abound, men become freer and nobler. Christ holds out to us the goal of perfect freedom.

June 4, 1957

Dear Mr. Crane:

I had just so far begun to write you this morning when I was interrupted and—bringing the mail back with me—received your note and list of books sent to the Freedom School. I do thank you, and I am sure that Mr. LeFevre does, and that the books will go on being helpful to his students for many years.

I was intending to write you to thank you again for your memorandum of the connection between Christianity and freedom, which I have read more than once and again this morning. It is most interesting and I don't doubt that it expresses the Christian view very nearly perfectly—that "very nearly" being the general qualification of perfection that both you and I apply to all things human. It is the only clear, direct expression of that view that I have seen, and if I had more sense I would have asked you for it years ago instead of being baffled by so many books.

It is not quite my own view for two reasons: Historically, I would *add* to the elements, or factors, that you see in the American phenomenon, (1), the Greek element in the 'gentleman's' education at that time, and, (2), the effect of direct experience in the wilderness upon the unlettered (comparatively) majority of the people here. I myself have stressed the Biblical influence, before. I believe that Greek monism, the assumption—not debated, but implicit in nearly all Greek thought and expressed in the use of "dike"—that there is "*the* way", of correct, proper, and profitable human living, which is knowing and acting according to (in the eighteenth century idiom) "natural law", whether in acting as farmer, potter, weaver, sailor or philosopher or politician or teacher or athlete or artist, had more influence in American thinking than is—so far as I know—recognized anywhere. I believe, too, that the effect upon persons of the European "lower classes" of being dislodged from all traditional social classifications and facing, individually, the fundamental situation of human beings on this planet—the "root, hog, or die" situation—taught them, certainly taught those who survived, more realism than so many as a million Europeans had ever known before. I think that something roughly analogous to the American development occurred on the Tiber in preRoman history, when a group of adventurers or refugees, or whoever they were, rationally came to a recognition of human equality that was, later, the foundation of the early Roman Republic.

Von Ranke's view is highly interesting and seems to me to be true but only partially so; it may wholly explain the development of liberalism in Calvinistic Europe, but does it account for the complete cleavage between American and Old World (English and Continental) political philosophy? A cleavage so profound as to amount to antagonism. John Adams said that no European thinker understood the American principles; George Washington warned against "entangling alliances:" with any European power, on the ground that basic principles are irreconcilable. These states then were not predominately Calvinist, nor even Christian in any European sense. The Christian revival here came a generation later. I am not intending to minimize the Biblical influence, certainly it was extremely strong, probably the strongest intellectual influence among people, by far. But it was the *whole* influence among, for instance, the Pilgrims, who in Europe were national-racist collectivists, and in Plymouth Colony became individualistic. It seems to me that another element entered the situation when Europeans encountered reality on this side of the Atlantic. So much for the historical question.

I'm not sure whether the rest is correctly labeled philosophical or theological. In either case, I am not arguing, not questioning your point of view. I am only saying that it is not wholly mine. You think and speak with assurance that I do not have.

I agree wholly, of course, that the universe is created, not an accident occurring by chance, and not without purpose. (I have just ended a controversy on this point by successfully erasing the atheist fallacies from a young college student's mind.) It seems to me obvious, self-evident, that—as you say—"moral law and all other laws are the design of God, the Supreme Being." And, that the universe is a unit, and a person is self-controlling. For me, it follows that "right" IS "natural law", simply because "natural law" IS; it *exists*. Created for a purpose, it serves that purpose—or aims at achieving that purpose. If anyone grants the existence of Creativeness and Purpose, he must logically agree that every particle in the universe attracts every other particle with a force . . . etc., etc. "rightly". The planets are right in following their courses, the leaf is right in its chemical processes, the righteous bee gathers honey and pollen and rightly makes a hexagonal cell of wax. It is inconceivable that any of these are acting wrongly, wickedly, in contravention of their creator's purpose.

This brings us to the problem, What is the purpose of man? I react immediately against the reply, which seems to me puerile, that man is created to praise and glorify God. This means that the Purpose of God is a vanity so cheap and silly that any parent would rebuke a child for it. I do not know, cannot imagine, the Purpose of Creation; but by analogy with the observable rest of the universe I infer that man is created to serve that Purpose, whatever it is; and, further, that a person serves it by acting according to "natural law".

The difficulty in doing so, as it seems to me, is that a person living today does not know what many such laws *are.* Being created as a self-controlling being, I must control my acts, I must choose (at every instant of time) one among almost innumerable possible actions, and perform it. In any action, I reject all other actions possible to me at this place and time. I must act; I cannot "do" nothing; not acting is also a choice, a decision of my mind, my will, my self. But I do not know *how* to act, in the sense that planets, leaves, bees, obviously do. In other words, they are controlled, obliged (nobody knows how) to act rightly, but I control myself.

I cannot say that God created man in His own image, because I have no image, no concept, of the Creator. And here I diverge from your concept. Because I agree with you that "all ultimate truth remains—must remain—a mystery" (to me, and I believe to all living persons) I do not have a concept of God in (what seems to me to be) the *human* terms, of power and knowledge and love.

To come down to human affairs, I have faith that human beings will serve the Purpose, whatever it is, for which we are created. Perhaps the dinosaurs did; who knows? I don't. Perhaps in some way human life is an end-in-itself; even perhaps it is the ultimate Purpose; I don't know. It seems to me probably that the *function* of man in the scheme, in the "design", is *knowing.* Our rational faculty is "given"; men do not create it. Perhaps we are created to add to the "design" an element of awareness, of self-consciousness, of the human quality of *knowledge* of "good and evil"; that is, knowledge of what the "laws" of Creation ARE. Perhaps the parable of the Garden of Eden has that meaning; that non-human life—plants, animals, insects —merely obey the Laws and are rewarded, each in its measure, by the results of obeying them without knowing what they are; but man is created to *learn* a human knowledge of what they are, by the process of ignorantly disobeying them and enduring the results. As a child learns a little bit about the nature of fire by trying to clasp the flickering bright thing.

Perhaps the theologians are mistaken in interpreting that parable to mean that "Adam *fell*" and all men inherit his sin. The human genes (according to biologists) carry an inheritance—in infinitely various kinds and degrees—of a *potentiality* of learning, of acquiring human knowledge of God and man; though all human beings are born wholly ignorant. What we in fact inherit from Adam, the human ancestor, is total ignorance and potentialities of developing ourselves. Poetically one might say that each of us re-enacts the story of the Garden of Eden; each emerges from automatic obedience to the laws of nature into self-awareness and self-controlled action, and each learns something of the Laws of Nature—quite a few even learn enough about time, space, momentum, velocity, to drive a motor car without wrecking it. And how do we learn to be "good", to act "rightly" toward other persons? Isn't it in the same way? either by acting "wrongly" and then wishing we hadn't incurred the results of that action, or by seeing what happens to others who act "wrongly"?

Here I leaped up, saying O my goodness! (Apropos; and right on cue, a practical example.) I had forgotten all about the coffee break for two men working for me; coffee break's at 3:30, and my watch said 4:15.—I have just been hearing them tell their adventures truck-driving, all over this country; what an incredible land this is. I hope I haven't bored you nor irritated you with stupidity; please forgive me if I have? Faithfully yours,

June 28, 1957

Dear Mrs. Lane:

I certainly agree with your very wise observations about the Greek element in our American thinking and also with the influence of the experiences in wrestling with the American wilderness. Only eight percent of the American colonists were members of Christian churches, but it does seem to be true that their most influential book was the Bible, and their predominant philosophy was Calvinistic. Collectivism had been the philosophy in Europe, but the breaking away from it and the move in the direction of freedom and individualism occurred in those countries which were Calvinist. That was so much more the case on this side that the discovery of freedom in America seems to me to be a valid statement.

You and I agree in our concepts of God and law. We believe in purpose and we wonder "What is the purpose of man?" When we say in our Presbyterian Shorter Catechism that it is to praise and glorify God, that does not necessarily indicate vanity. We can never know God's mind. We are tiny beings on a little speck of dust in an almost insignificant area of a small galaxy. Yet, we are persons and for whatever reason, which we shall never know, for which we were created, the simplest and most satisfactory idea is to be in harmony with our Creator. The purpose of man might be expressed better, but I would not know how to phrase it any better or more helpfully than praise and adoration and humble faith.

The amazing thing about it all is that along with our infinitesimalness we are responsible. We can learn something of the will of God. I once heard Willis R. Whitney, the great research chemist, express it this way: "It is silly to talk about the mastery of nature. Rather, we move aside a bit of the veil. Research is the appreciation of infinite creation." I love that expression, "Appreciation of infinite creation."

A lot of clergymen, perhaps nearly all of them, have too elaborate explanations, some of which are confusing, but the simplest explanation or appreciation of the mystery of life is probably the best. I have heard Billy Graham speak three times, and he is a grand person, preaching simply, sincerely, and it seems to me very helpfully. I don't get from him and many other great preachers too much and too complicated theology, but the simple expressions (with its two-fold meaning) of Christ in life.

Thank you again for your wonderful letter. I have learned so much from it. Indeed, I am so tremendously in your debt for the great amount of wisdom and the clarification of difficult questions and the development of understanding that I have gained from you. Whenever I can be of assistance to you to any matter in which you are interested, please do not fail to let me know.

July 5, 1957

Dear Mr. Crane:

I have your good—so good that I have no accurate adjective—letter of June 28, and value it so much that I need more time for answering it.

But today I have your carbon of note to Spencer Heath and I feel I should hasten to explain that I know nothing at all about him or—I infer—his Foundation; and therefore am not endorsing either, of course; also that "recommending" may be slightly too strong a word for my attitude toward his book. I think it very interesting, worth reading for its novelty and also a bit as news. After reading it I wrote Mr. Heath a note of thanks for the book, welcoming it as at last a scientific *approach* to "social science", saying that in detail I could question it.

I think its approach interesting, its implication sound that positive use of "rights" reserved to citizens by the tenth amendment is the correct means of resisting political encroachment on them; i.e. if property owners defend ownership by utilizing it to the fullest extent, politicians are deprived of pretexts for invading it. I think the reasoning fuzzy and the economics absurd. He presents for instance two mutually exclusive theories of value, as you'll notice.

July 11, 1957

Dear Mrs. Lane:

Your letter of July 5 has come in and I am glad to get this information about the Spencer Heath book which I, therefore, should read.

September 30, 1957

Dear Mrs. Lane:

I recently returned from attending the annual meeting of the Mont Pelerin Society at St. Moritz, Switzerland.

First let me say that promptly after arrival there I met Jean Pierre Hamilius and his wife. They are a darling couple. I was delighted with both of them. He is not only a strong libertarian but an aggressive one. He told me with some pride that his students—and he was among them—sacked the Russian Embassy in Luxembourg in protest of their cruelties in Hungary. Luxembourg had to pay indemnity to Russia of seventy million francs (as I recall the figure) but Hamilius said it was well worth while and that Luxembourg was the only country which made such a dramatic condemnation of Russia's aggression.

The Mont Pelerin Society was the most largely attended to date, one hundred and twenty members putting in an appearance, but the programme and speakers were not as good as they should have been. Hayek explained to me that this was because the programme was made up by volunteers. He had written all of the members asking who wished to speak and on what topic and accepted all those who volunteered. Unfortunately, that included too much from French members who compromised, quite eloquently, with the principle of freedom and also one contribution from an American who is not sound in the faith. These aberrations upset some of the American members, but we all agreed that such deviation could and must be excluded from the programme of next year's meeting if held in the United States.

I am getting quite busy in making tentative arrangements for a meeting at Princeton, September 8-12, 1958. The proposed subjects are the welfare state, governmental fiscal policy and the evils of inflation, the distribution of income in a free economy with emphasis on the effect of tools of production. About fifty foreign members are expected and if fifty out of eighty American members attend, the total number of attendants would be not over one hundred and twenty with guests strictly limited.

October 8, 1957

Dear Mr. Crane:

I am so glad that you and Jean Pierre have met, and that you like him. He needs to know—I was going to say, men like you, but what I mean, accurately is—you. I have truly GREAT hopes, expectations, of the increasing value of his work for centuries to come. By all disinterested reports, he is turning out annual classes of students who are sound, principled, individualists. . . . I'm rather amused by the boyishness of the sacking of the Russian Embassy, an exuberance of only momentary and superficial value, but the students are, I think, of incalculable value. The "little leaven", Jean Pierre's wife, Adrienne, I haven't met; from her letters she is both charming and most intelligent.

Any suggestion from me [about the Princeton meeting] is probably too late now. In general, it has seemed to me in the past that Dr. Hayek's selection of speakers is too academic—naturally, no doubt, since he lives in that world. I could wish that such a meeting in this country could hear such men as Congressman Gwinn, Dean Manion, T. Coleman Andrews, Dan Smoot, Bracken Lee, Willis Stone, and some young ones such as Dick Cornuelle, Roger MacBride, Bill Buckley if not in one of his pessimistic slumps. But in this I am thinking of the impact upon European listeners. All the men I have mentioned are a species unknown in Europe, their existence is news and their points of view are bombshells to Europeans. I do not know whether they could even be invited to attend a Mont Pelerin meeting, within the scope of the Mont Pelerin Society policy. If *ideas* are wanted, however, they have definite political-philosophical principles and, also, policies based on them, for strategical and tactical *action*. They could represent the real USA to Europe much more accurately and effectively I think, than any equal number of American professional thinkers in universities.

I suppose the first thing to decide is the aim of a meeting here. Is it to present the American revolutionary thesis to European intellectuals? (to whom it is as unknown as American history and geography and political structure). Or is it to startle and shock American intellectuals by showing them European intellectuals who question the collectivist assumption underlying all their Europe-oriented thinking?

In the first case, I would repeat my list of desirable speakers. In the second, I don't know what could be done other than to reject the *most* socialist of available Europeans. I suppose that in many persevering decades (if there proves to be so much time remaining) little by little the academic thinkers can be edged in a "left" to "right" direction. This is the Fabian "inevitability of gradualness" policy. It seems to work in England and the USA during the past century. Such men as Bertrand de Jouvenal, Ropke, Hayek, are a little off the "middle way" on its "right" side, which may be—I'm not sure—better than being Joad-like on the "left". I wonder whether Hayek, during this past decade, has moved so far as to abandon his advocacy of "Social Security", so-called.

I wonder, and this is an old, still unanswered question of mine, whether there can ever be genuine individualism in the halls of Academe. These institutions of learning seem to attract the parasitic minds and characters, the dependent, imitative, safety-seeking persons, cautious, timid, conforming. It seems to me typical that they repeat an error for thousands of years without ever thinking of questioning it; and when it occurs to a Galileo to drop a couple of weights and *see* how they fall, he is not *produced* by the universities; he is kicked out of them and followed by showers of brickbats. So any incipient Galileo who may be on a faculty smothers any rash impulse to think, considers his "tenure", his "standing", his safe routine, his easy living and continues to quote the quoter who quoted the quoter . . . way back to Plato at least. WHY does a mind like Hayek's think straight—rationally—from observed fact to logical conclusion almost through such a book as *Road to Freedom* and then duck out from under the final Q.E.D., turn a somersault and come up facing backward? WHY does a Ludwig von Mises do such a masterpiece of thought as *Human Action,* and then throw it all away by such crass idiocy as demanding "democracy" and declaring that "Any form of government will work well" if good men run it? If Henry Ford's mind acted like that, there never would have been a Model T. The correctly operating minds are not in the heads of professional thinkers; they're in woodsheds like Henry Ford's and bicycle shops like the Wrights', and telegraph offices like Edison's, and on surveying teams like George Washington's, etc., etc., etc.

Of course, a major difficulty is language. What to do with words such as liberty, freedom, democracy, competition. How to translate "competition" in American, into French which has no equivalent? What to do with "individualism" which to Alexis de Toqueville . . . means: a proud, haughty spirit which leads men to isolate themselves from their fellowmen and to live alone in remote places? As to subjects: The Welfare States. Will anyone *attack* the basic premises? which is, Physical force used by persons upon persons CAN make its victims richer and happier. The question to be decided is: CAN it? I fear you will find the discussion to be not CAN it? but, should it?

Governmental fiscal policy: Will anyone *dare* to suggest, even most timidly, even a possibility that banking enterprise, like all economic enterprises, can be free? Will anyone point out that banking, like production, transportation, communication, originally WAS a free enterprise, originated and carried on by persons acting freely; and that—like production, transportation, communication—historically it was seized by the Princes' police force—i.e. physical force used by politicians upon the bankers, producers, transporters—the inventors of these useful ways of acting? Will anyone think—much less say—that "government fiscal policy" is in fact a gangster's way of handling stolen loot? On the other hand, can you imagine any of these complacent discussers of "governmental fiscal policy" widening the discussion to include a logical consideration of the proper "governmental policy" of manipulating ALL weights and measures? It is obvious (though I doubt that any speaker will see it) that a government which from day to day changes the values of currency and credit should also, from day to day, change the number of ounces in a pound and the number of inches in a foot.

The disposition of income in a free economy strikes me as the most promising subject suggested. Though emphasis on tools seems to me rather superficial. . . . The *source* of tools is individual liberty acting in an environment of freedom; i.e., in an environment in which no use of physical force by persons upon persons inhibits human action (action both mental and physical; invention and production, as regards tools.) This is historical fact. The production of tools began, in the modern sense of "tools", in sixteenth century England, the place where men were least restrained by government at the time. Men have increased the invention, production, and use of tools only in those places on this earth where minds were least inhibited by tradition and custom, and actions were least inhibited by governments. Tools are an effect, not a primary cause; or, more accurately, a means of producing a further effect. Free men create tools; free men use tools to create wealth. And because wealth, created, MUST be consumed, the distribution of wealth must increase in ratio to the increase of production of wealth. The automotive industry does not produce cars to stack them up in Detroit; if it did that, it could not continue to produce. The cars must be consumed; to be consumed, they must be distributed. The increase of distribution increases the volume and rate of consumption, the volume and rate of consumption increases the demand for cars, which increases the production of cars. This process is inevitable, given human energy working freely to satisfy human desires.

November 12, 1957

Dear Mrs. Lane:

Your suggestions for the Mont Pelerin Society meeting are to the point and much appreciated.

Both are the aims of the American meeting; they are not contradictory. Therefore, the speakers should include men who can present the American thesis to Europeans. Beside that, the members will be afforded visits to manufacturing plants, farms, super markets, housing developments, and other activities, both in the East and in the Middle West—and in these exposed to the ideas of some truly libertarian directors of these activities—so as to give the European members an inkling into America. For the second aim, to present European thought opposed to collectivism, Hayek has made what seems to me to be a good selection of European speakers.

XII

December 26, 1957

Dear Mr. Crane:

I thank you so much—no, really, I can't begin to say how much—for this beautiful and fascinating *The American Past.* Nothing could have pleased me more—no gift to me could have pleased me more, as I'm sure you knew when you sent it. It is so perfectly done, too; even Bingham's paintings in it. I have enjoyed it very much and it is one of the few books that will never stop being enjoyable.

I thank you and Mrs. Crane, too, for your Christmas card. This year, again, I did not send any. . . . My house is not a house (to paraphrase Mr. Wilson's famous description of conscription) : it is chaos, its walls being removed in all directions in a process of remodeling, which was to be finished in October and may (I hope, I hope) be done before the turn of the century. But all this didn't mean that I wasn't sending you the warmest wishes for a happy Christmas and the best-yet of New Years.

I do not think that "tolerance" and "compromise" are virtues. I am damn certain that "to understand all" is NOT "to forgive all". I can "understand" impulses in myself, which I regard as not forgiveable, but as irrational, disastrous if not understood and therefore not tolerated but destroyed immediately. There is an enormous difference between a human fellow-feeling for other persons, and a toleration of, and compromise with, their human errors. Not many persons, if any, understand the motives and emotions and logic of Communists better than I do, or better than I understand the foggy-minded wanting to be "good" of the horribly destructive do-gooders; I KNOW that they all "mean well". I even understand the discouraged cynicism of the former do-gooder, or former Sincere Communist, who has become wholly vicious, cruel and wanting and enjoying destruction for its own sake, for its pure power. Anyone who has ever been delirious, in fever, can understand insanity. A fellow-feeling for these deluded *persons* is far from being a toleration of their fantasies and actions, and even further from being a "compromise" meaning a half-way "going along" with their actions.

It's absurd to say all that to you who know it so well yourself. But nowadays, it seems, so few persons do know it. There seems to be a sort of misty-mindedness, that so many are lost in. I am not a positivist, empiricist, materialist—all those labels that some pin on me; but I do wish that plain reason, logic, would go farther into some areas of mysticism. For instance: What sane person "compromises" such a statement as, two plus two is four? (Though certainly that's "abstract" and "theoretical"—in fact, mystic.) Nobody will compromise with the child who says that two and two are six, and "meeting halfway" will settle for two and two are five. But such a man as the late Robert Taft will know, and say, that "federal aid to education" is inevitably destructive of freedom in education, and therefore of free thinking and therefore of this Republic; and then he will meet in the Senate a bill appropriating $X millions for Federal aid to education, and—compromising, meeting it halfway—will support it when amended to $½X millions. There has come to be a general idolizing of the notion of "compromising," confused, I guess, with the idea of loving your fellowmen. I suppose it seems harsh, unloving, brutal, to resist, to oppose firmly, the other fellow; when you know him, you know he means well, you know he cares for his proposal, you know that defeat will hurt him, will make him hate you.

Loving-kindness becomes more important than truth—than truth as *you see it*—which is the only truth that anyone knows. And-who-knows?—maybe an Einstein knows that two and two are not four. Maybe what Mr. Taft knows about Federal Aid to Education is not what Arthur Schlesinger, Jr., knows. Maybe "everything is relative." Maybe there IS no truth. So let's all "get along, go along" with each other, let's not be "controversial" ever, let's have sweetness and kindness and harmony, harmony above all. In my opinion, that attitude is the "weakness of the West" against the organized Communists; every one of whom *knows* that he is right, and therefore everyone who is not a Communist is wrong, and to be destroyed utterly, by any means.

Truth crushed to earth does not rise by its own power. It rises again because living persons recognize it AS truth

—or, more nearly precisely, partially recognize some of it as truth—and stand for it firmly, at any cost to themselves or to others. That absolute conviction of being "right," i.e., of *knowing* a truth, is what is most desperately needed now, I think, in this country.

And there IS "controversy" between truth and fallacy, between fact and error. In the nature of things, there is this "flat open-and-shut" between them; there is no "compromise" between them. There IS a color, black; and a color, white. Black is NOT white, and white is NOT black. There is no "middle ground" between them. You can mix pigments but the colors cannot be mixed. Gray is another color; it isn't a "meeting" of black and white. There isn't, for instance, a "compromise" between Federal Aid to Education and no Federal Aid to Education. Anything *is,* or it isn't.

It seems to me that most Americans once knew that simple fact, and that nowadays too many are bewildered about it. I think we all need a lot more inflexibility than we have.

January 6, 1958

Dear Mr. Crane:

With all my other friends and correspondents, Jean Pierre has heard nothing from me all this past year, but somewhere on or over the Atlantic my thanks for their Christmas card has passed a letter from him, bits of which may interest you. . . . First a little gossip: you like it, don't you? Who doesn't?—"Adrienne has some fine clothes owing to the fact that she makes them herself, so we could "adapt" ourselves rapidly to the strange milieu of the Suvrette House at St. Moritz. . . . We were so glad and privileged to meet among others Mr. and Mrs. Jasper Crane; they are so very kind and pleasant people. They even invited us to lunch one day at the great surprise of some older attendants —the French Miss Genin who issued the French books of Mises (I told you that she refused to pay me anything for the translation of Mise's *Planned Chaos*) was terribly interested in our table that day and no more looks on me as if I were still a little boy. Mr. Crane told us about you at the great interest of Adrienne who is still looking for the pleasure of meeting you one day."

Now for the bits about the MPS meeting, which he reports at length, most interestingly; but you know all that. He says: "As to the congress, it confirmed what I already reported to you in 1953; there are two main tendencies: the orthodox liberals like Mises, Larrence Fertig, Milton Friedman, et al . . . on the other hand, dirigistic minded members: Ropke, Rueff, Gideonse (New York), Howard S. Ellis, etc. But this time I was not one young man among older persons; there were many young Americans, Germans and French. As to a famous (!) Frenchman's remarks (Giscard 'd Estaing) President of the International Chamber of Commerce, Paris, I could not agree when he took for granted in Europe the service of the post, telephone and telegraph is everywhere a government monopoly. I saw him as he was to leave the next day; when I asked him whether he really believed in Europe we could not turn these to free enterprise, he replied, "Monsieur, ce serait une mythe; c'est impossible. . . ."

"It was in order to refute his remarks that I had my name put on the list of those who would speak after the general discussion but there was not sufficient time available for me, two young Americans and other young to bring forward our modest ideas. A young American, [Warren] Nutter, complained later with me that the older gentlemen took too much time to say too little, whereas in the U.S. the discussion would be more vivid, owing to the fact that everybody could answer and ask questions in a direct range. I have to confess that this sympathetic Young American was right."

I wonder, too—I hope I needn't say, most tentatively—whether a session given wholly to "the young" might be an interesting feature of a meeting. On the ground, certainly valid, that they can give something of a preview of the "wave of the future," since they will help to make the future according to their ideas. Whether their ideas are wrong or right. After all, it is the older Europeans whose ideas have helped to make the past and present Europe. If, in the MPS meeting "young" Europe is more definitely and accurately liberal than the older European members, and if the older American members are, too:—two ifs—the effect on one session given wholly to the "young" should—and even might—shake that complacent brushing-off attitude of the Ropkes and the Rueffs, expressed in that "—a myth, impossible!" This attitude, I suspect, underlies the "dirigisme" of such men as Roepke. They may think it is impossible to liberalize Europe, but when young Europeans stand up and say they are going to *do* that, the effect should be disturbing at least.

January 17, 1958

Dear Mrs. Lane:

I have over the years noted a number of fallacies which have been widely accepted as truths. I wish I had made a collection of them. It is astounding what fads and fashions there are. Some idea sweeps the country and yet it is not based on truth. I have noted book after book by authors of good intentions, read one in fact last week, based on an utterly false premise. So the public accepts fallacy after fallacy—about money, inflation, big business and little business, depressions, financial support of education, and on such fundamental subjects as the nature of man and, therefore, the most suitable type of government, etc., etc. It is all very frightening. We wonder where we will end up, except that this sort of thing has been going on for a long time.

I am so glad to learn from your letter that Mr. Hamilius is so sound, not only in his philosophy but in his estimate of others. I earnestly hope that the addresses at the Princeton meeting of the Mont Pelerin Society are free from this fallacy of "dirigisme." It would be fine if Hamilius and his wife are able to come over for this Princeton meeting. I will see what I can do about that.

January 20, 1958

Dear Mr. Crane:

Your mention of fallacies inspires me. I do wish that you HAD collected them. Let's collect some now? And I will—or, more precisely, I will cherish an intention to—write an up-to-date version of Bastiat's sophismes economiques. It would be fun. And I am beginning to feel again like being what literary agents call "in production." Apropos, I am doing a quick rewrite of *Discovery of Freedom.* And shall be most grateful if you have time to put in your thumb and pull out the fallacies that you see in it. Could you? Would you? In that hope I'm sending herewith some early pages. If at your leisure—if any—you return them heavily blue-pencilled, I will remit my thanks on receipt.

March 26, 1958

Dear Mrs. Lane:

I read your manuscript with great interest and return it herewith. It is splendid.

When you discuss the effective uses of human energy in the United States, shouldn't New England with its rocky, unproductive soil, absence of minerals, and other lacks be cited, for it was particularly in these areas of the country that so many developments originated. A striking point should be made of this to counter the idea current in other countries that America is rich on account of our natural resources.

You have the makings of a great book here.

March 28, 1958

Dear Mr. Crane:

Thank you for your note with my manuscript, which came yesterday after the postman had taken my note to you. Do you sometimes wonder whether such incidents are simply co-incidence, or maybe what those professors at Duke have named ESP? When they occur I always remember Mark Twain's instructions for getting in touch with a mislaid friend or acquaintance. If you do not know where he is, Twain wrote, write him a long letter and stamp it, and lay it away. Within a few days you will receive a letter from him. This seems to work, often. What would happen if *he,* not knowing where *you* were, wrote and sealed and stamped an unaddressed letter to you, Mark Twain didn't say. Everybody knew where he was; I suppose he took it for granted that always it was the other fellow whose whereabouts had been forgotten. It's pathetic to think of those *two* unaddressed letters mutually waiting for a response that—so far as I can see—never would come. But perhaps Extra Sensory Perception would escape that dilemma somehow.

Goodness knows WHEN I shall get an opportunity to finish that book. You do encourage me to try, anyway, and I thank you. I have no self-confidence at all in non-fiction and can be stopped by the flickering of a leaf, though sometimes it does seem to me that it's *impossible* to write sillier nonsense than I read in pontifical and highly respected books. This so-called "conservative" movement, of the Russell Kirk ilk, impresses me as not only trying to scuttle backward, crabwise, to medievalism, but as being singularly asinine on the way. Commend me for mixed metaphors! Surely nobody has done more than to combine donkey and crab.

March 31, 1958

Dear Mrs. Lane:

I understand that you did not have quite the depth of snow that we had here and in New Jersey and in parts of Pennsylvania. Delaware was particularly hurt in that the electric current was cut off from 25,000 houses and the telephone service from a similar number. A great number of people out in the country were deprived of water and have been drinking melted snow or trudging through the drifts to nearby springs.

We were among the most fortunate, the only damage to the house being from leakage through the masonry, but our garden is a shambles. This has been the most destructive storm in my memory, and I recall the blizzard of 1888.

April 11, 1958

Dear Mr. Crane:

It has snowed here all night and is still snowing heavily, and I was mourning the harm that this winter's weather has done to your beautiful gardens. Here, there is nothing to damage, really; the woodlots' trees prune themselves doing themselves no harm, and so do the old apple trees, and the hemlocks are a lesson in gentleness, yielding so gracefully to all brutality that it doesn't harm them a bit.

I was intending to ask you a question. I am reading Tawney's *Religion and the Rise of Capitalism,* which I suppose you know, and he says: The most crucial and the most difficult of all political questions is that which turns on the difference between public and private morality. The problem which it presents in the relations between States is commonplace. But, since the essence is the difficulty of applying the same moral standard to decisions which affect large masses of men as to those in which only individuals are involved, it emerges in a hardly less acute form in the sphere of economic life, as soon as its connections ramify widely, and the unit is no longer the solitary producer, but a group. To argue, in the manner of Machiavelli, that there is one rule for business and another for private life, is to open a door to an orgy of unscrupulousness before the mind recoils. To argue that there is no difference at all is to lay down a principle which few men who have faced the difficulty in practice will be prepared to endorse as of invariable application, and incidentally to expose the idea of morality itself to discredit by exposing it to an almost intolerable strain. The practical result of sentimentality is too often a violent reaction toward the baser kinds of *Realpolitik.*

Of course I don't agree wholly with Tawney. But I find his theory interesting. And the statements in this paragraph raise a question that maybe I haven't the experience to answer. In my own, not extensive, business experience I did deal mainly with individuals, but it simply never occurred to me—(I am maybe TOO simple?—that every decision doesn't eventually "affect large masses of men," nor that a moral standard isn't always individual and always invariable. No doubt I am often "sentimental" but this attitude wasn't sentimental, it was an unexamined assumption, just taken for granted.

You have had experience in truly Big Business, which certainly does not deal with "the solitary producer," but with huge groups of producers, distributors, consumers, capitalists. Did you find that actually there is a difference? such that having faced the difficulty in practice, you would not "be prepared to endorse as of invariable application" the same moral standard applicable in relations with that "solitary" producer? or anyone else? IS there a difference morally, between dealings with groups of persons and dealing with a person?

I have argued that there is an enormous practical difference, consisting in the fact that in dealing with a person one is immediately aware of that person's reaction, whereas in dealing with large and, in space, distant groups of persons, a much more precise knowledge of moral principle is essential. The analogy, it seems to me, is with a simple person who can live very well, and never walk off the edge of a cliff, with only the vaguest sense of gravitation and no conscious thought about it at all, compared to the engineer who builds huge bridges or skyscrapers or outer-space rockets, and must know the principles and the mathematics of the attraction of masses to each other.

But this view is contradictory to Tawney's view that the moral *principle* varies in, so to speak, the volume of the mass; that the morality of dealing with a single person is not the morality of dealing with a "group" of persons. And I am halted by his confident assertion that men of such experience as yours must agree with him rather than with me.

He seems to me to confound Government with Big Business, to regard them as essentially the same. I suppose because both are large organizations. But men in "governments" have, as officials, nothing to use upon other men but physical force, and physical force per se is non-moral; it is simply kinetic energy. In strict morality, they should do nothing but intervene between an aggressor using physical force and the aggressor's intended victim; their only action should be the simplest police action, limited by legislation and courts. Their function—the use of physical force upon persons—is to diminish the amount of force used by persons upon persons in social relationship, just as the function of, say, a yarn-making factory is to diminish the amount of time-energy used by persons making yarn, in a given group of persons. By specializing in the use of force to protect most persons against the few aggressors, men in Government (so-called) relieve the majority of the necessity of self-protection. As the yarn-making specialist abolish the spinning wheels in kitchens. Protecting human rights has a moral justification, but the action of applying force to persons is not itself either moral or immoral; it is simply energy in action. The morality of the State consists in NOT acting, in refraining from action, excepting only when action is imperatively necessary to "keep the peace." Whereas the morality of all economic activity including Big Business, consists in increasing, extending, multiplying ways of acting, always according to the moral principles of human relationships.

* * * * *

In a letter crossing in the mail, Mr. Crane expressed his disappointment with the current American temper, and questioned whether a political party devoted to traditional liberal ideas could win an election.

* * * * *

April 12, 1958

Dear Mr. Crane:

I myself have never wondered whether a political party that "stood staunchly for the Constitution . . . for limited government and for sound principles of economics" would not sweep this country. Certainly it would. Only look at the record here. Hoover's administration suddenly developed the New Deal that Lincoln began; the RFC, the Farm Board, all those Commissions; the country reacted violently; in 1932 a landslide for Roosevelt's "twenty-five percent reduction in Federal spending," "a sound dollar," repeal of prohibition. The 1932 Democrat platform and all FDR's campaign speeches and promises, were sound and fine Americanism. The only reason that I did not vote for him was that I knew his New York State record. My parents and all the rest of Wright County's population did vote for him, and I knew why: they believed the platform and the speeches.

In 1936 what was the choice? Landon. A weak wobbler, whose only assets were business experience and the Kansas City *Star*. I was then in Columbia, Missouri, which went solidly Democrat, except one vote (mine) for Landon, and sixty-seven for the Communist candidate which, everyone said, were, "Oh, the University professors." Riverbottom Missouri has been Democrat since the Federal (Republican) military invasion of 1862, and, besides, no true-blue Missourian would vote for a Kansan if his life and salvation depended on doing so.

Then, FDR attacked the Supreme Court, and I've never been in a more furious community. Columbians would have lynched him if they could have laid their hands on him. You remember the roar from the whole country then. Missouri Democrats would have let their ancestors spin in their graves and voted against FDR in 1940, if they could have. But what was the choice? an imitation and obviously lying 'little' FDR. The word that made the difference in 1940 was, sincere. In every truck-stop and filling station and beauty parlor across the country what I heard was a rather wistful, "But I do think Roosevelt is sincere."

And then, Dewey; my God. That little mustache. That cheap cocksureness, so blatantly contemptuous of the voters. That silly yelping about "unity, unity." When the first rumor of Dewey as a possibility reached me I actually went to New York to see Mr. Hoover, to tell him that the American people NEVER would elect Dewey. I was asked to be one of Dewey's ghost-writers, but no money would have induced me to help him try to bamboozle Americans.

Finally, at last, a plausible hope appeared; a man who was not a politician, who seemed honest, who promised to "clean up the mess in Washington," who, as a soldier presumably would not try to defeat this country at war as Truman did, and what happened? a landslide for him. As soon as he was seen in action his popularity became a myth. Politicians and their publicist stooges keep on slavering about Ike's popularity; at the grassroots there never has been a less popular president since Lincoln.

Lincoln at least was shrewd, he knew that "you can't fool all the people all the time." If the political parties do NOT produce a platform and candidate that are staunchly for the Constitution, for reduction of Federal Government and spending and taxing, and for sound economics, there will be the bloodiest upheaval here that history has seen. There would have been civil war before now, if there were any geographical line on which to fight. It would surprise you, how often I have heard from how many 'little men' and women, here and there over this country, the remark that voting does no good, it's going to come to guns. This is a response that I get unexpectedly—from the last persons I'd expect it from—when I ask casually what do they think of a candidate, or how do they think an election will go. I wonder whether you and your friends and associates aren't perhaps rather isolated from the ordinary run-of-the-mill people? I can't visualize you in dusty shoes and sweater getting out of a battered Ford and drinking coffee at a diner's counter elbow to elbow with the truck driver and the local policeman and the Greek from the fruitstand next door; or loafing around the filling station while the car's up on the stand being greased; or stopping at the Chuckwagon to eat barbecued beef with the men from the round-up and the other passing tourists. But look at the labor-union-members' votes for Taft in Ohio.

Look at the plain record, and you see that the voters have never been given a choice, have never had a chance to vote, since 1932. All this time there has been in reality only one party here; one party under two names, Democrat-socialist and Republican-me-too socialist. It is the Soviet or Nazi situation; any vote is Yes. All that I, and undoubtedly multitudes of others can do is not to vote. Or to vote for the rare independent, anti-New Deal candidate, and those votes are not counted. It is impossible to know the vote for the States Rights party, for instance, in Connecticut. The written-in States Rights votes in Danbury were counted: seventy-five. But not the Connecticut vote; nobody knows what that was. Roger MacBride was a deputized poll-watcher in three New York City precincts; he found that only the regular party votes were counted, all write-ins were discarded without counting; he insisted that they be counted but was told that they "made no difference," and he is sure that none were counted in his absence.

One thing I am certain of: If the opportunity for peaceful change, which is provided in the Constitution continues to be blocked by the blindly stupid politicians, there will be a violent change. This country will not be totally wrecked without a fight. The general patience is long-suffering, but in this country it is not suicidal, as it is in Europe. Nothing like that yell, "I want meat!" that terrified Washington into abolishing OPA has ever occurred anywhere else. Beyond a certain point, Americans will not let politicians stop the operation of the American economy. I do not say that a majority *thinks* in terms of political philosophy, but the same drive that WILL keep the wheels turning in spite of hell and high water will keep them turning in spite of politicians. People here, in general, are not submissive; in general, they have no reverence for "upper classes"; in general they do not regard themselves as "little people, common men." And they do not think, they need not think, to *know* that the wheels must be kept turning. When OPA blocks the channels through which the steak comes from the ranges and pastures, they abolish OPA. The same fanatic union-members who strike against the Bell Telephone Company, even those who hate the "capitalists," will get out and work without stopping until they drop from exhaustion to keep the wires up and the telephones working, in fire or flood or hurricane or ice-storm.

What baffles me is not the reason, the cupidity, the dishonesty, of the Party bosses in both parties; what staggers me is their stupidity. The flaw—a fatal one—in democracy is that ordinary, moderately sensible voters have nobody to elect but a politician.

April 17, 1958

Dear Mrs. Lane:

My own experience in business has been, as you say, quite extensive, and I can only say that I have never noticed any difference between the morality of a man as an individual and as an employer in a corporation. Businessmen are honest in very large degree. In fact, the whole fabric of business is interwoven with the theory of credit; an oral bargain is almost always as good as a written contract. I encountered one corporation executive who lied, and I repeatedly told him so. Searching my mind for other incidents in big business I really cannot put my finger on any where I could not depend on the other fellow. Several men in small business tried to cheat me, and maybe others did, too, that I did not detect! One small businessman naively asked my advice whether it wasn't all right to employ the practices that he was, but I had to tell him frankly that they were not honest.

April 16, 1958

Dear Mr. Crane:

Thank you for your answer to my question, a question that I see I didn't put clearly. I don't want you to think that I was questioning the honesty of Big Businessmen as such. I know that business (anywhere above handcraft-and-barter level) depends largely on credit which absolutely depends on honesty; a business which did not "deliver the goods" as specified couldn't last at all. I think that is a fact that needs emphasis; the fact that modern business requires honesty, not only as Franklin's "best policy" but as an essential.

Practically all schools are teaching—and youngsters believing—that "buying cheap and selling dear" is dishonest and therefore all business men are crooks. I remember Henry Grady Weaver's little girl whom he adored (he told me this with tears in his eyes) who learned in school to be ashamed of him; she was only seven or eight, and used to beg and plead with him to stop working for General Motors and be a "good man" like the fathers of some of her classmates who were doctors or teachers. He tried to explain that business men were good, but he could not overcome the school's influence. After two or three years of this, the teacher read the class my mother's book, *The Long Winter*, and the little girl, all excited, came home and asked her father if he knew how important railroads are; people couldn't LIVE without railroads, she told him. So he explained that now cars and trucks were doing what once only the railroads did, and people now could not live as we do without motors. And she cried for joy because after all, her father was good, he helped to make things that people couldn't live without. Henry very nearly worshipped my mother after that. Mr. Earhart—Harry Earhart, did you know him?—had the same experience without the happy ending. His daughter in college—Smith or Vassar, I forget—learned so well to be ashamed of him, a "capitalist," that she never did change. It was the tragedy of his life. It was the reason he tried to use his money against socialism. But this is a far digression.

What I mean to say is that the question was, Is there a different KIND of moral problem in dealing with "large groups" of persons? That was the statement that rather puzzled me; the simple assertion as if it were self-evident fact, that a difference exists between "public" and "private" morality, which all men dealing with "large groups" know.

Does the *basis* of moral problems shift, or change? Is Honesty itself different? or does it seem to be different, when instead of dealing with John Smith you are dealing with 500,000 employees and 500,000 stockholders?

I think it must SEEM to be different. For example: Suppose that at one of those meetings in Princeton I had gone out leaving my purse on the table and Felix Morley had said to Mr. Pew, "Mrs. Lane owes me ten dollars; just take ten dollars out of her purse and hand it to me, please." I think Mr. Pew would not have done it. But I assume that Sun Oil Company every Friday takes out of its employees' pay envelopes money that they have earned and that Sun Oil Company has contracted to pay them, and hands that money to men in Washington who simply say that the employee owes them that amount. I hope I needn't say that I KNOW that Mr. Pew is honest. Doesn't he believe that there is a difference between "public" and "private" morality?

Of course I am not discussing Mr. Pew, nor expecting you to do so. I use him only as an illustration of the situation; it is the situation that interests me.

Now, if—as seems to be an evident fact— Big Business men in general believe that there is this difference, believe that morality (honesty, for example) changes its nature and becomes a different KIND of problem when they deal with "large groups" rather than with one person, do you, judging from your own experience with such problems, think that they are mistaken? Or is it your *experience* that there actually is such a difference?

If I finish the book whose tentative beginning I sent you in mss. I may want to say something about this, and I want whatever I say to be truthful and accurately so, of course. My own view is that there is no such difference. If there is not, most American employers today are simply robbers; and I would say that. Granting that few of them regard what they are doing as robbery, of course. But if there *is* such a difference, the problem shifts to a different basis, and as I have had no experience with morality on such a different basis maybe I'm not competent to have an opinion about it.

People say that I am too simple, that I do not see the

actual complexities of situations. At the time of the Pearl Harbor hearings a young lieutenant, supposed to know a fact extremely damaging to FDR and Marshall, was about to testify and there was tense speculation about what he would say. Two top Public Relations men with giant corporations were here and began talking about it; I said that from the lieutenant's point of view the problem seemed simple; they said I didn't realize its complexities. I said, Well, if he is considering effects on his career, repercussions on his family, the probable attitude of his friends, his longterm future, and so on, of course he's considering all kinds of complexities; but actually the problem seems to me very simple, just a simple Yes or No question: "Am I a Liar?"

Neither of my guests said a word; and what their silence meant I didn't and don't know. Did they suddenly see the utter futility of any discussion with the simple-minded? were they appalled by the revelation of such ignorance of realities? were they shocked by discovering their own mistake in having thought me intelligent. And WAS I an ignorant and unintelligent simpleton? I am not asking YOU these questions of course; they are questions I ask myself. It's because I ask myself questions that I referred to you this question about the assertion that there is a difference between "public" and "private" morality. You know whether there is such an actual difference; I don't. I have never dealt with "large groups" of persons as you have.

May 6, 1958

Dear Mrs. Lane:

It is mortifying and probably morally wrong for employers to collect taxes for the government. Almost the only person with a clean record in this respect has been Vivian Kellems. The Du Pont Company does it, my wife and I do it. I suppose it is because it is the law, an iniquitous law, but government is organized force and is, therefore, obeyed. Has anybody in this or other countries successfully resisted the government? There is not, however, a difference between the large groups and the individual in this respect. They both obey the government, even when it seems wrong to do so.

May 9, 1958

Dear Mr. Crane:

Yes, I can—happily—answer your question: Has anybody in this or other countries successfully resisted the government?—Of course, resisting the government (from 1760 to 1782) was what gave you and me everything we value; and I could reply by asking, In all human history, what progress or any other value has ever been achieved by any means *other* than "resisting the government?" But I can answer your question by mentioning an achievement right here and now.

The housekeeping women and their domestic servants in these States have most successfully resisted the Federal government by simply refusing to include domestic servants in so-called Social Security. The faintly publicized incident was the refusal of the Texas women, dubbed "the Marshall girls"—possibly you remember that? Cleverly, they nipped their money out of their bank accounts; what became of their legal resistance in the courts, I don't know. But certainly they have never even tried to inflict that "Social Security" fraud upon their "help." Because the women throughout the country simply did not do it, and that Act of Congress is now a dead letter. No attempt is being made to enforce it. I have never obeyed it; nobody whom I know about has ever obeyed it. And radio newscasts reported, two or three years ago, a public statement by the Secretary of the Treasury, who said—for publication—that enforcing it is impossible. "We would have to have a policeman at the elbow of every woman in this country who has servants."

When the Act was first passed, a woman came from Bridgeport to appeal to me for help. She was a domestic servant, habitually one of a bus-load of domestic servants who went every morning from Bridgeport to their various jobs in the Town of Easton (one of those Connecticut Towns that are really a country side covered by modest estates, five or ten acres and old Colonial houses restored and remodeled.) The whole bus-load, furious and lamenting, cursed and wept and raged, every morning, and someone had suggested that maybe I could "do something," so they made this woman a delegate to plead their cause. All I could say was, let them refuse to work for women who tried to force them into the fraud. I said, "Don't forget that your employers need you, as much or more than you need your jobs. I can't promise that this will work, but in your place I'd certainly try it." I don't know what happened.

At this time Stanley Parzuchowski came to me one day, in trouble. Stanley is a hatter in Danbury; he has worked for me in all his spare time—evenings, Saturdays and whenever the intermittent hat-factory's work stops temporarily—for the past fifteen years. He and his wife are my good friends and do everything for me. They are grand people. So Stanley came to me in distress, twisting his hat in his hands, and in a low shamed voice asked, "Mrs. Lane . . . Are you going to turn me in?" I didn't know what he meant. "I mean," he said. "I mean—are you going to turn me in to the police?" This staggered me; he is absolutely honest, a most careful driver, a kind and decent person. I couldn't imagine what he might have done; but after a moment I decided, and I said firmly, "No Stanley; no matter what you have done, I shall not turn you in to the police. What is the trouble? what have you done?" Astonished, he said that he hadn't done anything; he was talking about the new "withholding tax." Was I going to turn him in, on that? Of course I wasn't! I will have nothing to do with the fraud, myself; naturally I won't try to force anyone else into it. I said, "You realize, Stanley, this may mean that both of us will go to jail for evading the tax?" He said he'd take that chance; I said I would; and that's that. Stanley thinks the whole thing is morally wrong, and taking part of what he earns by working overtime for me was the last straw, he didn't know how he could put up with that, nor how he could quit working here.

The Internal Revenue Collector sent me a bill, including fine, for my not having paid the Self-Employment tax one year (no space for including it, no mention of it, having been on my tax form.) I sent a check. At intervals since then, various Authorities have been trying to force a Social Security number on me. They telephone and tell me I MUST have one; since I have none, they are giving me one. I tell them I won't have it. I get forms, my humble request to be entitled to Social Security benefits; with command, Sign here and return to—I put them in the wastebasket. I get orders to appear at such an hour, such a date, at such an office, with all records and receipts to show cause—I reply that it is not convenient for me to appear—etc., etc. I even get an order to appear and support with documents my claim for refund of the tax-and-fine that I paid; I return this, writing across it, I have made no such claim. The telephone rings, and I am informed that I am being given the necessary Social Security number; I say I have none and I shall NOT have one; I will have nothing to do with that Ponzi fraud because it is treason; it will wreck this country as it wrecked Germany. I won't have it; you can't make me.

Evetts Haley is resisting, too; he is fighting the Agricultural Adjustment Act's "wheat penalty" provision. You know about the Haley case? It is getting all the money I can spare. There is a lot of resisting in this country, and in the long run it is not going to fail. Because, if it did fail—if peaceful, legal resistance does fail, this country is going to live through times worse than Germany suffered before Hitler; Americans finally won't stand any more, they'll revolt with guns. It will be bloody chaos; it can't be civil war because there is no geographical line on which to fight. I think you do not know how much resistance with guns there has been already. The hope is the peaceful resistance that's growing fast.

XIII

September 25, 1958

Dear Mrs. Lane:

Trying to reach you on the telephone to urge you to attend the meeting of the Mont Pelerin Society, I found that you were out in Colorado and obviously, would not be able to attend. The meeting was carried out in accordance with the strong convictions that I had about it and which were so greatly influenced by you. Left-wingers were not invited so that throughout the academic world they may react as you suggested, that this important conference was held and they were not invited. Even from the Princeton University faculty only one economist was invited and participated by welcoming the members on behalf of the University; he was not felicitous in his talk—nor did he get into any points of economic theory. One of the most serious faults of the meeting was the lack of publicity, as the very able public relations firm did not receive adequate cooperation from the Secretary of the Society. So there seemed to be little notice of the meeting in the newspapers, but doubtless through journals of opinion and by word of mouth the academic world will hear about the meeting and what transpired.

September 28, 1958

Dear Mr. Crane:

In turn, I have pleasing news for you. I was at the Freedom School for two weeks, and it is wonderful. It is by far the best effort that I have seen yet. I hadn't expected anything like the reality. I think it absolutely sound, right, in principle and in method, technic and tactics.

It is about halfway between Colorado Springs and Denver, in the Rampart Range foothills—a half-section of wild forested mountain land. There are two shacks on the land, and a central house and two dormitories have been built of logs.

The staff is Mr. and Mrs. LeFevre, three young women and a young married couple, all volunteer. The young man gave up an exceptional job in Seattle and broke with his New Deal parents, to come with his young wife to help the school. He has a job in Boeing Aircraft in Denver; they live economically in a shack nearby and he works at the school weekends. The three young women have full-time jobs; two are secretaries, one a nurse; evenings and weekends they do the secretarial and much of the manual work of the school. Mr. LeFevre is editor of the *Colorado Springs Gazette,* a full-time job; by arrangement with the publisher he gets the day's work done before noon during the school's summer session, and gives afternoons and evenings to the school. All contribute their whole earnings to it. Mrs. LeFevre is young, pretty, chic, a trained singer with a marvelous voice. All rise at 5:00 A.M.; she gets breakfast for the others who leave for work at 6:00, washes the dishes; gets luncheon for the students, washes the dishes; gets dinner for the students and the staff, washes the dishes—a twelve-hour day in the kitchen. The food is *delicious.* She's an inspired cook, and a penny-fraction-saver, and gay and charming and pretty as a picture; and she bakes all breads, cakes, pies, etc. On Saturday she does the buying, wholesale and from ranchers (fresh eggs, cheaper; etc.) while one of the young women partially replaces her in the kitchen. (I did some baking myself.)

The school has a second-hand car, second-hand station-wagon and a tractor needed to get them out through the snow in winter; the staff lives there the year round. They do all the work themselves—cleaned, repaired, painted the original shacks, sawed down the trees, fell and saw the wood for the winter heating, and so on. The plumbers, electricians, carpenters needed to build the log buildings and modernize the shacks contributed part of their wages, unasked, and did a fine job. Each dormitory houses four students. The whole place is rustic but soundly built and perfectly comfortable. To get in fourteen students, two of the young women had to camp out through the summer, giving up their own rooms. They all want to be able to build one more dormitory next, so that they can take classes of sixteen, and still let these two stay in their rooms. Mr. Le Fevre intends to keep classes no larger than 16. But in time he hopes to keep the school open all year and to have another teacher, two classes of sixteen students each.

This is all background, of course; what matters is the —shall I say?—production. And that is what stunned me. I have never seen anything like it, and I know I can't give you any real idea of it. All I hope is to persuade you to go out there next summer and see it yourself. Can't you, please? The jets will be flying then; you could be there in no time, see it and be back in two or three days. You can't believe it until you do see it.

Mr. LeFevre gets back from work for lunch. He teaches from 1:00 to 5:00, and then from 7:00 to 9:30, and assigns work for the students to do next morning. He gives them really a year's work in the two weeks. He is a GREAT teacher. An e-duc-ator, genuinely. Within a minute, every mind in the room is working, intensely, eagerly. And they all go on working, through the whole two weeks. The result is—well, for example: In the class I saw, there were three college students, one just out of college, employed in Detroit. One had been working during and since High School in United Nations propaganda work among students. I have been up against the same thing myself, and listening to them the first day I was certain that nothing could change their views. By Thursday of that first week, they were individualists. I heard and saw Mr. LeFevre do it, and still I can't explain *how* he did it.

There were more students this year than last. In its two years, the school has graduated eighty, flunked three. Only convinced and informed—thoroughly grounded and understanding—individualists graduate. The students come from every state; they are mostly college boys and girls, going back to college, though there was one young married couple from Seattle in this class.

Now it goes without saying—which of course means that I'm going to say it—that all efforts to overcome or resist, or even delay the collectivist reaction are useful. They are all NEEDED. I am FOR all of them, naturally. And you know that for a long time now—since the early 1930s—I have thought that basically what we need is what Lenin knew in 1903 that the collectivist movement needed: persons who "give the whole of their lives" to this effort—as you are doing, and a few others, including this group at the Freeedom School. It is such devotion that actually makes history. This is what Communists call the "hard core." THEY know its value. There will be careerists, and exploiters, and lunatic fringe and time-servers, and—as Dr. Jordon said—"parlor individualists," the pseudo-intellectuals, but its the Hard Core that counts.

I like the Freedom School because it is real Hard Core devotion. And probably a little because it is repeating the socialist tactic that I saw in the 1890s and that put the New Deal into Washington by the 1930s. And, too, because it is grass-roots, and little, and poor, and squeezing every penny's worth of value out of every dollar. As well as every minute's worth out of every hour. I just have a personal liking for sound economy.

The staff has a gallantry that I like, too. They are gay and full of fun. With all that hard, intensive thinking and work, there's a lot of laughter. And somehow the work itself is a great joy. Everyone has a good time. There is no school on Sunday (though thinking and discussions don't stop). The cars take students to their churches in Colorado Springs, after or before a picnic breakfast in a lovely glade —pancakes, bacon, coffee, sausages from a grill that the young man from Seattle built. In the evening there's Open House—people come from all around, from the ranches and even from Colorado Springs and Denver for Discussion, with a leader—some point of individualist philosophy.

Sunday afternoon, I happened to come upon Mr. LeFevre and the Seattle young man sitting on the steps of the schoolroom; just sitting saying nothing, with tears in their eyes. Startled, I naturally asked what was wrong, and I learned that the school was done for. The land is bought on mortgage, amortized: $4,500 a year. They had saved $3,000 and the rest had been pledged but Washington had denied tax-exemption so the pledges could not be collected. Payment was due September 15. All appeals to the donors had failed; without income-tax deduction no contributions. This was the last class. The young women were already packing. They had improved the property, so the sellers were eager to take it back. If they had more time they still might get tax exemption . . . but they did not have time; mortgage foreclosure would begin next week. By the marvelous luck, I had $1,600 in the bank, a checkbook and pen in my purse, so the school was saved, at least until next year. This was a confidential transaction; I am telling you only to indicate my opinion of the school—that it is something that MUST go on. It was only by accident that I found out its danger; nothing at all could have been guessed from the way they were all carrying on to the end. They are really fine people.

The schoolroom is in the first log structure built. It is above the renovated shacks, on the mountain side; a covered stairway—or path under the trees—goes up to it. It contains the large classroom, the kitchen, dining room and beneath these a tiny bedroom and a showerbath, to which Mr. and Mrs. LeFevre retreat during the summer school terms. There are bookcases—containing the books you contributed and the LeFevres'—a fireplace, a blackboard, and 14 desks, also a teacher's desk, in the classroom. It has marvelous mountain views from the windows. The desks are oblongs of plywood mounted on cuts from tree trunks. Students supply their own notebooks, etc. The fee is $75 a week and fees cover running costs of the school. It will be self-supporting entirely when the mortgage is paid. But it does need another dormitory; one at least, and the staff dreams of a library building, too.

And if they, especially Mr. LeFevre, can someday give their whole time to the school and keep it open all year, they would need either another school building or living quarters for the staff. So far, the school is open only during the summer, when one can camp out. In the winter they live in the warmed dormitory and use the schoolroom as living room. A well built log dormitory for four, with bath, electricity, beds and desks costs about $5,000.

Don't you think that eighty young individualists produced in the first two years is a splendid beginning?

You ask me about the Laura Ingalls Wilder Home Association. This is a group of Mansfield [Missouri] people who are preserving my mother's home as a memorial library and museum. I gave them the furniture and a great deal of interesting Americana belonging to her, much of it mentioned in her books. If it is managed as well as most things in Mansfield are, for persons interested in Americana and especially interested in my mother's books, the house should be an interesting place to visit. Many schools are visiting it now, en masse, I am told. It is just one of those things, part of the reviving interest in American history that is going on all over this country now. I know that my mother's books are a real contribution to American values for children; so many parents have written me that they make all the difference in their bringing up their children to be real Americans, in spite of other influences. Preserving the house and things in it has some small effect in increasing the influence of the books, I suppose, but I can't attach my own natural personal interest in this project to the more important and imperative necessity of trying to save the Republic and the Revolution.[1]

October 28, 1958

Dear Mrs. Lane:

I am delighted at the news about the Freedom School, all except one point. As I understand him, Mr. LeFevre wants an absolute minimum of Federal Government. I believe in strong government, Federal, State and local, to protect us from external enemies, to deter or restrain people from using force on other people, and to provide the structure and the climate in which a free society can flourish.

October 30, 1958

Dear Mr. Crane:

I don't think there is any such difference between your view of Government and Mr. LeFevre's (and mine) as something has led you to believe. It's fearfully easy to misunderstand all of us, because we haven't even a reliable vocabulary.

There are two (at least) ways of looking at a discovered truth, you know; one is stating it as a principle—a fact, a natural Law; and the other is an answer to the question, How do I act according to it? The first is theoretical though I hesitate to call it theoretical, because that word is so often taken to mean, impractical. The second is tactical.

I'm sure we all agree theoretically: that is, we all believe the American Declarations that these truths are "self evident," etc. To say that a being or a thing—a person or an atom—is "endowed by the Creator" with certain attri-

[1]After Mrs. Lane's death the memorial was expanded to celebrate her life and work as well. There is now a new building housing memorabilia from both generations.

butes, functions, qualities, is merely a way of saying that their possessing these attributes, functions, etc., is a Natural Law. None of us—you, Mr. LeFevre, I—would quarrel with the Declarations-writers' view that God is "Nature's God." So, we agree that each person has, as a function of his human nature, inalienable self-control, control of his actions and therefore responsibility for them: i.e. each person is inalienably self-governing.

It follows logically that no person CAN govern another person's action.

God having created human beings as self-governing entities, obviously HIS will is that we act as such, obviously His purpose is served by our acting according to the nature with which He has endowed us, and it is NOT served by our acting otherwise—that is, acting contrary to His will and purpose. Yet, because we are endowed by Him with self-government, we CAN act contrary to our natures, contrary to His will, in opposition to His purpose in creating us; the choice is ours.

Now, if we are right so far, it must be that IF all living persons were to act as self-governing, responsible entities, knowing and understanding the Laws of our own natures and other Natural Laws of life and existence on this earth, God's will would govern the human world here, and that whole world would be good; it would be the God's Kingdom on Earth that the misguided socialists in the churches talk about.

In such a world, every person would be self-governing in his every action; no person would attempt to govern another mature person; there could be no organized group of persons acting as a Government.

That is the theory of individualism, extra-polated (as 'social scientists' say) to its full theoretical development as a hypothesis.

I believe that you accept it, agree with it, as such. If you don't, your objections would interest me greatly.

Now for the tactical view. As somebody said, We confront a situation, not a theory. Nevertheless, in the situation the "theory" exists as fact, just as gravitation does. The problem is, How to act according to the Natural Law, in the conditions *as they are.*

These conditions include the "external enemies," persons "using force on other persons," and—because of these

—no "climate in which a free society (our theoretical hypothesis) can flourish" as of 1958. Therefore, neither Mr. LeFevre nor I would want, now, "an absolute minimum of Federal—or other Government."

As Washington said, "Government is force. Like fire, a good servant and a fearful master." In other words, at present, as persons are and as the situation is, Government (the organized groups of men using physical force on other persons within an area of that group's power) is necessary and useful, *providing that it is strictly confined, restricted, and kept inside firm limits,* as fire must be. If it escapes, it becomes a devouring monster, which in the end destroys itself by destroying what it consumes.

You say that you "believe in strong Government." If there is any disagreement between us, it is simply—it seems to me—a question of the degree of the present Federal Government's strength.

I suppose the desirable strength of Government depends upon, varies with, the given conditions. The weakest Government that ever existed won independence from the British Empire in 1776-82, and established this Republic by 1815, by wars against the strongest government of the time. Evidently there was then no necessity for a stronger Government here.

On the other hand, the stronger the Government of the Roman Empire became, the weaker became the Empire; and under Diocletian's strongest Government, the Empire collapsed. Evidently the necessity there, from Octavian to Diocletian, was weaker Government.

At any time, in all situations, any Government gets its strength from the people outside that Government who live within the area of the governing group's use of force upon persons. A Government has no other source of strength; and it takes by force, that strength from that source. As a Government's available strength increases, the strength available from the source diminishes; and vice versa to a certain extent. I do not know the point of balance desirable; nobody does know, I suppose, because who has studied the problem? But certainly a point exists, at which a Government takes too much, or too little strength from its source of strength, its economic and moral and psychological support. As I read history, Governments have always collapsed as a result of destroying the strength of the people supporting them.

My own anxiety, now, is *for* American Government. What I dread—and unhappily expect—is not military danger from external enemies; it is the collapse of the Federal Government as a result of that Government's destroying us who support it. I am convinced that the only possible way to preserve the existence of the Federal Government is to curtail the powers that it is exercising, to stop its competition with private business enterprises, to restrict its taxing power to its constitutional limits (repeal the sixteenth amendment), to stop its attack on the local powers of the States. In my opinion, nothing else CAN save the present Federal Government; and I doubt that that way will be taken or taken soon enough, to save it.

Of course you know the economic situation as I do not. To me it is a situation of extreme danger for a Government, when that government owes more than all the capital resources of a country could pay, when it takes nearly one-quarter of a people's earnings annually, when its form of taxation increasingly drives the people into deeper debt, discourages earnings and production and trade, and diminishes capital resources, and when its invasion of basic human rights creates increasing resentment and contempt of laws.

Mr. LeFevre and I have engaged in heated, though amiable, controversy, about his attitude to Government. When the students in his Basic course—the one I attended—asked him, what should we *do*? his reply was negative. He said: Do not depend on Government; do not ask Government for favors and subsidies and support. I think that a negative is not enough; I say that if they do not know the right action they are too apt to take a wrong one; I think that the thing to do is to *resist* any further extensions and encroachments and usurpations by the Federal Government, by every peaceful legal means while such means exist for preserving the Federal Government. Because I am convinced that unless these means are used, and successful, the Federal Government must collapse, as inevitably as Bismarck's Germany did in 1932, and there will be chaos and violence here. In my opinion, the women who resisted the extension of the Ponzi fraud to their employees, the farmers who took no money, had no contract, with the Federal Government, and are refusing to pay fines or serve prison terms for growing grain to feed their stock on their own land, and fighting for their rights in the courts, are acting to save us from the terrible catastrophe of the Federal Government's bankruptcy and collapse. Nobody is more concerned for the preservation of the Federal Government than I.

I may add that when Mr. LeFevre was asked directly, Does he favor eliminating Government, he replied emphatically: NO. And in the course of his discussions with the class, he condemned the theory of anarchy much more drastically than I would. I condemn the tactics of anarchists but it seems to me that the absence of Government is the logical theoretical "extrapolation" of the basic American political principle (as I said in the beginning of this letter) and the definition of "anarchy" is no Government. Not that any sane person wishes for a practical realization of anarchy in foreseeable time .

November 4, 1958

Dear Mrs. Lane:

I am delighted to get your letter of October 30, and to learn from it that we are in such excellent agreement. I approve of every word that you say in your letter and am very glad to know that Mr. LeFevre is not unsound in his attitude to government. I agree with your position that we should resist in every way we can the wrongful and unconstitutional actions of the Federal Government.

The extensions of the Federal Government into more and wider unlawful areas proceed almost unchecked. One such abuse came to my knowledge only last week, and I am saddened by it. An educational institution in which I am very much interested and which has hitherto rejected Federal Government aid is now accepting half a million dollars from the Department of Health, Education and Welfare for research in health, but is specifically using the money as part of the amount needed to build a new biological laboratory. When I protested, I was told "this is a grant," but I still more forcibly pointed out how illegal and morally wrong it is for taxpayers' money to be devoted to building a building in a private institution, and finally had to say that I was just putting a small sum in my will for that institution but presumed that they would not want it as they were getting money from the Federal Government. The excuse is that everybody else is accepting it. And so the evil multiplies.

XIV

December 4, 1958

Dear Mr. Crane:

I am so happy—your gift to the Freedom School has made this whole dull gray cold sleety day change completely for me. It is so wonderful that you can help so much; I thought that you would want to, but didn't know how you might be tied by all these legalities that seem to be hindering everything nowadays. I know how glad, too, those girls and Mrs. LeFevre are feeling in their snowbound mountain cabin, did feel when Mr. LeFevre came back from work with the day's Freedom School mail. It isn't the money only, much as that's needed; it is the backing, too—the *support*—the feeling that someone's standing by, is *for* what you're doing, is wanting and helping your work to succeed. When there are so many discouragements, encouragement has such great value.

I'm glad that you had such a good Mont Pelerin meeting, and one at the Foundation for Economic Education, too. Yes, certainly there are many, many more efforts of all kinds being made now. Twenty years ago, do you remember? it was almost impossible to find *one*. I used to spend all my time, every day, at my typewriter following up every least little "lead" that I could find. Example: I heard a high-school "debate" among all pro-New Dealers on the radio, and wrote to each of them. One replied, with all the Welfare State collectivist notions that had been put into his head, but he didn't seem wholly unintelligent, so I kept on writing to him for some months, apparently with no effect, finally getting no answer. Now he turns up as publisher of *National Review*, telling people that I—i.e., my letters—changed his whole life.

Now there are literally thousands of college students in the ISI. I doubt that there was a single individualist in the colleges then. Roger MacBride went through Princeton and Harvard Law School hunting for someone not a socialist, and found only one in his final year in Harvard. Mr. LeFevre was a former business man in the army then; now he had made-over eighty socialists into individualists. The whole "climate of opinion" is changing. And every least little thing that you have done has helped to change it; never think that a bit of it failed, even when it seemed to. Bread cast upon the waters. . . . It returns, most unexpectedly, as publisher of *National Review*, even when you don't happen to see its returning. Your help to the Freedom School and everything else that you have done and are doing will be having effects thousands of years from now, in fact as long as this earth is inhabited by human beings. That isn't rhetoric, you know; it is simple fact.

March 12, 1959

Dear Mrs. Lane:

I had heard Dr. Sennholz speak about a graduate school of economics and have exchanged letters on the subject. We must have such an institution. The analogy I use is that the London School of Economics has been so influential and, unfortunately, heavily on the left. We must have a school in the United States with teachers of eminence in scholarship and sound in doctrine, sufficient to get such an institution underway, provided they could borrow or lease the necessary physical facilities. The problem would be to get honest money rather than funds that might be available to finance subversion.

March 16, 1959

Dear Mr. Crane:

I do so heartily agree with your view that "we MUST HAVE" an American-individualist School for Economics. It is at least a century late, but not too late, I believe.

Your estimate of $2,000,000 seems to me more than is necessary for a beginning. The London School of Economics was a slum-waif in comparison. Some money is essential of course, but where there's a will it doesn't need even butter on its bread. Do you realize that the "will" that put the New Deal into Washington in fifty years' time was financed by *dimes?* The thing of first, last and middle importance is men. We have the two or three needed for the start—Mises, Sennholz, Hayek for instance; and what they want (given enough to eat) isn't more money but an opportunity to do more effective work.

Just barely enough money to provide a slim chance is enough, and I think that more is *too much.* It is very, very easy to spoil a good man with money. It seems to me that persons who never have needed money—have never been broke, hungry, in *need*—cannot understand the pernicious effect that money can have on those who have needed it.

Let them begin *small,* and with not enough money to attract the sycophants and parasite collectivists; then—as the Webbs, et al., did—they can add to the faculty carefully, only *most* carefully selected and tested men, whom they know thoroughly; they will have no money to risk on anyone whom they're not sure is absolutely reliable and useful for their purpose.

I have been reading *Wedemeyer Reports* with intense interest, but so far have been able to only read about half of it. I think it is informed, intelligent, honest, and therefore most valuable history. I have not yet reached the invasion of Europe, and as yet the book merely corroborates a view of events which I suppose everyone interested held at the time. I am eager to read the part about China.

In my own opinion, the British were right in their effort to mark time and engage in only small attacks "on the periphery." That seems to me the proper strategy in this latest phase of the World War, as it was in the Napoleonic wars. The British error was in bringing the USA in; and Churchill understood that in the early 1920s when he raised the yell, "Americans, Go Home!" and added, "And stay there, stay out of Europe." The USA is intrinsically destructive to the whole Old World; the American Revolution has been wrecking the Old World since 1776, and will continue to do so; but would have done so more slowly, with less death and destruction, if Wilson had observed Washington's injunction and stayed out of "entangling alliances" instead of going headlong into them and starting this World War.

But Lord Grey lured Wilson in; and then Churchill let Roosevelt in (though it's a question whether anyone could have kept him out) and then tried to minimize the effect. From a strictly military standpoint—the object militarily being merely "Win the war"—General Wedemeyer doubtless was right in demanding frontal attack on "the Heartland." But from the political viewpiont, Churchill's effort to delay decisive action until Germans and Russians had worn each other out and Hitler's armies had been wrecked by logistics as Napoleon's were, and then to strike the decisive blow, as at Waterloo, seems to me sounder. After the USA came in, however, the headlong smashing destruction could not be prevented, nor the yielding to the Communists. I think this is a most valuable book and thank you for sending it to me.

April 8, 1959

Dear Mrs. Lane:

Your letter of March 16 is received and has been carefully read, as all of your letters are, but this one with special care. I agree with your thought that a graduate school of economics should start small. Two million dollars would provide an income of seventy thousand dollars a year and that really isn't very much with the present value of the dollar for doing a job of any reasonable effectiveness.

April 20, 1959

Dear Mr. Crane:

The value of money (to anyone) seems to be will-of-the-wispy—even more than most values. I remember how bewildering it was when I was traveling rapidly all over Europe early in the Armistice; once I very nearly paid $100 for a cute little cigarette lighter which, in the window, struck me as a most marvelous bargain. It was in Paris (franc 19 to $1) and I'd just arrived from Vienna (mark something like 20,000 or so). The figure, 1,900 looked to me like about a nickel. So, to you and to me a million dollars isn't at all the same thing. —Though I am surprised by your implication that a tax-exempt outfit's investment pay only three and one-half percent. I didn't know that.

Besides, as you know, I am a—maybe fanatic—believer in the uses of adversity. I do know about that; I've had such lots of adversity, as well as closely observing its values to others. I think, for illustration of my view, that the great harm that the New Deal did was the Federal intervention between the "depression" and its normally beneficial effects upon persons here. Even if all the Keynesian fallacies had been true—so that no injury would have been done to the political structure or to the "national economy"—still depriving persons of "fear of want" would have done them monstrous injury. Fear of want is wonderfully stimulating to anyone, really it is more useful than love in making "the world go round." Nearly—not all, but almost all—the good in our lives has come from fear of want. Persons who have never feared want, never come to grips with it, just don't know how valuable it is.

I remember once Mrs. Graeme Lorimer—Sara—and I were lunching; it was soon after Mr. Lorimer's death and his sons of course had inherited lots of money, and she was saying that it worried her because their children—Graeme's and hers—would always be so very rich; so much money is insulating in a way, and how can you overcome that effect by an artifical simplicity? bringing up the children *as if* they were poor, skimping their allowances, and so on—you can't keep them from knowing it's all a pretense; how can you teach them that money isn't important when even saying so gives it importance?—It is a problem and I was sincerely sympathetic. I said, Yes, but there are difficulties in every situation; living isn't easy in any circumstances; it is hard to be rich, but after all, remember that there are hardships in being very poor, too, and—I was going on to be consoling and encouraging, with all my heart and all the experience of my twice-her-age when our eyes met; and there was pure shock in hers. She had not meant a word she said; and when I took it all as simple fact, she realized that she hadn't meant it. The fact was that she didn't know what she was talking about; she couldn't; she never had known and feared want, she didn't know what she missed and lacked, and what her children would.

Now I think there is a lot of wisdom in the story of—Gideon, wasn't it? in the Old Testament. When with a few troops he was facing a force of many thousands, really overpowering odds, and Jehovah told him to send home every one of the faint-hearted; and when this left him with a small remnant by rejecting all those who did not pronounce the word shibboleth, with *absolute accuracy.* Then with the VERY few remaining, Gideon attacked and routed the scores of thousands. This, you remember, was Lenin's policy, ruthlessly enforced by Lenin on the few dozens of exiles that were the Bolsheviks of 1917. It was also the policy of the Christian Church during the first three centuries A.D. (Lenin copied it from the Church.) So far as I know history, it is the policy that always wins against the apparently unconquerable opposition. When a remnant faces a multitude, what the remnant needs is fewer numbers and greater desperation. They need to lose all the fainthearted and all the shillyshallying, and all who don't know the shibboleth *precisely*: they need to have want and fear it, and they'll win.

April 29, 1959

Dear Mrs. Lane:

Your letter of April 20 is received, and I am perplexed by a bit of it, coming as it does from one whom I looked upon as the "fount of wisdom"; particularly of the Bible. But you goofed badly; recorded in the book of Judges, Gideon on orders from the Lord reduced his forces from 10,000 to an absolutely dependable group of 300 by talking them up to the water to drink; those who cupped the water to their mouths fearfully looking over their shoulders were rejected; those who bowed down to drink were chosen.

Perhaps one hundred years or so later also in Judges is the story of Jephthah, the leader of the people of Gilead on the East of the Jordan. An army from Ephraim crossed the Jordan and attacked the Gileadites, but were routed. The fords of the Jordan were manned and the fugitives trying to cross the river again were asked to pronounce Shibboleth. Those who said Sibboleth were promptly slain and thrown into the Jordan. An interesting incident! And the word is used to this day to mean a test or watch word.

Here endeth the first lesson!

April 30, 1959

Dear Mr. Crane:

Ouch! I mean, *touché!* —Well, at the time I felt a bit uncertain and remembered something about lapping water like dogs, but in the fervor of composition, I did not pause to verify, mea culpa. My memory isn't what it once was. But my face is much redder.

I must read the Old Testament again. What barbarians they were, weren't they? And what a strange discrepancy between the Commandments—which as rules of human relationships based on the real nature of man haven't been equaled since—and the horrible brutality, but fraud and trickery and treachery among themselves. I think that story of the golden calf—set up behind Moses' back while he was away on Mount Sinai—and the compromise forced upon him which established a priesthood supported by taxes (share of the sacrifices) is symbolic of the beginnings (I mean, the very *first beginnings*—in Ur or thereabouts) of all political governments. I haven't verified this memory, either; O, don't tell me that *this* one is wrong!

May 11, 1959

Dear Mrs. Lane:

I have just heard about and am making a contribution to a project by two friends of mine, who are sending seven or ten trained young people to the International Youth Conference to be held this year in Vienna. This is a Communist activity, directed by the Soviet Government for indoctrination of youth, previous conferences having been held in Prague and Moscow with thousands of youth up to thirty-five years old attending from many countries. Now in Vienna, where the government and people are so widely and strongly anti-communist, the Soviet isn't going to have quite the control of this meeting as before; and these young Americans, well informed about Communism and articulate for freedom, will speak up, obstruct, argue, attempt to get across not only an attack on Communism but an affirmation of liberty. Two of them speak Russian, two of them Chinese, one of them is a Negro, and I am told that all seven so far chosen are dependable fighters. That sort of thing might do some good.

As to the brutality and inhumanity in the Old Testament times, there is no question the Hebrews' great gift to the world was the belief in one God, which was established by the Remnant after the Captivity when Judaism was born. The real heroes are Ezra, Nehemia, the Prophets, and the Psalmists. Our debt to them is immeasurable. And later Islam laid supreme emphasis to this very day on one God.

Yet, to the Jews the most sacred of their literature is the first five books of the Bible. Perhaps the justification for this improper emphasis on past history is the remarkable leadership of Moses. But I agree with you that the whole Old Testament should be read and re-read. But it gets better, not worse, in the later books. If you haven't a copy of the Revised Standard Version, which is so much clearer reading than any other I know, I will send you a volume!

Brutality and inhumanity seem to be so rife today that we may doubt whether there has been much progress in morals since ancient times. The Nazis re-introduced torture, which we all thought had long since been banished. The Russians have been practicing torture, famine, genocide, wholesale slaughter. The Chinese Communists are even worse; more ingenious torture—brain washing and the largest killings in all human history. . . .

We are now getting such an output of good books in the field of freedom: John Chamberlain, *The Roots of Capitalism;* Henry Hazlitt, *The Failure of the New Economics;* Frank Chodorov, *The Rise and Fall of Society;* Palyi, *Managed Money at the Crossroads;* William Henry Chamberlain, *The Evolution of a Conservative;* Jules Backman, *Wage Determination;* Sylvester Petro, *Power Unlimited,* and also *The Labor of the Free Society;* Merrill Root, *Brain Washing in the High Schools;* Leonard E. Read, *Why Not Try Freedom;* J. Edgar Hoover, *Masters of Deceit.* There has never been anything like it since you started the modern literature of freedom in 1942. *Liberty* by Friedrich Hayek and a new book by Felix Morley will be coming out in the Fall. I earnestly wish that your book may soon be completed and be the capstone of the current books on liberty.

The best part of it is that these books are now selling. John Chamberlain has just written me that he is amazed to find that his book and Hazlitt's are exposed for sale in a prominent book store. He says that couldn't have happened several years ago.

July 20, 1959

Dear Mr. Crane:

I'm happy to be able to tell you that my small Maltese has made a wonderful recovery; at thirteen I understand that his age is the human equivalent of ninety-one, so I can't expect to keep him many more years, but now he is as bright and gay as a puppy again. He is going with us to Colorado; he loves driving, I mean being in a car that's being driven. So do I. My English friend, Mrs. Jackson, will drive; after about a million miles (1911 to 1934, in these States and Europe) I stopped driving, definitely, on a sandy road over Tioga Pass, behind a loaded haywagon, when two dogs gaily attacked my front wheels. Never no more, for me. I never so much as scratched a fender, but what driving did to my nerves was always much too much.

I have read with interest the reviews of all the books you mention and would like very much to have them, but I am buying only books that I need for my own book. I have just got a marvelous one, which I know you would find most interesting: *The Forgotten Class* by Valentine T. Bill, a Russian-born woman educated in Germany and now working in I.A.S. at Princeton, with other academic connections here. Book published by Frederick A. Praeger, New York: $5. It's a history of trade and industry in Russia, pre-1900. I always was certain that there must have been a "bourgeoisie" in Czarist Russia; people can't *live* without one. This picture of the Czar's court, up above a flat expanse of serfs, with only idle Nobles in between, just CAN'T be true. But where do you get an inkling of what was true?

This book begins with the Morozov family. And isn't it curious? Morozovs, Fords, Rockefellers, all repeat the same pattern: Hardworking grandfather builds great industry employing thousands; his sons carry on; his grandsons finance destruction of "capitalism" and themselves. Grandson Morozov financed the Bolsheviks; Lenin's support (financially) was Morozov's contributions and Stalin's bankrobberies. But I am not doing justice to this book. I find every page fascinating, stimulating, new and undoubtedly authentic history. I can use it when I write the Reaction part of my book and come to the Third International. Have you an explanation of the third-generation reaction? It is from economic freedom, individualism, to slavery again, collectivism.

XV

Dear Mr. Crane:

Do you remember this in your old *Freeman?* See how it's still on its way, after all these years—piercing the self-made potentates with ridicule, that deadly weapon—

Ode To A Harvard Don
The Vital Center's Vital Center
by MORRIE RYSKIND

I give you Arthur Schlesinger;
Jehovah's Little Messenger!
(I trust the g is soft in Schlesy—
Or else the triple rhyme is messy.
Yet if the g be hard—as Harding—
It shall not stop this bard from barding;
Bless Harvard and keep blessing her,
She gave us Arthur Schlesinger!)

I speak, of course, of Arthur, Jr.
The Vital Center's Pet Petuniar;
The Darling of the Ada'ers,
The soothingest of all soothsayers.
If Yalta rankles, he with deft ease
Explains it to the Liberal Lefties
So well that, in their Ivory Tower
It's known as Franklin's Finest Hour.

Though some, misled by Fascist plots, damn
Yalta, Teheran and Potsdam,
By no such bug can I be bitten,
For I have read what Arthur's written;
I know the source: McCarthyism,
Intended to create a schism.
So I am deaf when Tory sots damn
Yalta, Teheran and Potsdam.

From Mounts Olympus and Parnassus
Art views (through Roosevelt-colored glasses)
The antics of the lower classes,
And passes judgment for the masses.

Objective, crystal-clear, impartial,
He hands the laurel wreath to Marshall
And gives his enemies the bird
(MacArthur is a dirty word).

I thought MacArthur patriotic,
But now I know that was psychotic;
Thought Wedemeyer knew the score—
But now I swear by Lattimore.
The very thought of John S. Service
Would start my stomach acting nervous—
But Junior's cleared up my confusions
And washed my brain of these delusions.

MacArthur right about Korea?
Says Junior, "Perish the idear!"
And proves, by Harvard's lucid lore,
MacArthur could have brought us WAR.
How better far the lovely truce
Since Truman cut MacArthur loose!
Men might be dying in the east now!
How nice that all the fighting's ceased now![5]

Are you depressed by moral ills?
Use Arthur's Little Live pills!
Must you arise, perforce, at night?
Let Little Arthur set you right!
Do you have spots before your eyes?
Let Little Arthur put you wise.
Does Jessup keep you from your slumber?
Call Arthur at his Cambridge number.

Let Schlesinger appease your
Misgivings on the Truman seizure;
Let him point out instead the barren
And empty workings of McCarran.
Let Arthur S. shampoo your brain
And you'll be innocent again
And ready for the Vital Center
Where no Republican may enter.

Though some detect a leftist odor,
He is a Middle-of-the-Roader;

---

[5]Written in mid-1952 while the Korean fighting continued.

Yes, there he stands, right in the middle,
Between Hank Wallace and Frank Biddle!
SO
I give you Arthur Schlesinger,
Jehovah's Little Messenger!
OR
Bless Harvard and keep blessing her!
She gave us Arthur Schlesinger!

September 23, 1959

Dear Mrs. Lane:

The international situation becomes clearer in that Russia's plan of world conquest, which has been their aim for two hundred years, now seems to be accelerating. Krushchev comes over in person to tell us what he wants us to do, and so many Americans believe that he can be appeased, a policy which has always brought on war throughout history.

I am glad to tell you that the Mont Pelerin Society meeting at Oxford this year seems to have been the best yet. The only discordant note was from Henry Luce. John Davenport has been getting sounder in the faith and has been a very active member of the Mont Pelerin Society; so when Luce needled him about the impractical ultra right-wing position of the Mont Pelerin Society members, John Davenport wisely invited his boss to speak. Thereupon, Luce seems to have been mildly critical, and he was promptly and effectively rebutted by Hayek and several others.

October 26, 1959

Dear Mr. Crane:

Russia's old imperialism, plus the Comintern, doesn't worry me. It doesn't worry Americans, either—excepting the little idiot groups of "serious thinkers" and their fringes. Just as common folks know there's nothing in all their hullaballoo but politics and taxes. And this attitude is it NOT "apathy"; it is a kind of subconscious common sense. My own view is that there is no *possibility* of major war—(if this isn't your view, I'll explain mine in detail if you like). Moscow (I add) has bitten off more than it can chew;

China can't take the rest of Asia—or if local Communists surrender their countries, the Chinese can't handle them. The USA is sitting pretty, internationally. Maybe the Federal Government is going to commit suicide and throw the States into chaos—certainly a *possibility* here—and maybe not. Either way the States will pull through.

And I don't believe for a minute these scare stories about high percentages of young Americans "gone soft." Were they "soft" fighters in Korea? It's Washington that's rotten. And Washington was sound fifty years ago. It takes more than a century for a rotten Government to destroy a country—just think of France; Frenchmen were not "soft" at Verdun; they didn't crumble till 1940, after "soft" Governments since 1793. It will take another century of FDRs and Marshalls to make Americans worthless, and I think prospects look better than that.

The Freedom School has just received the best of compliments—a quite clever "character assassination" began in Rockford, Illinois, reeking—to the initiated—with Lenin School technic. Started by a Freedom School student, picked up instantly by local labor press and immediately preached by a local minister using that smear book *Apostles of Discord* as his text, and bracketing the Freedom School with FEE and Christian Economics. The businessmen of Milwaukee acted to squelch it, efficiently, and beautifully. I am so delighted; it's wonderful to see real intelligence acting—ACTING—on our side. Don't tell me that this country isn't alive; it sure is. So far as I know, this is the first time that Comintern technic has not only been recognized, but met head-on and quickly and intelligently. And imagine its being done in Milwaukee of all places! Till now, the only political brains I've know in that state were among the Finns, poor wretches always defeated by the La Follettes.

November 3, 1959

Dear Mr. Crane:

Among letters held here while I was away last summer I found one from you. I put this with the letters to be read attentively. Next morning my little dog was killed. It was more than a week before I could recover at all. I don't know what I did with things. Some checks, bills and letters can't be found now, and the only one that can't be replaced is this one from you. I am sorry. *Really* sorry.

Roger MacBride has given me TWO puppies, Maltese, ten weeks old, charming little things and no end of trouble of course. They rip every stocking, they must most carefully NOT be stepped on, and they must be watched constantly as long as they innocently regard floors as what the French call dooble-vay say. One is completely a happy playboy; the other is an intellectual.

I have been rereading your letter of May 11. Thank you for offering me a Revised Standard Version, but I couldn't prefer anything to the King James. Modern phraseology may be—maybe—more precise than the modern King James' day but I never feel that I don't understand that, and I think I do understand it in all important matters. I don't see any more reason to "modernize" the Old Testament than to bring Shakespeare "up to date." Imagine Noel Coward's version of *Hamlet!* And remember H. G. Wells' version of Job. (I don't like tradition, so this is an example of inconsistency.)

What I meant to mention is our reference to brutality; brutes don't deserve the slander. And what I want to say is that I think the atrocities today don't mean that there has been little progress in morals. I think they mean that progress isn't *steadily* forward in Time.

Human atrocities to human beings are inseparable from the collectivist view (held by persons) of the nature of man. In the collective "the individual is nothing!" as members of the Comintern say, and believe now. But in all past history a majority of living persons perhaps have held that same view. Human sacrifice to the gods is intrinsic to all collectivist societies; one sacrificed for the good of the ALL. There are innumerable (well, maybe not; *I* haven't counted them) instances of that in the Old Testament. —Aside, were the Hebrews the first *racists?* I don't know. My impression is that other people in ancient times were tribal or what may be called national (subjects of the same god (or gods) and living god-king) and that instead of being assimilated when defeated and "carried into captivity" the Hebrews became racists.

Now morals are rules of human relationships, rules of human action in relations between living persons on this earth. Most of the Ten Commandments—and the Eleventh—are moral, nearly all of them prohibitions; thou shalt NOTs. The assumption underlying all of them is individualism.

As long as, or to the extent that, persons regard themselves and others as members of a human commune, a Collective Being (of any kind), they do not accept the basic assumption of the Commandments. Lenin and his followers are therefore entirely logical in saying that Judeo-Christian morality has no validity to a dedicated Communist, to whom "morality is an action that serves the Revolution."

Others in Christendom—or what's called The West—are simply human in more-or-less disregarding Commandments (orders) which don't seem to be enforced in "practical" affairs here on earth. After all, they read these orders in the same source of authority where they also read the wicked flourish as the green bay tree. Charles van Doren lied, but he got the $250,000 didn't he? and when I don't lie what do I get? are the semi-conscious observations. So you find, what I'm sure you have encountered often, the attitude: Oh, you are right, I agree with you absolutely, that's the *ideal* thing to do; but now let's get down to cases, we've got to be *practical.* —In other words, God's orders are moral-spiritual, other-world, enforced in eternity no doubt —or perhaps, but here in this earthly practical "real" world any strict obedience to them doesn't "pay." Of course I know that none of that is true at all, but I believe I do understand those confused minds.

Now, if the Commandments are valid—that is, if they mean any more than Jehovah's whims about Balaam and his poor ass—then they rest on "natural law" as solidly as Newton's First Principle does. Thou shalt not bear false witness has the same "practical" validity as Mama's don't go near that edge. If this is so, then a science of morality is as possible as a science of physics. There is no quarrel between a real science and a true religion. After all, it is not a man-made law that whosoever walks off the roof of the Nemours Building will be dashed to death. Mama's order to stay away from that brink rests on "practical" fact, not on her arbitrary preference; and God's commands given to Moses on Mount Sinai, have the same basis, in the field of human relationships, that Mama's has in the field of human relationships with inanimate forces, I think.

The difficulty is that "Because I say so!" doesn't satisfy the child who asks, Why? And when men ask, Why? they often are not convinced by the minister or priest or rabbi who replies, Because I say that God says so! The King Street minister told me the other day that Mark Twain said that God has said only one thing to *him*, which was—as he read in the Bible (and you'll correct my memory of the text, I'm sure) something like: When a man asks thee to go a league with him, go with him, Twain. Too many persons feel that God never said to *me*, Thou shalt not bear false witness. Evidently He didn't say it to Charles van Doren. Too bad for Charlie that the word didn't come from M.I.T. or Cal Tech.

I firmly believe that someday there will be a science of morality, i.e., of cause-and-effect in human actions in relation to other persons, as there is now in the field of human actions in relation to inanimate forms and forces. I think the First Principle of scientific morality is the American Declaration: All men are created equal and endowed . . . etc. (Atoms are endowed by the Creator with electrons, protons, ions, etc. We are endowed by our Creator with *our* functions and powers.)

The historical effects of this discovery have been an astonishing progress in morals, in a really very short time. You say, The Nazis reintroduced torture, which we all thought had long since been banished. Yes, we all thought that; but think again, I needn't tell you that it isn't two centuries since whipping slaves and seamen to death was commonplace, and crowds enjoyed watching men tortured to death in England and France. It was unheard-of-mercifulness to hang witches in Massachusetts instead of burning them.

Progress in morals began—for the first time in history—with the first glimmers of a perception of individualism; and regression to the habitual occurs with the communist reaction against that advance in knowledge. Progress in morals appeared only in "the West" and affected only relationships between persons with some perception of individual liberty. Torture, slavery, massacre, brutality, atrocities of all kinds, continued as before everywhere else on earth. The Chinese method of execution by "slow strangulation" was customary—and enjoyed as a public spectacle—in 1900 (eye witnesses have told me) and right along until now. In one of her books Nora Waln records it in the 1930s. The

Okrana in Russia used torture as the MVD continued to do. When Governor Bradford of Plymouth was a young man in England, dissenters were hanged, cut down alive, disemboweled, dismembered, and their heads displayed on pikes on London Bridge. Why does the Federal Constitution prohibit "cruel and unusual punishment"? because in 1789 such punishments were customary everywhere else.

I know Tex O'Reilly who was a policeman in China in 1910 and became Sun Yat Sen's Chief of Staff in 1911 and later. He was once a guard at an execution. The condemned was put in a cage at a street corner, standing on a pile of tiles, his neck encircled and held firm in a hole in the top of the cage. Every day one tile was removed from the pile under his feet. He lived more than a week. The criminal's wife had a bright idea; she put a large silk hat over the man's head, and charged I forget how much to remove the hat. She collected a considerable amount from the curious crowds. Nora Waln's Philadelphia family—traders with China—had traditional close relations with a Chinese family with whom she lived several years as a girl. During Chiang Kai Shek's revulsion against the Communists with whom he was associated during the 1920s, a son of this Chinese family was in college and had in his possession some Communist literature. This was discovered and he was condemned to death by slow strangulation. Nora Waln and his sister were permitted to see him to say goodbye. He said the sentence was just, he accepted it as merited because he had disobeyed authority; he had done wrong to read evil literature.

If you have read so far, please forgive this length. I mean to say, simply, it's true that "you can't change human *nature,*" but this doesn't mean that progress in morals (as in every way of human action) isn't possible; in fact, moral progress *has occurred,* demonstrating its possibility and the possibility of much greater progress.

November 10, 1959

Dear Mr. Crane:

Your reference to Greece gives me a wholly new idea. It had not struck me forcibly, before, that the Greek achievements were wholly mental and artistic for a reason.

There was the phenomenon of a great outburst of energy—one must grant Plato energy, if not brains—none of it utilized practically, no conclusions tested by demonstrations; therefore such fantasies as Ptolemaic astronomy and communism have perverted human efforts toward civilization for near 2,500 years, and still do.

The reason was slavery; traditional, accepted as normal, even explained by Aristotle as necessary because men do not willingly work, ergo, must be forced to work. A degraded person, a compelled person, a slave, worked; by association of ideas, work was regarded as degrading, despicable; an honorable man, a respected person could not work. All free energy went into mental and artistic action—creating inessential products, ideas and decorations. Ideas untested by demonstration tend to be fallacies, day dreams, systems of theory with no bases in reality. (Even ideas tested by demonstrations are only approximately "true.") The idea of the human commune is, in a way, as charming as the idea of the waters above the earth and the music of the spheres, and quite as unrealistic. I am not an admirer of the work of the ancient Greeks, not even of the Greek art which is nearly perfect form and wholly static, i.e., unnatural, artificial, false. But until now I had not thought of the reason that most of Greek thinking, too, is fallacious. Your letters are always inspiring to me.

Did Hamiliton have much to do with the Constitutional Convention? I know of course his work in the *Federalist Papers* and in practical politiking for the adoption. But my impression is that he went down to Philadelphia only once or twice, stayed briefly, was regarded rather as young and not (then) too weighty, and had very little part in the debates, little, if any, influence on decisions adopted. I forget where I got this impression, can't cite authority for it, of course may be quite wrong. Do you know? I know of course that he was *there,* Jefferson in Paris at the time.

November 17, 1959

Dear Mrs. Lane:

Hamilton was a rather small factor in the Constitutional Convention. That can be shown, I think, by reference to Madison's notes and the proceedings of the Convention.

It was believed that he would have preferred a constitutional monarchy to a Republic, but he was the chief writer of *The Federalist* and did a great service in getting the Constitution adopted.

XVI

March 3, 1960

Dear Mr. Crane:

Thank you for the *Saturday Evening Post* clipping, which I have read with interest. The article is good because it is sort of obliquely true, about the attitude of many young people now. Not that I think that the Affluent Society has anything to do with the case. Do you? Ascribing minds and morals to economic causes is the upside-downness of Marx. The state of an economy is the result, not the cause, of the state of minds and morals. You'd think that anyone a bit more intelligent than a moron would see that obvious fact. In my view, what has happened has been the stultifying of natural intelligence and the debauching of morals by the schools during the past forty years. Plus, so far as the army's concerned, causes are direct effect of socialism; the universal draft from the Jacobins of 1793; "progressive education" deliberately forced on American public schools by —now what's his name? Willi—is it Munsterberg?—the Comintern agent who came here in the early '20s, you know; and cooked up the idea with a few comrades in Columbia University.

And of course the morale of the troops must have been ruined by their treatment—Pearl Harbor—and FDR saying, "Nothing lost but one old battleship"—and Ike charming FDR's daughter and so being promoted over the heads of—how many? a couple of hundred or more, superior officers—and Walter Winchell swanking around New York night clubs in his Admiral's uniform. And graft, graft, graft. I met on a train once a non-com, taking a platoon or whatever it was of soldiers from one camp to another during the war, and he was sick with disgust and despair and figuratively wept on mama's shoulder; told me how he had tried to stop vast waste and been demoted for the effort. We all know scores of such stories, facts that we saw ourselves; and if they hadn't ruined morale I'd think less of the men than I do. They learned to despise politicians and top brass and to have no feeling but "Lemme

OUTA this," at least most of them did, and that's morally healthier than the cynicism that centuries of similar experience have taught Europeans.

As to the Communist 'brain-washing,' the surprise is that it was needed; if it was. The USA and Russia were democracies, weren't they? and allies against the monstrous Nazis; and Stalin was good old Joe and papers were full of pictures of Churchill and FDR and Stalin so happy together and Molotov and Krushchev are honored guests in the White House, and Ike is going to Moscow where Nixon has been; why shouldn't any American hobnob with any Communist? You just can't keep run-of-the-mill people from being logical.

March 14, 1960

Dear Mrs. Lane:

An interesting book that I am now reading is the *Freudian Ethic* by Richard La Piere. He calls the "Protestant Ethic" (though not confining it to Protestants) the great movement toward freedom, increased energy, advancing standards of living, and higher spiritual and cultural values, which was notably underway in the sixteen century, gained momentum in Western Europe and blossomed in America. This has long been my own belief; and mentioning it one day to Mr. Milione, a Roman Catholic, I was interested to hear him say that that was undeniably true. The present reaction, La Piere writes, is the Freudian ethic, agnostic and materialistic. He discusses the permissive home, "progressive education," the craving for security, etc. Perhaps his ideas may be useful for your book. If you would like a copy of it, I will send it to you.

March 15, 1960

Dear Mr. Crane:

I am sorry that you feel troubled by a possibility of a major war. Nobody knows and only time will tell, of course. But I, too, think that poverty will continue under the Communist regimes, and be a deterrent to war; and that uprisings will be a deterrent, too; experience has shown too plainly that the people only want a chance to turn against the regimes, or to get out and turn against them, and that war is their chance to do it. The cleverness of the Comintern is often over-rated, but its bosses are not utter fools. It's an old practice of men in Governments to make wars to distract their subjects from domestic grievances, but that works only when the subjects are such convinced collectivists that they will act "as a whole" against any alien "Whole." Russians are a small minority in the U.S.S.R. Krushchev, or his successors, know very well that there's no solidarity whatever to be relied on. Tartars, Armenians, Turkomans, Daghastani, Hungarians, Poles, etc., etc. (there were forty-seven distinct and antagonistic "peoples" or "clans" or "nationalities," with different languages, customs, religions, in Tiflis alone when I was there) may be Communists, but they don't adhere to each other, nor to Russians. They all hate or at least vigorously dislike each other. I think it takes all the energy that the Kremlin has, just to keep the whole empire from breaking to bits. What would the people in captive Germany do, if the Red army broke through the barbed wire to attack West Germany?

China is another proposition. I've no notion what's going on there. I think there's a possibility of a clash in Mongolia, where Chinese and Russian interests—Government expansions—certainly collide. If Communist ideology, and organization are strong enough now to hold Peking and Moscow together, I doubt if they'll continue to be indefinitely. Or, IF, just for once, "The West" would have sense enough to sit tight and let the gangsters eliminate each other. No more Wilsons, no more Churchills, no more Roosevelts. . . .

I ran across a fascinating bit about the Greek discovery of petroleum when Alexander invaded Asia. As an experiment, Alexander drenched a slave in the baths with the "naptha" which attracted fire if placed near fire, and put a torch to him. The slave immediately blazed up and his life was saved only by the interested bystanders who deluged him with vast quantities of water. I thought this an interesting bit for my book but only if contrasted with the discovery that was developed into the present uses of crude oil; and I can't find any data at all about that. Do you perhaps happen to know, or to know where I can find information as to who discovered, when, where, the nature or possible uses of crude oil, more recently? so that the discovery was developed to kerosene, gasoline, etc.

I think the *Encyclopedia Britannica* is the most pretentious useless set of books ever printed. It doesn't answer a single question that I want answered. Have you noticed its blithering about taxes? I have the origin of taxes in my notes—Tenny Frank or Toutain, I forget. Do you know that taxes historically originated in the idea of God's omnipotence—"The whole world is in His hands," as the Negro spiritual says—when ancient Chaldean and Egyptions believed that their living ruler was God? when they believed that Ur-Nammu, or Pharoah, or Ptolemy, was God Who owned all things and creatures, including persons, in His realm? So that when anyone used His land, or used his own strength in working, the farmer or worker naturally must, should, pay Him for the privilege. The extent and intensity of taxation in ancient Egypt is amazing. The Greeks got the idea from Asia, Rome got it from the Greeks, Europeans from Rome, and you and I from Europe. When you think about it, *Why* should you and I support—how many now?—millions of persons meddling with us in ways that we don't want to be meddled with? It's just a traditional custom that few have ever thought about at all.

Of course, I agree wholly with your remark that we must always vigilantly defend this country. And, that all these atom bombs, etc., are most useful in that way. I only wish Mr. Eisenhower would not often shout from the housetops that war is unthinkable. *I* can think of it, and if he didn't during the 1940s, he sure should have.

I should like very much indeed to have a copy of *The Freudian Ethic.* The author seems to express my own idea of Freud, and probably very nearly my view of the Protestant movement, or 'ethic.' And his material is no doubt more than I have, and will be valuable to me. I am not so completely persuaded that this country owes so much to Europe. It seems to me that the Reformation was reaction against the Church, which was all to the good in wrecking feudalism, but that much of Protestantism (if there is such a word) was reaction against the Judaic element of individualism in the Roman Catholic Creed, rather than against the collectivist element. The Catholic paradox: Man is free and not free, which Catholics resolve by believing that truth transcends human reason, was bound eventually to be just too much strain on the human rational faculty. When Thomas Aquinas admitted the value of reason at all, he made the Reformation inevitable. But think how many Protestants adopted the idea of predestination. How many Protestant sects kept the Catholic concept of the Church as a collective, the "mystic body of Christ." How Europeans continued to believe, with increased emphasis even, the ancient belief in the semi-divinity of The King. What was the attitude of the Capets? L'Etat, c'est moi. And of George the Third? And even now, of English people to their consecrated Queen?

An element of individualism is certainly traceable from the Ten Commandments to the Declaration of Independence, through the Dark and Middle Ages and the sixteenth, seventeenth centuries to the eighteenth and Virginia and Massachusetts. But it seems to me that the Revolution *began* here, and that its elements were Judeo-Christian, English common law, and most of all, human *experience* here. Throw a baby into water and he swims (it's said; I never did it). Throw a man into conditions where he relies upon himself or dies, and he learns self-reliance; he discovers that he controls his own actions and endures their results, that is, he is *responsible* for those results. You can't teach anyone to swim by telling him how, and I doubt that any amount of telling will teach a person that he is endowed by his Creator with liberty. Perhaps I react too strongly against this prevalent belief that Europe is this country's mama, to which the youngster owes all its heredity and upbringing—not to mention gratitude and support and defense. And hope of being as cultured, someday when we grow up.

I should send you a trained parrot to sit on your desk and repeat frequently, Thank you, Mr. Crane. I am truly indebted to you for so much more than I can ever repay.

I read with much interest Dr. Haacke's article and think it very good. But I don't agree with him about Carthage; my sympathies are with Carthage and I think he reverses the real positions of Carthage and Rome. Both were barbarians of course, but Carthaginians were useful traders and Romans were barbarian warriors, even forbidden by law to trade. They wrecked and looted the world, and then—after only a century's breathing spell, when their hapless subjects did recover and prosper a little—they governed it to death? Did you ever read Diocletian's economic plan? I think not; it would curl your hair into tight ringlets.

March 30, 1960

Dear Mrs. Lane:

My understanding of the Protestant Reformation differs considerably in certain details from your own. I agree about the teaching of Thomas Aquinas, and it is very interesting and important the way so many thinking Roman Catholics look to him for his teaching and philosophy. They call themselves Thomists. We all can gain so much from reading him. Predestination doesn't bother me at all if it is rightly understood. The way it was preached one hundred years ago was simply damnable but when the doctrine is accepted as illustrating the infinite wisdom of God, I can see no difficulty about it. And I believe in Christians being the body of Christ, to a very large extent from what I have learned from you. As you have stressed, we live in space and time, probably both illusions of mortal man. At any rate, we earthbound creatures can have little comprehension of infinity, eternity, reality.

March 31, 1960

Dear Mr. Crane:

Thank you for your letter of yesterday which—astonishly—came this morning.

I agree of course with your interpretation of predestination and "body of Christ." But do theologians? I don't know. I was thinking of the historical—as you say, 'hundred years ago'—usages of the words. And not that long ago, either. Only a few months ago I was reading a new book by a Catholic writer who explained that the church is the "mystic body of Christ" and, for good measure, that persons afflicted (as I am) with "invincible ignorance" are "members of the mystic body of Satan on earth." As I read this kind of thing, it's pure collectivism—this concept of a Mystic Being, a Whole in which living persons are component "members." And I think that it was this collectivist concept of the nature of man that anti-clericals took from the Church and—discarding God, as Marxists fancy they do, or setting Him respectfully aside, as Hegel or Burke does—attached to The Nation, or Humanity. Burke certainly treats "the Commonwealth" as a mystic Entity, a supernatural, super-individual Whole, a human Collective.

Something of this antique superstition, or myth, sort of haunts all our thinking, I believe. During those Princeton meetings, Felix Morley and I had an amiable little spat by correspondence; I saying that an institution—such as a college, or Du Pont—is a pattern of action which living persons follow, as a dance is, and that the institution ceases to exist when living persons cease to act in that way. Felix contended that an institution is a mystic thing, existing per se, and that the whole is more than the sum of its parts." Almost indignantly he asked me to think of Oxford; could anybody say that a great University is nothing but the people in it? Preposterous notion. That was, of course, precisely what I was saying.

I guess I am meek. Felix's view is Plato's Idealism, of course. And I am just struck speechless (Ha! fat chance) —I'd better say, I am struck by the, to me, stupendous arrogance of such claims to know, understand, and explain the Universe—the nature, purpose and actions of God. God creates Oxford? as a mystic, superhuman Being? and Emerson's Over-Soul of the souls of students, tutors, teachers, janitors, etc., who are co-operating in the institution named Oxford? Maybe. I can't say that God doesn't and in my opinion nobody can say that God does. I think only God knows.

But I can, and do, say that *so far as a living person can know,* any human institution is the actions of co-operating persons, and it follows that those persons are constantly creating and maintaining in existence that institution by their actions, and being the only controllers of their actions, they are responsible for the existence and nature of that institution. If the pattern of their actions exists on a supernatural plane, they have no means of knowing that it does. When they stop acting in that way, the institution—so far as they can know—ceases to exist. If the last surviving Catholic died, or became a heretic, there would be no Catholic Church on this planet. Just as there is no stagecoach line on the Boston Post Road now. If the Church or the stage-coach company exists externally as Plato's Idea or as Burke's or Bishop Sheen's Mystic Body, it exists in a way which I have no means of apprehending at all.

Do you ever read science fiction? I am addicted to a few science fiction writers: Ray Bradbury is one. (Though the experts in the field rather snoot him, as more writer then scientist.) I was struck the other day by a sentence in his *Martian Chronicles*: Science is no more than an investigation of a miracle we can never explain.

A person with my point of view is always encountering an assumption that it's the view that Science is God—the French philosophes' nonsense. It's really the view that man is not God.

This reminds me that you once wrote me your repudiation of a contention that man is perfectible. (Another idea I'm sometimes accused of.) And I have been meaning to write you that I don't know what that means. Is anything —can anything—be perfect? By what measurements? It seems to me that anyone who says that anything is perfectible must be hazy-minded and use words at random. And so must anyone who says that man is "good." Good by what standard?

I think that we are *what* we are, and don't know much about what we are. I think that we are created for a purpose and don't know what the purpose is, but that we are endowed with means of learning what the nature of man *is,* and that we serve the purpose of our existence by acting according to our real nature.

I think that the American declarations of the nature of man are a beginning of learning what it is. And that when, and so far as, living persons act according to those declarations (act as creatures endowed by our Creator with life, liberty, ownership, "among" other functions such as reason and characteristics such as human brotherhood) their lives and the results of their actions are more desirable (to them and other persons) than when they act otherwise.

In this sense, I am convinced that people become "better," that is, less cruel, more cooperative, more sympathetic to each other, more peaceful, more productive of such values as charity, knowledge, art, cleanliness, health, happiness. This process I'd call "progress"—progress *toward* perfection, if you want to ask Progress toward what? And if you ask, Perfection of what? I suppose the answer is: Human nature.

It follows that I don't think Hitler or Lenin or Stalin "evil." I think they acted according to false concepts of reality, which is what everyone, more or less, does. Only they did it more. How could Torquemada call Hitler black? both of them meant well, both of them intended to "do good," one by cleansing Humanity of Heretics, the other, ditto, ditto, Jews. Their views of reality were not yours nor mine, their methods were far different, but how does their motive differ from our motive of eliminating collectivist thinkers?

Which is why I think that actions are more important than motives. Human motives don't differ much. Everyone *means* well. It is our actions that produce effects in the human world. And because we act according to our concepts of the nature of things, it is our knowledge—the truth, the accuracy, of our concepts—that matters.

May 5, 1960

Dear Mr. Crane:

The Freudian Ethic expresses perfectly what I have been inadequately saying about Freud ever since I came briefly back from Europe in the early 1920s and found all my friends and acquaintances gone mad in Freudianism. These crazes that constantly—successively—overcome the intellectuals are fantastic. It's obvious that Freud's notions are nonsense.

I haven't said this before—because the reaction would be "You anti-Semetic fascist!" another bit of nonsense—but I think that Freud's theories are a product of the Jewish ghettos, of eastern Russia and Europe. They express an emotional reaction to the situation of Freud and his patients—a minority really in a dangerous and therefore rationally frightening, distressing world, and uncertainly trying to "adjust" to it, uncertain whether to face it or try to escape it. A human reaction; anyone's reaction who wakes in the night to know that an armed burglar is downstairs. Freud's error was his believing that the Jewish Ghetto was the normal human world.

A correspondent sent me recently a report of a lecture

by a psychiatrist, a Dr. Rogers, noted for his new "approach to emotional problems known as client-centered therapy." The heart of his doctrine is a search for ways to create an atmosphere of *safety,* warmth and *acceptance,* in which the client gradually loses *his fear of becoming openly* and honestly *himself.* This process, says Dr. Rogers, "is a fearful and shattering experience. It lasts through a lifetime, it is never complete." Isn't this a picture of the terror and misery of outcasts in a minority among a hostile majority—not necessarily Jews but anyone in that situation? Of course that has been the situation of Jews in Europe for almost two thousand years, and in old Vienna Freud and all his patients were Jews, not safe, not accepted, and naturally in fear of being openly themselves but unable to be anything else.

It is purely wonderful that now such a book as *The Freudian Ethic* is written and published with the authority of La Piere. Surely the times are changing in the Groves of Academe. I treasure this book; I am most grateful to you for your gift of it, and for your introducing me to its author. I have my second-hand book dealer, Mr. Pesky of Schulte's Book Store, watching for his other books for me. I do wish that sometime I can do something to say Thank You, more tangibly than these repeated words.

May 11, 1960

Dear Mr. Crane:

I am glad to have Hayek's *The Constitution of Liberty,* an interesting book, an addition to my library; but it does confirm a tentative view of Professor Hayek which I have held ever since his *Road To Serfdom.* Together with the *New York Times Book Review* of Ropke's *A Humane Economy*—with quotations—it convinces me that the only European individualist is Jean Pierre Hamilius, Jr.

There's something pathetic, as well as infuriating, in Hayek's bumbling around about freedom or liberty, or whatever—as best he can make out—it is. HOW can he be a collectivist without *knowing* it? Granted that he spends pages—probably hours and days—arguing that reason has little to do with human affairs (a view I think nonsense), still what does he suppose he is writing this book *with?* The man is a professional thinker; he makes his living thinking; if he can't or doesn't think, what's his excuse for living?

Take this bit, page seventy-four: "If we say that a person is responsible for the consequences of an action, *this is not a statement of fact* or an assertion about causation. . . . Rather, the statement that a person is responsible for what he does aims at making his actions different from what they would be if he did not believe it to be true. We assign responsibility to a man, not in order to say that as he was he might have acted differently, but in order *to make him different*." My italics.

Now, obviously, Professor Hayek would not write: "When I say that you are responsible for your action, *I* am lying for the purpose of deceiving you in order to make you what *I* think you should be."

When he writes "we" he means the "society" whose "forces"—as he says elsewhere—are the irrational traditions, prescriptions, habits, etc., that are products of "experience, not reason" and that control human actions and affairs for the most part. And by "we" and "society" he means (vaguely, without *thinking* it) a mystic human collective somehow "more than the sum of its parts," a human organic Whole which assigns responsibility to each of its parts in order to harmonize them in the Whole—in social order. Plato did a better job when he wrote this book 2,500-odd years ago. Europeans simply cannot get away from Plato. Hayek includes even the Platonic immorality—the lie, a privilege reserved to "we" the State, which has the right to lie for the public good. "We" do not state a fact when "we" say that a person is responsible; "we" say it to make him believe it and therefore act as he would not act if he did not believe it.

Does Professor Hayek advocate lying? Yes. But I doubt that he knows it.

And Roepke. Years ago Leonard Read sent me a book of his, in French, for my opinion of it. I read about half of it and reported that it was implicitly collectivist, and nonsense. Now Regnery publishes his latest, *A Humane Economy*; I haven't seen it but read the *New York Times Book Review* of it, Sunday, which contained direct quotations. According to these, the Jacobinism of the French Revolution, giving "equal access of all men to law and property" always endangers liberty and leads inevitably to Communist or Keynesian national planning, with a decline of individual responsibility and an enormously expanding "mass society." The clamor "for the rights of this mass society" comes from the United States and has spread to Europe, Asia, Africa, and Latin America and the insatiable demands of the "mass men" for consumer goods destroy social order and stability, and taste, because mass taste is always vulgar. And apparently even vulgar mass-man does not profit from this spreading clamor for the rights of his mass-society, for there is another quotation in the review: "If everybody has the same chances of advancement, those left behind will lose the face-saving and acceptable excuse of social injustice and lowly birth." —What an admirable defense and justification for The Elite. For legal and enforced social inequality, a class society, the organic collective national Whole, stable, orderly, and with the best taste. It would be funny, if not so appalling.

May 19, 1960

Dear Mrs. Lane:

Your letter of May 11 is received, and I agree with you about the defects in the books you discuss. Yet, Hayek's writings have had a most useful and desirable impact on the thinking of scholars. Roepke, too, was so influential with his advice on Erhard and especially on Mueller-Armack in turning Germany forward on the path to freedom.

May 23, 1960

Dear Mr. Crane:

Thank you for your letter of the 19th. The question of the value of such writers as Hayek and Roepke is one of those that I never quite decide—I mean, of course, the strategic or tactical value. Lenin who was (I think) a truly great tactician, demanded *absolute* "correctness" of every associate, as Marx did too, of course; an "almost right" ally, he said, is more dangerous than an open enemy. That position is logical, because in a crisis of action the not-quite-with-you ally turns out to be the Achilles heel, or Trojan horse, or Fifth column; he compromises, appeases, betrays you. And Lenin's *policy* won, in practice, against what seemed to be insuperable opposition. (Though, in the crisis of action, he did abandon it for alliance with Trotsky, a Menshevik.)

On the other hand, the Fabians, with their "inevitability of gradualness," appeased and compromised the whole way through, and *their* policy won . . . well, did it? Enough, at least, to destroy the British Empire and the "class" that they aimed to destroy. The British Labour Party, when Fabian-controlled, was (Lenin said) "The Second-and-a-half International." But it does seem more than doubtful that the Third—or, the Bolsheviki in England—*could* have seized the islands as the Bolsheviki seized Leningrad (St. Petersburg, I mean) and Moscow.

I don't know. I have opinions but no firm decisions about strategic and tactical problems. But Hayek and Roepke and many, many more, seem to me to be neo-Adam Smiths. *The Wealth of Nations* certainly is a great book, of great influence in history; only its little error of Marxian theory of value proved to be the basis of Marxian theory and Lenin's conquests. Would we today be better off, or worse, if Adam Smith had never written it? I don't know; do you? I can't even guess.

What it comes down to, I suppose, is that anyone must do his best, and that is all anyone can do.

June 1, 1960

Dear Mrs. Lane:

It is good to know that Hamilius is making such good progress, as is indicated by the enclosed newspaper clipping and other news about him. The other day Von Mises suggested he might be a good man for secretary of the Mont Pelerin Society, indicating the high regard he has for him.

June 3, 1960

Dear Mr. Crane:

Thank you for your note and clipping about Jean Pierre. He is certainly whole-hearted and doing wonderful work, especially considering the small opportunities of which he makes so much. I suppose he did not tell you—and I do rely upon your discretion and silence—that he is in serious difficulty with a knife-in-the-back communist who may get him thrown out of this University that was his own idea. Of course nobody would believe that the man is a Comintern agent, so it is impossible to say that he is; I was able to verify the suspicion for Jean Pierre. It is at least a compliment to Jean Pierre's value, as the "McCarthyism" furore was to McCarthy. I can only hope, not as fatal. I wonder if Professor Mises knows the situation.

June 10, 1960

Dear Mrs. Lane:

I am not surprised at what you write in your letter of June 3, because in all countries anti-communists are subjected to smears and other attacks. I have written down a list of quite a few men who have been driven out of public life by such campaigns. The communists are well financed, always active in various situations, and venomous in their attacks—although the real perpetrators in such attacks are almost always well concealed. We must do everything that we can to protect our young friend and advance his interests.

XVII

August 23, 1960

Dear Mr. Crane:

You are SUCH a darling, and I am grateful, and so pleased. I did feel quite sure that you would send Jean Pierre the books he wanted, but all these others that you have added will be an overwhelming delight to him, redoubled because he will eagerly read them himself and know, too, that his efforts are spreading their influence in Europe, Asia and Africa. Your letter, and then the arrival of the books, will be GREAT DAYS for him and Adrienne and even the little girls. And the librarian whom Jean Pierre has so laboriously contrived to get into the key position to promote their reading by the foreign students.—An ironic little incident, trivial because Jean Pierre is on guard and acted quickly: A visiting American Professor, whom Jean Pierre considers "very naive" and doesn't name, urged that the Communist agent (on the brink of being pushed out of the faculty) be given the charge of this University library! After swatting this notion down, J. P. regards it as comic. Thank heaven for laughter; where would we be without it?

Hans and Mary Sennholz were here for dinner last Saturday; they MUST leave at 8:00 p.m. but did go at 2:00 A.M., though urged to spend the weekend—they had a Sunday morning appointment elsewhere. They are certainly a wonderful couple; a more-than-equivalent of the Sidney-and-Beatrice-Webb force on "our" side. They have all or more than the Webb energy, the same concentrated purpose, and certainly much more intelligence and the honesty that the Webbs weren't so firm about sometimes. It is amazing, what Hans has done. Arriving here nearly penniless, getting his Ph.D., publishing a good book, then having an $8,000-a-year job, translating that mighty tome, Boehm-Bawerk or something like that (I have not been able to read it, and forget the spelling) while contributing articles to all "our" publications, buying and with his own hands remodeling, painting, tiling, etc., two houses, saving thirty percent of all gross income, investing in two apartment houses whose rentals are paying for them, planning the new post-graduate university, getting it chartered, applying for its tax-exemption, while turning out trained young individualists to teach in other teaching jobs—two are placed this year, he told me, and he anticipated four next year; and they are well instructed to repeat the process. Hans sees no reason why American universities should not be thoroughly permeated with individualist professors within the next twenty years or so. . . . Of course Mary works right along with him editing, typing, filing, etc., as well as housekeeping and mothering; and he always says "we"—which is rather more than I'd expect from the indubitable German master of family and household.

I doubt that *anything* can stop them—while they have life and health. The idea of a naive young German prisoner-of-war in a concentration camp in Louisiana in the 1940s being, twenty years later, Hans Sennholz, Ph.D., individualist, capitalist, American citizen, author, and subverter of the whole trend of American academic thinking. I honestly believe that that is what he is. Of course hundreds of others are working along the same lines now. . . .

It is things like this that support my optimism. They aren't in the papers, on the radio, in political conventions or party platforms, or the UN or Washington, London, Paris, the Congo, or Indonesia. But they are the things that make history. As the books you sent Jean Pierre will be doing.

September 2, 1960

Dear Mrs. Lane:

I wouldn't call the visiting Professor naive, as Professor Hamilius has done, for this practice of putting communists in charge of libraries, or in other important contacts, is a frequent communist technique. Sometimes the perpetrator may be guileless, but normally the instigation is communist. In the Hoover Tower—the Library of War and Peace—at Stanford University, an institution that is very valuable in the struggle for freedom, the curator was a left winger. Mr. Hoover told me two years ago of the trouble that he was in, having discovered this; he got him out and the successor proved to be a left winger also. So recently, he has told me that he has got the second fellow out, and the Trustees of Leland-Stanford have conferred on Mr. Hoover the authority to pick a sound man to run the library. We had an instance right near here of a communist librarian in the Plymouth meeting (Friends); when they wanted to fire her, pinkos from all over the country rushed to her defense. The Soviet strategists know the importance of literature.

You mention the "mighty tome" translated by Hans Sennholz. Eugen von Boehm-Bawerk, 1851-1914, was one of the pillars of sound economics and a most effective enemy of socialism, one of the most important economists of the Viennese School. His *Capital and Interest,* translated by Hans Sennholz and partly by Huncke, also, the English translation being only copyrighted last year, is one of the great works of economics. I have it, but I am not going to read it, so perhaps you ought to! Three volumes!

Still on the subject of literature, have you now read John Chamberlain's *The Roots of Capitalism?* It is a wonderful book, interesting and readable, as well as uncompromisingly sound. He pays you tribute, as he should, for your influence has been so strong. It is grand of him to turn out such splendid stuff, and with quite inadequate monetary reward.

You ask about Barry Goldwater. My opinion without qualification, is that he is the best man in public life today. His *Conscience of A Concervative* is simply tops and it only takes two hours or so to read it. He is still young, and I hope we can elect him President one day.

September 10, 1960

Dear Mr. Crane:

Thank you for your most interesting letter. I am so glad to know that Mr. Hoover has been able at last to get back control of his Library at Stanford. After a lapse of some time, we have lately exchanged a few letters but neither of us mentioned the Library. YEARS ago I wrote him that it was Communist-controlled but he did not refer to the information when he replied. I think it will take more than a sound man, as curator, to get rid of that infestation. From the little I have known of it from time to time, I feel that the situation needs the FBI and a new Supreme Court.

Probably you are right about the American Professor in Luxembourg. And maybe Jean Pierre was not wholly unsuspicious, but giving an American the benefit of all possible doubt. (After all, Europeans do regard us as artless babes, you know.) By a triple play across the sea we may have lowered the boom on that Comrade who's been tangling with Jean Pierre; it looks so. But "we" are at such an enormous disadvantage, against the worldwide organized conspiracy that's been operating and perfecting itself since 1919. And so few can believe, even now, even that it exists.

Ah me, that's what I feared—that I "ought to" read that mighty tome: Boehm-Bawerk. Now really, couldn't he at least have had a reasonable *name?* I didn't know it was THREE volumes; Hans mentioned his translating two, which seemed to me more than enough. No doubt I should. But can't I hold the thought of them, as a treat to be looking forward to? Seriously, it would be a treat if Herr von Boehm-Bawerk wrote as enthrallingly as Ludwig von Mises does, and did especially in *Human Action*. But somehow I doubt that. Have you read Mises's latest one, which you sent Jean Pierre? And is it *good?* Somehow I hadn't heard of it.

Yes, I read John Chamberlain's *Roots of Capitalism* quite awhile ago—soon after you sent it to me. I think it really a superb job; beautifully written and packed with information and, of course, brilliantly right. What a loss that Princeton Panel was, what a sorrow that it ended just when it was starting so well. It would be so easy to be a superstitious fatalist, answering the question: WHY are all "our" efforts so baffled? and all the Communists' so consistently smoothly carried out? with some such reply as *The Wave of the Future* or *Kismet.*

I agree heartily with your view that Senator Goldwater is "the best man in public life today"—taking "public" to mean "party-political," and the whole not meaning much. He would be a fine President provided that the misnamed "conservative" movement was a tremendous force behind him. But then, any man would be, in that situation; even Ike or Nixon.

Mr. Goldwater strikes me (all I know is what I hear

on the radio) as sort of blindly, "instinctively" anti-socialist —as Americans generally are; and as a competent "politician" as competence goes among politicians; but as lacking ability to think in philosophical terms and having absolutely no "sense" of the intangibles in a human situation, no intuition of historical trends, but the reactions of the human "common man." I think the attempt to draft him, in the Chicago convention, in order to make a show of "conservative" strength in the party, was ill advised; Mr. Goldwater has steadily insisted that he was not and would not be a candidate; and his anger, his fury at being used as a martyr against his will was only natural. As party-political strategy, his refusal of the nomination was imperative, i.e., if he had not stopped the attempt to draft him when he did, his political career would have been killed dead as Knowland's. His action was clever, but in my opinion far from clever enough, not intelligent at all but showing the lacks I have just mentioned.

Not by any means all "conservatives" were trying to draft him, trying to *use* him (and ruin him) for The Cause; that group was a small minority. He stood on the platform and vented his fury on all of us. It did not please me, listening to the radio, to be assailed as a silly fool, told to "Wake up!" told to "Have some sense!" told to know better than to demand perfection and to stop "getting mad" because not every detail was precisely what *I* wanted.

Now I am an ordinary middling person—middle west, middle "class," middle aged—plus just enough of whatever-it-is that makes me a fiction-writer, to be able to see that that's what I am. And I have found, hundreds of times through the years, that my reactions are the general middling reactions. So I said to me: the man is antagonizing tens of thousands of voters, cooling the admiration of hundreds of thousands whom, if he understood people and situations, he would have made his loyal following. Then as he left the platform, some woman reporter snatched him, and asked, "You are campaigning for Nixon?" and he snapped furiously, "There's nowhere else to go!" There is no way to settle a bet but if there were I would bet—I would bet even my little Maltese pups that, by count, thousands of voters who heard that will not vote at all in November. "Nowhere else to go" is too old hat; it has been heard too often; it is exactly the attitude of the Republican party leaders who cater to every other minority in this country but despise us because we "have nowhere else to go." And Americans *react* to that kind of bullying. Do you want to bet a nickel that the stay-at-home voters won't be more numerous this year than ever before? One nickel gets you ten. I say Mr. Goldwater is a clever party politician but not clever enough, and not intelligent at all.

Did I tell you that Roger MacBride has bought a place in Vermont? land for investment. And, he says, to enjoy meanwhile. He bought 1,000 acres "more or less" (as deeds read hereabouts) and found after verifying titles and boundaries, that he has nearly 1,200 acres! with two lakes, two gently high mountains, nine lively brooks, innumerable distant views of the Green and White Mountains, herds of deer, stands of growing valuable timber, bears, beavers, sugar-maple grove with complete "sugaring camp," two miles of country road snowplowed in winter, comfortable house with six bedrooms (ONE bath), living room, dining room with fireplace, electric kitchen, and laundry, telephone. . . . You know his two little Caxton books, don't you? on Electoral College and on Bricker Amendment. They have sold, are selling amazingly well.

September 15, 1960

Dear Mr. Crane:

I hope it is not too much to ask of you, busy as you are —Could you read these few pages of manuscript for me? and tell me what you think.

I have tried very hard to say exactly what I mean, but writing is communicating and I don't know whether or not I have succeeded until I know whether a reader knows what I mean. Religion isn't my subject so I don't want to go into theology at all, but people do act on a basis of their —the Germans have the word for it (which I forget)— world-view; or rather universe-view. Religious philosophy.

All kinds of problems and difficulties harass me, in trying to do these few pages. Keeping them simple enough, not baffling and stopping readers of women's magazines and *Saturday Evening Post*. . . . When *Saturday Evening Post* printed *Give Me Liberty* an attorney wrote begging me to use words that his wife, a college graduate could understand. And I don't think there was a word of more than two syllables in the whole piece. . . . Then have I used a a phrase that is offensive? Does a Christian object to "the God of Abraham *and Jesus*"? If so, how should I say that? A Christian believes that Jesus was, is, God—Sotir, Christus —But if I say, "the God of Abraham and Christ," it seems to me to become nonsense, "The God of God. . . ." The God of Abraham, Moses, of course was named YVHV, transliterated Jehovah in the Bible, and they were monotheists; Jehovah was One God; and that concept is not challenged, indeed it is supported, in the Gospels. The belief that Jesus is Christ is Christian theology, and I don't want to raise any theological questions, or imply any theological attitude. Should I cut this whole phrase, and list Jehovah, Christ, with the names of the other Gods in the sentence? But would this seem to imply an equality between Mithra and Jehovah and Christ which would anger Jews and Christians? I would like to leave out this whole bit, but it really is essential (it seems to me) to a serious consideration of human action.

I think I shall be right without so much trouble when Christianity comes in historically, as a change in belief, later in the book. This bit is very early, in discussion of kinetic human energy per se.

September 30, 1960

Dear Mrs. Lane:

Where does Roger MacBride live in Vermont? I visit that state occasionally. If he has trout in these brooks, I wish he would invite me to go fishing.

Now as to the few pages of manuscript which you sent me and which I return herewith, I think your approach and treatment of this subject is very striking and will make a strong appeal. Your thought, expressed twice in these pages, that action only occurs when man expects to obtain a profit, is identical with von Mises' statement that man always acts to remove uneasiness, which, in those words or with such alteration in expression as may occur to you, might emphasize your thought of expectation to gain a profit. I think the removal of uneasiness is the lowest denomination, or the simplest, spring of action.

Your true and wise characterization of atheists reminds

me of what Werner Heisenberg, the great German physicist, who is a Christian, said to me: "Dirac, the English physicist, says 'there is no God and Dirac is His prophet!' "

Now, on the main point that you inquire about, I see no reason why you shouldn't speak of the God of Abraham and Jesus. I see no objection to the use of that phrase that indicates the God of the Old and New Testaments. I always prefer the word "God." For there is the true God who is sought by all men everywhere but under various names, as men try to create God in their own image. That is natural for finite creatures reaching out toward the infinite. So I respect the use of various names by other peoples—Jehovah, Yvhv, Allah and so many other names—accepting none of them as final, but believe with all my heart that we only come to God as Father through Christ.

October 1, 1960

Dear Mr. Crane:

I thank you for your letter of yesterday and your help with my book. You can't know what a worry you have taken from my mind. You are the only person I know who could have done it and it is generous of you to do it—to want to do it—with all else that you are doing.

There ARE trout in those brooks, and I'm sure Roger would be delighted to have you go fishing with him. Though he is there so seldom that how good the fishing is, I don't know. *Hordes* of hunters swarm over the place killing the game in hunting season, and neighbors say that his road is solid with cars then, also that the hunters are lawless and dangerous; last year they shot a warden. Roger is posting the place, and intended to be there this fall to defend it in person but I hope I have persuaded him not to. The danger seems to me disproportionate to the possible gain. It will be much easier for hundreds to shoot him, than for him to patrol 1,200 acres of woodland and hills. And the warden, whom he saw, advocates hunting and opposed his posting the land, also said that he was too busy to be in that part of Vermont in hunting season. So, as I was going to say, the brooks may be pretty well fished out. I don't know. Roger caught his suppers when he was there for a week-end a few weeks ago.

November 4, 1960

Dear Mr. Crane:

Of course you have seen John Chamberlain's piece about the neo-radicalism of college students, in the *Wall Street Journal.* Splendid, I thought. But one little item in it troubles me; that I.S.I. (Mr. Milione, I suppose) thinks of changing the name, I.S.I. to get "conservative" into it. I think this would be a mistake now, and a worse one later. I do wish that I knew Mr. Milione at all, so that I could protest to him. The trouble with using "conservative" in the name is that it invites controversies and alienates some persons and groups, ESPECIALLY among the youngsters in colleges and universities. The self-styled Conservatives are a distinct group, the *National Review, Modern Age,* Buckley, Burnham, Russell Kirk group; certainly doing necessary and fine work, but by no means appealing to all the young neo-radicals who are rapidly multiplying in the colleges. It is a question largely of emphasis; the theoretical, metaphysical, idealist-philosophical position of these Neo-Conservatives is consistent with, but does not include the—for instance—political-economic position of Hayek's disciples. In one group, individuals find Conservatives boring and unrealistic; in the other, some exclude the Neo-Liberals as materialists if not positivists. Both, however, are anti-collectivists, i.e., individualists. It is individualism, not conservatism, that is the antithesis of collectivism. A conservative CAN be a collectivist; in U.S.S.R. a Communist must be a conservative now. But an individualist cannot be a collectivist, ever, anywhere.

Now the Intercollegiate Society (I.S.I.) today is, as John Chamberlain says, historically a repetition of the Intercollegiate Socialist movement of sixty years ago, in reverse. Like that young Socialist-organizational movement, it must be inclusive to be effective. This is not the time for I.S.I. to amalgamate (or SEEM to) with any special group of these new-radicals. Its appeal should be general, inclusive, non-partisan; basic; individualist, as opposed to ALL socialism. Just as the young Socialist movement was all inclusive, opposed to all individualism, embracing all the "anti-capitalists" from anarchists and International Workers of the World to "social service workers," from the young Marxists to the young Lillian Walds. A generation later the Socialists could split into Socialists and Communists, and soon into

Communists and Fascists; but then they had grown strong enough, numerous enough, to afford to split and still act effectively. This is not the time to lose the all-inclusive, general, anti-collectivist movement that I.S.I. may be.

Roger tells me that you welcome the idea of fishing his streams next spring. If you pass by my kitchen without stopping enroute, I shall be disconsolate. Roger *always* stops, for dinner and breakfast or for a weekend, and I tell him that he must bring you. He was here last night for dinner and drove on to be on the job with the bulldozers this morning; bulldozers are remodeling one of his little lakes, replacing a washed-out dam, and building a small island. I told him, when he asked me to suggest a name for the place (Deer Park isn't his choice) that the only suitable name for a newly-incurred "country estate" is: Little Wotting. How true. The adjective, however, more aptly applies to my seven acres than to his 1,200.

December 13, 1960

Dear Mr. Crane:

You are totally right about the proposed debate in India. But whether any European can possibly understand. . . . Collectivism is so rock-bottom to all European thought and culture that anyone questioning it is a Copernicus to Europe. If American intellectuals hadn't always been European-minded, perhaps in nearly two centuries they might have made a small dent in the Greco-Romanism of Europe. As it is, John Adams is as sound today as he was 150 years ago, when he wrote on the margin of a book: "The logos of Plato, the ratio of Manilius, and the mind of Condorcet, all plausible and specious as they are, will be three thousand years longer more delusive than useful. Not one of them takes human nature as it is for their foundation." I remember reviewing for NEC a book by Dr. Jewkes; very sound and good (like Hayek, or Henry George) until (like them) he threw it all away without even knowing what he was doing. It's fantastic, the unconscious self-contradiction in their minds. As obvious and salient as: "I like you, you are absolutely right and I agree with you completely, except that of course you are wholly wrong, I denounce and totally repudiate you." Yet they imagine that they are consistent.

Hayek's *Road To Serfdom.* Flabbergasting. Clearly, truly, sincerely, wonderfully describing and opposing the whole "road" since the 1880s, and then approving its beginning, with a hearty "come along this way, boys! this is the right road to good"; and Frank Meyer told me, actually, that it converted his whole thinking and yanked him out of the CPUSA. All I can do is fall back for solace on my always comforting N. J. Birrell's *Man's Emerging Mind.* It's just absolutely essential to hold on to a faith that human intelligence is (or will be) beginning some day to emerge.

XVIII

December 23, 1960

Dear Mrs. Lane:

I [have been] laid up at home with a cold for a few days.

The piece you sent me about the United Nations [by Orval Watts] is excellent. My only question is endorsement of Dr. Malik's views, for, sadly, Dr. Malik has twice recently praised the Universal Declaration of Human Rights lavishly. I have in my file a memorandum of how to tackle him on this error. Indeed, I, too, have quoted Dr. Malik in my attacks on the Declaration and have been confounded by his recent statement. This piece by Dr. Watts is something we have wanted for a long time to help fight against the widespread approval of the United Nations.

December 28, 1960

Dear Mr. Crane:

I am sorry that you have—have had, I hope—a cold; but how sensible of you to stay at home until you haven't it. Everyone has a remedy for a cold, so I have one. (Remember Mark Twain's "Everybody drank from the public drinking-cup, so I did"?) My remedy cures a cold: as everyone's remedy does. But mine DOES—as everyone says. Mine is: Stay in bed three days (and nights, of course) and eat Sunkist oranges; eat them, don't merely drink their juice; the bioflavonoids are in the pulp and anyway, I *like* eating oranges. So everyone should, don't you think? I don't know why this reminds me of my favorite Albanian proverb: "I think this will be a good year for pears," said the bear. "Why?" asked the other bear, and the first bear replied, "Because I like them. . . ." I almost gave that gem to you in Albanian!

Weather has been freezing here since a week ago last Friday; my driveway down the hill is glare ice, so I can't get to my mailbox. Roger's larger lake was being repaired —some years ago a flood broke through its bank (not injuring its concrete dam with spillways, but lowering the lake several feet) and left its rim marshy; the contractor was clearing away the messy edges and rebuilding the bank to restore the lake's level. He was to finish the job by the first of November. He brought in some $60,000 worth of machines and had men working them now and then, in the maddening way that so much work is (isn't) done nowadays. Why is it, that I am so at the mercy of my employees? when somehow my employers are never at MY mercy? The job isn't done *yet*, and all is buried under yards of snow. I'm afraid that there'll be fishing only in the brooks and the smaller lake next spring. You know Roger is anticipating your fishing with him then. He is going to the Human Events conference in Washington the first week in January—rather prodded by me, because I am curious about it. Senator Goldwater may be the best in sight but I wish there were better, don't you?

December 30, 1960

Dear Mr. Crane:

A note from Orval Watts says that the assistant to the President of Pepperdine College wants 300 copies of the UN pamphlet (done for high school debates, copy of which I sent you). Adds that this assistant "is another excellent young fellow-conspirator for individualism." Another cheering instance of hope in the on-coming generation.

Orval continues: "I know of three small colleges—Pepperdine being the largest, 1,000-1,200 students—which would take me on as a part-time lecturer—if businessmen would come in with donations for that particular purpose."

I thought, perhaps if Mr. Hoover would do nothing else, he may know someone who would support such a course, indefinitely, as a permanent tax deduction, a contribution to education. Pepperdine by all I hear is a good small college, good from our point of view, I mean; not vigorously promoting socialism.

Orval does not "sell" himself. He tries to sell his wares—his knowledge, his philosophy—but as a shopkeeper who knows his stock is so good he expects customers to come in. A "kissin' kin" remote "cousin" of mine, Laura Ingalls, was the first aviator to fly from Pacific to Atlantic across the

Andes; a most daring and spectacular feat for any pilot, and she was a teen-age girl. She expected that the achievement itself would bring her such renown and backing that she could continue a career in the air—the one thing she passionately wanted to do. Nobody but pilots ever heard of it. Years later she was first—or one of the first—aviators who wanted to fly from Minnesota to Moscow over the North Pole; she was trying to get the flight financed, and I arranged a luncheon for her with "public relations" Bernays and the Communist (or fellow-traveler) arctic explorer, Stephenson. She told them what she had expected from the Andes flight itself, and they laughed heartily at the naivete which expected any recognition of unpublicized achievement. The incident has bothered me ever since. I don't know whether the whole world has changed (in that regard) since I was a girl, or whether I am wholly mistaken about life in the nineteenth century. But I do see personal salesmanship getting not only more cash and publicity, but more opportunity—which matters—than genuine value does. So the value is lost because the smart salesman needn't have much and usually hasn't. Amelia Earhart was not the pilot that Laura Ingalls was. But if anyone remembers Laura Ingalls at all, she's remembered as the hapless foolish flyer whom some "public relations expert"—after I'd lost touch with her—induced to fly over the White House, all innocent of any illegality. She was arrested, sentenced, served a term of imprisonment, and stopped flying. A total waste of real ability, as well as of a life. Q.E.D.?

Brought up on McGuffey's *Readers*, I keep on trying to make a real-life incident reach a Moral. But what is it here? if any. "Full many a flower is born to blush unseen and waste its sweetness on the desert air" for lack of expert Public Relations?

February 1, 1961

Dear Mr. Crane:

I myself—well, after all I was young in Dakota Territory where strictly good and moral men frequently said, "A man that won't steal from a railroad ain't *honest.*" (Background, of course, was resentment against the railroad builder's getting subsidies from Lincoln's Administration, and later. Idea: the RR stole from me, via Washington; what I steal from a RR is only getting some of my own back.) I don't feel so about railroads now; heaven knows they brought the Interstate Commerce Commission on themselves, for their sins. But I do not think that any honesty is involved in paying taxes. Taxation is plain armed robbery; tax-collectors are armed robbers. I will save my property from them in any way that I think I can get away with. If you wake in the night with a flashlight shining in your face and a masked man with a gun ordering you to tell him where your money is, do you feel that you're morally obliged to tell him the truth, the whole truth, and nothing but the truth? I think you might. I don't. I will try to get out of that predicament with as little loss as possible. In regard to taxes, this means taking advantage of every legality that any attorney can find in the tax "laws" so called, and regulations. I have no scruples about this whatever, anything that I want to do with *my* money, and that I can in any way slip under any legality so that the robbers won't find it and rob me of some of it, I do. They make the legalities, trying to be smart about who gets how much of my property; and to keep as much as possible of my own, I'll out-smart them if I can.

I can only hope you are not too shockingly shocked, but this is so and I do tell the truth to everyone but "the Federal men." Moonshiners I sympathize with, too, and all bootleggers and smugglers, who in the worst times keep the free market working and people alive, at the risk of their own lives. And all the (fairly accurately estimated) 100,000 families of Americans (not gypsies) displaced from homes and living as nomads in this country, illegally, by unlicensed selling and useful unlicensed work. I spent part of a summer among them once; they are good ordinary American families, much above people living in the "lawless lands" between the Midwest's big rivers and their levees. (They live untaxed and free, too, but they are like wild animals or gentle young children, and their lack of brains frightens me; I feel that they might tear me to pieces on an impulse, meaning no harm but not thinking what they are doing.) The Green River Law was passed in Green River, Utah—really an ordinance—to stop the nomad Americans; and all over the west the towns have highway signs: GREEN RIVER LAW ENFORCED.

But it didn't stop the nomads. Only last fall a neighbor here told me of a (she thought) curious happening. Her car was standing in the driveway with a flat tire; she hadn't noticed it until a Buick sedan stopped in front of her house and a pleasant man, well groomed and clean, in overalls, got out and came to her door and said he had noticed the flat tire. He said, If you'd like me to change the tire, I'll be glad to do it for fifty cents. He did, she paid him, he thanked her and left in the Buick. She didn't know what to make of the whole thing. His wife (she supposed) and two children were in the car, and they looked like "nice folks" and fairly prosperous; neighborly to change the tire, but why the charge? and if a charge, why only fifty cents? An incident typical of the nomads' life; in a day he picks up enough to provide a comfortable living and save a little, because all he earns is his; no property taxes, no sales taxes, no income taxes, no license fees. And all across this country are places the nomads know, where they buy *untaxed* gasoline—for seven cents a gallon in 1939 when I was meeting and talking with them. A couple had been on the road for thirty years, had a whole machine shop in a big truck; he did machine repair work for farmers all over the country. Nobody knows what "the Government" has driven people to in these States. And, of course, everywhere else, more people are driven to worse.

February 8, 1961

Dear Mrs. Lane:

I do not disagree with your dissertation on tax returns. I always try to take advantage of any exemption that is legal, but I always bear in mind that signing a tax return I take an oath that I believe the items in the return are truthful and in accordance with the law.

I may shock you when I tell you that several years ago when a statement from Washington was made of the considerable degree of counterfeiting in this country, I suggested to Harry Hazlitt that he do a piece praising the counterfeiters because they are helping along the Federal Government's programme, although only in slight degree(!), of putting more money in circulation and that the counterfeiters themselves were probably no more unworthy recipients of this additional currency than were government agencies insofar as they were creating new money and spending it on unlawful purposes! Harry thought that too flippant!

I haven't had the contact you mention with nomad Americans, except that I know that here in the effete East many farmers and stockmen work on what they call a "cash basis." No damning records! Once, too, as I was driving outside of Philadelphia and a tire went flat, one of the doingest little fellows you ever saw pounced on it immediately, changed the tire in the twinkling of an eye, and then asked the price of thirty-five cents—"What they charge at a service station." So I gave him a dollar.

Yet, we aren't anarchists, but patriotic and law-abiding citizens. Hoping you are the same, I am,

XIX

February 14, 1961

Dear Saint Valentine:

Happy birthday to you.

Herb Cornuelle used firmly to refuse any and all confidences, asserting unequivocally that absolutely everything he knew was in the public domain. In the years since he went to the pineapples in Hawaii, my appreciation of this wisdom has risen into orbit. I haven't adopted his policy, however. Maybe a pride in skill handicaps me; I am truly expert in never NEVER telling; the ivory casket behind my placid brow is cram-jammed with never-told secrets.

But, see how wily Herb was, and I suppose is. Days ago I had an airmail from—enclosing Leonard Read's formal note to him and beginning, "Dear Rose, I wonder if Mr. Crane or somebody is behind this? . . . But I'm taking it . . ." etc.

To this I replied, Horray! Horray! and if you have any sneaking notion that *I* was behind this, all I can say is that I didn't even know that FEE had any such arrangement, and wouldn't have done anything like this if I had known. (If this be duplicity, need I ask anyone to make the most of it?)

So, as the columnists say, I "envisage" the moment when—will tentatively express thanks to you and you, in shock, will be unable to doubt such evidence of my untrustworthiness. O, Herb, how wise thou art!!

To me the very word, patriot, has collectivist connotations. Pater, father; patria, fatherland; patriarch, generating source and ruler of a family-Whole. And patriotism is everywhere regarded as obedience to, dependence upon, self-sacrifice for, the divinely ordained Ruler: The *Government* (whether Emperor, Queen, Parliament, or FDR).

Detour: Look for instance at the whole American press, even the *Wall Street Journal,* on these anti-trust cases against the electric companies; all condemning the hapless victims on "moral" grounds. The assumption is that obedience to Acts of legislators is *moral.* In that case, genocide is moral: "liquidating" Jews or kulaks was and is obedience to absolutely *legal* orders from absolutely *legal* authorities. Price-fixing (if done by men other than politicians in office) is a *crime* but certainly no sin; morality has nothing to do with it. At the same time that brother Kennedy is sending men to jail and wrecking corporations, (ruining hundreds of thousands of little small stockholders in them) for the crime of price fixing, big brother Kennedy is all set to bribe, intimidate and blackmail legislators into fixing prices. And the whole American press yaps about the immorality of the criminals, while discussing the expediency of the proposed legislation. This is only a little indication of the practical effect of patriotism; patriotism being a lingering tradition of the Divine Government of a human Whole, which is at least as old as the first Living Gods: Ur Nammu, Khammarubi, Pharoah, Ptolemy, Augustus Caesar. Every one of them, and men in all Governments, since then, and now, was or is a robber, murderer, treacherous betrayer of trust, and all have been and still to some extent are, worshipped as somehow holy, somehow having some quality or attribute of God. It is incredibily fantastic, but it is a fact.

I have immeasurably less respect for "the office" of President or for any President personally, than I have for you. And I do not go into rhapsodies about "my country," its rocks and rills, its super highways and wooded hills, as Bob does in that "Tiger" piece you sent me. This whole world is almost unbearably beautiful; why should I love Oak Creek Canyon or California's beaches or Washington's Sea Island counties any more than the Bocca di Cattaro or Delphi or the Bosphorus? Because *I*, me, the Great RWL, was born in Dakota Territory? The logic seems weak, somehow, don't you feel?

My attachment to these USA is wholly, entirely, absolutely to The Revolution, the real world revolution, which men began here and which has—so to speak—a foothold on earth here. If reactionaries succeed in destroying the revolutionary structure of social and political human life here, I care no more about this continent than about any other. If I lived long enough I would find and join the revival of the Revolution wherever it might be in Africa or Asia or Europe, the Arctic or Antarctic. And let this country go with all the other regimes that collectivism has wrecked and eliminated since history began. So much for patriotism, mine.

As to anarchy, you can find me with Woodrow Wilson (that lying treacherous scoundrel who began this World War; truly a Platonic "idealist," he was) who said words to the effect that increase of freedom is decrease of Government. The difference between W.W. and me is that *I* mean what I say. I am not wildeyed and whiskered and I do not contemplate throwing a home-made bomb at Mr. Kennedy but I am FOR any and every way of diminishing the size, the activity, the extent of Government per se, and all respect for Government, to the eventual end of eliminating Government totally. Anarchy is absence of earthly Authority over human beings, by definition and etymology; so I am an anarchist.

I am not a utopian, though, so I am not impatiently trying or expecting to establish the Kingdom of God on earth next year, or next century, or even next millennium. I will even concede that progress toward it may be the ancient Greek's—I forget his name at the moment. Who was it who described that progress which perpetually advanced half the distance to the goal in each successive period of time, and therefore never arrived at the end? It is the *direction* of the movement that matters. Progress is advancing *toward* a goal. That old Greek's racer never quite reached the goal, true; but in time he was much nearer it than he would have been if he had perpetually backed away from it. When Jefferson said that the least Government is the best Government, what was he advocating but anarchy? The lesser and lesser and lesser the Government the better and better and better, and the nearer no Government.

As to being law-abiding, I deny that legislators make *law*. They create legal Acts, statutes, which may or may not coincide with real Law, and in fact seldom do. Generally a statute is an order which "executive" Government uses physical force to "enforce" upon persons not in The Government, but believed to be subject to it, and the great majority of such legislative Acts are intended to prevent or hamper or stop harmless and useful human action, so the enforcement of them has that lamentable effect. Consider the so-called "laws" that we more-or-less obey nowadays; how many of them do no harm? Is it virtuous, or desirable in any way, to concur in doing harm?

I am "law-abiding" purely for expediency, for self-defense, in the main against my conscientious principles, so at bottom I am ashamed of not being a conscientious objector practicing Ghandi's or Thoreau's civil disobedience. I did refuse to be rationed; I do absolutely refuse to be Social-Secured; but I should refuse to pay taxes and be in jail, only what would become of my little Maltese puppies? and my own little area of freedom? and my books and my friends and correspondents? I shall be reluctantly a martyr, only when backed into the last corner of the last resort. No heroine, alas.

I do think that immeasurable harm is being done by the general and increasing, self-defensive "lawlessness" in this country. Not because it is disobedience to statues, but because it is training nearly all of us (I suppose, not Eleanor Roosevelt. But does she need such training?) in trickery and deceit and lies and distrust of everyone; it is Europeanizing us. Americans used to be simple people, more honest, trusting, neighborly, generous than people were or ever had been anywhere else. Those qualities are a tragic loss.

My sundecks were cleared of snow yesterday so now the downstairs windows are covered quite to their tops and above. But a tunnel to the mailbox remains open, though the sky is promising more snow. Hoping your windows are not the same.

June 14, 1961

Dear Mr. Crane:

How are you? —Perhaps on your vacation. Anyway, it seems a long time since I heard from you. I hope all's well and cheerfully busy. Roger MacBride last winter was eagerly anticipating your fishing with him in Vermont this spring and even preparing for it but in February he met a girl and sort of vanished—he wasn't here even when he was, if I may say so. A week ago she said Yes, and I've seen them a couple of times since in a clear sky at an altitude of about 20,000 feet. He is getting the Vermont house remodeled as fast as possible and I expect they will be married this fall.

Everything is so much, much better than it was thirty years ago. I was writing Orval recently that I'm inclined to believe that historians someday will say that Wilson saved this country by starting the World War. His idea of course was to rule the world and what he really did was to wreck Europe and make Marx's "spectre" a reality armed with nuclear bombs. But the effect was to startle Americans into thinking about principles, as they haven't done since the 1840s. And not only Americans, either—a leaven of people everywhere else.

XX

June 23, 1961

Dear Mrs. Lane:

A month ago Mr. Crane had a cerebral vascular accident and had to undergo surgery. It is a pleasure to write, however, that he is recovering beautifully, and it is expected that he will be leaving the hospital the first of next week. It will be sometime before he is able to return to the office, but he is already expressing anxiety to resume his activities.

Yours sincerely,
Mrs. William D. Wendle
Secretary to Mr. Crane

June 27, 1961

Dear Mrs. Wendle:

Thank you for writing me the good news about Mr. Crane's health. I am so VERY glad that he is making, as you say, a good recovery. Would you please tell him that I sit here *wanting* to *do* something—*any*thing, like sending flowers or candy or telegrams or calvesfoot jelly? and being baffled by the absurdity of everything I can think of. If, as—was it Madame Blavatsky?—wrote, 'thoughts are things and their airy wings fly faster than carrier doves' such swarms of them would surround him that he'd have to be protected by a mosquito net. I can only send him my love and gratitude, as I have been doing for years.

September 1, 1961

Dear Mr. Crane:

I am so happy that the doctors have released you from bondage, so really truly you are feeling better. Now—inconsistently of course—I beg you PLEASE do every single thing that nurses and doctors say, and then some, to take care of "our" Mr. Crane. Nobody is more valuable, and the whole responsibility for his welfare is yours, because none of the rest of "us" can do a thing.

Oh, yes, there's a good time coming ("It's almost here, it's been long, long, long on the way") when I shall dance on the rooftops caroling, "I TOLD you so!" Twenty-eight years ago I began—in Garet Garrett's car in Kansas when we were looking at FDR's AAA repetition of Emperor Domitian's agricultural policy—to resist "All is lost" pessimism. And as you know I've kept up that resistance (in spite of all evidence to the contrary) ever since. Showing, maybe, a tough faith in A Final Cause; certainly showing that I deserve less credit than those who kept on doggedly working for, they believed, a lost cause.

I know about the Wisconsin students; met them at the Freedom School, corresponded with them, and didn't I once send you a copy of their *Insight and Outlook?* And I've exchanged some letters with the Yale group, sent them Roger as a speaker, VERY successful. But I know nothing of those at Chicago and Pennsylvania.

Orval Watts is greatly encouraged by the general trend around him in southern California, says it is nothing short of miraculous, the recent change and its increasing impetus. Have you seen Morrie Ryskind's column? I had some clippings of it; they're marvelous, as Ryskind's wit always is. If I can get hold of them again, I'll send them to you. I don't know where it's being printed, I believe it is syndicated in California.

Dear Mr. Crane, don't bother to answer all this chatter. I'm only a visitor whom the nurse is now shooing out. I'm happy because you are"gaining every day" and all I want is that you'll keep on doing that. It's a grand world that has a few persons like you in it.

November 7, 1961

Dear Mrs. Lane:

I am sending you the latest issue of *The American Behavioral Scientist* in order to get your opinion about it.

November 15, 1961

Dear Mr. Crane:

The term, Behavioral Science, is new to me. My ignorance would guess that it's the name of some relatively new branch of the mythology that Comte (wasn't it) named sociology and that I've known as Social Science.

If there's anything in this guess, then the name might indicate some dim glimmer of normal common sense—an unlocalized perception that persons, not Societies, act: behave. But I don't find this fact suggested in the copy of *The American Behavioral Scientist* which you sent me. If the puzzle were originally mine, I'd ask Orval Watts, Ph.D. because he knows trees in the Grove of Academe.

The magazine seems to be well edited. Contents are written in the vocabulary of the cult, which I know fairly well (except its higher-mathematical reaches) though really it makes no sense. (Example—for locating judicial ideal-points in the psychological space: . . . classify, as either an assent [plus equals agreed with the majority who controlled the decision] or a dissent [minus equals disagreed with the majority] each vote of every justice for all cases in the sample. To arrive at a measure of relative dyadic agreement, tabulate all votes for each pair of justices. There are four possibilities for each pair of justices in each case: they may agree in assent, as they may agree in dissent, or one may assent while the other dissents, *or vice versa* [! my italics]. The tabulation yields a four-fold table for each of the thirty-six pairs of a nine-justice court. A phi correlation coefficient is then computed for each four-fold table. The resulting correlation matrix is factor analyzed and the first three orthogonal factors are extracted . . . etc., etc.—) This example is probably brilliant work in its field, but to me it is a commonplace product of the group of "social scientists" who are trying to make sociology one of the real sciences by using mathematics. "I say it's spinach."

November 27, 1961

Dear Mrs. Lane:

I grow roses, not too well I am afraid, but most enjoyably. So last year I wanted to make some crosses between several varieties, which I thought would result in new varieties of promising character. I looked up the latest article on rose breeding and there I found it set down that crossing two hybrids of different ancestry would produce sixty thousand billion new varieties. In other words, no two of the resulting new varieties would be exactly alike.

Roses are comparatively simple things compared to human beings, but this bit of analysis indicates to me how no two people have ever been alike—not even identical twins. So the whole socialist theory, which is based on treating people as if they were all alike, is quite absurd and I agree with you that using mathematics to try to make sociology a real science is "spinach."

December 11, 1961

Dear Mrs. Lane:

I am sending you a little pamphlet, put out by the *National Review*—Dorothy Sayer's *The Lost Tools of Learning*. I was greatly impressed with this, although it seems to me that there are, in her view, a great many subjects to be studied.

Yet, looking back on my own education, I think I was amazingly blessed in the manner of it. In grammar school, Miss Crosby, a fine old lady, taught us very wisely. We had English grammar, spelling, arithmetic, and, both in school and at home, science in a most valuable little book, *The Story of Familiar Things*. We also had geography, where I used to draw maps of different countries, and history, where I read (as soon as I learned to read) the history of every prominent nation and all sorts of stories and fairy tales. I only remember one author's books that were forbidden by my Mother, the Elsie books, which she said were "sissy." Then at home I had simple theology, forming my beliefs retained to this day.

In high school I had four years of Latin, three years of Greek in one year part time, German, English literature, mathematics (through trigonometry), history, and a most inspiring course called physics. We had wonderful teachers in the Newark, New Jersey, high schools, not realizing until many years afterwards how fortunate we were to have been given such sound education. They are so clear in my mind to this day. We even had a course in economics, which was poor. Besides the school work, I used to stop at the public library several times a week and get and read books that are frowned on today—Alger, Oliver, Optic, Henty and Conon Doyle, etc. I even began to get into rhetoric in my last year of high school, leading a debate, which was probably rote, but learning quite a lot from it nevertheless. One of the most valuable educational influences in my high school years was my interest in chess, which is the only thing perhaps I was good at.

As sixteen years of age I went to Princeton, loafed for the first year and then got interested in chemistry and studied really hard in the chemical laboratory. We had at Princeton in those days wonderful teachers. After graduating, a trip abroad was most educational. I went to work in a chemical laboratory where my duties were rather light, gradually, however, becoming heavier, so I had much time for research in industrial chemistry and, particularly in the chemistry of cellulose, which was my specialty.

So I go along with Dorothy Sayers in her criticism of the teaching today in school and college, believing that I was unusually fortunate in really having an "old fashioned" education.

You are one of the wisest people I know. How did you get that way?

December 13, 1961

Dear Mr. Crane:

Thank you for the copy of Dorothy Sayer's *Tools of Learning.* I am a fan of hers (have you read her detective stories?) and have read this before in some English print; I am glad to have it in this form for cataloguing and study shelf. She is, was, intelligent, so she wrote nothing that doesn't give pleasure to a reader, as everything of Chesterton's does, though both of them are so English, deal so exclusively with English situations and problems, that their conclusions seem to me to have little practical application here.

Tools of Learning with its advocacy of teaching "how to learn" rather than "a subject" can too easily be misunderstood here and become the American educationist's grinning idiocy: "We do not teach a *subject,* we teach a *child,*" ending in the NEA's official position that reading and writing are skills which, like law or medicine, require special aptitude, therefore, it is as absurd to expect everyone to read and write as to expect everyone to be a lawyer or a doctor.

In substance, Dorothy Sayers seems to me to have been advocating an English equivalent of the old-fashioned American methods—remember that it used to be called "pedagogy" and studied in "Normal Schools" and teachers' summer schools?—before the reaction at this century's beginning, which instituted compulsory State schooling, and the Communist infiltrating of the system during the 1920s which has since then been deliberately preparing the coming generation for the inevitable collectivist state—in the words of the Guggenheim report.

Your view of my wisdom astounds me. I can't doubt that it is sincere though. And wouldn't doubt its accuracy if it were your opinion of anyone else. Also I do often think that all the world is queer but thee and me and sometimes (deviating only slightly from the mythical Quaker's modification), sometimes I think I am.

How do I get that way? you ask. I suppose by not being able to go to college. As Mr. Ashmore said editorially in the *Little Rock Arkansas Gazette,* that time I raised all the furore about the textbook leading the planned Keynesian invasion of grade schools, I am an illiterate with not even a high school education. In fact, had he but known it, not a grade school one.

I learned to read from sheer curiosity when I was three years old. Someone gave me a little book of pictures and letters, printed on cloth, a year or so earlier, and I learned the letters by asking what they were, and being told to stop asking. My only memory of the tree-claim shanty in Dakota[6] is of standing in front of the cook-stove in the kitchen and seeing letters on the cover of the jutting-out place that held the ashes, about on the level with my chin. I reached up and over, put my fingers on each letter and said, "P A T, what's that?" My father said, "Pat." "Pat who?" He said, "Pat Murphy." I remember it because I couldn't understand it; I felt some discrepancy between those three letters and something as long as Pat Murphy, and I kept trying, and failing, to cope with it in my mind.

[6]See *The First Four Years,* by Laura Ingalls Wilder, Harper & Row, 1971.

This is all I remember about learning to read; so far as memory goes, I have always read.

I learned to write in kindergarten in the De Smet school, when I was five. Six was the age for admittance, but my father was sick, my mother working, my grandfather was the first settler in the Territory, the town patriarch, so I was admitted at five. Miss Barrows was the teacher; I worshipped her. My seatmate was in *Second Reader*—McGuffey's. There was not room on the desktop to spread out the penmanship book, so I learned to write sidewise—not left to right but from me to away from me—and I still do. The Spencerian copy was at the top of each page, to be copied precisely on each of ten lines beneath it. Procrastination is the thief of time. Evil communications corrupt good manners. Sweet are the uses of adversity. *a*, exactly between the first two ruled lines; *t, I, h* exactly between first and third lines; *p, g,p* between first and and second with tail down to thin line below. I wrote every line, every page, all the way through the kindergarten book and the primer book, and was taken out of school with a malady called "writer's cramp." I wonder what it really was, which nearly deprived me of a right arm. But I had read the *Primer, First Reader* and *Second Reader,* anyway; and while convalescing, I read *Robinson Crusoe, Gulliver's Travels,* and the weekly *Inter-Ocean* after the grown-ups had finished it. I didn't understand all of it, but I read it. And I voted for Cleveland on the sample ballots that used to be distributed for studying before elections. I didn't know why, but the grown-ups used to ask me to do it, to show disbelieving onlookers that I would.

Then we traveled in one of the covered wagons that filled the roads, going in all directions, during the Panic of the early 1890's. We went to the Land of the Red Apple, the Ozarks. I walked two miles to school—the only school thereabouts, the town school. For one reason or another (I don't remember what) I never finished a school year, never was there on Last Day. But I read all the McGuffey's *Readers,* the *Geography,* the *Physiology, American History,* and a fat book, *Ancient, Medieval* and *Modern History.* When I was in the upstairs room, must have been *Fourth and Fifth Readers,* there was a shelf of books which could be borrowed, and I read them all: *Green Mountain Boys; John Halifax: Gentleman; Ivanhoe; Mill on the Floss.* At home in the evenings, my mother read aloud to my father and me Prescott's *Conquest of Mexico*; *Conquest of Peru;* Parkman's *Oregon Trail.*

We moved to town, and a family arrived in town who had a whole wall of books. The lady lent them all to me. I remember Gibbon's *Decline and Fall of the Roman Empire;* and I remember my first literary criticism, which one day spontaneously rose in my mind and amazed me by my brilliance. It was, "Marie Coreilli's use of adjectives is *masterly.*" I fear you never read Marie Coreilli, and will not justly appraise my achievement. She wrote: *Sorrows of Satan, Thelma, Wormwood* and many others, novels of the wickedness of London Society, and her use of adjectives was lavish. I also read Eugene Sue's *Wandering Jew,* in two volumes. And Bulwer Lytton, the whole set, and half a dozen other English novelists, in sets.

So when I was sixteen, or rather fifteen, and could not afford to go to an Academy (they cost $4 a week, board and tuition) my aunt invited me to come to Crowley, Louisiana, and go to high school. It was not quite a high school yet; it was, ambitiously, a Ninth Grade, that year added to the eight grades of the school. This was in 1903. No compulsory schooling, yet, no educational theories so far as I have ever heard. My Aunt took me to see the Principal; we told him that I wanted to graduate from high school. He asked me what schooling I had had, and I hadn't had any to show on a record. So he said, politely regretful, I would have to pass examinations. To enter the new class I must know: American History, two years English history, two years Latin, Algebra, Plane Geometry, Civics, American Literature. I said, All right, I would take examinations in all but Latin. I knew no Latin but I passed the others; I would do three years of Latin to make up the lack. He was doubtful but finally consented and I did. Came out top of the class of seven in Latin. Wrote a Latin poem and read it at Graduating Exercises. This ended my academic career.

You may wonder—I knew algebra and plane geometry because I was purely crazy about them. I never did learn arithmetic and still cope with figures on my own methods. But somehow I got an algebra textbook and being out of school I could do all the problems as fast as I liked. Usually I was not going to school because for some reason I was "mad at the teacher." I used to spend all day in the haymow in our barn in town, lying on my stomach, eating apples and solving algebra problems. I had got through plane geometry in that textbook, luckily, before I went to Crowley. And, luckily, most of the English history questions had been covered by the English novels I had read.

My being mad at the teacher was not quite as unreasonable as it may seem. For example: One year I went to school not quite half a day. The First Day of School was in *Fifth Reader*. The teacher was new and to get us Fifth Readers out of his way while he got the names of the Third and Fourthers, he gave us an exercise in transposition: "Transpose Tennyson's lines, break, break, break on thy cold gray stones, O sea,/ And I would that I could utter the thoughts that arise in me."

When his attention returned to us, he asked for my transposition. I said the lines could not be transposed, they were poetry, and what they meant was not what they said. (You really must sympathize with the pitiable teacher, hearing *that*.) He turned to a boy, Charlie Day, and asked him for his transposition. Charlie Day stood up, proud in successful achievement, and read:

Smash on your rocks, O Ocean, and I wish that I could say what I think about it!

This I could have borne, suffering but enduring, if the teacher had not turned the incident to my moral profit. Let this be a lesson to you, Miss Wilder, he said; you fail because you do not try; you see that Charlie succeeds in doing what you did not attempt. Perservance is the chief virtue; without it you will accomplish nothing in life. If at first you don't succeed, you must not weakly give up; you must. . . .

I stood up, slammed my books on the desk, said in fury, "I will not stay here to listen to such stupid, stupid!!" and went home.

This is becoming another *Gone With The Wind*. And city editors used to tell cubs that the creation of the world was written in 600 words. I was, a telegraph clerk, a telegraph operator, a telegraph officer manager, a space-buyer (advertising), a real estate salesman, a newspaper feature writer, a free lance writer. Selah.

I never intended to do any of it. I can't explain any of it. About thirty-five years ago I began to know something about education, universities, colleges, entirely from the outside of course; and to meet VIPs in the field; and I ceased to grieve because I never had their opportunities. Of course, what I would have done with them, or they would have done to me, if I had had them, is unknowable. But when Mr. Ashmore calls me an illiterate, incapable of understanding an economic textbook, I am sincerely amused, and that is all. I know some of my inferiorities, but inferiority to Mr. Ashmore isn't one of them. Even our nation's President from the London School of Economics doesn't awe me.

This attempt to answer your question has failed. I'm sorry. At least I hope I have entertained you. And if pursuing the problem of how I got this way will continue to interest you entertainingly, I'll be glad to answer any questions that occur to you.

You'll have a happy Christmas, I know, and I hope you're feeling fine and fit again, and will have a Merry New Year's Eve and the best of new years.

January 13, 1962

Dear Mr. Crane:

Thank you for your note of yesterday. I am so happy to know that you are recovering good health. Mr. Crane, you must not leave this world before I do! I cannot bear it. Mr. Older went, and Mr. Lorimer went; you must stay; you must swallow handfuls of vitamins (as I do) and never work when tired and always do what you enjoy doing and be happy and well and stay on this earth with me. Please, make this a New Year's resolution and keep it?

In this morning's mail I have the announcement of the YAF Ralley of 20,000 on March 7 in Madison Square Garden. This is where I came in, while you were absorbed in science I believe. I knew all about the socialists from 1904 on; I was reading *The Appeal To Reason* even earlier, and by this century's teens I was one of our little groups of forward-looking thinkers, humbly following the Fabians and never questioning the then-current cliche, "Germany is fifty years ahead of us in social legislation." So I knew the Socialist-into-Communists all the way from the slums of New York to the penthouses of Park Avenue and the East 80s, and all those roaring rallies in Carnegie Hall—behind the scenes as well as in front.

The only differences between then and now are, first, that the "trend" is reversed and, second, that the police are not out with clubs now; the Terror now is so much more subtle. In those days unlocked doors were rushed off hinges, furniture smashed, people thrown out of windows (a whole night-school class of Russian refugees from Bolshevism, trying to learn English, was beaten up, thrown out of the windows, and into police wagons and jail, where one of them, a pregnant woman, died unhelped. I remember this because I spoke about it indignantly to some "bourgeois" friends, who reported to others that I was becoming "hysterical"). There were knocks on doors at midnight, and suddenly vanishing people, frantic wives unable to learn what had become of husbands, etc., etc., etc. The Department of Justice men knew nothing at all and were incredibly stupid. They filled ships, overnight, with any and all kinds of "radicals" yanked out of their beds, a few in nothing but nightgowns and pajamas, and shipped them out to Russia before dawn. Imagine shipping Emma Goldman, fanatic anarchist, into the clutches of Lenin! We could do profitably with some such violence now; it MADE the CPUSA and the New Deal; But maybe the Soviet rockets well serve the same purpose now. Let's hope.

XXI

January 4, 1962

Dear Mr. Crane:

I am sending you what, I hope, may be an interesting occupation of some lazily idle time, an interlude from all current events. It is the diary-notes that my mother made while we were traveling from Dakota to the Ozarks in 1893, with a bit of explanatory introduction and a postscript by me.[7]

You must have been on this planet at the time and a comparison of memories may be entertaining. Also I think the 1893 prices are interesting now. I remember the whole trip quite vividly and could tell scores of incidents that aren't in those short notes. Paul did drive all the way, except through cities where he had to let his mother do it because the horses might be frightened; humiliating as it was to him, at nearly ten, to have to give up the lines. Sometimes I was allowed to ride with him and George in the Cooley's second wagon and once I bullied him into permitting me to drive for almost a mile. You are the first person ever to know this guilty secret, which to this day Paul and George and I have kept.

February 7, 1962

Dear Mrs. Lane:

I remember '93 so well. My father's business failed, and he was out of a job for many months and took a very minor job for some years. I was twelve years old, and I recall saying to myself that that ended my chances of going to Princeton—a selfish thought, but it hit me hard. And I remember the subsequent years and, particularly, the routing of the unsound leaders in 1896. So I did go to Princeton after all, in '97, and some years later borrowed money and had a year at MIT.

---

[7]Published later in 1962 as *On the Way Home*, Harper & Row, Publishers, Inc.

Walter Wyckoff, whom we called "Weary" Wycoff, professor at Princeton, had his historic hike across country during the panic, succeeding, however, in getting a job and supporting himself at each place he stopped on his way. There is a lot of sound economics in his volumes. Your writing will be so helpful to the cause of liberty that I want to see this in print! I am still insatiable! How is your great book getting along, and when do you think you will have it written?

February 21, 1962

Dear Mr. Crane:

I believe that those who made their money in happier times do not realize at all the present cash-costs of sincerity and self-respect, our views being 'given.' Of course nobody who pays the costs howls about them. But for instance—and I mean, only *as* one instance—in 1930 I was tops in my profession, easily earning at the rate of about $100,000 a year; the crash reduced my prices about twenty-five percent but did not affect my market; in 1932 I was best-selling and getting back to top prices. I lost nothing in the crash, but did lose everything in the Palmer & Co. failure in 1932. I was supporting a number of persons and owed incidentally about $10,000, so a little later I came to New York (with $7) to recover, quick. I wrote *Free Land* and broke even, debts paid. I didn't need to be told but I was told, explicitly in plain words, that I could increase my former income if I'd 'go along' with the Communists then in complete control of the literary field.

So ever since I have known you, until lately, I have lived on less than $1,000 a year. Lately I have inherited property giving me an unearned (so not "social security" liable) better income. I know a woman more conscientious than I who lives on less than $600 in order to pay NO federal taxes—for war and support of Communists regimes. I draw the line only at the Sozialpolitik fraud which will inevitably destroy the American political structure. This makes it impossible for me to earn money by writing, of course. Since the self-employed are "benefited."

The situation handicaps us in ways perhaps not quite understood. During those Princeton meetings, for example,

I did pay transportation but could not pay hotel bills, so I was a guest, not in a wholly independent position. Anyone can be wholly frank without being rude, of course; but if complete frankness might be unpleasant to a host, courtesy requires a guest to be silent. I think this is the reason that Foundations generally fill with persons unscrupulous in dealing with "capitalist" and "capitalism" (regarded as their unscrupulous enemies). If you are dependent on politicians for privileged status, and dependent on "capitalists" for your income, you must either be a fawning (or silent) sycophant, or a treacherous one; and most of them are treacherous because they blame and bite the hand that feeds them instead of blaming themselves for selling their self-respect.

You could serve Du Pont with self-respecting loyalty because you agreed with the company's aims and because your relations with the company were contractural, essentially equal; *quid pro quo.* But imagine IF you can, that Du Pont had engaged in the international narcotic traffic.

That is the position of a real 'libertarian', an individualist, employed in a Foundation supported by men who advocate tarrifs, Social Security, Federal Aid to Education, rent controls, public schools (State Schooling), etc. He has a choice of suppressing his own views and continuing to take their money, or quitting or hanging on till he's fired. If he continues to take their money and pretend agreement with them, he hates (such is the irrational pressure) *them,* and does them all the harm he can. Meanwhile the place fills up with socialists and Communists who in principle agree with them and in practice work to destroy them; so the fake eventually loses his job anyway. So all the Foundations are collectivist, excepting a few tiny ones, most of which are futile because of their non-profit shackles.

There really is no place, at present, for a John Adams or a Madison or a Patrick Henry who must earn his living. Oh, that's an exaggeration; but what few places there are. Hans Sennholz does have his job at Grove College; and he is turning out sound economists. But his work is stymied because it's near impossible for a sound economist to get a teaching job, and Hans is spending years trying to get an American College of Economics started to give them the necessary academic degrees. While a Fund for the Republic can get all the millions that they want. Still, it is cheering that Hans can earn a living. In the 1930s he couldn't have done it.

Things are not as bad in the literary field, either. Little, Brown has got out of the Communist Party control; *Collier's* is dead; the Party grip on several publishing houses is weakening somewhat. I am running a really Right Wing Extremist series of articles on needlework in *Woman's Day*; Eileen Tighe, that editor, has always been WITH us. And the reader response is terrific; astounding; tens of thousands of letters saying, Thank you, THANK you, for American history, American spirit. Six publishing houses have asked for the series in book, though certainly some of them want to sabotage it; their editors bragging at cocktail parties of their houses' "right wing" books that they have killed. I get no money from the series, have no ownership in it, so the Internal Revenue Service hounds are still baffled.

Did I ever tell you about the one, enraged, determined to get me into "Social Security" who shouted at me" "I am a PUBLIC SERVANT, I have no time to listen to *you*; you will do as I say, or ELSE!"? They are really very funny sometimes.

February 24, 1962

Dear Mr. Crane:

A young man, Robert Adams, has just called me for some data to use in a debate next Tuesday at Yale, between the individualist students there and their opponents. He says "things are hopping" at Yale, and his only fear is that there may not be time enough for "us" to save this country. Bless these youngsters; aren't they wonderful? After all these years of fighting the good fight, the reserves are coming up at last.

March 7, 1962

Dear Mr. Crane:

Speaking of religious ecstatics recalled the "miracle" I once saw done by Whirling Dervishes during the Ramazam (or Ramadan) in Tirana. I knew several leaders of the

Sect in Istanbul and Damascus, highly intelligent, learned, cultured men. These in Tirana were ordinary rank-and-file members of it, merely performing its rites during the sacred month. Equivalent, or parallel (I guess) to the "Holy Roller" rites here, of suffering the bites of poisonous serpents or "speaking in unknown tongues," or flagellation.

For days and nights, without stopping, these Dervishes whirled chanting and circling in a small ring. There were a dozen or so of them, in the open air, in the midst of the holiday crowd. I mean in the crowd at night. Ramazan came in the heat of summer that year; the day-long fasting, without water, was terrible and people came out only at night, after sunset, when they could drink and eat and celebrate till sunrise, but the Dervishes whirled all the time without stopping until they dropped. When one collapsed another came out of the crowd into his place.

One night I stopped to watch them. I was in the edge of the crowd-circle around them, near enough to touch any of them as they whirled past under a big arc light—electric; this was after Ahmet installed electric street lights in Tirana. They looked haggard, exhausted, and seemed asleep though their eyes were open. I was thinking this is an exhibition like the horrid Walkathons in the USA, when the chant rose into a kind of howl, they all pulled daggers from their sashes and stabbed themselves through their cheeks, right through, the hilts hard against one cheek and the knives coming out through the other cheek. Blood spattered, a few drops on me. They kept on whirling by, I guess three times, I couldn't count, then they pulled the daggers out, and their cheeks healed. I suppose I stood there ten or fifteen minutes. A Christian Albanian friend was with me, an American Registered Nurse, trained in Massachusetts General Hospital. I couldn't believe what I saw, and asked her; she said, Yes, the Whirling Dervishes always did this. Their cheeks were really healed, not a trace of the wound. Only a little blood drying on their jaws. The healing was not instantaneous; it took a little time while they went on whirling but I did not precisely see it happen; I saw the wounds in their cheeks plainly enough and then I didn't see them, I saw the smooth dark skin instead. Hypnosis? Power of mind over body? It scared me; and still does when I remember it.

In Istanbul one evening I was a guest of the head of

the sect, who had just returned from the pilgrimage to Mecca. He told us every detail of the whole journey and of the rites in Mecca, a fascinating tale. And his Nubian slave served us each, as climax of the evening, a tiny cupful of water from the Well ZemZem, the miraculous well in the desert near Mecca which saved Ishmael's life when he (and his mother) were dying of thirst after Abraham cast them out to satisfy Sarah. God created the well in answer to Hagar's prayers, and preserved Ishmael to be the ancestor of all Arabs. I am probably the only person in Danbury who has drunk water from ZemZem.

When you asked me where I got my ideas, I should not have forgotten the Moslems. I went to Europe accepting all the socialist assumptions, never having heard anything else in this country. Seeing Europe shocked me and dislodged most of them, but I was still bewildered and floundering until, in this country again, I began to work from the "We hold these truths to be self-evident . . ." sentence. Then many talks with Moslems in Albania, Turkey, Syria, Egypt, Baghdad, began to fit into my thinking, most usefully. The Hadj in Istanbul was a firm individualist; I wish I had asked him to explain that dagger-rite of his sect; at the time I was too diffident about discussing religions; I merely listened.

March 20, 1962

Dear Mr. Crane:

Springtime again—arriving, I believe, at 9:0- something this evening—and no doubt your crocuses are blooming. Mine only poked cold little noses up into the snow which now is melting under rain. So, happy springtime to you.

You will like to know that Harper is publishing my mother's diary of the 1894 trip, manuscript of which I sent you. You are right, of course, about the value of such real Americana now. Many hundreds of letters from parents, during these thirty years, have shown how much good my mother's books have been—and are— doing in their quiet way. And this diary is more of the same. By the way, did you ever read my mother's books? It would hardly occur to you to read a series of eight books for children, but I believe you will find them purely delightful to YOU, if you have time for simple enjoyment. Parents who buy them for the children write me that—well, a letter today says that father and mother *sneaked* reading them straight through because they couldn't wait for the every-evening chapter they read to their pre-school children. I don't believe they'd bore you for a single minute. The Little House books,[8] or The Laura Books, they're called, by Laura Ingalls Wilder. The first one is *The Little House in the Big Woods.* My mother wrote it only to preserve the stories her father told her and her sister when she was three years old, in the Big Woods of Wisconsin. The second is *Farmer Boy,* my father's childhood near Malone in northern New York State; the others follow my mother's childhood; my father reappears in the seventh and they marry in the eighth. They are true autobiography in the third person.

March 27, 1962

Dear Mrs. Lane:

The news in your letter of March 20 that your mother's diary is being published in book form is very good indeed. With the illustrations, if they are good, and your additional pages, it should be an inspiring book to rank along-side *Let The Hurricane Roar.*

April 3, 1962

Dear Mrs. Lane:

Deists, as well as Jews, and Moslems, can be ardent individualists; indeed they must be if they put their ultimate reliance on God. I don't see how an atheist can be. If one's philosophy is entirely secular, the last word is attributed to man, and force is resorted to.

April 5, 1962

Dear Mr. Crane:

Actually there are no genuine atheists. Harold Stearns was the only one I ever heard of who ever *acted* according

---

[8]Published by Harper & Row, Publishers, Inc.—ed.

to what he erroneously believed that he believed. Do you at all remember Harold Stearns, I wonder. Later had had a minor reputation as a minor critic of America's bourgeois capitalistic materialist lack of culture; published a book, maybe two. He was Harvard, class of 1920 or thereabouts, and one evening he was expounding his views as a senior to a group of inferior intellects, explaining that "there are no principles," and suiting action to philosophy, he stepped out of third-story-window. Had to be carried to hospital; broke a leg.

Persons who say they are atheists merely have another name for their God. —History, for Marxists, for example. —So they may inconsistently act; and even say that there are such laws as gravitation and I suppose could agree that persons are inherently self-controlling and responsible for their actions, which would be agreement with the basic implication of the Ten Commandments. But, consistently with atheism, in fact they cannot say anything of the kind; they cannot *act* at all, they can't *live.* If Chance—nothing but an accidental collision of atoms accidentally happening to be—creates everything, how could anyone dare to walk—to step on a floor which at that instant might happen to be an abyss, or seawater or air or a rattlesnake? Atheism is merely an instance or irrationality, which according to N. J. Birrell comes from the as-yet-incomplete evolution (creation) of human minds. I suppose I've said to you before, WHAT an encouragement to optimism his *Man's Emerging Mind* is.

I suppose the uniqueness of each person makes it impossible that anyone's idea of God be *precisely* identical with another's. The same words haven't exactly the same meaning to two persons. So agreement on a creed cannot be perfect, no more than anything else human. And sometimes someone disagrees with all forms of religion that he knows and, being actually deeply religious, he declares that he is an atheist and sets up a God of his own, as Marx did. Really irreligious persons don't think about it at all; they simply live as animals do and conform to whatever church rites may be usual where they are.

April 22, 1962

Dear Mrs. Lane:

No matter how devout a person is he should resist the tendency to create God in his own image. I was quite shocked to read in an article in the February *Reader's Digest* of the teaching of this space age, which stated the probability of encountering beings from other planets more intelligent than ourselves, and that that, forsooth, would emphasize the teaching of the grandeur of men and his possibilities for self development. To get this feeling, we were advised to go out on a clear night and look at the stars, reminding us of how wonderful a man is. This is quite contrary to my own reaction. I think pride is the greatest sin and humility the basis of all virtue. I wondered why DeWitt Wallace permitted such an article.

April 25, 1962

Dear Mr. Crane:

Mr. Wallace probably had nothing to do with the article about the grandeur of man. He is in Europe, or lately has been for some time; also I hear that he is trying to disengage himself from the management of *Reader's Digest* as much as possible; I'd surmise that he hopes to leave the enterprise in shape to continue flourishing after his death. He and Lila have been really the indispensables. Truly great editors, and apparently the last of their kind in the national field. I suppose others are budding now on the numerous little new publications. If not, there's an end of the American magazine. They simply *cannot* be made, nor kept alive, by Soviets. So now they're dying off, everywhere.

I agree with you about humility, of course. But too often humility is supposed to be Uriah-Heepish, don't you think? This looking at the universe and saying how tiny, how negligible, how worthless is man, seems to me merely the obverse of the sticking in the thumb, getting a plum and saying What a GREAT man am I! I remember an anecdote of someone's saying, after seeing the stars through a telescope, how puny is man, and someone's replying, Yes, but he made the telescope.

I suppose the necessity may be, not so much pride nor

humility, but a just sense of proportions. One might say, Who am I, to be either proud or humble? Am I properly my own judge at all? CAN *I* say, accurately, more than: I *am?* Can I do more than my best, so far as I can know what is my best? I can measure my achievement by my own intention (and it will always fall short) but that's a relative and temporal measurement, isn't it? How can I know how well or how poorly my life serves the ultimate Purpose of Creation? or even of human life on this planet? And without that knowledge, how can I judge my own ultimate value?

I don't "resist the tendency to create God in his (my) own image" because any such tendency was left out of my make-up. I simply lack it. I know too little about everything, or anything. It's all I can do to create a logical thought, or a house or a book or a platter of ham and eggs; and I've not yet done one of those ever-nearly *perfectly.* When I try to imagine creating so much as one little bush, much less the visible (to me) universe . . . I'm stymied; my own limitations stop me there, without any effort to imagine the Creator, the Purpose, the Final Cause. All I know is that, obviously, there must be one.

Man's Emerging Mind is a a joy to me because it is a view (though probably tentative, insufficient) of *continuing* Creation. It seems to me self-evident that there is a continuing creative process; that God did not complete the universe in six days and stop on the seventh, to become then and thereafter a changeless Authority ruling a static, timeless, changeless Reality. That Platonic view seems to be too inconsistent with facts, phenomena, which are within the grasp of human (limited) means of perception; senses and mind and that mystery named 'inspiration.' We *see* a creative process producing new, tangible things, even such little things as red grapefruit.

Do you know how they "happened"? I knew Luther Burbank, who made new kinds of fruit by understanding a little about processes which certainly he didn't himself create. And in McAllen, Texas, I talked with the man in whose orchard the red grapefruit appeared. He had only an acre or so of trees, so he knew each one intimately; and he said that one spring one branch of one tree seemed "peculiar" (his words) and puzzled him. It seemed healthy, he couldn't say how it was different, exactly; it was on a thriving tree that had been bearing well for some years, all the leaves on the branch appeared and unfolded and were green and well shaped, as all other leaves were, it just somehow didn't look quite "natural."

So he watched it; it blossomed and produced and ripened grapefruit, quite normally; and when he cut one open, its flesh was ruby-*red*; not pink; a deep rich red. And with a new flavor. So he grafted twigs from that branch onto other trees, and all the *red* grapefruit existing now have come from one branch. The other branches on that tree produced the usual fruit. Of course, this is commonplace, the branch was a "sport," the ordinary way in which countless fruits and vegetables have appeared and are appearing all the time. Why should the spirit of man be proud? when no man can create so much as a red grapefruit? On the other hand, why should man grovel, when it is given to us to learn enough about these mysteries to act according to our little observations of them and be Luther Burbanks? We can have our little limited share in creating things and in creating ourselves.

Vocabularies are inadequate. We need a word between *hubris* and *humbleness,* it seems to me.

And if astronauts from this planet meet on other planets beings more intelligent than human beings, all I'll say is, So what? Any of us meets every day, in every garden or lawn, intelligence greater than ours. (If "intelligence" is the word.) What man ever changed grass seed to a blade of grass? The starry heavens declare the glory of God and the firmament showeth His handiwork; and if they say anything about the grandeur or the insignificance of man, I don't know what it is.

XXII

The Gold Dust Motel
7700 Biscayne Blvd.
Miami, Florida
July 2, 1962

Dear Mr. Crane:

News of me: I have been here since May and will be here until the end of this month, trying to finish the revision of *Discovery of Freedom* for publication. I have a pleasant room, at back of the motel away from the boulevard and fronting on Biscayne Canal (from and to Indian creek), a lovely expanse of water with bridges over it, an occasional boat on it, large tropical houses, pink and white, in lots of tropical foliage, and its other bank mirrored in it. A good coffee shop almost next door and a truly excellent restaurant and shopping center a block away. I have nothing to do but work.

My house caught fire in my absence, but King Street volunteer firemen saved it with very little damage to it and none to books and furniture. Thereafter a rainstorm flooded the sundeck and brought down the ceiling plaster in two rooms. It is really funny, I sit here laughing. But it isn't so pleasant for my good friends-of-all-work Stanley and (his wife) Julia Parzuchowski and daughter Marybeth who are puppy-sitting in my house while I am away. Still, they say they are comfortable and enjoying living in the undamaged part of the house. My silver lining is that Stanley is now doing nothing but working at repairing the damages, so most of his summer's wages are tax-deductible. Roger's telegram to me about the fire began: You have another casualty-loss deduction. Now it sure is a Welfare State that makes people thankful for calamities and prosperous from debts. When I see ads in the *Wall Street Journal* offering, or asking for, a business losing hundreds of thousands of dollars a year, I am Alice in Wonderland crying, Curiouser and curiouser!

I have to be at Freedom School late this month, and hate it. They have insisted on giving my name to their newly finished big central building, and I have to be there when it is dedicated. Bob LeFevre has a fantastically mistaken feeling about me because *he* changed all his ideas and the rest of his life while reading *Discovery of Freedom.* I am not responsible for what he thought and did; and this isn't an opinion, it is demonstrable fact. He is not the only reader of that book, and all the others haven't made Freedom Schools. It isn't even a good book. He embarrasses me, but I have not been able to talk—write, rather—him out of it.

Gold Dust Motel
7700 Biscayne Blvd.
Miami, Florida
July 4, 1962

Dear Mr. Crane:

Orval and I are wrangling about a definition of "freedom." We agree to use "liberty" defining as an intrinsic inalienable function of self-control existing (as human life does) only in an individual human being.

A major obstacle to revolutionary (American political philosophical) thinking is a lack of a vocabulary. It is necessary first, as Euclid said, to define the terms. Actually there are no precise definitions of liberty (*libertè*) or freedom (*freiheit*). Dictionaries define liberty as freedom and freedom as liberty. I say, there must be one word for a function and another for the environment in which that function can be exercised, used, e.g. seeing is a function; light is the necessary environment. So we are trying to define an *environment* of freedom.

Did you ever frivolously waste time reading any of the *Saturday Evening Post* series of stories about Botts, the tractor salesman? In one of them he finds a small-business customer on the point of shutting down and quitting because of taxes, and a school, non-profit small foundation, on point of closing for lack of pupils. Brilliantly he combines the two, changes the school into teaching the small-business craft, giving its six skilled employees scholarships instead of wages, makes the owner the school's principal, keeps the teacher as teacher of the craft (she needn't know anything about it, how many teachers do know what they're supposed to teach?) and eliminates the taxes—the whole multitude of them; and sells the school the tractor. Saves the business.

July 9, 1962

Dear Mrs. Lane:

In the "all about everything" memorandum of 1949, to which you were much the largest contributor, we defined liberty as "the individual person's control of himself, his freedom of choice, his responsibility for his own actions. . . . Freedom, which is a condition external to the individual, is the absence of force to coerce him; with it . . . he is unrestricted, except for not harming others, in worship, speech, writing, cooperation with others, choice of occupation, handling of property, enjoyment of all of his faculties." "For what is freedom but the unfettered use of all the powers that God for use has given?" (Coleridge.) We went on to say that "personal responsibility is the indispensable condition for ethics. There is no mass liberty, no group control of the individual self."

July 31, 1962

Mrs. Rose Wilder Lane
The Freedom School, Inc.
Box 163
Colorado Springs, Colorado

Dear Mrs. Lane:

Probably if we all were ready to go to jail we could have stopped the present iniquitous course of affairs. Schecter—wasn't it?—defied the government and sold chickens in the free market. Another man was jailed for cleaning pants for fifteen cents. But these actions and several others helped to kill the NRA. I always wished afterwards that I had bought some gold and locked it up when it was so illegally taken away from us in 1953, but I didn't have the common sense to appreciate what was going on until too late. Vivian Kellems courageously refused to withhold wages and accept the role of government tax collector and was dreadfully persecuted for it. How did that turn out? It seems to me that she finally was beaten, but I am not sure of the outcome.

August 23, 1962

Dear Mr. Crane:

I do wish that you would visit Freedom School in Colorado. Can't you possibly? I am so sure that it would be an experience so cheering that it would always take all the sharpness out of all the disheartening ones that we keep encountering. It is really almost incredible what those few persons are doing there. . . .

It is a beautiful place, on the mountain side among the huge pine trees, mountain air and stllness, and far views, and in the evenings herds of deer come out of the woods and browse on the open slopes. You could not find a more restful place, or a more interesting one. Do please tell me that you will visit it? I know that they would all be delighted to have you there, any time that you choose.

The students come from all the States, and they are most interesting, not only in class where they respond so vigorously to the teacher's ideas but in their constant talking about them. You have never seen more lively interest or heard more enthusiastic discussions and clashes of opinions. It is the most ALIVE place that I've ever seen. Hundreds of young people are going out of that school every summer, thinking about human rights and Welfare States as Americans thought in the eighteenth century, as you and I want people to think, of individual responsibilities and moral values. Young Jeffersons and Madisons and Franklins; you can't see and hear them and doubt me when I repeat, this century will end in a great upsurge of liberalism, as the eighteenth century ended, and this time its success will be greater than before. I shan't be here to see it, but I have seen the Freedom School, and I do want you to see it.

August 30, 1962

Dear Mrs. Lane:

Your letter of August 23 urging me to visit the Freedom School is very greatly appreciated. Mr. LeFevre has invited me to come there several times, and quite emphatically, too, so I definitely assume that I would be welcome, and I would like to go.

The possibility is among several other wishes of mine which can only be fulfilled if and when I am able to travel.

So far I have not been anywhere, except about three weeks in Cape Cod, reached by automobile in easy stages. I haven't even been to nearby Philadelphia yet, but I am improving in health and strength, and I hope that some of these wishes of mine will come true. Certainly a visit to Colorado Springs would be very important and is much to be desired.

September 1, 1962

Dear Mr. Crane:

[On] my first visit to the school, afternoons and evenings for two weeks I sat in [Mr. LeFevre's] class and watched his teaching and thought it almost incredibly inspired, getting the most marvelous response from those college students. I'd say that his method is Socratic, only I think him right where Plato's Socrates wasn't, and a thousand times as good a teacher. He opened the course by asking What is truth? And before that hour ended he had the class hunting truth like a pack of hounds on a hot trail. He not only listened, he seemed to know what they—each—would think before they thought it (I used to do that with prospects, when I was selling land in California. I know what a strain of concentrated attention it takes.)

September 5, 1962

Dear Mr. Crane:

I thought in 1933 and still think, that the men who stopped Bryan in 1896 (men in the same positions) could have stopped FDR if they had acted to defend themselves. I was astounded that they didn't. All the active opposition came from thousands of the 'little men' such as those who sold chickens and cleaned pants, and the countless farmers who drove the 'Federal men' from their farms with guns, to protect their little pigs and their crops, and the dozen or so who went to jail or lost their farms. The most "important" person who acted was Vivian Kellems. She explained the situation to her employees, and each of them individually paid the taxes; Miss Kellems simply refused to work for the Government against her will and without pay, on the Constitutional ground of the amendment forbidding involuntary servitude. Two Federal men went to her bank and demanded her money, and the banker gave it to them. She sued in the courts to recover it, and lost. She closed her factory.

It is really simple enough to abolish tyranny if even a considerable minority of persons want to do it. It can't be done by isolated single individuals when the media of communication are controlled by the tyrant. I spent ten years doing nothing but writing letters twelve hours a day; I got hundreds of letters saying in effect, "I am against this, but I guess nobody else is, but you. Can just the two of us do anything?" I wrote the letters just to let people know that each one was not alone, that many others thought the same.

There was no necessity at all that employers collect withholding taxes from their employees. If they simply had not done it, they would have saved this Government ultimately, and much of their own property immediately (all the costs of collections and reports). I still cannot understand why the managers of the larger corporations did not protect their own immediate interests. The housekeeping women did, when "the benefits of social security were extended" to their—I believe the word now is maids; when I was younger they were hired girls. Only a few of the women were mentioned in the press, the Marshall Girls? The Government tried to make an example of the women in Marshall, Texas (a small town, I don't know where in Texas) and Federal men went to their banks and took their money, as they did Vivian Kellems. The women simply closed their bank accounts and continued not to collect the withholding taxes.

I can only suppose that the big industrialists, I mean those employing thousands of workers, by 1933 were educated in colleges, where the influences had been strongly socialistic for a generation. In 1896 they were mostly "self-made men, up from the bottom, realistic, practical, and tough fighters. In 1896 they had BUILT their railroads and their factories; in 1933 they were only running them, and the organizations were so big that it must be difficult to feel, "This is *mine;* I control it, *I* am responsible, *I* am the boss." Also, generally speaking, there was no admiration for businessmen in colleges, there was a strong element of the European artistocratic contempt for "trade," and of the socialist scorn of the "bourgeois." And the sudden stock market crash and the depression must have been a terrible shock. Add that since the Founders died in the early 1800s, there had been no intellectual development of the American political philosophy.

How fortunate that there is so much of that now. Never mind, the past is past, and there's a good time coming. To which you, Mr. Crane, have contributed so much that I'm sure you should be much happier than any kings are. Thank you.

September 11, 1962

Dear Mrs. Lane:

We have agreed before that business executives are so greatly responsible for the mess we are in. Hitler commented on this, I think in *Mein Kampf*, to the effect that business men would dig their own graves if properly paid to do so.

September 15, 1962

Dear Mr. Crane:

Hitler, the misguided boob from eastern Europe, knew NOTHING about business men, and even less about Americans.

What seems to be happening (or maybe, to have been almost happening) here is a recurrent historical phenomenon, which I cannot understand in any instance. But it happens so invariably as to suggest an axiom—well, it's said: Whom the gods destroy, they first make mad. I'd say the same thing: A destroyed class or group invariably has produced its own destruction. What I CANNOT understand is: Why?

Think of the French aristocrats, who first concurred in being made useless appendages to the Kings' Courts and then supported the writers and thinkers whose ideas inspired the Terror and the guillotine which cut off their heads—. The German, Italian, Russian plutocrats who financed, respectively, Hitler, Mussolini, Lenin and Stalin (when Stalin was Lenin's bankrobber, pre-1914-18 war). —The elite Greeks who supported and applauded Pericles.

—The Gracchi and their noble Roman followers to and including Julius Caeser, who attacked their own class and destroyed it and the Republic.

Hitler's idea of "Capitalists" is ridiculous. Men do not dig their own graves for pay. Henry Ford II is not financing "Leftists" for money. I needn't labor the point; you know the names of a dozen or more big organizations amply supported financially by the men whom they are destroying. And the names of half a dozen men whose fathers made them rich who are Corliss Lamonts, openly and proudly pro-Communists. Why? What has happened to the normal and proper human motives (in them) of profit and of self-defiance? Why are they suicidal? and, like Samson blind in Gaza, pulling down the pillars of their country?

OF COURSE, as you say "Business executives are dedicated to producing goods and services, thus making a great contribution to the welfare of the American people"—indeed to all human welfare, since history began. In 1896 in this country, they *knew* it. They were properly aware of their value and they acted to defend it; and maybe some of them were merely *self*-defending (which human beings *should* be), but many of them were wise enough to see that they were also defending the Revolution for "life, liberty and property." What happened to the next generation?

In 1896 when the Boy Orator of the Platte came out of the west with a popular whoop and hurrah behind him (at the time, I was all for Free Silver, sixteen-to-one, and Bust the Trusts!) the business executives defended themselves and this country. In the second century B.C. when the Gracchi, full of Greek learning, roused up the rabble and attacked the Senate and the Republic, the Senators killed them. Smashed up the wooden benches in the Senate House and personally killed Tiberius and 300 of his supporters and threw the bodies into the Tiber. By the time that Caesar, descendant of Zeus, crossed the Rubicon, most of the Roman nobles had been killed in the Terrors and the civil wars.

But when Mr. Roosevelt with his Harvard brain trust moved into Washington, American business executives were still right here, hale and hearty; no Terrors, no wars, had disposed of them. Many of them were all for their own destruction; I remember seeing—Who was it? Mr. Young?—on a movie screen on election day, pleading for "heart" and FDR, rather than "head" and Mr. Hoover! And when the destruction is actually occurring, in the early '30s, the resistance comes from "little" farmers and a barber and a grocer.

The resistance grows, from the "grass roots." It will save this country, and, incidentally, in spite of themselves, most of the business executives. It's superfluous to mention what you and Mr. Pew are and have been doing to help it. And some others of whom I know little. But how many others? You know; I don't. I could name perhaps a dozen of the hundreds in this country. What I do not understand are those silent motionless hundreds. If you understand them at all I would be grateful for a clue to the puzzle.

Some of them seem simply to be scared. But surely they can't be, actually? That seems as fantastic as Hitler's idea that they can be paid to dig their own graves. Even if they could be, they are being robbed. Men know when they are being robbed; there is a notion that factory workers are too stupid to know that, but they do; and surely the factories' "Management" does.

I guessed at the universities' influence because so often I meet a scorn of "commercialism" in men whose occupation and source of wealth is commerce. The scorn is general in the Groves of Academe. It seems inexplicable. . . . Well, here's an instance. Years ago a factory worker in Bridgeport brought me an excellent pamphlet, well written, beautifully printed (at great cost), signed by the president of a corporation owning many factories, employing thousands. He said that just before the lunch hour uniformed messengers had come through the factory carrying baskets full of this pamphlet and giving one to each employee. The men took them and threw them out of the windows. When the shift changed and the men went down to the courtyard to eat their dinners, they walked on a carpet of those thousands of pamphlets. He picked up one to bring to me. While they were eating a young man in overalls, a Communist, came in and talked to them about being wage-slaves, and their exploiting employers; he was friendly and the men liked him. My informant said that so far as he could determine, he was the one man in the place who even opened one of those pamphlets.

It was really a good pamphlet; and at that time I was doing nothing but writing letters and mailing out anything in print that was any good. I wrote to the President author praising it; asking if I might have fifty copies, and making a mistake. I was then almost automatically urging all writers of pamphlets to sell them, so I did this: I pointed out that people never value a give-away offered them as they valued something that they pay for, and that to get the circulation and attention that this pamphlet deserved, it should be given at least a nominal price. Its obvious cost was at least fifty cents; sell it for ten cents and get a hundred readers, and it will be immeasurably more effective than a thousand copies given away.

It didn't occur to me that the President might infer that I intended to sell the pamphlet. I intended to send it only to persons who, I knew, would read it. The President did not reply, nor send me any copies. But Freda Utley, who was working with him, met me later and mentioned his having read my letter. "Of course," she said, "He wouldn't *commercialize* the pamphlet." Where does a man engaged in commerce get his scorn of commerce? And, having it, how can he continue in commerce and keep his self-respect? Miss Utley's scorn is understandable; she is, or was, by way of being "an intellectual." A disillusioned English Communist. But an American business executive? where did he get it and how did he maintain it, in his own mind?

September 20, 1962

Dear Mrs. Lane:

I don't look on Hitler as a "mis-guided boob." It is quite clear that he had paranoia, the most dangerous form of insanity. He was a killer and the greatest foe to freedom up to the emergence of communist Russia.

Why these prominent people down through the ages have supported the tyrants that you cite is a repeatedly occurring conundrum of history. May the reason be the lack of understanding of liberty plus the instinctive approval of the use of force? Going into church leadership circles and into the National Council of Churches, I was amazed at the socialistic philosophy of so many leaders. I keep on my desk a quotation from Philip Wylie: "When Christians are organized, they begin to behave in an un-Christian manner." Whatever the reason, it seems to have taken almost eighteen hundred years from the teachings of Jesus to establish a government fashioned after the nature of man. Then it wasn't appreciated. The meaning of liberty was unknown and our heritage was almost wasted away. Then a book appeared called *The Discovery Of Freedom.* A new literature developed and has now reached great and influential volume. Yet, most people in this country still do not understand freedom, and in other lands the situation is much worse and well nigh half the world is dominated by communists.

October 9, 1962

Dear Mrs. Lane:

Do you know the novels of Helen McInnes, which contain much anti-communist material? I don't know how large the sales of these books have been and, therefore, how effective they are as propaganda for our side. I have read *Neither Five Nor Three* and now *Decision At Delphi.* She makes one interesting point that I never heard before, that Lenin added Nihilism to Marx's theory, and that is grim.

October 11, 1962

Dear Mr. Crane:

Yes, I know something of Helen McInnes's work, because for years the only readable fiction has been detective and science-fiction. (The vogue for the Faulkners and Hemingways, their imitators, I'll NEVER understand.)

Neither Five Nor Three was, I believe, the first of her anti-communist stories. It was a best seller for months, and I think that all her books sell well. How effective they may be is another question of course. I remember the hopes pinned on (1) saving Richard Kreb's (Jan Valtin's) life by getting his exposé into print; then, (2) on *Out Of The Night's* effective arousing value—when, not only in print, it was Book of the Month, tremendous best seller and sold to movies. And I remember the reaction of one intelligent reader who said, "Well, it certainly kept one reading, I couldn't put it down, but really I didn't like him much." I murmured something about its exposure of the Comintern underground and she said, Oh, *that,* that was just made up, of course; and overdone in spots, just *too* melodramatic.

(The fact was that it was toned down and deleted, to make it credible.)

Nihilists were all through the Russian revolutionary movement, of course, but it's news to me that Lenin anywhere adopted the theory of nihilism, explicitly at all. The attack on profit-motive is essentially nihilist, because profit-motive is essential to human action. Without hope of profit —that is, hope of obtaining by acting something worth more (to the acting person) than the time-energy expended in acting is worth (to them)—nobody ever acts.

This definition of profit of course includes hope of avoiding loss; as a slave will work to remain unwhipped, for instance. And of course the "something worth more" is most often not a material thing.

It is the communist effort to destroy the profit-motive which tends, in effect, toward death; it stops the human effort towards more abundant life, more abundant in both quantity and quality. Lenin therefore *was* nihilist in theory and action, but it is astonishing that he knew it, if he did. I'm sure that most persons who denounce the profit-motive and praise the virtue of un-self-ishness, of altruism and self-sacrifice, haven't the faintest inkling that they are nihilist. They have a beautiful vision of a world-organism in which each human cell lives for all and all for each, and time does not exist (history stops as in Communist theory); there is no more change, no progress, because perfection has been achieved.

The absurdity is their belief that they are the revolutionary "wave of the future," working for a better world, when they are simply wanting to return to the primitive tribal consciousness which anthropologists call "pre-individual," existing in all infants and in the aborigines who have no clothes, no tools, no fire, no man-made shelter and no word in their language for "I." Actually these "revolutionists" are the superlative reactionaries.

Anyway, the sun is shining here today and I hope in Wilmington, and I'm wishing you all the best of everything.

November 4, 1962

Dear Mr. Crane:

Helen McInnes's *Decision At Delphi* came Friday and I have read it with the greatest pleasure, and thank you VERY much, for that enjoyment and for the book which I am glad to have and keep.

Memory clicked when I read the reference to Lenin's debt to Nechaiev; of course! (I thought.) That was the Menshevik retort to Lenin's "deviation" at the 1903-04 winter conference of the Russian section (in exile) of the Second Communist International in London. And true enough as far as it went, which was tactical. Lenin—and Nechaiev, for that matter—were no more anarchist than Marx; they all assumed that eventually a classless state must "wither away." Marx and Lenin would destroy ownership of property and thus destroy the State by leaving it no function; Nechaiev et al. would destroy the State and thus eliminate ownership of property, leaving it no use of force to maintain it. The real difference is one of strategy, the eventful end being the same.

What Lenin took from Nechaiev was not aim nor strategy, but the tactic of organized conspiracy and the use of "force and violence." This tactic plus his contention that capitalism is not an essential preliminary to communism, was his "deviation:" from strict Marxism. Marx relied (in theory) upon inevitable mystic processes of History to produce the victory of the proletariat. So the Second International in practice relied upon propaganda and popular suffrage. Which Lenin denounced as ineffectual; and eleven years later the German section (voting war-credits to the Kaiser in the Reichstag) dramatically proved (or seemed to) that he was right about that. His bolshevik faction of the Russian section proved it again, by the coup d'etat of 1917 in Petrograd. Why am I recounting all this, anyway? you know it.

I rather felt that Helen McInnes weakened *Decision At Delphi* by vaguely referring to "extremists." Actually she was using routine procedure in the underground half of the Comintern everywhere, and softening it very much, at that. I suppose in order to be believed, if possible. Incidentally, do you remember the incident of Mrs. Browder's being held up at the Canadian frontier, refused entry till Eleanor Roosevelt intervened and brought her into this country? and do you know that she was not Mrs. Browder but an expert agent whom the Politburo had "married" without ceremony to Browder against his will? Probably by this time quite a lot of the truth would be accepted as plausible fiction, but of course the book (it uses the Browder incident—the Party giving the villain's girl to the rich Italian) was written some time ago.

Americans generally can't believe the facts, so foreign to experience here. And I really feel worse about the "innocence" that they are losing than—well, almost—than about anything else. This country, of unlocked doors and open mailboxes and "make your own change" newsstands and innocence assumed until guilt was proved—never in history was any place or people anything like it before. Its ruin is tragic.

And do you remember what a wonderful upspringing of poetry and fiction and painting there was here, in this century's early teens? So suddenly killed by Wilson's starting this World War. I remember a silly little verse of about 1919:

> Of all the literary scenes
> The saddest are to me
> The graves of little magazines
> That died to make verse free.

which is wry laughter at a real tragedy. Lost forever, never to be known, what American art, American culture, would have been. If Wilson hadn't killed it in its childhood. What will be now—Heaven knows *when*—is worldwide, or nothing.

I remember one Easter at Delphi, in steadily *pouring* rain. The hotel was then the usual Balkan hotel—two story, rough boards, stone-paved ground floor cafe, stairway to bare rooms with iron bedsteads (no rugs or curtains) and candles or kerosene lamps. Blow out the light and the onrush of roaches and bedbugs was *heard.* Before you could scratch a match, the whitewashed ceiling was black—and I mean literally black—with the bugs. But my photographer, Peggy, and I were Balkan adepts by that time. While the lamp burns, you order four dishes, set one leg of the bed in each, and fill the dish with kerosene. Over the lower sheet on the bed you spread evenly a layer of Keating's powder:

when ready to sleep, you roll yourself deftly in the upper sheet, tucking in its ends to make a neat package of yourself and bringing the last end over the tucks so that no folds lead inward (not easy to describe, but it can be done). The final last fold, held open, lets you blow out the light and, quickly, quickly, you roll that and lie on it. All snugly wrapped up, lying in Keating's powder and in wrappings more or less smeared with it, on which the bugs patter down like rain from the ceiling. But I have slept many nights so, and often in the morning found that not even one survivor had penetrated the wrappings.

In the cafe the coffee was Turkish, excellent; the food was lamb, stewed or kebab, and *kos*. Have you stayed in Delphi? If you have you know that Helen McInnes did not do justice to the view, but nobody can. That Easter I walked alone in the rain (no tourists then; no buses) up the Sacred Way, past the ruined temples, the lovely columns . . . at night in the rain, all the way down that long, long narrow valley to the sea. The Pascal lambs were roasting over the bonfires in the darkness, and after the feasting there was singing and dark figures leaping over the flames. Rites at least two thousand years older than Christianity, of course. All indescribably WILD and strange.

I don't have the admiration for the ancient Greeks that Mrs. McInnes—all knowledgeable persons, indeed—seems to have. Do you? After a half century of deferring to education opinion, I begin to wonder—Did you hear of the motorist who stopped to eat at a diner because seven trucks were standing outside it; and in conversation with the seven drivers, he learned that one was there because the waitress was his sister; the other six because food is always good where truck-drivers stop?—I have diligently tried to admire the ancient Greeks. Grant that a few Ionians had flashes of remarkable thinking (if they didn't get ideas from sources not yet excavated) and that Magna Graecia had a lot of brainy traders and Archimedes, it seems to me that their achievements were small compared to the idiocy of their philosophers and politicians generally. Their customs were barbaric-savage; their living was squalor; they never got food enough to keep them alive, and personally I don't like their art. It is all form, static, motionless, a perfection containing nothing—like the empty, dried carapace of a beetle; I mean a locust.

Those artists had no sense of Time, of energy, of action, of reality, of *life*. They lived like Plato in a dream, supported by serfs and slaves whom they casually despised for working. What is so wonderfully admirable about them. Their architecture? Not comparable for grandeur with the Hittites' or the Egyptians, for grace with the older Cretans, and for taste—just think of their caratides, my goodness. You can clothe the ruins with your own fancy and marvel if you like; I think that if you (all their admirers) saw them in their glory, all daubed with raw colors, every hue helter-skelter and glittering gold in that fierce sunlight you'd squawk and flee.

Or is this only my own reaction against the unanimous? which always makes me tired. For almost thirty years now I have been going to meetings of King Street Dorcas Society, the nicest good women imaginable, the "American 'innocents' " so incomprehensible in Europe, Africa, Asia and the seas' islands. In the minutes of last month's meeting, the secretary writes, "Moved that . . . " which is plenty because whatever is moved, seconded, is always voted unanimously Aye. So one day I offered a motion, it was seconded, Madame President said, "All in favor . . . " and I said, NO. Shocked silence, then unanimous outcry, "But you *can't* . . . ", and I explained, Just *once* I wanted to hear a NO.

Who was it wrote, Stand a sheep on its hind legs and you do not have a man; stand a flock of sheep on their hind legs and you have a crowd of men? It is explained to me that everyone always agrees with everyone because everyone is afraid. Afraid? but of *what?* Still, everyone does seem to be. And who is afraider than Professors? more timid than mice. Probably none who knows Greek *dares* venture to murmur that there might be a possibility that someone might suppose there to have been perhaps a flaw in ancient Greek brilliance. But doesn't (for instance) Helen McInnes know that Plato is the grandpappy of all her Communists?

XXIII

November 16, 1962

Dear Mr. Crane:

One of the girls at Freedom School has sent me the enclosed clipping, written by a Filipino whom I know and who called here this summer (she knew it would interest me for that reason). And I think it may interest you because it is a foreign point of view.

It hadn't occurred to me exactly, *how* this country puzzles foreigners. This boy explains that. Not having the unspoken *basic* assumptions that most Americans have—whether aware of them or not—they see a confusing conflict, where we only see shades of differences of opinion. The value to him of Freedom School is that it deals ONLY with basic truth. Nothing about super-structures—tariffs, taxes, welfare, etc. The idea is, Get the *basis* right, and the particulars will be subjects for discussion and maybe differing opinions on that basis. Be clear as to the moral nature of men, first.

There was another student, from Argentina, who came to see me in bewilderment. He cried out bitterly, "You say it's your Constitution, and we in South America, we believe it's your Constitution and we HAVE your Constitution—at least, well, with just a little, a few small changes here and there, for our other circumstances. . . . But YES, we DO have your Constitutions, all over South and Central America, but they don't work for us. WHY don't they work for us?" So I tried to tell him that it isn't the Constitution, that the Constitution is an effect; it is an act, a human act, which always comes from an idea; that it is the American idea of the nature of man which produced the Constitution and American history so far.

November 21, 1962

Dear Mrs. Lane:

My warmest thanks to you for sending me the autographed copy of *On The Way Home*. It is a charming book and an important contribution to American literature. I had read it before, as you know, but read it again several evenings ago and am enthusiastic about it.

December 7, 1962

Dear Mrs. Lane:

I have mentioned to you how the Brandywine Valley area has made valuable contributions to America; in the settlement of New Sweden with its freedom prospectus, in introducing to American pioneers the log house and the Conestoga wagon, in becoming the first center of industry in the United States after independence with one hundred and twenty mills established on twenty miles of the little stream. When your extensive travels bring you to Wilmington again, which I hope will be soon, you should see the Hagley Museum of early industry!

December 11, 1962

Dear Mr. Crane:

The brochure of the Brandywine Valley Association is interesting, and I do approve of the effort, though with approval qualified by existing circumstances. These make the laudable effort to handle such things instead of leaving them "all . . . to government" perhaps too late.

Because the intellectuals deserted the Revolution immediately (as Lenin said that intellectuals always would desert revolutions) an element in the American federal constitution has never—so far as I know—been noticed. The "system of checks and balances" restricting the use of police force upon Americans consists in giving certain specified powers (to use such force) exclusively to each of three groups of officials: legislators, executives, judges. The check upon each group is the *use* of power delegated to it. The theory is that each group, jealous of its own power, will always resist any encroachment upon its exclusive use of it, by either of the other two groups.

This same check is provided in each State, and between each State and the groups in Washington to whom the States delegate their specified powers.

Now, the ninth and tenth amendments make explicit a fact which the men who wrote the federal constitution said, truly, is implicit in the whole system: the fact that "all powers NOT delegated" are reserved, and remain, in the hands of individual citizens; who, in this structure (and in fact) are the original sources of all human energy acting on this earth, in the human world here.

The legal, as well as actual, check upon the whole political system—upon all politicians in all the functioning groups—the legislators, executives, judges—is the *use* of citizens' legally reserved (and real) powers to act, to handle their affairs instead of leaving them to be handled by those politicians.

What happened was that first, being still influenced by old traditional habits of mind, industrialists asked the politicians to use police force to manage transportation and trade; to enforce tariffs, to subsidize railroads. Indeed, at very first, steamboat owners got the States to give them monopolies and to keep rival steamboat owners out of their ports; the Supreme Court stopped that, denying such power to the States. And in the interim, before politicians in Washington began the New Deal in the 1860s, Americans were more free than people ever had been, and made the greatest progress in history. (The far greatest progress was made, of course, before known history.)

The checks as between politicians worked fairly well until subjugation of the States by the Union Armies in the 1860s. Then came the period of politicians selling privileges of various kinds to the active economic builders—franchises, licenses, tariffs, Acts of various kinds. In the cities, States and Washington. This brought into play (what I believe to be) an inevitable action, a Natural Law of human energy; a praxeological axiom.

Any government action intended to benefit a minority of a population causes an equal reaction against that minority.

There were the Muck-rakers, the graft prosecutions, the "Bust the Trusts!" legislative Acts. The politicians found it more profitable to use police force against, rather than for, "The Capitalists." The tables turned; the builders, instead of being required to pay for privileges, and bossing the politicians whom they bought now were bossed by the politicians —and robbed by them.

Through all this, the individual citizens simply did not *use* the powers reserved to them as a check on the actions of politicians to whom we delegated only a few, specified, limited, uses of police force. Not until the 1930s, when some thousands of farmers drove "federal men" off their property with guns.

The Brandywine Valley Association should have been, ideally, formed in 1800. Ideally, individuals should have understood their function in their new, unprecedented, political system; they should have formed companies (for instance) giving such good postal service so cheaply that their customers never would have permitted the "Government" to seize and monopolize postal service in these States. They should have built the roads and highways and dams —not only built them, as they did indeed build the Lincoln Highway, the first transcontinental highway since Ancient Rome, but effectively resist "the Government's" taking and monopolizing roadbulding here. And so on. This is enough to express what I mean.

IF (the always piteous historical IF) American intellectuals had stayed with the Revolution, developed its principles, instead of (if I may be Biblical) whoring after Europe's socialists from the 1840s until today, then today the Brandywine Valley Association would not be sending money to Washington and to State treasuries and begging for some of it back, and creating a County Authority, to get dams built in its own land. When you look at this from a practical, sensible, good-business point of view, the situation is absurd. Do these men NEED police force, to build a dam that they want to build and need? Did the first Du Pont need a policeman to take his money and give some of it back, and plan and order the building of his little powder-factory? Does the Brandywine Valley Association NEED the Federal Soil Conservation Service, the Pennsylvania Department of Forest and Waters, the (created for the purpose) Chester County Water Resources AUTHORITY, to buy land and build a dam?

Not in reality, NO. In the lamentable circumstances, YES. Because if a group of Americans now undertakes to—even to build such a little powder factory as the first American Du Pont did, the police will stop them.

If I undertake so much as to build a kennel for my little Maltese on my own property here, without asking and paying permission to do so, the police should stop me; it's their duty to stop me. They won't because they are afraid of stirring me up again. So I do build what I want to build, without permission. This is the resistance, this is the *use* of power NOT delegated to any legal group in American political structure, which once would have saved the Revolution and developed it, without violence.

Nothing but resistance to "Government" will keep police force limited to its proper function. Eternal vigilance AND constant ACTION is the price of liberty, which Americans failed to pay. So there are only two possible alternatives: collapse into Dark Ages again, or collapse into violence from which, perhaps, the revolutionists now called "Conservatives" may rescue these States and resume the Revolution. I hope so; I really expect it.

March 13, 1963

Dear Mr. Crane:

Roger and Susie are having a—I believe the current word is "fun"—time; though overworking themselves as only youngsters can. Vermont is in a bubbling stew; Senator Aiken squawks in Washington; Roger moves in a cloud of incredulous reporters; he has been twice on Vermont television, four times on radio; Susie and I are intermittently convulsed with laughter. Roger's purpose is to get Vermont endorsement of the Liberty Amendment; Vermont never ratified [the Sixteenth Amendment]. Roger has introduced a flock of bills, to abolish the State Recreation Commission ("It is costing taxpayers $36,000 a year and it exists to teach people to play. I think people know how to play."), to sell the Vermont State Morgan Horse Farm ("I have nothing against the Morgan Horse. I admire the Morgan Horse. I am confident that in private ownership the Morgan Horse Farm will yield a pleasing profit to its owners. It is costing taxpayers $42,000 a year."), to sell, on long-time easy terms, the Vermont State magazine to its present management ("It is costing the taxpayers $28,000 a year. It is an admirable publication. Certainly its able and enthusiastic publishers will profit from owning it."), and many others similar, plus a bill cutting the State income tax ten percent to yield the Treasury a profit (assuming that the Legislature passes all the other bills) of $1 million; the savings being $3 million and the cut being $2 million. (I make no claim to accuracy of the figures in other bills, as above; I don't remember them exactly. Roger has them down to a penny.) Susie's scrapbook is fattening with clippings; hardly a day and hardly a Vermont paper without headlines, usually with photograph of Representative MacBride, the Legislator's intellectual; or Representative MacBride of Halifax, population 286 (Nasty slam, what? This is where Susie and I weaken with laughter.) Roger says: Well, anyway it's making people think.

I am sure he will be flabbergasted if the legislature passes those bills. He is still blocking passage of Vermont ratification of the poll tax amendment (on the ground of constitutional law) which Senator Aiken announced to the press, four weeks ago, would be passed "this week", but it will pass, I'm sure. I am glad that Roger is too sensible to be broken-hearted by failures all too probable. He and Susie went to Halifax Town Meeting last week and Susie tells me on the phone it was a "riot". All Halifax was there, cheering and cheering and telling Roger to keep on, keep on; and even the eleven who voted against him in the election; everyone of them came separately to shake his hand and say they're FOR him and only hope he can do it. But what people want isn't what they get from politics. Conservative Republicans (three or four) have asked him to run against the up-coming "liberal" Republican candidate for Governor in the primary; it's possible he could win in the primary— and elect another Democrat Governor.

During his first days in the legislature, an Old Republican professional was guiding his infant steps, and spoke about the former Republican governor's defeat for re-election. He said the former governor, in his first campaign, promised to reduce taxes and believes that he was defeated in the second campaign because he didn't. Roger asked, Why didn't he? Answer: Oh, the party won't stand for that. Roger, all wide-eyed innocence: Why didn't he try, anyway? Answer, with withering scorn: You don't think *that* would be very smart politically do you?

Maybe it isn't logic, but it is politics.

XXIV

April 24, 1963

Dear Mr. Crane:

From the age of five when I first heard the story of the wandering Jew—"Stay thou till I come"—who at the age of thirty-five is living until the end of the world, I envied him. In the swing by the Ozark cabin I used to day-dream of having endless time, learning the whole world, all languages, all history—imagine *knowing* from experience everything that's occurred since the year 1 A.D.—traveling on trains and ships *everywhere,* living all kinds of lives—farmer, lawyer, merchant, miner, railroad man—did you ever hear the 1880s song,

> I wouldn't marry a farmer,
> He's always in the dirt,
> I'm going to marry a railroad man,
> Who wears a striped shirt, etc.

And pirate, the bold buccaneer, HO HO HO and a bottle of rum! whose buried treasures would amply finance all my other lives in other occupations. Being the Wandering Jew under a curse, I couldn't be hanged. So I dreamed blissfully in that swing under the oak tree. And though I stopped dreaming about those lives later, until recently I have thought that to be thirty-five years old until the end of the world would be enviable.

Now I know it wouldn't work. Here I am not yet quite eighty, and in my own country I don't even know my own language, much less the views, habits, customs, manners of the youngsters speaking it. By the time rockets are running on regular schedules to the moon and planets, I'd be totally helpless. Imagine the misery of the wretched Wandering Jew, wherever he is now in this world of radio, television, jets to the Coast in four hours, frozen foods, vitamins, speedways, "household appliances", elevators, and the UN. Oh, Yes, and "mental illness". He must be out of his mind.

Roger is astounded by the wholly unexpected. He introduced all those budget-cutting bills I sketched to you—to reduce State income taxes, with profit of $1 million to the State treasury. And, Machiavellian, he put them all into one package-bill, so that at the hearing ALL those whose subsidy-graft was threatened appeared and ALL viciously attacked him, personally. There he stood alone, friendless, unsupported, attacked from all sides with increasing fury, but there he *stood,* quiet, courteous, making no reply to multiplying *personal* attacks—a newcomer, a smart-aleck Harvard graduate, city slicker from New York, etc., etc., etc.—answering only the few relevant objections with facts, figures, and courtesy. The spectacle was, on the one hand, so atrocious, and on the other so "brave" that a few persons present hotly denounced the attackers and left in fury, and at least some reporters reported the meeting as an outrage—crassly mercenary mob unscrupulously ganging up upon the people's friend, who with courage unheard of stood his ground. Roger's purpose was to show his fellow legislators that the opposition to the bills was from porkers only trying to keep their noses in the tax-filled trough; and in that he succeeded perfectly.

He was slightly surprised by even the Democrats' resentment of the attack on him as an attack on *legislators,* but that was all right. What staggered him was the State-wide reaction; a deluge of telegrams, letters, postcards, all yelling Good for You! Don't quit! And a State-wide attack on him by all the "liberal" (Democrat-Republican) editors and reporters. The Governor himself (Democrat) denounced him as a member of the John Birch Society. And then came with his wife to dinner with Roger and Susie and (privately) apologized, saying he knew it wasn't true but implying somewhat mysteriously that he had to do it. Susie filled a scrapbook with clippings and half filled a second; Roger was asked, and did appear several times on radio programs and local television. Editorials urging his nomination for Governor multiplied in Susie's scrapbook, and three legislators decided to form with Roger an anti-liberal bloc; they added seven more and met to discuss tactics. Word of the meeting brought twelve more asking to join the bloc, and proposing to make the number thirty. They decided on a second meeting, of thirty, at the hotel. Senator Aiken, alerted in Washington, flew to his fences in Vermont. Until more than fifty came to the bloc's meeting they didn't know that the Senator was conferring with his buddies on the same floor. Members of the bloc are now insisting that Roger run for Governor, and swearing to elect him.

Roger intended none of this and doesn't really want it. As he says, his socialist opponents, the fools, have stirred up all this publicity. He has no experience at all "in politics," doesn't know the ropes, doesn't know what's going on in the "organizations" of both parties. The Lieutenant Governor, heir apparent to the governor's job and a Republican, is his most determined opponent. With, of course, Senator Aiken. I have a wholly baseless sense—a "hunch"—of peril in the situation. Do you care to make any comment?

Is it possible to be elected without making the smallest "compromise" in principles? Roger has made none yet and will not make any. Is it justifiable to take the chance of having to "betray the party" in the middle of a campaign by refusing to "compromise"? *Can* the "grass roots" without organization or funds, beat both party organizations, with funds? Is making a campaign and losing worthwhile as education of the voters?

Well, as my *bonne* in Paris said so frequently, Qui vivra, verra. At least Roger's life is not all invested in politics. He has his law office and a number of other interests as well. Biographies of Legislators I Have Known—Howard Buffet, et al—don't incline me to believe that he will be there very long. He is buying a 100-acre improved farm near Montpelier as an investment; it looks like a VERY good one.

I trust that you're well and enjoying springtime in your lovely gardens. Daffodils, early cottage tulips, stocks and muscari are blooming here, and forsythia. I am having my little walled vegetable garden changed to a cutting garden, with brick walls crossing it both ways and a bird bath, in the middle. I shall still have Golden Bantam corn and tomatoes in it, but the rest will be flowers for cutting. I hope I shall have the firmness to cut them, I never have had, but it is so silly to cherish flower beds and borders and buy flowers for the house from the florists. On the other hand, should I admit that I am silly?

May 10, 1963

Dear Mr. Crane:

Yes, I think Hannah Arendt is very sound. I do not know her, nor anyone who does know her, personally, but I have her *The Human Condition* which seems to be excellent though I have read only bits of it. It is a book that I look forward to reading carefully, when I can get time. She has written *Origins of Totalitarianism,* too.

By the way, do you happen to remember what Englishman said, or wrote, that the difference between an intelligent man and an intellectual is the difference between a gentleman and a gent? I can't remember who he was. It sounds like Disraeli, doesn't it?

I hope you're feeling fine and frisky in truly spring weather and that your gardens are thriving beautifully. Weather here is plumb crazy—breaking all records for heat today, and frosty tonight; and only last week the pups and I woke to find two inches of snow on the sundecks and lawn. In MAY.

We Missouri children never understood the poet's, O, what is so rare as a day in June?/ Then if ever come perfect days/ When Nature sees if the earth be in tune/ And over it gently her warm ear lays. . . . If I recall correctly. One bright boy answered the question factually: A day in February. The poem was simply inexplicable to the rest of us. Now I know what it meant, and those words "IF *ever*" mean something to me, too.

May 12, 1963

Dear Mr. Crane:

I have long been worrying at property-ownership as a small puppy with a big bone. It seems to me that thinking goes askew on that word, "right," which connotes "law," which easily slides into "authority" (either divine or human) which traditionally is "compulsion." I think it more accurate to use the word, function. I arrived at this view years ago when I first began trying to think in this field, and could find nothing to begin with but the "We hold these truths" sentence in the American Declaration. Obviously, life is a *function* of a living creature, it isn't a "right" with all the connotations of that word; and if the sentence makes sense, liberty (equated with life) is also a natural function of a human being. And, by the Virginia Declaration, so is "property," i.e., *owning* property. Everything I have been able to think since then, in the 1920s, comes from that original source in my reading of the "We hold these truths . . ." statement.

Now it seems to me that owning property is an innate, inalienable natural function of a living person. A man is an owner, as a bird is a flyer or a fish is a swimmer, because of his intrinsic *nature* in his environment. Other forms of life *are adapted* to their environment, they are equipped with inner controls of their actions which keep them living passively in relation to their environment; but man survives only by actively *adapting* his environment to himself.

Now primitive aborigines do exist "like animals," naked, without fire or tools or manmade shelter, eating leaves, worms, roots, nuts, shellfish; but they exist by no means as *well* as animals do, most of them die in infancy or starve to death young. Men begin to *live* as successfully as animals when they begin actively to change their environment. And to do this, a man MUST *own* a part of that environment.

The collectivist view of course is that individual ownership is unnatural, and that it is robbery, because God gave all the earth to all men. And socialists propose to see to it that all men have it all. The fallacy is their illusion that "all men" are ("as a whole") one organic Whole, a mystic Being. But the comic aspect of their position is that it never occurs to them that God doesn't need their help; IF GOD gives all the earth to all men, no single man CAN own a part of it.

And Bastiat pointed out more than a century ago that nobody does own any part of the earth that God gave to all men. What a person owns is a *change* that *men have made* in the environment that God gives us.

Bury's *History of Greece* mentions the origin of ownership in Greece, which I surmise is its origin everywhere. He says (pages 99-100; Modern Library Giant) that in ancient Greece families occupied and cultivated areas of land—apparently as the Sioux Tribes in Missouri did—but nobody possessed, controlled, was responsible for its control and disposition, as nobody possesses anything in "public ownership" now. But "side by side with the undivided family estate, personal properties were actually acquired. At this period there was much unalloted wild land 'which wild beasts haunt,' especially on hill-slopes, and when a man of energy reclaimed a portion of this land for tillage, the new fields became his own, for they had belonged to no man. We can thus see generally how inevitable it was that the old system should disappear and the large family estates break up into private domains; but the change *was not accomplished by legislation* and the process by which it was brought about is withdrawn from our eyes. It was only when private land ownership had become an established fact that the law came in and recognized it by regulating sales of land and *allowing* men to bequeath it *freely*." (My italics.)

We could have guessed that, from seeing what Governments are doing now; they always seize what men not in Governments *have done,* and "regulate" it and then grant permission to *only* a few men to keep on doing it. One thing Athenians did was to prohibit sales of farms, and to establish serfdom.

When a man cleared trees, brush, grass off a bit of land, dug it with a hoe, planted seeds in it, then he MUST keep that land, defend it from animals and other persons, in order to get the harvest which is the end for which he spent his life-time-energy. The decisive element here is Time, the forth dimension, the measurement of movement in space—the dimension that collectivists ignore. The man MUST *hold* that land while the seeds move to be plants, flowers, seeds again. But the land per se is useless, worthless; what the man has made, what he owns, is a *field,* the *change* that he has made in his God-given environment. The unchanged environment is still *free* for anyone's taking.

But others want the *field* more than they want the unchanged land. And if they can't bargain with him to get the field, they will take wild land and change it to a field only because he has shown them (1) that a field is desirable, that they want one, and, (2) that they can change their environment as he changed it.

Bastiat has shown that in all our buying and selling, the God-given environment is always free, there is never a charge for *that.* We buy and sell land that has "value" to us because men have made it desirable by exploring, surveying, mapping it, building roads, towns, cities near it. There are millions of miles of land that anyone can have for nothing; e.g. the valley of the Amazon. The earth and the oceans are full of materials and creatures that cost nobody anything but the life-time-energy spent in taking them, because nobody has yet changed any of them into anything that anyone wants. You can have a wild horse for catching it, or a sealskin by killing and skinning a seal. We buy a horse *trained* to saddle or harness, or a colt that can be so trained; we buy the sealskin tanned and cut and sewed and lined. What is *owned* is the *change* that men have made in man's environment on this planet.

So here is the theory of the "natural right of property" (as I see it, stripped of all the mystic connotations, "abstractions," twisted notions of Law and Authority.) Ownership is a function of a living person, the function of possessing, controlling, etc., what human life-time-energy creates. That is, the "natural right of property" is a labor-theory of ownership. And this is darn risky, because this is the socialist contention: that labor creates all property, therefore a person is entitled ONLY to the product of *his* labor, and entitled to ALL of it. So what do we do about Barbara Hutton? or Henry Ford the Second?

Up to this point I am sure (as sure as *can* be) that I I am right. The collectivists go haywire, of course, because of their assumption that the human Unit is a collective Whole composed of persons; whereas in fact the human unit is an individual person. The theory that ownership of property is not a "natural right" but a "civil" right, *granted* to a person or persons by the Whole (the King, Legislature, State, Society, or Community) rests on this collectivist fallacy. (In *Discovery of Freedom* I said that ownership is a civil right, without seeing that I was contradicting myself.)

But, rejecting this fallacy that a "General Will of the Whole" (or Mr. Kennedy maybe) grants a person permission to own a house, there is so far nothing but the theory of "natural right" (or function) as an alternative. And I can't seem to get it applied satisfactorily to modern industrial conditions.

At the moment, the theory of natural ownership is old-fashioned; and it never has been solidly thought out. Schlatter says that it is abandoned (incidentally by NAM) because it is untenable; "labor" does NOT get all it produces "under" capitalism; therefore defenders of private property have fallen back on utilitarianism, claiming (as NAM does) that private property is essential to *liberty,* which is preferable to economic security in communism. This obviously is nonsense; all known history demonstrates that "liberty and property" *produce* economic security.

Such freedom as has existed since the sixteenth century (only partially handicapped by police and military forces in this country and the British Commonwealth during the nineteenth century) and ownership of property have produced this new world of unprecedented economic plenty and security. The only rational conclusion that I can see is, that in freedom and with ownership of property, men can act "naturally," i.e. in accordance with the real nature of man. Because certainly we are on this earth to *live* here, and to live better in every way than animals do. If there is Purpose in the Creation (as I believe) then the purpose of every creatures' existence must be to live *according to his own nature, using* the functions with which he is "endowed by his Creator."

And I must say, it's a tough job for a human being. When I look at the birds or at my pups, I can't help *thinking* how much easier it must be to live *without* thinking. And I'm sure my own personal difficulty is that my rational function is just plumb inadequate. Then again I take comfort from N. J. Birrell's *Man Emerging Mind;* it gives me hope that after a few more millions of years at least a few persons will be able to reason correctly. But this is off the track.

What I am trying to do is to see the natural human function of ownership AS IT *IS.* The historic theory of the "natural right of property" was blurred (it seems to me) by irrelevant connotations of the idea of "right" and it never has been clearly reasoned or established. I'm certain that it should not be abandoned, either for the old antique fallacies of collectivism or for a nonsensical attempt to defend ownership of property on the ground that liberty is preferable to ownership of property. (What is "economic security" BUT ownership of property?)

The complication comes in with trading, and that's another natural human function—the one that promises someday, a civilization. Ownership is the first essential to trading; you can't exchange what you don't possess and control the disposition of. And every little advance toward a possible civilization has been made by traders. Trading goods stimulates men to produce more goods, more material goods sustain more human lives, more human energy producing more kinds of "goods"—knowledge, charity, kindness, art, inklings of a new human world to be made in time. Trading for instance, transformed this continent from what it was in 1545 to what it is now. So, what shall we think about, for example, Barbara Hutton?

Not a good example because I know too little about her. But I know even less about Tommy Manville. As an example, a man creates a great organization of persons producing a huge volume of goods for multitudes of persons. He does this, and *can* do it, only in comparative freedom and by owning property. Ownership of property includes control of its disposition; therefore he bequeaths this property to his heirs. The heir in question merely *possesses* the property; he does not control its uses—men in *the organization* are doing that; he does not control its disposition—that's done by trustees chosen by his father or grandfather. Thousands of persons are acting co-operatively in the organization, actively changing their environment and obtaining "goods"—values—material things, leisure, prestige, learning, etc., etc.—in exchange for their life-time-energy spent co-operatively in the organization; and the heir who "owns" the organization is also obtaining those "goods" while exchanging nothing for them. Barbara Hutton is spending her life-time-energy in divorcing her fifth husband; Tommy Manville is spending his in marrying his tenth wife. They couldn't hold a job in Macy's basement.

So collectivists don't just stand there, they do something; they used armed force to rob the producers; the State "distributes the wealth more equably" with progressive taxes, death taxes, rules and regulations and even plain honest confiscation. Benevolent Mr. Roosevelt proposes to see that no American has an income exceeding $25,000 a year, and does a lot to approach that end. And I'm ag'in all that. But what am I FOR?

What is wrong with the operation of the natural human function of ownership, that produces this malfunction, so that a person can *possess* property without controlling its uses or being responsible for them, and thereby obtain "goods" which other persons *are NOW producing?*

May 15, 1963

Dear Mrs Lane:

It is so interesting to have you write me so enthusiastically about the coming (?) of spring. Last year and the year before I was in the hospital after major operations, but this year I have been enjoying our garden. We have been developing this garden for thirty-five years, and I think over and over again, and keep thanking God for it, that there is so much beauty for us to enjoy in our old age. (The "we" and "us" are not in any sense collectivist philosophy, but simply the statement that my wife and I planned this garden and have seen it develop over the years.) A week ago Saturday was Garden Day and nearly four hundred people visited our garden. So we are not entirely selfish in our enjoyment of our garden, and it is being passed along to one of our daughters, who is such an enthusiast herself. So was my mother and my grandmother, and we have a rose bush, the flowers from which decorated my grandmother's wedding one hundred and ten years ago. So when *The Rose,* Journal of the National Rose Society of Britain had a friendly competition of what member had the oldest rose there was no competition, the next oldest being something like fifty years old.

May 22, 1963

Dear Mrs. Lane:

I enclose a copy of a report by the President of Princeton University, entitled *Federal Financing and Princeton University.* If you are willing to do so, I will very much appreciate it if you will read this report and send to me any terse comments that you may have upon it.

I may say that I am critical of some points of this report, particularly receipt of Federal funds for unspecified research, for buildings and for scholarships, and also of some of his reasoning in favor of Federal aid to education.

May 24, 1963

Dear Mr. Crane:

I do not know how sincere Mr. Goheen is. The report appears to be a defensive reply to critics, and an appeal for larger or continuing private funds, by an honestly confused writer. He seems to be trying to be both dependent and independent.

First: "Government is *force*" used by persons upon persons. Education is an individual person's self-development; e-duc-ation. The two are absolutely incompatible. Schools should be free-enterprise institutions, profiting from selling opportunities for learning. Any institution that cannot profit from satisfying a demand should not exist; because to exist it must be a parasite upon the usefully productive institutions. Therefore, the whole basis of present education systems is wrong.

The report's defence of political subsidies by "sets of facts" is flimsy.

1. The history is irrelevant; so is popular "concern." "Old" or "new" have nothing to do with truth, which is timeless.

2. "Federal investment . . . in the national interest" is Keynesian collectivism. An investment is a use of capital for profit. Federal spending is a politician's use of other men's capital (taken from them by force) to increase the politician's power—i.e. usable force.

3. He who pays the fiddler calls the tune; properly. The political use of universities distorts their purpose; Mr. Goheen is defending political use of universities while apparently trying to resist the distortion.

4. Phraseology is wholly collectivist. Q. Do not the "fruits of advanced research" enable Du Pont, et al., to profit from satisfying a demand? profit sufficiently to expand and improve advanced research without being subsidized? This report's approval and encouragement of increasing Federal "investment" in Princeton is asking for increased distortion of real educational opportunity in Princeton. The end of this course is totalitarian state schooling.

Mr. Goheen's concept of freedom is fantastic. "Milton . . . reminded us that freedom is but choosing. In this true sense, Princeton is freer today. . . ." That is, Princeton has more money. Freedom is in ratio to cash in the bank? Nixon is freer than I because he can choose to buy a $100,000 apartment and I can't? The man is nuts.

It seems to me that Princeton is in the business of selling opportunities for learning, as a restaurant sells opportunities for eating. Neither should ask nor take charity. If either can't profit from satisfying a demand it should cease to exist.

If either is entitled to exemption from taxation or to being maintained by taxes, it is the restaurant; food is more essential to human existence than education. But what happens when "Government" undertakes to feed "its people"? They die in famines. An equivalent famine afflicts minds wherever a "Government" undertakes to educate them, as in the Roman Empire or the Kaiser's Germany. Or the U.S.S.R.

I object to taking *any* unearned money, which is money that someone else has earned, for one thing. I would object strenuously to Princeton's taking money for specified research, for that reason and for the reason that (I'd think) it is setting up Government competition with free research, such as Du Pont's. And compelling Du Pont to support that competition. (I use Du Pont as a figure, representing real—because free—research.) This is distorting research per se.

XXV

July 11, 1963

Dear Mrs. Lane:

The difference between you and me on one point is important. I am, therefore, expanding to you my view on what is proper for the Federal Government to do: that is, because the Congress is charged in the Constitution with the national defense and general welfare of the United States. Adequate defense means a vast amount of weapons, and keeping up with or exceeding our enemies development of weapons. Offensive and defensive equipment rapidly becomes obsolete, and the United States is only properly prepared to defend our country by continuing research and developing projects for all the military services.

I remember after the first World War when the agitators were claiming that the private munitions industry led to war that Newton Baker said that when he became Secretary of War he found there was no munitions industry. He went on to say that in times of peace ninety-five percent of ordinance production was in government arsenals, but in times of war the production would be so enormously increased that the government could only turn out five percent of the requirement and private industry had to produce ninety-five percent. I don't know what the figures are today, but we are at war and must be prepared in every way to protect the United States against the adversary. So now it seems to me that it is quite proper and in accordance with the Constitution for the United States to make contracts for research for all the services. Contrariwise, it is quite improper for it to spread money around in universities and colleges for every subject taught, for building, for expenses of students, for general research, etc., etc.

July 13, 1963

Dear Mr. Crane:

Your letter to Dr. Goheen seems to me perfect—or, if nothing is perfect (as I'm told) then so nearly so that I can't pick flaws in it. And I'm a top flaw-picker, as you know. Of course I am accepting your view of defense contracts—your expression of that view—while reading the letter.

I hope you may tell me more, from time to time, about this situation in Princeton. It interests me very much. I needn't tell you that earnestly I hope that your views will prevail here. Nothing but my absolutely incorrigible optimism saves a faint hope that something may yet rescue Harvard and Yale.

Our little discrepancy of views about defense contracts touches again my almost-constant dilemma. In *principle,* I cannot accept, as in any way good or beneficial, the use of physical force upon persons by other persons, in their habitual relationships. You and I (and George Washington) agree that "Government is force" used in that way. "Government" is a misnomer, a traditional usage of a word not applicable to the political institution, which in fact is the *actions* (in space-time) of persons organized in a group and holding the monopoly of the legal use of force upon other persons living in a certain geographical area.

Since all persons are endowed by their Creator with *inalienable* liberty (function of self-government) it is impossible that one person govern another person. Mr. Kennedy et al. in fact have NO power to govern anyone but themselves. All they CAN do is to use physical force upon other persons. The institution in which they are acting, therefore, should not be named "Government." But to date there is no other, no accurate, name for it.

Now, the dilemma: I am convinced that the only human action producing desirable results is action *according* to the laws existing in the nature of things. (It is only by such action that men produce food, buildings, bridges, engines—the necessities and satisfaction of human living on this planet.) I am certain that there are laws existing in the field of human relationships (called, with incorrect etymology "moral" laws, or "morality") and that one person's attempt to control another person's actions by physical force is NOT according to those laws, and therefore can produce nothing but disaster.

Yet, accepting the present general assumption that "a foreign power" designs and is planning to attack these States with military force, I cannot quarrel with your position that those men in Washington should be spending all that all of us have and much, much more for the "defense" of all of us. True, they are destroying the economy of these States, and thus inevitably destroying their own institution of "Government." But I am not prepared to stand so rigidly by principle as to advocate the abolition of military force here. Actually I am even inclined to advocate using it in Cuba. So, dear Mr. Crane, precisely *where* am I?

I would "go along" far enough to make no vigorous objection to a University's accepting a "Government" contract, agreeing to do a certain research job, for a certain amount of money. This at least preserves the dignity and independence of the party of the second part, in a contractural relationship based on the equality of the contracting parties. At least, in theory, and maybe in legality. (Though the legal equality of a citizen with his "public servant" was abolished, wasn't it? with the decree that a citizen cannot sue "the Government" without the "Government's" consent.)

I think that our dilemmas both political-economical and moral, come from the old, old traditional belief that the Government is God Incarnate; literally, actually, God Himself.

It is astonishing, and frightening, how unquestionably and firmly people held that belief for thousands upon thousands of years, actually for some six thousand known years (how much longer before that, nobody knows yet.) The very name, Government, originated in it, and implies it. And what else, *precisely,* do men mean when formally they adopt such resolutions as, for instance, "Government should do for people only what people *cannot do* for themselves?"

If that means anything at all, it means, doesn't it, that "Government" has some power to do what *people* can't do? that somehow it has a more-than-human power? that it, The Government, is more than human, that it isn't simply an organization of persons as General Motors is.

Would persons who adopt such resolutions (and say the same thing again and again, all the time, everywhere) put that idea in realistic terms and say: "Government should do nothing but compel other persons, by force, to do what those persons do not want to do?" (Because, obviously, if those other persons *want* to do it, they *will* do it, if it can possibly be done; so it will be done, if it can be; if they're simply let alone.

I find that everyone I know is startled by the fact that until lately (within the last three or four centuries) the Governments were believed to be Gods Incarnate, or at least Divine in nature. I don't understand why educated persons don't learn such things in schools. Or even see them on television screens. Millions saw the coronation of Elizabeth, the screen drawn around her to shield the holy moment when God Himself bestowed upon her the Grace, by which she is Queen of England, etc., Defender of the Faith, etc., etc. Everyone reads in the newspapers, even the tabloids, that the Mikado was the Son of Heaven, and that the Great Lama is God Incarnate of the Tibetans but nobody seems to *notice*.

Almost everyone I know is a college or university graduate, but my acquaintance must be too small. Surely *in* universities, among the faculty . . . ? But the books they write. . . . I have nearly 6,000 books, catalogued, and they are like a strawpile in which a few scattered grains can be found by searching. To me, the striking fact about Julius Caesar, for instance, is that he believed he was descended from Zeus through Aphrodite, and that Cleopatra was Isis Incarnate; but Mommsen writes four volumes of adulation of him without mentioning that. I have shelves upon shelves of learned books about Rome, Republic and Empire; and no more than two mentions of Augustus (after defeating Anthony's troops in Italy) setting up an altar to his Deified great-uncle and sacrificing 300 war prisoners on it. I have only two or three quotes—from archeologists, not historians—verifying the divinity of the ruling Gods Incarnate in Mesopotamia and Egypt. Do you happen to know that deed of property, from Ptolemy the Saviour to the other two gods from Xerxes had expropriated? (Alexander, of course was the God Amon in Egypt—Ammon-Ra Himself recognized Alexander as his son in his desert-oasis temple;

and the Ptolemies were the Sun Incarnate.) The deed reads:

"I, Ptolemy (etc.) I restore the territory of Patanut to the Falcon-God Horus and to Buto (the Cobra-Goddess) as from this day forever, with all its villages, all its cities, all its inhabitants, all its fields, all its waters, all its four-footed beasts, all its birds, all its herds, everything begotten and grown there, in the condition in which it was of old and with everything that was added to it by the gift of the Pharaoh Kaabash. Of all this that Kaabash gave, Ptolemy has restored the gift, forever."

The people living in Egypt—for thousands of years—were not chattel slaves; they were simply the property of God, the Sun, together with all else "begotten or grown" on God's earth, by His power. They were governed in groups by the Incarnate God's overseers, and Pharaoh's priests counted and numbered them and used them in Pharaoh's manufacturing and building and trading and took whatever the God Incarnate wanted, from whatever they produced under his orders. And education, of course, was Government education; Pharaoh's priests trained such boys as they wanted, for Pharaoh's service in the enormous bureaucracy.

When Augustus, in his turn, became Ammon-Ra in Egypt, he transferred the whole system to Europe, and continued and improved it in Asia, Africa and Egypt. That was what wrecked the Empire in two centuries. (Of course Augustus was descended from Zeus, himself, through Julius Caesar's niece, his mother; but Zeus and Amon were identical; Roman Emperors were divine in nature, worshipped in the Provinces and often formally deified by the Roman Senate when they died, as Julius Caesar was.)

I think that *historically,* the great achievement of Christianity was its separation, *for the first time,* of the two ideas (in men's minds) of God and of Government. There was a Manichaen dualism behind the two ideas, behind the separation of "this world" from the "spiritual world" and I myself see no such duality in the nature of man or the universe. But when—as what Pope said?—"God set two powers to govern men, one to govern their souls and one to govern their bodies" (my quote, from memory, isn't precise) the King's use of physical force was separated in men's minds from the Church's spiritual influence, and the relation of man to God was different from his relation to the King. Add the Judaic element of individualism, implicit in the Commandments and preserved in Church doctrine, and the eventual outcome (given the human rational faculty) was almost inevitably the Reformation and the American Revolution.

The Revolutionary view is that The Government is merely human, a human institution, no more Divine than any other man-made organization. But this view is so new, so unprecedented, and so rare on earth, that it is being almost overcome by the reactionary ideas—the old "feeling" that a group of persons (a Nation, State, Society) is an organism, a "body politic," governed "as a Whole" by a super-individual, in some sense as super-natural, mystic Power inherent in The Government.

The Government is supposed to be responsible for the "welfare of the People as a Whole (as logically it would be IF it governed the Whole). Human minds always are logical; the fallacy always is in the premise, the basic unquestioned assumption, upon which the process of reasoning is based. So in logical return for The Government's benefits, we are supposed to "owe a duty" to It. The custom of taxation is a remnant of the Incarnate God's ownership of "his people." WHY do you *owe* money to Mr. Kennedy? If you need to guard your property, you hire and pay guards, nightwatchmen; if you are a banker you buy and pay for armored cars and hire guards to transport the bank's gold; if you manage an insurance company you hire and pay detectives to investigate claims against your company. If a foreign power attacks your country, *you* defend it; you man the tanks, fly the bombers, fire the guns. Is there a need, in reason, to compel persons—by force—to defend their property and themselves? Is there a reason why "people cannot do for themselves" in a free market, everything that The Government is supposed to be doing for them?

"The people" have in fact done everything that is done; they build the houses and roads and railroads and telephones and planes, they organized world-wide co-operative institutions—the oil companies, the banks—and the postal services, and the militia companies, and the schools—What didn't "the people" do? What happens is that, after they do it, The Government takes it. The Government takes the roads, the postal service, the systems of communication, the banks, the markets, the stock exchanges, the insurance companies, the schools, the militia, the building trades, in Europe the railroads, the telegraph and telephones, the radios, AFTER "the people" have done all these things for themselves.

And I'm sorry I have made this letter so long. But am I wrong? If I am, what is my mistake?

What I had in mind to write is that I think there is no danger whatever that men in the Kremlin will ever take any military action against these States. And I could explain my position in another five pages. Briefly, there is no warrant in Communist theory or practice for any apprehension of military action by the Comintern or by the Soviet Government against what's called "the free world." If these States were totally disarmed, with no army, no navy, no air force, the American Communist underground would—or might—try to "seize power" by coup d'etat (in arms), though federal organization—even in its delapidation—makes such an attempt almost impossible. There would have to be fifty simultaneous coup d'etats here, when one will work in any other country. An attempt to "seize power" by force here would produce unmanageable chaos. THEN a Red army might come in "to restore order." But—let a Red army out of the barbed wire frontiers, march them through the Berlin Wall—and the whole Soviet empire will crumble. If the Soviet rulers don't know that, why do they guard and barbed-wire their frontiers? and build the Berlin Wall? If they do know it, are they likely to start a military invasion of "the free world"?

I am not advocating unilateral disarmament, but I think this spending "for defence" is idiotic and suicidal. It is falling into Lenin's policy-trap: "We will induce the capitalists to spend themselves to death."

July 19, 1963

Dear Mrs. Lane:

I am afraid that I cannot speak with any authority about property ownership. You have given so much and such wonderful thought to this matter that it ought to be a part of a book, and, thus, available to the public. My own simple thinking is this: We have been endowed by God with the right to live. In space and time the right to live must be supported by some items of property; such as, tools of production and means of safeguarding and sustaining our lives. If the ownership of property is taken away from the individual and seized by the collective, the individual no longer has the means of sustaining his own life. His God-given liberty is also lost in slavery to the collective. I see that this is really quoting you, that "private ownership is necessary for liberty."

XXVI

October 15, 1963

Dear Mr. Crane:

Some education sure is needed. *Human Events* is running an educational (and subscription-getting) contest on American history and Constitution. Current question: What was the first State admitted to the Union? (Six states are listed; one is to be chosen as correct answer.)

Well, Delaware could be the first, being the first to ratify the Constitution and thus "admitted to the Union" technically made by the Constitution.

Virginia was the first, being the tenth to ratify the Constitution which provided that nine ratifying States effectively established the Union.

Neither Delaware nor Virginia is listed. Vermont is, and therefore, is the only possible answer. But, after four States had been "admitted to the Union," the *fifth* accession was the Republic of Vermont. So *Human Events* requires contestants to give incorrect answers in order to win prizes offered for correctness. The editors should go back to McGuffey's *Fifth Reader* Class in the nineteenth century. The ignorance prevailing today is purely fantastic.

October 19, 1963

Dear Mr. Crane:

Have you read *What Man May Be,* by Dr. George Russell Harrison, Dean of the School of Science at M.I.T.? If you haven't, I think you would enjoy it tremendously. I have read only about half of it so far; Orval sent it to me. I think it is one of the most cheering, encouraging, of the many straws in the wind of changing opinion. And it lifts one's mind right out of all these temporary troubling things to the long view of human life in this marvelous order of all Creation.

October 25, 1963

Dear Mr. Crane:

Thank you for telephoning this morning. I do appreciate highly your telling me so personally your views and some of your interesting experiences and observations. If I may say so without sounding flattering, I think you very wise (of course, since I agree with you!).

I agree completely with your view that nothing should be done to aid Mr. Goldwater's election without the knowledge and at least the tacit approval of the Senator and his managers.

It seems to me most important, however, if not essential, that a vigorous *attack* upon the smearers of Mr. Goldwater be made, and it can be made effectively only as an independent effort, outside the official campaign organization. What can his representatives do but deny charges after they are made? They can't attack the *originators* or the smears, publicly prove what they and their motives are, and thus discount the effect of their organized campaign *before* it gets fully started full steam ahead, supplied with nearly unlimited funds and helped along by all the "liberal" publicists as it is.

Furthermore, Mr. Goldwater and his associates are naive in this field. Though nobody can more wholly agree with your approval of them in *their* fields than I do. Sound economists, able politicians, honest and patriotic men, are still what Communists scornfully call "innocents." You remember that when Mr. Kohlberg started *Plain Talk* he said to Don Levine, "NOW the truth can be told to Americans," and Don replied, "Oh, no, we can print the truth but we can't tell it; nobody would believe it." (I knew Mr. Kohlberg slightly and thought very highly of him; only sometimes names escape me momentarily.)

The "extremists" tactic is already being used with beginning effectiveness against Senator Goldwater and he is not sufficiently wary of it; obviously he doesn't understand it or its source. If it isn't intelligently countered, it can split the Republican Party and stop Goldwater's nomination.

Consider one incident, a straw in the wind. Someone trapped Mr. Goldwater into repudiating the elected leader of the Young Republicans, as an "extremist" of course. Now Susie, Roger MacBride's wife, was a delegate to the San Francisco convention and—with another Vermont delegate

—led the "extreme" right faction, some thirty to forty delegates. There were three candidates for President of the YR organization—roughly, and not too accurately: Right, Middle, Left. The chairman was Left; and every tactic of Communists and racketeer labor bosses was brazenly used to control the convention—to the point of disconnecting the public address system when any Right or Middle delegate tried to speak. Therefore the election was pandemonium.

Susie's faction (for short) was for the Right candidate. Practical politicians—Stan Evans for one—argued desperately that there would be only one vote; that votes for the Right would defeat the Middle and elect the Left candidate. Those in the Right faction insisted that they would stand for their principles. They gave more than thirty votes to candidate Right; and the election of candidate Left was announced. Convention then went crazy, in convention style; while furious practical delegates attacked the Rightists, the triumphant Leftists paraded the Left candidate on their shoulders yelling for Rockefeller; Rockefeller banners and buttons appeared by the scores. (The Leftists had vehemently denied any Rockefeller attachment, before.) Meanwhile, some of the practical Middle leaders fought through the roaring crowd, got hold of the tally clerks, and of the chairman, and proved, no election. There was a fist fight for possession of the loud speaker system. "No election" was announced. In comparative quiet the Right candidate withdrew. A second vote elected the Middle candidate, Susie's faction voting for him this time, giving him the plurality or whatever it was. Susie tells me all this in more detail two days later.

So, what happens? Papers and radio report the "extreme Rightists'" rough-house tactics at the Convention, ascribing to them what actually were the Left (Rockefeller) tactics. Mr. Rockefeller himself makes the charge, including the "well organized lavishly financed" lie. Time passes, and last week Mr. Goldwater repudiates the "extreme rightist" Young Republicans of California. The Middle candidate *National* President of the YR (an 'innocent' himself, I surmise) has unwarily made some statement which the smear organization can use, and it is instantly used on Goldwater to get him to repudiate YR "extremists." He then tried to retrieve the mistake, and "makes up" with the YR National

President. So here come cartoons, WHERE *DO* you stand, Senator? I see them in the little Danbury paper.

The smear organization *is* "well organized, heavily financed." All its parts mesh, it runs like an oiled machine. And "nobody" will believe it even exists. Do even you yourself see it, Mr. Crane? If people saw it, it couldn't work. But who is printing even a quarter of the truth?

I have watched it working since the early '20s, and in high gear since the early '30s. One tiny instance, amusing in a way: Franklin P. Adams' career on the *Herald Tribune*. It's unlikely that you'd happen to know this, and it serves as an illustration.

In the early '30s (I'd have to verify precise dates) the paper was running in the red, some millions a year. It was eating up the Reids' capital. Union workers agreed to small cuts in wages, to hold their jobs. Feature writers were on contract; they agreed to a ten percent cut. Only FPA (Franklin Adams) refused; his contract was for $25,000 a year and he would not take less. So when the contract expired, the Reids did not renew it, but immediately came a deluge of letters—thousands by count, thousands of letters from the whole area of *Herald Tribune* circulation, asking in thousands of ways, Where is FPA? saying, "I take the *Herald Tribune* only for FPA." Panicked, the Reids renewed FPA's contract, at $25,000. Other employees were NOT pleased, but hung on to their jobs by their teeth. The paper kept on losing millions, another year. The Reids argued and pleaded with FPA; he was adamant. They HAD to let him go; they did not renew his $25,000 contract, he refused $22,500. Again the deluge of letters, letters by the *thousands,* and postcards, typed, handwritten, signed, certainly personal individual inquiries and demands for FPA's column. The Reids collapsed; FPA got his $25,000 for another year. At the end of that year, the same repetition, and again Mr. and Mrs. Reid gave up; they had sent for FPA to come back when a man came up from the mailroom with handsful of letters and showed them the postmarks. These letters from up-state New York had been posted on the first day that the paper had appeared without FPA's column, but at an hour earlier than that issue of the paper could possibly have reached those towns.

Thus FPA lost his job on the *Herald Tribune,* and he and others had to get on the air with their *"Information*

Please" program. It took them a year or more; meanwhile Esther Read, FPA's wife, supported their family in less than the way to which they had been accustomed. Let me stress, please, that this incident is a most trivial use of the apparatus, just a favor in passing to a useful publicist, a minor exploitation of a (enemy by definition) capitalist; nothing of any importance. It simply serves as an illustration of the functioning apparatus that helped to destroy Taft, and that Goldwater is up against. THEY were important, are important. The attack on Goldwater is starting and it will be carried out with much more care, skill, and effectiveness than any trivial favor to an FPA.

Do please forgive this long letter? I do wholly agree with your view that it is not wise to act without an understanding with the responsible men in Mr. Goldwater's organization; it is not wise to act in opposition to the organized hidden apparatus now geared to destroy him without an understanding of *that,* and I doubt, unhappily, that he or any of his associates understand it at all or perhaps even know that it really exists.

November 5, 1963

Dear Mrs. Lane:

What a stunning surprise! Your book on American needlework[9] seems to me to be a monumental achievement. How wise it was of the editors of *Woman's Day* to invite you to write this story!

I was especially pleased to see illustrations of needlework in the Newark, New Jersey, Museum, an institution with which our family has been associated since its beginning.

November 7, 1963

Dear Mr. Crane:

I am so glad that the book pleased you; I hoped that it might be a bit of cheer in the morning's mail. Now I

[9]*Woman's Day Book of American Needlework,* Simon & Schuster, 1963.

think I should have told you about it earlier, its history is so encouraging.

It began in the 1930s—Do you by any chance remember a lead article by me, in the *Saturday Evening Post,* entitled "Credo"? That had an amazing history—another story. What mattered was its terrific reader-response success when it appeared. George Horace Lorimer told me that for more than a week more than TWO-THIRDS of *Saturday Evening Post* mail was applauding that article; I myself received more than three thousand personal letters—all but a dozen or so (which threatened my life) were enthusiastic about it. Mr. Lorimer told me that in his whole editorial experience he had never known nor heard of a reader-response equaling it; the article was by for the most successful ever published in this country. He said he told me this because the *Post* would never take another of its kind; he would gladly continue to take any fiction from me BUT not a political word nor inference even in fiction. The essence of the article was individualism, anti-communism, inferentially anti-New Deal, though wholly theoretical, not mentioning "politics." At this time (I am coming to the point) Mr. Hanson and Eileen Tighe came to see me. Mr. Hanson an executive of A&P. The magazine *Woman's Day* was happening to A&P in spite of them; Eileen was its new editor and they wanted me to write a piece for it.

When the 1929-32 depression struck, A&P managers observed thousands of young-married customers who—brought up in the boom—had no idea how to spend money on food. In pity for malnourished children, they tried to advise the bewildered mothers, and they suggested some printed advice. So A&P got out a leaflet, give-away of balanced-diet menus with prices. When times were a little better, A&P tried to discontinue it; but customers raised such a clamor for it that managers demanded it; so to kill it, it was priced at five cents. Then at ten cents. (I, or any sensible person, could have told them that anybody values a purchase higher than a give-away, but I guess they were listening to "public relations" experts.) The demand became a furor, of course, A&P *couldn't* kill the thing. Mr. Hanson then began to fight for, first, giving the buyers their ten-cents' worth, and later, making a bigger and better magazine out of the incubus. Other executives kept trying to kill it, saying that A&P *sells food,* what's it doing in the publishing field? The paid circulation was about 1,200,000; the leaflet magazine carried only A&P ads. Eileen could offer me only $50. My price *had* been $1500. But she said she would print anything I wrote; and she did.

So in the late 1930s we concocted a pro-American, anti-socialist series on needlework. It was quite successful, not disappointing, but response was almost wholly about patterns, materials, etc.

So last year Eileen "pressured" me into doing an American needlework series again. And this time the response was tremendous, more than we hoped for, actually all we wanted. An avalanche, tens of thousands of reader letters; very nearly ALL overflowing gratitude for the *Americanism.* Orders for patterns, etc., engulfed the business department too, but the patriotic, individualistic, anti-Welfare State response overwhelmed the editorial staff so that twelve more typists had to be added to the Answers-to-Readers department. And seven publishers asked for the series in book.

So Eileen and Roger MacBride handled the publication in *Woman's Day* and in book. They had virtually decided on one of the major houses when, in one of his clubs, Roger happened to hear an executive of that house bragging about how he had destroyed a "conservative" book by accepting it and suppressing it.

They decided finally on Simon & Schuster, an extremely "left" house, but those boys are primarily money-makers. And they are so tied up financially in the book ($15,000 advance; $100,000 manufacturing costs) that their staff can't hurt the sale too much. Besides *Woman's Day* is advertising the book and S&S are obliged by contract to supply *Woman's Day's* demand for it. So I expect a good, and indefinitely continuing, distribution; in addition to *Woman's Day's* already impressed 8,000,000 circulation.

You should be very happy about the Newark Museum. In the 1930s it was the best—by far the best and almost the only—one that had a fine collection of American folk-art. I used it almost wholly for material and illustrations. The Metropolitan Museum in New York had just then opened its American Wing, with a lot of fanfare; and when I inquired there for American needlework, the curators were dumbfounded; they had not heard that there was any. Quilts? Well, now, quilts. . . . Maybe some prints in the print department? Oh, yes, yes of course. . . . And after half an hour's searching, they brought out a print of an Indian palimpore, the Persian Tree of Life. The proud Americana experts of the new American Wing shrank and shriveled under my courteous contempt, and I enjoyed gently informing them that the Newark Museum had an admirable collection of American needlework, including a truly superb representation of the unique American folk-art, patchwork, both pieced and appliqued, and American quilting. You know New York's ridiculously haughty provincialism; imagine the agony of the Metropolitan Museum's curators, informed that *Newark* far surpassed their acquisitions AND their knowledge.

What happiness it is, to recall now and then a bit of such pleasant malice. Also, maybe by this time the Metropolitan Museum's American Wing is a bit more authentically American.

In general, museums are MUCH better in that respect now than they were thirty years ago. There is a real American renaissance going on, though as yet it shows on the surface only in the Goldwater boom. In its museum-aspect, the Newark Museum certainly led it. And Henry Ford probably with the first follower. Boston and Salem had some good things but they were sort of left-over, not proudly displayed and added-to as they are now.

So here is another long letter from me, excuse it please. You know my letters can always wait for attention at leisuse—if any leisure—and they don't require answering.

November 15, 1963

Dear Mr. Crane:

What an opportunity you have, knowing the great physicists. Their science arrives at coincidence with religious mysticism, doesn't it? Both reach the First and Final Cause of existence and find . . . Spirit, Energy, Anti-Chance, square root minus one, a transcendence beyond the (to human grasp) tangible and visible, which as LeCompte du Nouy wrote, "they might as well call God." As the Arabs say: "God has a hundred names; the hundredth only the camel knows."

It was Robert Louis Stevenson who wrote, wasn't it?

something like: Thus we bombard each other with missionaries, to the amusement of the angels. —All the hatreds, wars, massacres, about *names,* words, nothing but different symbols for the same truth beyond utterance. —A thousand years of Christian slaughtering Jew because the Jew worships One God, the Christian worships One Triune God. And now Jew and Arab hating, killing each other, because one says Jehovah and the other says Allah. If we would bombard each other only with missionaries!

Still it is a beautiful world "with the beautiful waters around it curled," and man is not *only* vile—we all have aspirations and faith and some bits of loving kindness, and slowly, so very slowly, we do learn and become a little better, bit by bit. You once wrote me that you do not believe that man is perfectible. I was surprised; does anyone believe that? *perfectible?* Of course not. But becoming better is not becoming perfect; and who can say that Americans in their churches are not better than (only 2,000 years ago) Romans at their atrociously obscenely cruel "games" honoring their Gods?

I trust you will have a truly happy Thanksgiving. I shall be at Roger's and Susan's in Vermont, being thankful —among other blessings—for my fortune in knowing you.

November 29, 1963

Dear Mrs. Lane:

My family association with the Newark Museum happened this way: My father, as well as myself, was well acquainted with John Cotton Dana of the Newark Library. He was an outstanding librarian and a fine man. He wanted to start a museum and, about that time, my father was returning from a trip to Japan and met Dr. Shelton, a Presbyterian missionary, who had been almost the only American to live in Tibet. On his furlough, he was bringing back a number of Tibetan articles which he wanted to sell, the proceeds to be devoted to his work with the Tibetans. My father purchased these articles and presented them to the new museum where they are still on exhibit as the Edward N. Crane gift.

Some years later, my uncle, Arthur N. Crane, became, I think, the President of the Museum's Board of Trustees and added to the Tibetan exhibit many more articles which Dr. Shelton brought to this country on subsequent trips. My brother is on the Board of Trustees of the Newark Museum. A month or so ago, my daughter, Mrs. Willard A. Speakman, Jr., who is very fond of antiques and works in the Winterthur Museum, not knowing of our family's interest in the Newark Museum, learned what excellent American articles were on display there, made a special trip to the old home town, and was delighted by what she saw.

The political situation now seems to be very greatly changed by the assassination of the President. That is so lamentable, so horrible. Throughout history the assassination of a ruler has almost always been followed by evil effects. Let us earnestly hope that in this case it does not mean the further advance of the welfare state, the police state. We should, rather, draw from this deplorable incident a further illustration of the evil of the use of violence, of the terrible behavior of communism.

December 4, 1963

Dear Mr. Crane:

As for the political effects of those shots in Dallas, I think as you do, though perhaps not wholly for the same reasons. It seems to me that Goldwater's strength in the South is gone; Lyndon Johnson is one of their own, he is not a damn Yankee, *he* did not (they'll feel) invade the South with Federal troops, he is a Democrat and that's important—decisive—to the professional politicians who want to hold their House and Senate committee positions and their White House connections. Also, the Republican Old Guard money-men would prefer Johnson to Goldwater, if it came to that choice. You know so much more about all this than I that this may seem childish prattling to you, but for whatever it is worth (if anything) I expect the Republican convention to be a 1964 version of 1896: The Eastern Big Boys against the Southwest.

Mr. Goldwater will support whoever the convention nominates for he is a party man, at all costs. So if he isn't nominated, his supporters are left—again—with nowhere to go. And I would not be surprised if he saw his chances somewhat as I do and declined to enter the contest at all.

I doubt that, personally, he has any wish to be President; I believe that he would undertake the responsibility and strain (which probably would shorten his life) only reluctantly, from a sense of duty, with none of the ambition that drives such men as FDR and Lyndon Johnson. So, IF he sees nearly no chance at all of being elected, he may very well decide to support someone else for the nomination.

I do not think, however, that the Kennedy "Image" which the leftists have been trying so vigorously to establish will last long enough to matter. . . . They tried even harder to make a Lincoln myth of FDR, and who is worshipping him now? He is not even a memory to the millions of new voters, the youngsters, and he is a faded one to those who adored him once and more recently have been adoring Jack and Jackie and those cute children Carolyn and John. People generally felt more warmly to Mrs. Kennedy than to him—and did you notice that hair style—huge mass of 'teased' hair—lasted only one season? It, and similar wigs, were a rage for their first year in the White House; last year the vogue was the 'small head' with hair smoothed sleekly down, though Mrs. Kennedy's style was still fantastically bouffant. These trifles are indicative. So were the many letters to magazine editors from fed-up readers saying "For goodness sake, can't you print anything but the Kennedys?" The publicity was already overdone; last week's image-making roused nothing like the hysteria whipped up when Roosevelt died; and I think that the Kennedy "image" will fade away even sooner than the Roosevelt one did.

I was driven across Connecticut and Massachusetts a week ago Monday, the day of the funeral. *Everything* was closed, not a gas station open, not any goods available, all flags at half-mast, but the people everywhere were having a good time, a holiday, lots of fun.

December 26, 1963

Dear Mrs. Lane:

Certainly, I agree that the advocates of individual liberty and our form of government should be ready to stand up at any cost in the endeavor to recover, retain and advance these principles. On the theme of "Are there any more at home like you?", I would mention a few: The Chairman, President and Vice President of the Du Pont Company, Edward P. Neilan, President of the Bank of Delaware, who is now doing such a superb job as President of the U. S. Chamber of Commerce; Senator John J. Williams of Delaware; J. Edgar Rhoads, retired manufacturer and a leading Quaker; and several other businessmen in Wilmington. Now farther afield: J. Howard Pew of Philadelphia; Lawrence Fertig and Henry Hazlitt of New York; Herb Cornuelle of Boston; Frederic C. Crawford of Cleveland; Charles M. White of Cleveland; John Stuart, Donald Lourie, Alfred P. Haake of Chicago; William J. Grede of Milwaukee; Robert Gaylord and James Rogers of Rockford, Illinois; Lem Jones of Kansas City, Mo.; H. F. Langenberg of St. Louis; W. C. Mullendore of Los Angeles; The Trustees not named above of the Foundation of Economic Education; Fred G. Clark and Richard Rimanoczy of the AEF; Howard Kershner of the Christian Freedom Foundation; Billy Graham and some other ministers that I could name; several of the Social Science faculties at New York University, Princeton University, University of Pennsylvania, Johns Hopkins, University of Virginia, Grove City College, Wabash College, Pepperdine College, Carleton Men's College, The Freedom School; Victor Milione at ISI; F. A. Harper and others in the Institute for Humane Studies, and a long list of others.

And think how the signers of the Declaration of Independence pledged "Our lives, our fortunes, and our sacred honor" and stood up to that pledge, suffering grievously for their principles. Their successors exist today and are increasing in number.

"Wherefore, seeing we also are compassed about with so great a cloud of witnesses, let us lay aside every weight . . . and run with patience the race that is set before us."

XXVII

February 5, 1964

Dear Mr. Crane:

The belief that God establishes Government is older than history. I can quote you its earliest known record, written in the third millennium B.C.:

> "After the world was created and after the fate of the land Sumer and of the City Ur had been decided, An and Enlil (The gods of sky and air) appointed Nanna the Moon to rule the city. One day Nanna chose Ur-Nammu of Lagash. He defeated Lagash and put Namhani to death. Then with the power of the Moon Nanna, king of the city, Ur-Nammu did justice in Ur."

This record is in the Museums of the Ancient Orient, in Istanbul. Ur-Nammu is historic; he founded the Third Dynasty of Ur. You know that the belief in the divinity of Governments prevailed thereafter, that the Pharaohs and Ptolemies of Egypt, the Emperors of Rome, were believed to be God Incarnate, worshipped as such, and that George the Third rules the British Colonies by Divine Right.

I have realized only lately how strong that belief still is. It is Catholic Church doctrine, of course, firmly believed by many fine minds and spirits. Pope Innocent expressed it: "As God has placed in the heavens two great lights, one to rule the day and one to rule the night, so He has placed in the world two great powers, one to rule the souls of men and one to rule their bodies." (Quote from memory.) It is said to have Biblical authority in the text —doubtfully authentic—"Render unto Caesar. . . ."

As I understand the American Revolution, its basic principle is that God creates no human institution; that He creates individual persons and endows each one with *inalienable* powers, functions, of free choice and *self*-government.

If this is true, then the institution named—from antiquity—"Government" cannot in fact *govern* anyone; as

Washington said, "it is force," force used by persons upon persons. It is a human institution made by living, self-governing persons, and no more divine than any other institution that human beings make.

The difference between the Old World and the Revolution is illustrated in the coronation of Queen Elizabeth. She rules the United Kingdom and the Commonwealth by the Grace of God, which she received in the sacrament. Her power is thereby divine, a power given to her by God, and given to no one else.

An American official undertakes, himself, to assume certain duties, and promises God that he will perform them faithfully. He has no more power than any other person; his relationship to God is no different from any other person's; he is held to his function in "Government" only by *his* assuming it, and *his* conscience.

In the minds of some persons, The Government has a sanctity which other institutions do not have. They do not regard the Government as they regard, e.g. General Electric or a Chamber of Commerce. It seems to me that the old traditional belief that Government is divine, holy, sacred, lingers in their thinking as an unnoticed assumption. (IF it is not maintained as an article of religious faith, consciously.)

I would say that the real question at issue is "Do you believe that God institutes the Government?" Or, do you believe that the political-police-military institution is man-made, as any other human institution is?

If those who attach a peculiar sanctity to The Government propose to restrict its action, they are inconsistent. What God makes, men *cannot* change, or resist.

Those who believe that "Governments" are man-made (by persons using their God-given liberty as best they know how) regard that institution as justified only by its usefulness to human beings, and as subject to their maintaining or changing or abolishing it. They believe that they are self-governing, and therefore, entitled, by their Creator, to ignore the Government as far as possible, to suggest that more useful institutions can be made, and to try to make them—as men made railroads which replaced and thereby abolished pack-trains and stage-coach lines.

Opposition to that position seems to me to be supported only by the traditional (and to some extent still religious) belief that The Government institution has a sanctity much more than merely practical, that somehow it is more divine than a stage-coach company.

Of course colonial Americans carried their revolutionary views of the nature of man into action; they openly disobeyed The Government, as Ghandi did and as American conscientious objectors to war do. They finally resisted their Government in armed rebellion.

This is the only country on earth, or ever, where people constantly remake this institution. Americans have abolished and replaced literally *hundreds* of "Governments" in these States since 1782, and they are still doing it. Nothing is more commonplace here than a "constitutional convention." We hardly notice reports of them in the newspapers. Why should this process be stopped? Why try to return to the pattern of 1789? What is wrong with fundamental thinking about the nature of man and the nature of institutions of "Government," and an effort to invent still better organizations of human relationships?

March 11, 1964

Dear Mr. Crane:

When I finish this book on which I have been working twenty years and more, it will not support the institution called "Government," either historically or theoretically. I am trying very hard to make this position clear and I do hope that in the book it will be clear and I do hope that in the book it will be clear to you.

The question, Do you believe in the monopoly of the use of force by persons upon persons, inaccurately named Government? seems to me to be in the same category of questions as, Do you believe in war?

My answer, honestly, is Yes, and No. In given practical situations, I am a pacifist; I will fight; I will cooperate with other fighters. At this moment, this year, for instance, I want these States equipped with plenty of the very best munitions. I want the next Administration in Washington to be Senator Goldwater.

But do I believe in War? NO. I believe absolutely in the existence of a principle of Natural Law, (not yet discovered and stated in the way that principles of physics or chemistry are) on which the Commandment, Thou shalt not kill, is based. The Natural Law, implicit as the basis of the Ten Commandments—and the Eleventh—is individualism; i.e., the free will and inalienable self-control of each living person. The first *statement* of that *principle* existing in the Law of the nature of man, is the American Declaration that "all men are created equal and endowed by their Creator with . . . unalienable life, liberty . . . etc."

I *believe,* firmly, that a similar principle is implicitly assumed in each of the Commandments, though these principles, these Natural Laws, are not yet stated. Unless, He who lives by the sword shall die by the sword, roughly indicates the Law producing the (now) obvious results of war.

Now you know that objections to war per se are very recent in history, and far from prevailing generally. I remember in France in the 1920s trying to express an anti-war position which, until then, I'd supposed was everyone's, and meeting blank incomprehension. Servants, tradesmen, etc., stared, shrugged, and dismissed the notion as if I'd objected to weather; saying, "There'll always be war!" Thinkers reacted (they thought) intelligently; saying that war rejuvenates Nations spiritually—and I just couldn't see that because I was a "materialistic American," unable to perceive "spiritual values." I think that now this country's anti-war policy is totally misunderstood abroad, regarded as hypocrisy and a cover for vicious designs upon other Governments; hence the fury of the people in the new African and Asiatic countries who wreck American embassies in the fervor of their patriotic nationalism.

I think that war is evil, necessary while a majority of people on earth *believe in war*—as naturally inevitable, as a "spiritual value" in a "Nation's life," or merely as the honorable and glorious occupation of an admirable man. I remember Mimtax Bay of Elbasan, with whom I talked behind the Government barricades during the battle of Tirana in 1922. He was feudal lord of more than thirty villages (he had never counted them exactly) and brought 1,000 of "his" men to defend Tirana. He had lived three years in the USA, holding more than twenty jobs in that time and spending $35,000 from his Elbasan estate. He despised the States and Americans with total contempt. Why? "You work," he said. "You all *work,* even the richest Americans *work;* per Zoti, why?" I asked what we should do. He said there are only two occupations for an honorable man: hunting and war.

I believe it is desirable to abolish war; I believe it is possible to abolish it totally—in the long, long run. So if you ask, Do I believe in war? (as the Europeans I've mentioned did, and millions do) my answer is, No.

That answer is the tiny beginning of an abolition of war. Not until a majority, or nearly, of the whole earth's inhabitants believe, (1) that war is evil; (2) that war is not necessary, and (3) that it CAN be abolished, replaced with something better, will it be possible to disarm the Governments and have peace on earth.

Meanwhile—and it'll be a long, long while—I am for nuclear submarines and plenty of ICBMs in the hands of a sane "government" in Washington.

Those NO and YES answers do not seem to me to be inconsistent because they are in such different fields.

Asked, Do I believe in Government? I make the same answers in the same fields. Logically, I must, because the *function* of "Government" is war: the use of physical force by persons upon persons.

Since God endows each person with an *unalienable* function of self-government, it is impossible that one person govern another.

People do not act according to that fact, because they don't know it; as they didn't sail around the earth because they didn't know they could. Most living persons (and everyone, more or less) still have the prevailing antique beliefs that, (1) persons are passive parts of an *organic* human Whole governed by a power of the Whole (as any real organism is governed). This power, The Government, was originally conceived to be God's appointed agent (Sumeria, 5,000-2,000 B.C.) then to be God Incarnate (Egypt-Rome, 5,000 B.C.-400 A.D) then to be endowed by God with His Divine Power, by birth and by anointing, i.e., by the Grace of God (into our own lifetime).

Not long ago some Americans discarded that belief in the Divinity of the human institution called Government. It had been doubted before; Americans first tried actually to abolish the Institution's power to *govern*. In any rational consistency with their discovery that God endows men with *inalienable* life, liberty, they had to deny that any man CAN *govern* another; and if The Government is not God, God's agent, or God's power, then it is a human institution like any other. The Founders tried to make it subordinate to individual persons, they tried to make public officials *governed,* instead of governing. It was unfortunate that they still called the institution "Government" but there was—and still is—no other word.

Americans try to say what they did, and the word, "Government," makes literal nonsense of the efforts. "This Government is the servant, not the master, of the people." But to govern and to serve are two different things. The saying is nonsense to everyone outside these States, because it *is,* literally, nonsense.

I don't know all that the Founders wrote; I wish I did, but I shall if I have time enough, in Time. But what they did was to try to abolish *government,* in the political institution they made; and in their situation, the institution was necessary (though so many said it wasn't, and fought to prevent it) because without it the Revolution would have been destroyed by France, England and Spain, their Governments.

The "Government" that the Founders made was not to *govern;* the men in it were to *be governed,* restricted, limited, checked in their actions. "Bind them down with the chains of the Constitution." They were given explicit *permissions;* they were told what *to* do, and what *not to do;* and they were explicitly prohibited from doing *anything whatever* that they were NOT told to do. In such a position, a person is controlled, he is governed; he is not the governor, the master, the controller; he is a hired man, obeying orders.

If Americans had used the powers they had, and the methods of using them provided in the Constitution, to continue to add to the restrictions, limitations, prohibitions upon men in the institution erroneously called "The Government," their power would now be much less than it was in 1789; and the Founders' purpose would be more nearly achieved. The "Government" would be more nearly approaching abolition. For to limit the use of a power is to reduce the power; to reduce it more, little by little, is progress *toward* abolishing it.

Instead of pursuing that course, Americans have little by little *increased* the power of "Government" in the USA. They have done this because of the old traditonal "belief in

Government," i.e., belief that human beings naturally *are governed* beings, parts of a human Whole governed by a Power somehow greater than that of a person's. "The Government should do for people only what they cannot do for themselves." —But there is nothing here *but* people; people do ALL that *is* done.

Even the brief limitation of "Government"—of the use of force by persons upon persons, here—gave Americans an opportunity to create innumerable institutions—organizations—of persons willingly co-operating, without any use of force. The multiplicity of these voluntary organizations is the outstanding characteristic of these States—something unique in history and in the world.

It is impossible that there can be a society of persons working together voluntarily, without war, without any compulsion?—as millions are doing now, in General Motors, General Foods, Red Cross, churches (what an innovation here: un"Governed" churches), radio, publishing, innumerable charities. . . . The Better Business Bureau *now* "policing" businesses without using police force; because in (comparative) freedom men discovered that honesty is the best policy. And honesty is merely obedience to two of the Ten Commandments. The knowledge hasn't spread around the world yet, but wouldn't you say that most American business men are acting according to it? Human beings cannot be perfect, but certainly we can always be better than we are—as certainly some are much better now than people ever were before—and the better people are, the less is the need to stop their actions by force.

The use of force in human relationships is evil. I do not believe that persons can't choose to abolish any evil existing in their relationships with each other on this earth, when they know enough to do it. In less than three centuries, some millions of us have abolished customs thousands of years old—slavery; torture as routine procedure in law courts; executing heretics, witches and bootleggers by slow torture in public; human sacrifices to the gods, etc., etc., etc. Only yesterday, all these evils were established from time immemorial, and regarded as proper and permanent.

Nothing that we do on earth is necessarily permanent. None of our ways of thinking and acting, none of our customs, habits, institutions is so perfect that we cannot make them a little better. If the use of force by persons upon persons is evil, human beings can reduce that evil; and this means, they can reduce the legal monopoly of that evil, the institution mistakenly named "Government." They can continue to reduce it, indefinitely, aiming and moving toward abolishing it completely.

Human beings are units of energy *acting* in time-space on this planet. In the human world, nothing is static; nothing can be kept immobile, unchanged. The question is one of the direction of movement since movement in some direction is inherent in the nature of life.

As regards any human institution—any organization of human energies—the direction is toward growth or toward extinction. That is as true of the "Government" institution (accepting it as human, not divine) as it is—was—of stagecoach lines, pack-trains, sailing ships and is of railroads, airplanes, General Motors, Studebaker, Uneeda Biscuits, etc., etc., etc.

The Founders tried to abolish *government* in the unique institution they created and called "Government," because they did not believe that men *can* actually *govern* men whom God endows with self-government. And they did not "believe in Government" as all their ancestors (*almost* all) always believed; they did not believe that Government was divine, in any sense that any man is not.

They believed (as I do) that a monopoly of force was necessary in the given circumstances; they knew that it is evil. They kept it as well *governed* as they knew how to do; they provided a method by which future Americans could keep on reducing it, in a movement toward eliminating it. This is a sort of preview of my book.

March 18, 1964

Dear Mrs. Lane:

Of course we don't believe in the divine right of Kings. Government is a human institution, a necessity in this imperfect world. As it was expressed in *Christianity vs. Totalitarianism,* and you were the principal contributor to that and wrote me that you approved it, "*Government.* But evil exists. No one is righteous. Some persons molest others, kill them, steal their property, interfere with their liberty, attack them with lies. They cannot be stopped from their evil doing. Crimes cannot be prevented by force, but to discourage violations of law and deter the wrong doing of a minority and, thereby, to restrain them from infringing on the rights of other persons in society, an instrument of force is needed in Space and Time. A government is set up and empowered to use force, which is known as police power: 'Government is organized force.' (Woodrow Wilson). Government, strong and effective government, is needed to protect the rights of the people, defend them from aggression, punish evildoers, provide justice, preserve order. Sound and wise leadership is conducive to the welfare of the people and promotes progress. But the power of the government is exceedingly dangerous and must be confined to its proper purpose."

We might almost say that our limited Federal Government stood up for over one hundred years in spite of innumerable attacks on it. We still also agree that in recent years there have been unconstitutional, unwarranted, and undesirable increases in government at all levels—national, state and municipal. We denounce the excesses, extravagances, and excrescences of government. The remedy is not to abolish government set up by the founding fathers. So our job is to restore the proper practices of government.

Bad as the situation is, we still can maintain that in America a better job of government has been done than anywhere on earth. I am deeply grateful every day of my life for the inestimable privilege of being an American. I want to help, not destroy. So I try to help anybody who is in a position of leadership and influence to correct unwise and indiscreet language, which is so harmful to the cause of freedom.

We look forward to the solution of human problems to a final time known as the millennium "when the lion will lie down with the lamb," but it is pretty tough on the lamb if we think that is possible today.

XXVIII

November 18, 1964

Dear Mrs. Lane:

Referring to our telephone conversation about the election, I think your characterization of your feeling about it is the same as mine—"heart sick," but optimistic of the long-time future of the United States.

As you have also indicated, we have lost the Republic and the American people have been badly infected by socialism. It seems to me that that is the major lesson from the election, that the people want the welfare state. That is very sad, indeed. I have had personal contacts with and have been a close observer of the disastrous results in several European countries and in several South American countries which have adopted or have been led into the welfare state philosophy. The sequence of events seem to be almost always the same, although differing in the time involved—coercion by centralized authority, overspending by the government, inflation of the money supply, rising prices, depreciation of the value of money until it reaches a runaway stage, fall in the standard of living, increasing poverty. Why cannot the lesson of history and of contemporary occurrences be read and understood by people?

Milton Friedman has pointed out how in the under developed countries there is widespread belief in socialism, particularly of the Fabian variety, and it seems almost impossible to knock this fallacy out of their minds. This even goes so far in country after country that if one tells them that socialism never succeeds, back comes the reply, "We are going to make it work."

November 20, 1964

Dear Mr. Crane:

I am not yet persuaded that anything like a majority of Americans want what they voted for this year. They do not know what they are doing—and in this world people are NOT forgiven because they know not what they do.

Natural Law (in the field of human relationships, where it is still called morality—from *mores* tribal custom —and not yet discovered and stated; as in the field of human action upon animate things, where it is called physics and since the sixteenth century has been somewhat discovered and stated) *produces the result* of human actions, regardless of whatever the acting persons believe and want the result of their action to be.

Americans, the great majority of them, of us, do not know what they are doing. Because we all tend to take for granted the conditions we find prevailing as we grow up. Because all children are brainwashed in the "compulsory, free" system of State schooling. Because the socialist reaction operating here since the 1860s has corrupted the vocabulary until NOBODY *speaks* the truth. (Lenin was extremely intelligent, a truly great mind tragically working from the ancient false premises. His "First Instruction" to his "professional revolutionist" was: First confuse the vocabulary.)

Take the words in their true meaning: Don't *you* want a welfare state? a state of general welfare? Don't you want social security? a society in which everyone is safe? especially safe from hunger, cold, beggary, starvation—as a minimum. Don't you prefer a liberal person, generous, "neighborly," to a narrow, selfish, miserly, skinflint? Are you for Progress, for progressing ideas and actions rather than for stick-in-the-mud minds and keeping the status quo?

Would you vote *against* welfare, against security, against liberality, against progress?

I think we wouldn't, and if we wouldn't we can't misunderstand others who don't, can we?

In the beginning of the overt, open and visible-to-everybody socialism in Washington, in Hoover's administration, there was a landslide vote against it; remember? FDR won on his explicit promises to stop it. He won again by unscrupulously clever politicking plus the Brain Trusters' and Communist agents' monopoly of all national means of communication. With these, plus the war-scare (like Wilson, he "kept us out of war") he won again. Through the 40s and 50s there was only one party here: socialist, under three or four names. Yet, after all that, twenty-six plus millions of voters still try to get rid of the whole thing.

The number is truly amazing, even discounting whatever number merely automatically voted as they always had voted and father did. It is astounding when you think that they got no help from the Republican campaign.

Was there ever a more inept national political campaign than the 1964 Republican?—if it can be called Republican. Goldwater was defeated by Republicans, of course; as Senator Knowland was, and how many others since 1936? It is a flabbergasting mystery—HOW *could* the Goldwater people—whoever they were—be so fantastically naive as not to know that they had to *fight?* and to fight on two fronts? the labeled-Democrats in front, the labeled Republicans with knives, in back? This country is full of "little people," registered Republicans who knew that. And were stymied by—was it the National Committee? (By the way, I hear that the National Committee's public relations man is a partner in the law firm of the Lyndon Johnsons? Is that so?)

Whoever, besides the Senator, were the VIPs the *real* ones, managing the campaign, I don't know. I am merely a voter. And a spend-till-it-hurts contributor to the campaign. I even carried self-sacrifice so far as to watch on television every campaign program I heard of. I mean "heard of." They were not listed on any list of next-week's TV programs that I saw—the *TV Guide,* the *Herald Tribune's* Sunday TV booklet, the local papers. There was a nest of Goldwater workers in Brookfield; they telephoned news of programs around to each other. I *knew* the press would not publicize them; why the VIPs didn't know that, and *advertise* them, I can't imagine.

In this century's teens when socialists were making the fight that "we" should be making now, the whole press was antagonistic. So they scraped together nickels and dimes and offered ads to the papers, announcing meetings, speeches, etc. And when the paper refused to take the paid advertisements, the socialists HOWLED—they picketed, they stood on street corners and handed out leaflets, they stood on soapboxes and protested till they were arrested. It took them thirty years to get a President into the White House.

Today, the whole press is antagonistic. So, the whole press smothers the campaign. I cannot blame "the people." The people is uneducated, uninformed, uninterested persons with all kinds of immediate interests on their minds and a touchingly innocent faith that VIPs are as honest, truthful, patriotic as themselves, with much greater learning and wisdom to boot. I blame the managers of a national political campaign of utmost importance, whose job is to know all the elements of the situation, and to ACT intelligently. And who don't do their job.

So, I saw *one* short TV broadcast, the Reagan-Goldwater one, that was straightforward, honest, truthful, down to brass tacks. I know six ardently pro-Johnson, born and bred and registered Democrats, who saw that broadcast and put on Goldwater pins, argued and voted for Goldwater.

I saw the Senator on TV, three times.

1. A Travelogue of Mr. Eisenhower's farm, beautifully photographed, lovely landscapes, charming cows, handsome house, the Senator and ex-President wandering and admiring the prospects and the herds. They sat to rest at a table near which a man—evidently a servant—was frying hamburgers or something. The Senator tells the President that people call him a reckless war monger; he asks, Does Mr. Eisenhower think so? With a slight hesitation, Mr. E. says, nonsense, of course not. They agree that the Presidency is a great moral responsibility. They rise (and, inexplicably, ignoring the hamburgers or whatever they were) walk slowly away from me, slowly, slowly, their backs recede up a long, long lane, walking together in silence.

2. I see the interior of a *radio* station, the walls of light-blinking mechanisms, the engineers attending them. Enter the Senator escorted by the manager, who introduces him; he shakes hands with the mechanics, he listens and presumably learns how the mechanisms work. Blink! He appears alone in an office occupied by a number of clean, dusted desks and empty desk-chairs. He walks about the office aimlessly, talking to its emptiness, about morality, crime in the streets—I forget what else; a kind of mother-home-and-heaven discourse, against sin—while he listlessly sits on a corner of a desk, moves to a chair, rises and walks up and down, finally walks away, slowly away down a corridor, and gone. Another face tells us that TV costs money, lots of money (I have that day a letter from Goldwater HQ, saying it costs $100 a second; please contribute) and asking for contributions.

3. On the eve of election. Senator and Mrs. Goldwater sitting in their patio; he asks her how she enjoyed the

campaign, she says it was wonderful; he suggests their visiting the Millers. Blink! The happy Miller family, saying nothing I can remember. Blink! The Senator strolling toward a patio wall—desert mountain beyond: Camelback. Boyishly he leaps onto the wall, sits facing us, assures us that he is not a war monger, smiling asks us to vote for him.

These are my memories—those of any voter seeing the programs, I'm sure; and vaguely in all the scenes there was an attitude of defense, a repeating of accusations against him, and a denial of them. He denied that he wanted war; he said several times that he has children and hates war. He denied that he would injure Social Security—he *said* "Social Security." He would only strengthen it. He was FOR one thing: strength; as Dewey was FOR one thing: unity.

Really, Mr. Crane, if you had never thought about political questions—say, when you were twenty-one, if you remember your first voting—and if all you knew about the Senator was what you read in the papers and happened to see on TV, would you have been aroused to campaigning and voting for him? And if you hadn't been, could you be accused of *wanting* enforced collectivism?

If it is possible, if there is an available tape of the Reagan Broadcast, I wish you would get it; I do hope you can hear it. The address was: Reagan-Goldwater TV, P.O. Box 80, Los Angeles 51. I'll bet it got an astounding sum in contributions; it sure got votes.

Reagan attacked. He scored Communist influences in Washington; he used old-fashioned patriotic rhetoric. He ridiculed the War on Poverty; quoted figures, cost of $4,500 a year per "youth" in the camps; "Why we can *send them to Harvard* for $2,700.—Don't mistake me, I'm only suggesting sending them to Harvard. Only, there seems to be a lot of overhead here, somehow." He attacked the fraud called social security. They say your money is going into a fund; they'll pay it back when you need it. But look at the fund—there's nothing there. —He *explained* the fraud, in terms as simple as that. He was speaking to a small audience, a couple of hundred, who responded to every point; they went wild at last, when he advocated saying to Moscow: "There is a price we will not pay, there is a point beyond which you do NOT advance." Somewhere he quoted, Is life so sweet . . . as to be purchased at the cost of chains and slavery? And he made it perfectly clear that the "welfare state" IS chains and slavery. He did not call it, as I recall, a "welfare state." He did not call his opponents liberals, he did not advocate morality and peace nor deny any charges against him or his views.

The Goldwater supporters whom I know were sickened by his campaign. Who on earth were his advisors? WHY didn't he have sense enough NOT to keep *repeating* the lies about him, to deny them? I contributed enough to the National Committee to pay for those TV seconds, and it annoys me that they were used to say again what his antagonists were saying: *I* say, Let COPE pay for *that*. But Senator Goldwater used those dollars to tell voters, "They say that I. . . ."

I kept remembering the convention and hoping that real work was being done unseen, as it had been done before the convention. There was organization in San Francisco; the organization is working now at the grassroots, I kept thinking. Do you know what happened? I hear from two Goldwater supporters in Michigan that Republican organization stymied them there; and from one in Illinois, the same. She saw no hope for Goldwater, and worked for Percy. Since 1936, this is the first national election day on which the local Republican HQ didn't call and offer me transportation to the polls. What became of the delegates who gave Goldwater the total support in San Francisco?

To me the vote does not at all prove that "the people" *want* socialism, as "everyone" has been saying since FDR double crossed those who first voted for him, *against* the socialism appearing in Hoover's administration.

Socialism everywhere else is traditional, plus reaction against the American Revolution. As you say, the sequence of events is almost the same, everywhere. The pattern appeared first in France; when "les Americains"—Franklin and Lafayette's group—tried too soon to take the Revolution to Europe. Centralized authority is taken for granted; it's immemorial; prevailing since history began in Sumer. In reaction against American individualism, since 1789 the pattern has been: Socialists seize centralized authority from monarchs; they try to enforce socialization, with coercion, spending, inflation, till the political-social structure collapses; enter the Dictator, after or with a Terror. This occurred in every government on earth, from France in 1792/93-1800, to Mexico in 1820, all European governments in 1848, China in 1911, Russia in 1917. And since then they have all been trying somehow to recover balance, stability, in increasing world chaos. The pattern you describe as you have seen it recently and are seeing it, is a variant repetition of the eighteenth century French one, seems to me.

Why can't people understand the lesson of history and contemporary events?

December 30, 1964

Dear Mrs. Lane:

I haven't yet answered your letter of November 20, but I did appreciate it very much and agree with your analysis of the situation. My overall view is that the American people are so obsessed that they are bewitched by the fallacy that appeasement is the way to peace. Yet, all the evidence from history and the contemporary world indicate quite the contrary.

February 5, 1965

Dear Mr. Crane:

I have just been "down in the Valley" in Texas for ten days, and have bought a little house there, in Harlingen, snapshot enclosed. It is an escape from the trap into which I have boxed myself here, with books and pups and winter weather.

What do you think is going to happen? Or if you'd rather not claim to be Mohammed's successor, a later prophet, would you tell you what to do? I am so FURIOUS at me, for not *knowing* what to do after living through three, count 'em, THREE "runaway" inflations: Germany, Russia, Greece. I observed at the time—and times—that really huge fortunes are to be gained by traffic in currencies. But, (1) I don't want millions; I only want to survive in comfort; (2) that traffic requires quick mobility, quick thinking, quick action, a kind of smartness and rashness and chance-taking that doesn't interest me any more; and, (3) so far as I can see, this is a situation wholly unprecedented; not *one* good currency anywhere on earth, since the "Washington dollar" is no more. How can anything be relative when there is nowhere anything to be ultimately relative *to*. When *every*thing is relative, nothing is.

The Swiss Franc was supposed to be solidly on gold. (By the way, de Gaulle seems to be sane and sensible about currency, surprising me.) But Swiss bankers say that when the dollar goes, the Swiss franc will. Which I do not understand because what do they mean, "when the dollar is devalued?" What's the value of the dollar *now*? 'way back yonder Mr. Herbert Hoover told me that the dollar was then worth twenty-five cents on the free gold market. The dollars seems to me like those old old barns around New England, standing on who knows what? since the sills are rotted and vanished away and even the bottom ends of the studs are mostly gone. (I was amazed to find, when remodeling this house, that under one corner post there was nothing left but air, the corner stone being a good foot below the end of the ant-eaten timber.)

The other evening I heard Mr. Johnson's speech to the Anti-Defamation League. I heard it on radio, not on television; I honestly believe that seeing as well as hearing him would have made me really ill. Radio made me only *feel* ill, and I kept turning him off, partially recovering and turning him on again. How is it, WHY is it, that in every time of special stress this country is represented by a blatantly ignorant stupid and vain-glorious idiot? Wilson, FDR, Johnson. Even Grant, I suppose. The little I know about Grant is the Missouri view—the ne'er-do-well who failed in everything he tried, not trying much, and lived off his wife's folks until he got on an army payroll. In time to profit from the collapse of the already ruined South and be elected President.

I hear that an ex-minister, Congregational, writes Johnson's speeches. Sounds more like a Holy Roller exhorter, fervent, ignorant, complacent, brainless, proud of big-sounding words—such superior-class words as e.g. "concensus," sounding big and impressive and beyond the speaker's understanding. I am glad I am not in Europe not in England, surrounded by those joyously cruel smiles and polite references to "*your* president."

February 16, 1965

Dear Mr. Crane:

Minimal Religion strikes me as very good indeed. I truly have not been able to read it every word, as thoroughly as I wish, but I have read about half of it, different parts at different times. This is not the way to read a book, I know; as soon as possible I shall read this one properly.

Meanwhile, I think it remarkable—fascinating and unusual, and sound. I would have a few small arguments with Mr. Nymeyer, so small that they don't matter; such as that Suetonius isn't too trustworthy about Tiberius; that the labor theory of value was Adam Smith's, not Marx's—except by theft, or plagarism; that *I* would say—indeed, have said in mms.—that the profits from co-operation (division of labor) come from the *diversity* of human beings. (Diversity is not necessarily inequality: "all men" are in fact equally human—none is mineral, vegetable, or animal"; all men are created *"equal"* but no two identical.) I might raise a question: Are not all equally necessary, equally indispensable, in any division of labor? I said this once to Ayn Rand. Aren't the skills that make paper, ink, typewriter as necessary to a writer as the mind that writes is necessary to the craftsman? She was infuriated and answered that all the fools would be good riddance, without them "we," the intellectuals, would do all that they do better and cheaper and faster. I don't see why Mr. Nymeyer regards the various crafts, or the men with various skills as *unequal.* (pages 98-99) I am surprised by "Polygamy does not work" and "A mate is 'property.'" (page 283) Mr. Nymeyer should stay out of Utah and avoid the Society of Women Voters.

But all that does not matter at all. Fundamentally he is perfectly right and he seems to have thought it all out for himself by himself, given a good library probably accumulated by himself.

March 16, 1965

Dear Mrs. Lane:

I, too, have had intimate contacts with runaway inflation in Germany, France, Italy, Brazil, Argentine, and Chile and it is frightful. There is no sure way of prospering through a period of inflation. Lifetime savings are wiped out and only a few successful gamblers seem to profit.

Let me tell you about two men that I knew and did business with in Germany, where I used to visit eight and ten times a year during the 20s. One, an industrious and able businessman, had a twenty year endowment policy to pay him the equivalent of one hundred thousand dollars, which, invested at six percent would afford him an affluent living for the rest of his life. The policy came due in November 1923, and with the proceeds he bought a pound of butter. The other was a clerk in the Metal Bank of Frankfurt, twenty-seven years old, who acquired a chemical factory, mortgaged it to the hilt, bought another and another and as the value of the mark kept going down and borrowed everything he could, paying it back in the further depreciated mark. When the currency was all scrapped and the new and stable reichs' mark was introduced in late 1923, he turned lender, as money was still commanding the grotesque interest rate of ten percent per day. He cashed in his holdings into gold and foreign securities and amassed a fortune equivalent to twenty-five million American dollars, and married the boss's daughter.

We do not know whether our U. S. inflation will reach runaway proportions or when it will do so. The announced national debt is not the whole story of the long-continued bad fiscal policy of the Federal Government. To the little over three hundred billion dollars national debt must be added the liability for those now on the social security rolls of our hundred billion dollars, against which there are no reserves, but which must be liquidated by further borrowing of an improvident government. Millions of others are coming on to the social security rolls, and all of these and other payments by the Federal Government make its expenditures far in excess of any possible income.

There may, therefore, be a public realization of some of these basic facts and failures of these grandiose and unsound schemes and a return to fiscal sanity. The value of the dollar can't be kept intact. It must be devalued very considerably, but how much we do not yet know. Meanwhile, there are some investments, some equities, a few convertible securities, and land which may ride the tide of inflation—but it is not easy to find them, nor can we feel any security.

But Shakespeare wrote:

> "For we all know security
> Is mortal's chiefest enemy."

March 21, 1965

Dear Mr. Crane:

It is generous, kind—so like *you*—to write me your views of the general situation here. Thank you. I have hoped that there might be some refuge in land. Unless expropriated, it is at least a source of food. I have only four acres "more or less" (as Connecticut deeds say) here, and most of that is woodlot, but during the late fighting I lived really quite lavishly from it, with no ration card. I know, it seems childish at best, but I was born in Dakota Territory and *asking* some snippy pert official for permission to LIVE is just more than I can do. If I can't live without permission, I'll die. All that pseudo rationing was so ridiculous, anyway; and so nauseating. Have you ever suspected that in being so nice to me you are consorting with a criminal? All through the fighting I was diligently breaking laws every day.

First, being listed as a farmer, I received a bulletin of decrees thicker than the Income Tax Instructions. I was permitted—emphatically NOT to sell food produced from my own land by my own or regularly employed labor; provided, (1) that it be prepared on my premises, and, (2) consumed on them; and, (3) consumed only by myself, members of my family, and employees regularly employed; and, that it be prepared for consumption in a kitchen as defined on page (I forget), paragraph, etc., etc. So I looked up the legal definition of kitchen; and by (then) law a kitchen is a row in a domicile in which food is prepared for consumption on the premises, daily, for a family of not less than four persons, consuming three meals a day.

Imagine me, then in the not-yet-remodeled tiny house, 23′ x 24′, cooking not in a kitchen but in a pantry, for a family of me and one Maltese, I eating two meals a day and the pup eating one.

You wouldn't believe the quantity of foods that I produced from my gardens year after year, and canned. I lined my 23′ x 24′ cellar with shelves and filled them with cans; when you turned on the light you were in Aladdin's cave glittering with jewels—all those colors in glass, with the gold-colored metal rings on the tops of the jars.

Coming from the nineteenth century Midwest, I am an incorrigible food-hoarder, always buying in quantity (my instinct is, flour by the barrel, salt and sugar by burlap sack) so by pure chance I happened to have fifty pounds of flour and twenty-five of sugar when the ration-edict struck; and until the fighting sort of fizzled out in whatever we have now, I didn't buy a bit of food, nor need to. Except, that from criminal neighbors (this was farming country then) I bootlegged the carcass of a hog and carcasses of two or three dozen fat hens every year. The pork I processed through brine and smoke, and canned ham, bacon, sausage, chops in half-gallon jars and stone crocks; the hens I cold-water canned in two quart mason jars. Every conceivable vegetable and fruit was in glass; there were shelves of jams and jellies and preserves and compotes, too. I processed sweet fruits in their own juices, having no sugar to use for that, and jellied them with quinces from the trees; and you never tasted anything so delicious—MUCH better than with sugar. And since I was doubly a criminal already—no ration card, and cooking illegally—I compounded the crimes by *giving away* case after case of mason jars full of foods. The pup and I and all our friends lived high and lavishly through those years.

What do you think of these civil-rights and other outbreaks of violence?

Persons from whom I used to get information have died. I keep wondering, Is it possible that the Communist *cadres* (who are so ignorant of the USA) actually estimate that the time is ripening to "seize power" here? They were intelligent enough to see the invincible obstacle—the federal structure, the (then) forty-eight centers of political-police-military power—and to attack it with the plan of Seven Authorities; beginning with TVA and proceeding to MVA, the second planned, but the tactic was stopped there. Since then, the authority of the States has been nibbled away—Federal troops in Arkansas; the take-over of National Guard in Alabama, which so startled and stunned Governor Wallace when he realized what it means—did you see that instant on TV? And the Supreme Court decisions, blatantly unConstitutional; to which even the State Legislatures are supinely submitting. . . . It is surely not impossible that all this may seem, in Moscow, to mean that the time is near-ripe here; and all these disturbances all over the place *are* the preliminary move. If there's anything in this conjecture, the comrades will get a shock; this country is not to be "seized" in any such way, of course.

But what IS happening? How is it possible that this man calling himself Martin Luther King can seize fifty miles of a State Highway and charge U. S. taxpayers—you and me included—$360,000 for his use of it for four or five days? with no effective endorsement of law and order maintaining State authority over that highway? If this can occur, what can't?

June 18, 1965

Dear Mrs. Lane:

Did you know that George Bernard Shaw designed a window for the grave of Beatrice Webb with a coat-of-arms for the Fabian Society—F.S.—and a wolf in sheep's clothing? That seems diabolical to me—the gentle Fabians really ravening wolves. This is illustrated in a new book, *The Great Deceit,* published by the Veritas Foundation, Colonel Archibald Roosevelt's Foundation. It is a forceful attack on socialism. Have you seen this book?

[Many of] these acts of violence you referred to on March 21 have been instigated, not only in this country but throughout the world by the communists. The Soviet propaganda apparatus of five hundred thousand fully employed people, with an expenditure of two billion five hundred million dollars, operates all over the world. It is one of their most effective instruments for subversion and conquest.

XXIX

Fairmont Hotel and Tower—Atop Nob Hill
San Francisco
June 27, 1965

Dear Mr. Crane:

I am sorry I had no time to answer your latest letter—I have been coping with Washington till now. Am leaving Tuesday—Honolulu, Guam, Manila, Saigon; Thursday—Address Hotel Caravelle, Saigon—One or more articles probably in fall in *Woman's Day,* 8,000,000 circulation all bought, no subscriptions—very good medium, most influential opportunity I could not refuse.

All the best to you.

Hotel Caravelle
Saigon
July 13, 1965

Dear Mr. Crane:

A note from home says that there is a letter there for me from you. I wrote you hurriedly that I was coming here—you must have written me earlier, or my note went astray. I am all right here but the Lodge appointment has taken the heart out of the Vietnamese generally, and the Americans. They take it as the first move in a betrayal to the Communists, as in Laos and Cambodia and the 1954 Geneva agreements giving most of the Vietnamese to Ho Chi Minh. Let's hope and pray that this time the USA does not betray our friends. But who can blame the Viets for fear and caution? They are splendid people—after twenty years of frightful war on their own soil, they would do this job themselves (with American arms) if they could be sure that the US would not betray them. I have just returned from Qui Nhon, both ways in a military plane crowded with exhausted Viet troops—flying over the sea to avoid shots from mountains held by the Viet Cong (they hold most of the land outside some twelve urban centers by murder, torture and terror). When peasants do not obey them, they line up and kill all men in the village and take the women, raze the village. Cities are full of refugees, from the land. But if the USA abandons this point, Americans will one day be fighting Communists in our States.

All best wishes,

July 22, 1965

Mrs. Rose Wilder Lane
Hotel Caravelle
Saigon
SOUTH VIETNAM

Dear Mrs. Lane:

It is simply amazing to me that you should undergo the hardships and dangers of your present visit.

I deeply hope that you are safe and well, and I look forward to seeing you again when you return.

435 Woodland Drive
Harlingen, Texas

December 25, 1965

Dear Mr. Crane:

It is so long since I heard from you—not since before I went to Vietnam. I am hoping that you are having a very happy Christmas and that the new year will be nothing but generous to you.

Also, I meant to send you a copy of December's *Woman's Day* in which my piece about Viet Nam appeared. Now I am trying to get some copies of that number and IF I can, I shall send you one. The editor, Eileen Tighe, intended that twenty should be sent to me but—you know: Organizations. Something went wrong.

Weather has been and is magical here, for me from Connecticut. Sunny and sea-breezy and full of flowers. It is now COLD—bitterly cold, everyone tells me; 'way down into the sixties and once even to forty-eight in the night.

I have the air conditioner off, but doors open to my back yard full of blooming roses, poinsettias, gardenias, hybiscus —can it be, do you suppose, hybiscuses?—and the orange tree and the Ruby Red grapefruit tree. My bananas will not be producing bananas till next year—at eighteen months of age—but they are thriving.

The odd thing here is that oleanders, poinsettias, gardenias, bougainvillias and all sorts of exotic annuals (growing wild as weeds) are disregarded as commonplace, while the prized things are geraniums, chrysanthemums and roses. And ordinary white daisies, of all things. A neighbor has a bed of those and the whole neighborhood is waiting eagerly to see them bloom. She had an orchid tree in full bloom which excites no second glances.

May 4, 1966

Dear Mrs. Lane:

I don't know Texas well, having visited there only two or three times, but I am very interested in what you say about it. I had no idea that it would be so flowerful.

Thank you for your inquiry about our health and your good wishes to my wife and me. Sadly, we are both beginning to show our years, so much older than you! Our memory is faulty and our physical strength quite lessened but we are comfortable and well taken care of and are grateful to God for all the blessings that we have had.

May 16, 1966

Dear Mr. Crane:

I remember your helping Pepperdine College; doesn't it make you proud to see Pepperdine refusing Mr. Lewis's million dollars because of the condition that the college give Dan Smoot a degree? Isn't it heartening, that a Pepperdine degree can't be bought? That college must be turning out good men and women—if it's co-education? I don't know. Anyway, good for the future is coming out of that college.

Do you hear from Orval Watts? I hope so. He is doing so well at Northwestern Institute which is going great guns—expanding now in Texas. Orval will be in Dallas this winter, starting the Economics Department there; he seems to have done good work last year in Brazil. (Because of Viet Nam and other complications in my 1965 affairs, I was out of touch with him for months.)

Temperatures here are flickering around ninety. But all buildings and cars are air-conditioned, so my house is deliciously cool. I don't know yet whether I shall go to Vermont this summer.

May 24, 1966

Dear Mrs. Lane:

What you write about your new home is very interesting, but I am a bit bewildered at not knowing whether you are a nutmeg Yankee, a Texan or a Vermonter.

May 31, 1966

Dear Mr. Crane:

You say you're a bit bewildered. . . . But really it's easy: I am a nutmeg Yankee, a Texan, a Vermonter AND a Missourian, not born in the USA but addicted to ALL these states, from Padre Island to the Sea Island Counties of Washington, from the deserts of Maine to Disneyland. You didn't know that I can't, by birth, be President of these United States? No; I was born in Dakota *Territory*.

Seriously, I have further news of the World Youth Crusade for Freedom. This is a proposed development from the International Youth Crusade for Freedom in Viet Nam. It seems that *that* YAF project aroused enough response in Siam, Japan, Australia, Taiwan, Korea, Viet Nam (naturally), Hong Kong, India, Belgium, Denmark, Norway, Sweden, Italy, Honduras—etc., etc. and in the United States, even, to inspire an idea of a permanent world anti-Communist youth organization. This is the intended World Youth Crusade for Freedom.

It has a Senior American Advisory Council including scores of names, almost all the "Rightist" names you can think of, from Gene Lyons to Hans Sennholz to George Schuyler to John Chamberlain and of course all the *National Review* people. Temporary headquarters in Bloomington, Indiana, temporary Secretary General of the International Secretariat, Tom Charles Huston; national USA secretariat will be established in New York City, chairman Davis Keene, University of Wisconsin. Activities of anti-Communist youth groups USA, to be co-ordinated with those of World Youth Crusade. Enormous funds required; must of course be supplied by Americans.

I don't know what I think about this. It may be that I am only old-fashioned, unable to understand this world of 1966. Or may be I am biased by my living among Moslems for years. Or may be I am right. In any case, I believe there can be—and often is—too much organization. Too much organization costing too much money, in enterprises not checked by profit-or-loss in cash terms.

It seems to me that we successful in free-market enterprises use a way of thinking suitable to buying-and-selling (or buying-making-and-selling) in other fields of human action where that way of thinking isn't applicable. If you want something that can be bought, of course the more you buy the better, up to total satisfaction of your need or demand for that thing. And the more money you spend for it, the more you can buy. I remember a man starting one of "our" education foundations saying to me with enthusiasm that all that was needed was money, money in $ hundreds of thousands; no worry about writers—"writers are all over the place, writers can always be hired. . . ." Dear Mr. Crane, you know me; need I describe my explosion at that point?

Do you remember, I think it was in 1933—apparently quite suddenly some men with lots of money realized what FDR was—there was loud fanfare for $ millions, out with trumpets to save the country—Was it the Liberty League? some such name, with the word Liberty in it. If money could buy what was needed then, there would have been no New Deal.

I wish that young people were being left alone to work for freedom with their hands—to WORK for it, as the young socialists were doing sixty years ago. Nobody organized Senior Advisory Councils and gathered large funds together for Lenin in 1904 or Jack Reed in 1919—or the

Eastmans, Max and Crystal, or Gene Debs, or Rose Paster Stokes. The Communists are winning the world—so far as they are winning it—because they have and use what cannot be bought—faith, hope, convictions, courage and devotion. They DIE for their faith, communists do. And there are young Americans who would die for ours—more of them than there were in 1776.

But it seems to me that their energy is damped down and diverted by organizations and money. Take IVS—International Voluntary Service. Started privately, evidently on a shoestring, just a little group of young Christians in foreign countries being "neighborly" in the American (unique) sense of that word. The President seizes the idea, calls it Peace Corps, clobbers it with money. The difference was visible in Viet Nam, and enormous.

Twelve men, without money, started historical Christianity. How many began the American Revolution? without waiting until they got the money from France. How many Bolsheviks seized Russia? How many college students belonged to the Intercollegiate Socialist Society in 1904?

It is human ACTION that creates human history; and human action comes from individual belief, purpose, will. None of these can be bought. It is individual's belief, purpose, will that's needed. Not an organization, a suitable staff, transportation, printing presses, expert public relations men, etc., etc., etc. IF the belief and purpose exist, in time they will succeed. "An army of principles will march on the horizon of the world, and it will conquer." If they do not exist, no funds, organization, staff, etc., etc., etc. will do anything at all—but waste the money.

As a bit of gossip: Orval Watts mentioned to me that he believed Northwood's English Department could require better reading than Steinbeck's *Grapes of Wrath,* and asked me for suggestions. Me, of course, I rose up and RAGED, so Orval *read* Steinbeck's masterpiece and went as beserk as that mild gentleman can. And he read some of that book to the President whose hair stood straight up. And *Grapes Of Wrath* is ejected from the English Department of Northwood Institute. Orval says the English Professor is bewildered, saying that *Grapes Of Wrath* is an American "classic" and what's wrong with requiring students to read classics? I fear you never read that dirty piece of obscene communist propaganda which the Comrades made the renowned best seller of the 1930s, slandering the generally decent "Okies," as it did. So you must take it from me that chucking it out of a college is a minor victory for us. At the time I began a counter novel of the "Okies," but the Communist blockade of the literary field was so solid that I knew it couldn't be printed.

June 14, 1966

Dear Mrs Lane:

Thank you so much for your letter of May 31. I don't dispute a word of it. All through history progress has resulted from individual men and women, often in the garret. Also, research is now organized in corporations which appreciates the value or, rather, the virtual necessity of developing new ideas, new applications of science, if they are to meet competition and survive. This is a prime example of voluntary cooperation.

On the other hand, government enterprises, lacking the spur of competition, do very little indeed in the way of research. Numerous books have been written on this theme. Yet, the failure of government to develop any new ways is too little recognized. In all enterprises money is required. That is true in propaganda also. It seems to me that thoughtful study and great discrimination are needed to determine where to place one's gifts.

June 20, 1966

Dear Mr. Crane:

Thank you for your letter and the enclosure. The Church League of America does seem to be doing good work. I know little about it, though my mother was a close friend of Mr. Robnett, had the highest opinion of him. Major Bundy was here recently. Rufus Shackelford financed his speaking tour and radio-television programs throughout the valley—a whirlwind campaign lasting some weeks, at a rate of several dates daily. Major Bundy was at a last gasp when I saw him.

Rufus Shackelford, one of nine brothers, sons of a salt-of-the-earth 'dirt farmer' couple is himself a whirlwind-energy; he farms some thousands of acres in California, Florida and here, flies his own plane, is a motive-power of the Confederate Air Force (building a museum, collecting and aiming to hold and display at least one of every model of plane used in World War II—the latest phase of Mr. Wilson's World War), distributed 50,000 copies of *A Texan Looks at Lyndon Johnson,* went after Bishop Pike tooth and nails when that hypocrite dared to address High School children in Harlingen . . . ; he is also happily married and adored by his seven sons and one small daughter who are splendidly healthy and disciplined youngsters. Incidentally, he totally lost 600 acres of tomatoes near here, by bad weather this spring, and is now in California with his family seeing to planting there. He plastered the Valley with announcements of Major Bundy's campaign; his family and his brother's and I stuffed thousands upon thousands of envelopes.

Major Bundy is one of those apparently awkward and ineffective speakers who makes a terrific impact on an audience. He quoted endless reports of Communist activities, from House and Senate Committees, FBI, etc., etc. This was his final speech in the Valley at the end of some thirty days of them, many every day, and breakfasts, luncheons, teas, dinners, banquets. . . . He was extremely effective. Afterward mobbed by the audience, which also bought masses of 'literature' from tables in the lobby. The campaign was a brilliant success, educational and financial. By that, I mean that it showed a satisfactory profit above the costs which Rufus Shackelford contributed.

Major Bundy's peroration seemed to me, in a sense, a non sequitur. After showing the Communists' dangerous *activities* in undermining the Republic's political structure, debauching education and morals and infiltrating the churches, he ended by declaring that the ONLY—the ONE and ONLY—hope of resisting them is to be reborn in Christ. This seems to me a shift from physical action to spiritual being. It isn't by believing that there is no God that Communists have taken all Asia and Cuba and north Korea and North Viet Nam and, in part, the National and World Council of Churches. It isn't by being a Christian that Rufus Shackelford demolished Bishop Pike; it was by writing and paying for page advertisements all along the Bishop's trail. But in a sense I suppose Major Bundy was right; the answer to atheism is theism. Anyway I heartily applauded Major Bundy and the work he is doing.

Yes, I don't doubt that the Comintern (under whatever alias) is spending $ billions a year, maybe even employing—especially if the word means using, not hiring and paying—hundreds of thousands of persons in agit-prop alone. ("Agit-prop"—agitation and propaganda.) But I remember and so do you, when it was a rare socialist who was sure of being able to pay next month's rent. And it was the socialists—members of the *Second* Communist International—who laid the foundation for the destruction of every government and society on earth and who "seized power" in Russia in 1917. The *Third* International has billions of dollars *now;* but even in 1917-20 the men and women working for the future Communist World Commonwealth hardly had enough to eat; they lived from hand to mouth on contributions from Vanderlips, Vanderbilts, Astors, Marshall Fields, etc., etc. Straights. Kahns. In 1919 *I* knew where to get say $1,000 to finance a Communist's speaking tour "around the circle" in this country; but the girl who went to the lady and got it had no place, herself, to sleep; she slept on a cot or on the floor in some sympathizers room in the slums of New York. And I was rather despised by almost everyone I knew, because I was burgeois; I worked; I paid my bills; I wore fairly good clothes—clean, at least, and I paid the cleaner instead of giving the dollar to the Mooney defense.

It isn't money that moves the world; it is faith, conviction, ardor, fanaticism in *action.* They will move mountains; even the Bible says so, though not as a manual for revolution. Lenin was hungry, printing *Istra* in Switzerland, when Stalin pulled off that murderous bank robbery in Tiflis and sent him—how much? I forget. A fortune—Lenin spent it for propaganda, for printer's bills. And he was broke and hungry again.

I remember someone, some English person, telling me of seeing those gaunt, ragged, almost barefooted and soaked-in-the-rain Russians around Soho in the winter of 1903-04, hot-eyed and chattering madly to each other, and he never dreamed that they amounted to anything at all, or ever would or could.

The socialists (Second Internationalists) whom I knew in Greenwich Village—they were the ones that educated

Eleanor and FDR—who joined Lenin's Third International lived on scraps, handouts, and banquets that promoters spent masses of money on; they traveled in box cars or steerage, or stowed-away by comrade sailors; they wore clothes that some bourgeois gave them. They went to jail. They gave up careers; Bob Minor was cartoonist of *great* ability. He did cartoons, gratis, for *The Masses;* he refused huge offers from newspapers and syndicates and he wrote a most amusing piece for *The Masses,* autobiographical and titled: "I Get Arrested A Little." And the outcome of all this is such things as Social Security, "Civil Rights" destroying civil rights; and Medicare and The War on Poverty. . . . Sure, they have money NOW. They have the heart-wealth of all the countries they are looting. They have billions to spend. And they are losing their power to conquer the world. They can't do it with money. Money will NOT do it.

XXX

November 18, 1966

Dear Mr. Crane:

How are you? It seems a long time since I heard from you. I do hope that you are feeling well and approaching next week's feast with appetite and every cause for thankfulness. And I KNOW that you are enjoying the recent election.[10] Do you remember my wild enthusiasm for Ronald Reagan in the disastrous (and I must say, most annoying) ineptness of the Goldwater campaign? I hope you do remember it, as if you do, I am spared the embarrassment of having to say 'I TOLD YOU SO!' . . .

Look: California is rotten with "leftness." The State is a bigger, stronger center of Communists than New York; it is brutally unionized; its huge universities are militantly "anti-capitalist" and you know its Democrat registration, overwhelming since FDR. And even in 1916 it was the State that elected Wilson, though I must add that it did so because "He Kept Us Out Of War." But after he didn't, California very nearly elected Upton Sinclair's EPIC (End Poverty in California) and rah rah rahed for Thirty Dollars Every Thursday, remember?

Yet what the voters of California really wanted was just one honest candidate telling the truth. The landslide for Reagan would have been a national landslide for Goldwater if that admirable man had had the courage of his convictions instead of soft-pedaling and evading and backing down and denying charges, on the advice of idiot advisers who must despise the American "masses." Or, does Mr. Goldwater *have* convictions? does he understand political philosophies at all, or is he simply reacting against anti-Americanism without being able to *think* why? as I believe most Americans do.

Well, anyway.

I spent September-October in Vermont, among my books in the new wing to his house that Roger had built for them and me when I'm there. That wilderness is gorgeous in

---

[10]In which Ronald Reagan was first elected Governor of California.

autumn, as I'm sure you know; the air so fresh and clean and cool, the sky so blue and trimmed with white clouds, the mountains so vividly colored and all but the air reflected in the lake—twenty-five acres of lake that beavers and Roger made beyond the pine grove by the house. A marvelous place to visit, but . . . Twelve miles to the nearest town is still twelve miles to me, though of course to the youngsters it's twenty minutes. Roger and Susan have a jeep, a sedan and one of those strange four-wheel-things called Scouts, this for use in deep snow and during "the mud season," when bottoms fall out of the melting country roads. And Roger hopes for a small plane. He is a licensed pilot of both land and sea planes, but he owns neither.

He was in Japan at the Mont Pelerin meeting in September and three girls from Viet Nam were visiting Susan. They are incredibly beautiful in their *au dai* (pronounced as spelled), their native dresses, gorgeous colored silks, brocades and velvets. They were a huge sensation in Vermont, very successful in overcoming a lot of "left" propaganda about the war.

I am expecting two of them here next week for their Thanksgiving vacation from college; they are students at the University of Southern Illinois. One of them Nguyen thi Hong Phan—called Phan (Fan), the name of a small blue flower, but since Viet is one of those sung languages Americans usually say the name on a tone which makes it mean "dung." Phan says she is used to that now. She is a charming person, in her twenties and unwittingly—well, no, it is the missionary who did that to me. He helped Phan get a scholarship which he told me meant all expenses, and in addition she would have part-time work in the University offices, giving her plenty of money for sightseeing vacations, etc., etc. But she could not take all this for lack of transportation; cost of travel to USA being some 75,000 piasters, equivalent to her refugee-from-the-north family of $75,000 to an American, though because of the inflation-exchange, only some $600 to me. Phan is a sister of my interpreter in Saigon. It seemed a shame that she should miss all that, for lack of $600. So I gave a check to USOM for her transportation, and thought no more of it.

It was nearly a year before I found out what was happening. An assistant teacher at Southern Illinois University finally telephoned me, saying that Phan was with them

—his family—trying to write to me but not succeeding and he and his wife thought best to explain that "NOBODY is paying for Phan's food and shelter." This he repeated and emphasized; "Nobody is PAYING." Apparently the missionary's wife emphasized this to Phan, as later she did in a note to me. The assistant professor wrote me in detail; in addition to the scholarship, which covers only tuition, the University charged $39.95 a quarter; $160.00 a year. Phan is employed in the University offices four hours a day, five days a week, at $1.00 an hour. She can live in a cheap room with five other girls for $30 a month. "With economy," she can eat, but it is impossible to pay the $160 a year charges. And my informant mentioned that he did not include her clothes; he omitted these because I would know more about them than he did. —That'll be the day! When Phan shows up in classes omitting clothes! —His wife interrupted the telephone conversation to tell me not to worry about Phan, "We'll take care of her somehow, we LOVE her!" and he wrote that she was welcome to live with them but she was not sleeping with their two daughters; their house was small and fourteen blocks from the campus, which would be VERY difficult for Phan in winter as she is so small. (She wears size three.) I believe, too, that his family has so little money that her food would be a burden. Assistant Professors usually get starvation wages.

So, it figures out that simplest decent living, adequate food, essential clothes (shoes, stockings, wear in four years) and added University charges require roughly $800 a year plus Phan's $1 an-hour part-time earnings. And I'm elected; or, in other words, the fall guy. Being responsible for the girl's being here in the first place, a hungry stranger in a strange land. . . . And I'll have to pay her fare back to Viet Nam. She had intended to save that from her salary. So much for putting trust in missionaries. I should have known better. I knew missionaries decades ago in the Near East. They lack brains and they rely on Providence. And after all, Phan is cared for, isn't she?

My pinched pennies will be adequate and I like Phan a lot. Also I and everyone else liked her Buddhist companions, one of whom is named Grand Daughter of the King; she is a grandaughter of Bao Dai, whom, incidentally, the State Department should have supported; he had Viet loyalty as the Mikado had the Japanese, but Moscow and China didn't want a free Viet Nam. One question always asked in Vermont was about the conflict between Catholics and Buddhists and Phan always replied, "There is no *real* antagonism; it is a Communist fake. I am Catholic; my friends here are Buddhist. And we do not quarrel, I assure you." This was most effective.

Every good wish to you and Mrs. Crane, as always. One thing I am thankful for, and shall remember next Thursday, is that I've known you. I doubt that you know at all how valuable knowing you is, I'm sure to many persons, in keeping alive hope and faith and optimism.

December 7, 1966

Dear Mrs. Lane:

Republicans are rejoicing over their victories in this year's elections. That is natural, because it may well be the first step toward the restoration of the Republic. Yet, the election wasn't a victory. The Democrats of socialistic views still control the executive, legislative (both houses) and judicial branches of our Federal Government. A shocking state of affairs in New England is revealed. The people there, the part of the country which had been since colonial times so strong in upholding liberty, now seems to be possessed by desire for government aid and ready to discard freedom for slavery.

There are some good signs of growing away from socialist philosophy throughout the nation. . . . In art, the popularity of modernism, in vogue for thirty years, is declining. The recent sale of modern art in Christy's of London was a flop; whereas, in Philadelphia, the exhibition of Andrew Wyeth's paintings of real sound artistic merit was the best attended that has ever been held in their Museum. In New York, his son's exhibition was so crowded that one reporter who went there to write it up complained that he couldn't even get to see the pictures.

Through history, it has been noticeable that after great wars there is a decadence in public taste in the visual arts, whereas, in healthy countries in peace, public taste has had high standards.

December 8, 1966

Dear Mr. Crane:

I shiver when I think of the post office during the week before Christmas. Lately I have seen actually FOUR suggestions in print selling the P.O. Department to private enterprise. The suggestion has been so obviously sensible, ever since Mr. Wanamaker's offer of 5 million for it, that I suppose there's no hope of Congress' actually adopting it. What really is occurring is the development of methods of communication so much swifter and more efficient than letters that if Government hadn't monopolized postal service it would now be as extinct as horse-and-wagon transportation. It is mostly distributing trash—of course, at huge cost to us who daily chuck the trash into wastebaskets. Oh well. —

It is so good to hear from you. I hope that you are comfortable in, I suppose, winter weather in Delaware. Here the days are too hot. Landscape artists have been "doing" my grounds. I have bought a lot connecting with the Woodland Drive one, which gives me frontage and backage on two streets, and lots of land between, now almost all planted to trees, shrubs, flowers and grass, with brick walls interspersed cunningly, and a bird bath *without* a statue of Saint Joseph. I never could bear that sugarily sweet saint, and someone once said exactly what I thought about him. "Saint Joseph said, 'My little sisters, the birds.' If Saint Joseph had looked even once at a bird, he would have known that he might as well have said, 'My little sisters, the Grenadier Guards!'"

Down in the Valley, here, there is a green jay. The green jay is to a blue jay what a blue jay is to a blue bird. There is also a large bird, name unknown to me, which spends its winters plunging its long, long slender bill into ripe oranges and Ruby Red grapefruit, just one plunge to one fruit. Its motive is a mystery. Its action destroys the fruit of course. Why? Audubon knows. (I suppose.)

October 2, 1967

Dear Mrs. Lane:

Concerned about your safety when I read that Harlingen was in the flood area [of Hurricane Beulah—ed.],

I tried for three days to reach you by telephone, but every time was told that the wires were so busy that no calls could be accepted. I did get Mr. and Mrs. Kamp on the telephone, and they told me that they had succeeded telephoning you and assured me that you were in good spirits.

October 4, 1967

Dear Mr. Crane:

Thank you for your concern for me in hurricane and flood. The Valley is indeed a Disaster Area, many thousands of acres and some of Harlingen are still under water. Fortunately I and my place escaped any serious injury.

Harlingen was seventy minutes in the Eye of the Hurricane Beulah, a unique and marvelous experience which I wouldn't have missed. The hurricane destroyed almost all of this year's citrus crop but did little other important damage; the trees generally survived. The disaster was caused—as usual on American rivers—by the obstinacy of men trying to do the impossible. So far as I know, Egyptians and the farmers of Cul de Sac in Missouri, at the juncture of the Missouri and Mississippi Rivers—who have fought Army engineers tooth and nail since the 1840s—are the only people who know that man cannot control great rivers. So those farmers and the Egyptians prosper greatly, accepting floods with gratitude for the enriching silt, and never suffering from them.

June 24, 1968

Dear Mrs. Lane:

I haven't heard a word from you or about you for a long time and am greatly concerned, hoping, however, that you are well.

There is a tremendous lot of developments to be discussed and understood.

I am doing quite well, being in much better health than I was two years ago. I spend part of the mornings in my office almost every day and the afternoons at home.

* * * * *

Mr. Crane's letter arrived in Harlingen while Mrs. Lane's maltese, Pepe (del Camino Real in Danbury, naturally) was dying. During August and September Mrs. Lane made preparations for an extended trip through Europe, and departed by car for the northeast in October. She died in her sleep of a heart attack in her Danbury home on October 30, 1968. Mr. Crane followed her a year, a month, and a day later, in Wilmington.

In summary and valediction, here is a letter from Mrs. Lane dated April 19, 1966, and the first paragraph of the letter from Mr. Crane dated May 4, 1966—omitted earlier.

* * * * *

April 19, 1966

Dear Mr. Crane:

Here, "down in The Valley," there is no spring at all. One day all decidous trees are totally leafless, budless; next day they are all in full heavy leaf, shading the fast-growing lawns, and the whole town in a brilliant bouquet of bouganvillia, oleanders, orchid trees, hibiscus, roses, petunias, geraniums, lilies, even chrysanthemums. I never heard of such a thing as chrysanthemums blooming vigorously in March-April outdoors, but neighbors tell me that mine will bloom more-or-less all the time, busting out massively in November-December. Temperature here today is 98° F. in shade on north of my house. All buildings and cars, are air-conditioned. One day my conditioner was working on HEAT; next day, on COOL. I suppose Springtime went by in the night; all vegetation thought so.

Now, dear, Mr. Crane, don't be anxious about this country; all sensible persons know that the politicians are running it straight into the worst times yet, but the youngsters are going to pull it through—the youngsters and the millions of simple decent people that nowadays are never heard from. These fifty States are NOT that feverish little eastern littoral, full of eggheads full of European reactionary notions; Fulbright and Morse don't represent this country; the beatniks and SANE don't; the Negro "leaders" don't represent even the Negroes; the newspapers and radio and TV don't report facts. You and I know that the truth prevails, always, in time. As Paine wrote: "An army of principles will march on the horizon of the world and it will conquer."

For years, indeed decades, I have hated Wilson for starting this World War, deceiving the voters (I voted for him myself, in California, being so young and stupid as still to believe a politician and believing the implication of his campaign slogan, He Kept Us Out of War. When already he had promised Lord Grey to prevent a negotiated peace by putting the USA into war if he were re-elected) and betraying his trust, his oath, the United States, in his moronic egotism. But now I think that historians a few centuries from now will see this world war as a great—if not essential—impetus to the World Revolution. Throwing American energy from here into the whole world situation has smashed the empires, wrecked all governments and nearly all social institutions outside this country (perhaps inside it, later) and set everyone on earth who can think to thinking about basic principles, of human nature and human relationships. Billions of people who had always taken for granted (as their ancestors always had) collectivism, social classes (ruling, and working) and the flatness of the earth, are encountering such new ideas as individualism, human equality, liberty, and Copernican astronomy. The whole world is stirred as a hornet's nest is stirred by a stick. There is nothing but confusion, destruction, wreckage. Confusion is the beginning of greater wisdom (or less ignorance, if you want to put it that way). Destruction is the essential obverse of construction. The new building begins in the destruction of the old one. Human *life* as such is indestructible while this planet lasts; and it is indubitably true in history that human knowledge increases in Time. It is impossible, in the nature of man, that the Revolution for human rights will not transform the whole human world on this earth, in time.

So don't be distressed—not really—by the day's news of the year's losses. Or by not being at the office and doing more than you are doing. You have done far more than your share, already. You and I must leave the tasks to the young ones—as they must, someday. A real world Revolution is not won in a couple of centuries, maybe not in a millennium or two. Remember that Heron invented the steam engine in Alexandria two thousand years before his discovery of the nature of steam had any effect on human actions. In those centuries how many thousands of persons, unnoticed then and unknown now, did little bits to encourage rational thinking and discount baseless superstition, preparing a time when Kepler and Copernicus and Galileo could tell a fact and survive; as they in turn made it possible for people to accept and use the principle according to which steam works in engines. I myself have done almost nothing at all for the Revolution but the little I've done can never be lost. You who have done so much should be wholly contented, and glad, serene and untroubled no matter what immediate transitory occurrences may be.

With every good wish to you and to Mrs. Crane, as ever,

Rose Wilder Lane

May 4, 1966

Dear Mrs. Lane:

Thank you for your letter of April 19, which I have had read to me three times. It is a most encouraging message, keeping high my hopes for the future of this country. Many years ago, I was thrilled by the thought coming from the austere, but really very kindly, Francis L. Patton, then President of Princeton, a Briton—"America is the last hope for the human race." In spite of the lessons of history, I, too, simply cannot believe that America will fail.

Very sincerely,
Jasper Crane

Index